Emancipating the Female Sex

The Struggle for Women's Rights in Brazil, 1850–1940

June E. Hahner

To my mother

© 1990 Duke University Press
All rights reserved
Printed in the United States of America
on acid-free paper ∞
Library of Congress Cataloging-in-Publication Data
appear on the last printed page of this book.

The publisher and author gratefully acknowledge the
support of The Department of History, State University of
New York at Albany.

Emancipating
the Female Sex

The Struggle for Women's
Rights in Brazil,
1850–1940

Duke University Press
Durham and London 1990

Contents

Illustrations

Tables

Preface

Although women have always comprised an essential element in the evolution of Brazil, their activities have received scant scholarly attention. Never mere passive components of society, women of all classes had their own areas of influence and played significant roles in the nation's historical development. But histories and general studies of Brazil traditionally have been written as though women scarcely existed. For years, the sparse literature on women in Brazil was largely comprised of impressionistic, rather than factual, studies, general appraisals of women's contributions to society, statements of belief as to the nature of women, or brief biographies of exceptional individuals that told more about the preconceptions and orientation of the authors than about the women themselves. Only in the last decade have more Brazilian scholars sought to study women and their roles and activities within contemporary society. And this research still lags far behind that on their counterparts in the United States or Western Europe.[1]

Historians are largely dependent on written records and on the availability of those records. Female illiteracy in Latin America renders the general problems of sources for women's history very difficult, obliging us to explore a range of conventional as well as less conventional documentation. Historically, far fewer Latin American women than men had access to education, no matter what their class. Before the late nineteenth century, very few women ever learned to read and write. Even literate Latin American women rarely kept diaries and wrote fewer letters than North Americans or Europeans, thus largely negating the possibility of inquiries into a woman's world through such personal writings. Much energy must be expended by historians in collecting and organizing scattered data, ferreting information from diverse documents, and reevaluating material previously neglected or overlooked. The problems of locating sources on women in a country like Brazil lead to difficulties in reconstructing feminine institutions, let alone the lives of ordinary women.

Hence it is not surprising that in Brazil, as in other Latin American countries, the new scholarship on women is largely a social science scholarship. Historical studies there have lagged noticeably behind those by sociologists, anthropologists, and political scientists, who have written on late-twentieth-century issues and have tended to concentrate on questions of development, work, fertility, population, and politics, while demonstrating less interest in values or attitudes. Brazilian investigations into historical subjects often are produced by nonhistorians who use printed rather than archival sources. Even Brazilian feminists demonstrate less interest in restoring the female past than women in the United States or Europe, reinforcing the old saying that Brazil is a "country without a memory."[2] Although a few studies have appeared on women's suffrage activities in other Latin American countries, there is no comprehensive history of the long struggle for women's rights in Brazil.[3]

The very existence of women's rights protests in nineteenth-century Brazil may prove surprising to many readers. After all, according to the traditional view, women in Brazil still suffered from centuries of Moorish seclusion and obscurity, and to an even greater extent than their sisters in Spanish America. How, then, could some Brazilian women have advanced arguments and undertaken activities similar to those of better-known opponents of gender inequality in the United States and England?

This book examines the growth of women's rights activities in Brazil from their early manifestations in the mid-nineteenth century to the successful conclusion of the suffrage campaign in the 1930s. It explores uncharted empirical territory, focusing on the social, economic, and political situation of women in Brazil and the strategies, struggles, and ideological positions of the nation's feminists, while probing the relationship between feminism and social change in that complex, diverse, deeply stratified country. Since changes in women's status and position within Brazilian society came first to urban upper- and middle-class women, from whose ranks rose the nation's small but determined women's rights leadership in both the nineteenth and twentieth centuries, this study concentrates on those women, situating them within their society. By examining the historical dimensions of feminism in a particular cultural situation, this book can contribute to an understanding of feminism, and its range and diversity, across national boundaries. However, the complex problem of defining the term *feminism* remains beyond the scope of this study.

In both the nineteenth and twentieth centuries, female activists working to improve their position in Brazilian society sought more "rights" for women, or, as many said in the last century, for the "female sex." They advocated the "emancipation" of women, a concept which assumed a broader significance as the nineteenth century progressed, and which would still be invoked well into the twentieth century. Although the words *feminism* and *feminist* appeared in Brazil by the first decade of the twentieth century, few women's rights advocates, or their detractors, would adopt them until the 1920s.[4] While we generally seek to avoid the anachronistic use of terms, *feminist* is nevertheless a useful adjective for describing over time these opponents of gender inequality: women angered by, advocating an end to, or actively seeking to eliminate this inequality; hence the term is employed broadly in this historical study. It is just as unnecessary to limit feminism to a specific time period as it is unwise to expand the term to cover every advance undertaken by women. In this book, feminism embraces all aspects of the emancipation of women and includes those consciously collective struggles designed to elevate their status—socially, politically, or economically; it concerns women's self-concepts as well as their position in society. However, organized women's rights movements only arose in Brazil in the early twentieth century. There, as in the United States, the women's rights movement generally overlapped the suffrage movement, a specific aspect of what should be seen as a broader struggle. Women's rights movements all over the world are dependent on a class of educated women with some leisure. But the nature of each movement depends on specific historic circumstances.[5]

Neither women's rights activities nor the mobilization of women for social change are new to Brazil. During the second half of the nineteenth century a small band of dedicated women voiced their dissatisfaction with the traditional male-determined roles assigned to females. Primarily through their long-forgotten newspapers, which appeared in cities of south-central Brazil, they endeavored to awaken other women to their potential for self-advancement and to raise their level of aspirations.[6] These opponents of women's subordination sought to spur changes in the economic, social, and legal status of women—that is, those women most like themselves—in this highly stratified, slave-holding society. Although their assistance has since been largely ignored, in the 1880s some Brazilian women also contributed to the movement for the abolition of slavery.

As members of the growing minority of literate females, the early advocates of female emancipation emphasized education for women as a source both of increased options for economic independence and of societal improvement. While some opposed only the subjugation of women, others also sought advanced education for women, since, as they well knew, women could not move on to prestigious occupations without a university degree. These believers in progress drew inspiration and promises of future successes from women's achievements in other countries. Well aware of male opposition, female indifference, and the limited acceptance of their own ideas, these brave women remained convinced of the importance of their cause and its eventual success. Unlike many of their male detractors, who assumed women to be easily corruptible should they step outside the home, and the family to be weak and in need of defense, these pioneers displayed their confidence in women and their abilities. Part of the groundwork for changes in the status of some women in Brazil was laid through their persistence and efforts.

By the end of the nineteenth century, increasing numbers of women were receiving education, although large segments of the population remained illiterate. The doors of Brazil's institutions of higher learning finally opened to women, as the early advocates of female emancipation had demanded. More women found employment outside the home, especially in the classrooms, government offices, and commercial establishments. By 1920 they were competing for high-level positions in government service. The women who succeeded in entering the traditional, prestigious professions like law and medicine represented only a tiny fraction of the total female labor force, and the professions remained overwhelmingly male dominated. Yet from their ranks came most of that minority of Brazilian women consciously working to change their social and political status in the twentieth century.

In Brazil as elsewhere, gender clearly signified relationships of power, and women were excluded from the political process. The suffrage issue in countries with limited as well as larger electorates reflects and illuminates divisions and inequalities in society. If women obtained the vote, other aspects of gender relationships might be threatened. The processes involved in securing the enfranchisement of even part of the female populace must be investigated in the context of time and space—in this case, in Brazil's large urban centers during the early twentieth century.[7]

Prior to the abolition of slavery in 1888 and the overthrow of the empire in 1889, universal manhood suffrage, let alone universal suffrage, could not become a political issue in Brazil. But during the first decades of the twentieth century, increasing numbers of educated Brazilian women advocated female suffrage, a demand first voiced in the late nineteenth century after the establishment of a republic but denied by the Constituent Congress of 1891. Formal women's rights organizations appeared as the suffrage cause gained limited acceptance among sectors of the Brazilian elite who noted the achievement of the vote by women in Western Europe and the United States after World War I. While Brazilian feminists demonstrated a willingness to learn from experiences in other countries, they sought to develop strategies appropriate to the Brazilian context. The women's suffrage campaign in Brazil was not tied to any political party or other social movement. Coherent national parties occupied no prominent position on the contemporary political landscape. Hence women could not be relegated to "women's sections" of competing parties, as in Chile, or form a branch of an inclusive national party, as in Mexico. Political discontent and protests against the entrenched oligarchy mounted during the 1920s; for some people, women's suffrage found a place among urban middle-class demands for electoral reform.

In 1932 the Brazilian suffrage campaign achieved its stated goal. Led by Bertha Lutz, a biologist and one of the first women to compete successfully for a high-level position in public service, the suffragists obtained the vote for women, subject to the same literacy qualifications as men. This victory was confirmed by the Constitution of 1934. In the 1920s and early 1930s Lutz's lieutenants included lawyers, doctors, and engineers, both inside and outside government service. Those occupying high-level public service positions possessed the necessary organizational skills and determination—as well as the personal contacts—to lead a successful women's suffrage campaign. Although their movement lacked the widespread following and vociferous enthusiasms of the U.S. suffrage movement, it proved larger and better organized than most subsequent ones in Latin America. The Brazilian suffragists tackled problems of concern to the working class such as salaries, shorter hours, working conditions, and maternity leaves, but interclass link-ages proved very difficult. Women's suffrage in Brazil was a largely middle-class movement for a judicial change to give the vote to women who met the same qualifications as men, not an attempt to revolu-tionize the role of women in society, or that society itself.

Although the Brazilian women's rights movement grew more con-servative and respectable as it broadened its appeal and widened its basis of support among the upper classes, it did help to raise the level of consciousness of middle-class women concerning their problems in a changing world and add legitimacy to many female activities beyond the home. And it prepared the way for other women's organizations formed after the fall of Getúlio Vargas's Estado Novo (1937–45), a dictatorship which smashed the first small wave of feminine political activism in Brazil. The same kinds of well-educated upper-middle-class professionals who had worked for women's suffrage would con-tinue to lead most of the organizations concerned with women's status, both before and after the 1964 military coup d'etat. The new feminist movement that emerged in Brazil in the mid-1970s reveals certain sim-ilarities with the suffrage struggle, although sharp differences separate contemporary feminists working for a more equitable society from Brazil's pioneer fighters for women's rights and societal betterment.

Changes in Brazilian orthography can cause confusion. Throughout this book, names or words in Portuguese in the text will be given in the modern Brazilian Portuguese spelling, but in the footnotes and bibliography authors' names and titles of works will be cited in the original orthography.

This book's origins can be traced to the discovery of previously unknown source materials on women in Brazil. In 1970, while I was conducting research in Rio de Janeiro on the urban lower classes in the Old Republic, I located a variety of nineteenth-century materials and documents on Brazilian women, particularly their forgotten wom-en's rights protests. In 1974 I was able to return to Brazil, with the aid of a grant from the State University of New York Research Foundation, and commence research on this lost history of Brazilian women, which I felt had to be recaptured. By then I was also teaching about the history of women in the Americas and had helped to develop, and for a time headed, a program in women's studies at the State University of New York at Albany. For the next decade I continued to gather material for this book and for other works on Latin American women in the nineteenth and twentieth centuries. Grants from the Fulbright Commission and the National Endowment for the Humanities provided essential financial support, and I am profoundly grateful to these institutions.

Much of the research for this book was conducted at the Biblioteca Nacional do Rio de Janeiro, which underwent major changes during the years I worked there. The resources of the Arquivo Nacional, especially the archive of the Federação Brasileira pelo Progresso Feminino, the major Brazilian suffrage association, proved crucial. Of major importance were the collections of the Instituto Histórico e Geográfico Brasileiro, Arquivo Geral da Cidade do Rio de Janeiro, Arquivo do Estado de São Paulo, Instituto Histórico e Geográfico de São Paulo, and Biblioteca Municipal de São Paulo. I am deeply grateful for the aid given me by so many members of the staff of those institutions. I was also fortunate in being able to consult the personal papers of Carrie Chapman Catt, the U.S. suffrage leader, in the New York Public Library, and related materials in the Sophia Smith Collection of Smith College.

So many people in Brazil helped me during the last decade while I was gathering material for this book, especially the many women in Rio de Janeiro and São Paulo who generously shared with me their ideas and observations, that it is impossible to single them all out by name and thank them individually for all their kindnesses; and it would not be right to mention just some of them. I only hope each and every one knows how deeply grateful I am, for I owe them much. Without them, this book would be impossible.

Albany, New York 1989   June E. Hahner

Introduction

Women and Society in the Mid-Nineteenth Century

In the mid-nineteenth century the empire of Brazil contained only seven million people scattered across three million square miles of the eastern half of South America. A highly stratified society with an economy dependent on slave labor, Brazil appeared backward in the eyes of visiting Europeans. The majority of its racially and ethnically diverse population remained concentrated on the coast, living on the land and farming with crude techniques. Most towns seemed sleepy places with muddy streets frequented by pack mules, pigs, and chickens, although they also served as social, religious, and market centers for nearby areas. Methods of transportation were rudimentary and manufacturing industries practically nonexistent. While foreign travelers admired the country's natural beauties and often noted its social diversity, they commented far less on the activities of Brazilian women, whether empress, plantation mistress, or slave. In the major urban centers, however, a few visitors detected signs of change in some women's lives.

According to the common stereotype of the Brazilian patriarchal family, anchored in the observations of male visitors from abroad, the authoritarian husband, surrounded by slave concubines, dominated his children and submissive wife. She developed into an indolent, passive creature, kept at home, who bore numerous children and abused the Negro slaves. Among the foreign travelers' accounts supporting this image is one by John Luccock, a British merchant who, in 1808, caustically commented on the premature aging and increasing bad temper and fatness of Rio de Janeiro's upper-class women. At thirteen or fourteen, attractive girls with "a sprightly laughing air" commonly

A Brazilian woman of the elite and her slave attendants, who are making lace, as depicted by the French artist Jean Baptiste Debret, ca. 1823. *(Courtesy of the Biblioteca Nacional do Rio de Janeiro)*

Wife of the owner of a large plantation, or *fazenda*, sitting cross-legged and receiving her female guests and relatives, ca. 1823. The slave fanning her is wearing the type of mask often placed on a slave considered an earth eater. *(Debret, courtesy of the Biblioteca Nacional do Rio de Janeiro)*

had to assume "the cares of a household." At "eighteen, in a Brazilian woman, nature has attained to full maturity. A few years later she becomes corpulent, and even unwieldy; acquires a great stoop in her shoulders, and walks with an awkward waddling gait. She begins to decay, loses the good humour of her countenance, . . . and at twenty-five, or thirty at most, she becomes a perfectly wrinkled old woman." Luccock attributed this deterioration to habits of reclusion and indolence, claiming that these women "were seldom seen out of doors, except when going to mass. . . . The exercise which these ladies take is almost wholly confined to the house . . . they are surrounded by slaves, and it is their privilege to be waited upon."[1]

This stereotype of the secluded and guarded female was not universally valid; actual behavior varied according to class. The constraints surrounding elite women reflected considerations of female honor, which remained closely related to family honor. Some of the same elite males who sought to confine female relatives to a cloistered family environment where they could be defended from presumed dangers of seduction or sexual assault might themselves seek opportunities for sexual aggression. But this aggression could most readily be directed against the unguarded and more vulnerable lower-class females. Questions of female and family honor remained closely connected with the social hierarchy.[2]

Among the poor in nineteenth-century Brazil, as opposed to the planter, merchant, and professional groups, far fewer efforts were made to mold women into passive creatures. And attempts by the authorities or their employers to control their behavior might be resisted. Impoverished free women struggling to survive in São Paulo traversed public squares and streets and congregated by fountains, water tanks, and river banks, working as laundresses and ambulatory street vendors or seeking to hire themselves out as maids, cooks, wet nurses, or seamstresses. Sometimes street sellers battled not just hunger but also the police, bureaucratic regulations, and taxes imposed on their petty commercial activities.[3] Even servant women living in their masters' households asserted a measure of independence; those whose work took them into city streets and markets could conduct their private lives there, far from employers' prying eyes.[4]

At times, slaves too might achieve a degree of personal autonomy, particularly in the cities. Although all remained "private property," slaves' specific situations and experiences differed widely. Not just gen-

Laundresses working at the large tanks by a public fountain, Chafarriz da Carioca, in Rio de Janeiro, 1824. *(Courtesy of the Biblioteca Nacional do Rio de Janeiro)*

der but race, occupation, and location also helped to determine many aspects of their lives. However, while some scholars stress slaves' resistance and adaptation, others emphasize the privations slaves suffered. Certainly female slaves, unlike free women, might be forcibly separated from their children and even obliged to serve as wet nurses to their owners' offspring. And slave women remained subject to sexual violence and the advances of their masters. Yet some still succeeded in constructing limited family or personal lives, even though ultimate control remained in their masters' hands. At night some slaves, like some freedmen and -women, managed to hold dances, religious rites, and festivities, or just to meet with husbands, lovers, and friends working in different households. In the cities, slave women sometimes enjoyed considerable personal freedom, going about the city (with their masters' permission) selling food they prepared or fruits and vegetables they raised, while their mistresses generally remained cloistered at home, shielded from the perceived vulgarities or dangers of the street. Some slave women even accumulated sufficient funds through their commercial dealings to purchase their freedom. Within the Afro-Brazilian religions, as contrasted with the official Roman Catholic church, poor black women could occupy leadership positions.[5]

Even among the elite, not all women were confined to the private sphere of the home and excluded from the public sphere assigned to men. An often-repeated Portuguese proverb stated that a virtuous upper-class woman left her house on only three occasions during her lifetime: to be baptized, to be married, and to be buried. But in Brazil, as in other countries, the ideal did not necessarily correspond to the real. Active widows sometimes ran plantations, known as *fazendas*. The Reverend Robert Walsh, chaplain to the British ambassador, traveled through the interior province of Minas Gerais in the late 1820s and observed that widowed wives of fazendeiros often managed the farms and slaves by themselves, "and in all respects assume[d] the part and bearing of their husbands."[6] Widowhood provided a release from some of the legal restrictions imposed on married women and conferred on them the authority of the family head.

In the cities, elite women who remained largely secluded in their homes often directed sizable establishments full of relatives, retainers, and slaves. They supervised the production of clothing, food, domestic utensils, and other necessities of a largely self-sufficient household and were responsible for the family's health care, numerous religious obligations, and training of dependents. As peddlers and sellers of other goods came directly to the door, the mistress of the house could engage in petty commercial transactions without setting foot outside. Such women certainly could and did exercise behind-the-scenes influence on men occupying formal positions in the public sphere; nevertheless, the authority of the husband and father remained paramount, and the wife was subject to him.

In law, as in custom, the ideology of male supremacy prevailed. The Phillipine Code compiled in Portugal in 1603, which basically remained in effect in Brazil until the promulgation of the Civil Code of 1916, specifically designated the husband as the "head of the couple"; only on his death could the wife occupy the position of household head. Under the existing civil law structure in nineteenth-century Brazil, an extension of the Phillipine Code, women were perpetual minors. (And the Civil Code of 1916 did not really change matters.) A married woman had to submit to her husband's authority in decisions regarding their children's education, upbringing, and place of residence. The law denied wives the right to engage in commerce, alienate their immovable property by sale or gift, or even to administer that property without their husbands' consent.[7]

Upper-class women had little choice in matrimonial partners. Maria Graham, a cultivated Englishwoman and governess to Princess Maria da Glória who socialized freely with members of the imperial court, found that "Master Cupid" was very seldom allowed to play a part in marriage arrangements.[8] Like other foreign visitors in the early nineteenth century, the Reverend Mr. Walsh reported girls being married off by their fathers "at the early age of twelve or thirteen," often to much older men.[9] In the 1860s John Codman, an American sea captain, noted the continued existence of such disparities in the age of marriage partners and complained that women were used to "advance the fortunes of their parents by being sold in the matrimonial market when they should be at school."[10] Although celebrated as a holy sacrament according to the rituals of the Roman Catholic church, marriage, for the elite, focused on property. A proper alliance involved marriage partners with equal wealth and status whose union would preserve the families' financial standing and position. To maintain prestige and social stability, elite families sought to limit racially mixed marriages as well as those unequal in birth, honor, or wealth. Since marriage served to guard property and social arrangements, it could not be left to individual discretion, and certainly not to female preferences.

Sons, far more than daughters, might sometimes succeed in choosing their own marriage partners. Although females could legally marry at twelve, and males at fourteen, they were still minors needing parental consent. But a son who graduated from medical or law school automatically attained legal majority upon receipt of his degree and could marry without parental permission. Daughters, who were denied access to higher education, as well as those sons who also lived at home, remained directly under patriarchal control and subject to the plenary power conferred by Brazilian law upon the father to determine his children's marriages. In 1831 the age of legal majority was lowered from twenty-five to twenty-one, thus theoretically benefiting both sexes, but in reality providing more opportunities for males.[11]

Under Portuguese law, family, property, and marriage remained inextricably joined. The complex and unwieldy Phillipine Code, together with a stream of subsequent Portuguese and Brazilian enactments, governed the spouses' rights over conjugal property and established the line of succession. Portuguese law decreed that in the absence of a prenuptial agreement, a valid marriage resulted in a system of complete community of goods between the spouses. A prenuptial agreement could establish complete separation of the spouses' property, complete community of goods, or some specified combination. Under Spanish law, in contrast, complete community of goods between spouses did not exist. In the Spanish colonies the dowry, one among several kinds of goods in a marriage, served as a form of protection for the wife, for it would be restituted to her intact if she were widowed. But in Brazil, where the practice of dowry generally disappeared in the nineteenth century, the dowry represented an advance on the daughter's inheritance. Under the Portuguese system of complete community of goods, the dowry brought by the wife disappeared into the pool of marriage goods, and she was not guaranteed a fixed sum upon widowhood. But as owner of half the joint estate, she retained that half in widowhood and could dispose of it in her will. Portuguese law, however, severely restricted the free disposal of property by testament. By law, two-thirds of a person's property automatically passed to his or her descendant, ascendant, or collateral kin, leaving only one-third to be freely bestowed. Within this system of bilateral, equally partible inheritance, all children, sons and daughters, were the forced heirs of their parents and could not be disinherited. No doubt this equal division of property for legitimate heirs was a strong force promoting endogamous cousin marriage and marriages of women to political or business allies. Through careful matrimonial arrangements an elite family could avoid the dispersal of their patrimony and perpetuate the family's social position.[12]

Legal marriage remained more of a rarity among the racially heterogeneous lower classes. Nor did patriarchal or extended families prevail. Recent studies focusing on the provinces of Minas Gerais and São Paulo demonstrate the wide variety of family types that existed in the late eighteenth and early nineteenth centuries, suggesting that marriage practices in Brazil varied by race and class. Nuclear families predominated among the bulk of the population, although the number of female-headed households loomed large. The Roman Catholic church did not approve of the common occurrence of concubinage and illegitimacy, wishing coition limited to procreative purposes within indissoluble marriages. But the poor were least likely to be able to afford the high cost of legitimate church marriages or to overcome traditional barriers to matrimony such as the presentation of positive proof of marital status. Legal marriage served as an indication of social differentiation even among those segments of the population with little property to transmit.[13]

Modifications in customs and institutions proved most noticeable in the cities and in the aftermath of the removal of the Portuguese court to Rio de Janeiro in 1808. The Napoleonic invasion of the metropolis forced the Portuguese royal family to flee to Brazil, initiating a series of economic, political, and social changes which accelerated Brazil's development and led to political independence from Portugal in 1822. João VI opened Brazil's ports to foreign commerce. He not only installed the royal court in Rio de Janeiro but also created the royal press, a public library, medical and military schools, and a botanical garden, introduced European cultural missions, and oversaw urban improvements such as paving additional streets, filling in more land for construction, and the melioration of the water supply, all of which contributed to an intensification of the urban life of the city. The presence of some fourteen thousand Portuguese who accompanied the royal family to Brazil, plus members of foreign diplomatic missions accredited to the court, could not but influence the habits and behavior of Rio's elite. Festivities sponsored by the royal family to commemorate birthdays, weddings, and political events increased social interaction among members of the upper classes as well as with foreigners. The capital evolved far more rapidly than the countryside and the disparity between the two increased, for the changes wrought directly and indirectly by the arrival of the royal court were overwhelmingly concentrated in the urban areas, primarily Rio. For thirteen years, until the establishment of an independent Brazilian empire under Pedro I, eldest son of João VI, this city served as the seat of an empire extending far beyond America. Rio's population, over sixty thousand in 1808, doubled by 1822, surpassing that of Salvador, with Recife in third place.[14]

Upper-class Brazilian women began to follow more European modes of behavior after the arrival of the Portuguese court in Rio de Janeiro in 1808. According to two Bavarian scientists, Johann B. von Spix and Karl F. P. von Martius, women participated "in the change which the removal of the court hither ha[d] occasioned and [were] now more frequently seen in the theatre, and in the open air."[15] Even at home their appearance and behavior were modified; in more stylish, Europeanized dress they could no longer sit with legs crossed on mats or low platforms when receiving female visitors or directing household tasks. The intensification of commercial and political life in mid-nineteenth-century Rio de Janeiro required larger, more complex social gatherings and formal receptions in which upper-class women had to display proper social skills and graces in order to promote the family's position. Daniel Parish Kidder and James C. Fletcher, two American Protestant missionaries, noted this increased tendency of upper-class women in Rio de Janeiro to venture out to parties, church, and the theater. But, like John Luccock decades earlier, they contended that these women quickly grew stout from a lack of outdoor exercise and were constantly surrounded by slaves.[16] Elizabeth Agassiz, wife of the American biologist, found upper-class female life more stifled and limited in the northern cities and provinces than in Rio de Janeiro, which had its "progressive aspect."[17] Several years later, Herbert H. Smith, an American naturalist traveling in the Amazon, reported the decreasing seclusion of upper-class women in the city of Belém, but not in the smaller towns of the area.[18] Far fewer changes, however, could be seen in the lives of poor women, even in the cities.

While rich and poor often lived in closer physical proximity in Brazil and other Latin American countries than in the United States, an immense social gulf continued to separate the two groups. With the traditional disdain for manual labor which permeates a slaveholding nation, wealthy Brazilians felt themselves far removed from the rest of society. As an American zoologist reported, the upper classes would "not soil their hands with tools" and looked down on even skilled craftsmen as members "of an inferior class."[19] An English newspaperman observing the great regard Brazilians paid to "distinction and rank," claimed that "perhaps in no other language are these so precisely determined."[20]

Dress, like income, occupations, and housing, sharply set off the elite from the urban poor. Only the wealthy could appear publicly in full sartorial splendor. Although upper-class women dressed simply and sparingly in private, if not as carelessly as in colonial times, at balls and parties they appeared in elaborate low-cut gowns that were full of ruffles and ribbons and designed to please men. On such festive occasions upper-class men, with their beards, canes, and other symbols of dignity and sobriety, and women, with their clothes and jewels demonstrating family wealth and status, could meet under somewhat freer conditions than usual.[21]

Like Americans and Europeans in far cooler climates, a gentleman walking the streets of Rio de Janeiro or Recife in the mid-nineteenth century wore a "stiff silk hat" and a "double breasted frock coat of black cloth, closely buttoned even in the warmest weather." Some donned gloves as well as garments of English wool. Europeans commented on the oddity of such male attire "in a climate where light weight and colored clothing and straw hats were naturally advisable." Only in the far north of Brazil, in a city like Belém, would upper-class men stroll the streets dressed in white linen and upper-class women wear flowers in their hair instead of French bonnets.[22] In contrast, the poor wore lightweight cotton clothing, "often much faded and patched." Pants and a shirt sufficed the men year-round. Women wore just a blouse and skirt. Some men sported black felt hats, and skilled workers like typographers might take pride in their caps. Not only slaves but also many free laborers went barefoot. The unshod could find themselves barred from some streetcars, and men without coats were not supposed to enter public buildings.[23] Dress reflected class position and indicated the type of treatment due each person.

Social mobility proved difficult, perhaps in part as the middle ground between the wealthy and the mass of the population remained narrow and uncertain. While poorly paid primary school teachers,

Wealthy urban family going to mass, ca. 1850. (Kidder and Fletcher, *Brazil and the Brazilians*)

A street vendor (*quitandeira*), ca. 1850. (Kidder and Fletcher, *Brazil and the Brazilians*)

bookkeepers, and white-collar employees might consider themselves far above the lower classes, the wealthy saw fewer differences. Minute in size compared with the middle class in Western Europe or the United States, Brazil's so-called middle classes lacked unity and attempted to imitate the upper classes in their life-styles and appearance whenever possible.[24]

Legally separate from other urban workers yet performing many of the same jobs were the slaves. As late as 1872, the date of Brazil's first national census, slaves formed 15 percent of Brazil's total population, comprising 18 percent of the inhabitants of Rio de Janeiro, 12 percent of the city of São Paulo, 13 percent in both Salvador and Recife, 14 percent in Belém in the far north, and 19 percent of the inhabitants of Porto Alegre in the far south.[25] Urban slaves ranged in employment from skilled craftsmen to day laborers, domestic servants, and prostitutes. While many female domestic slaves performed menial tasks such as cleaning, carrying water, or kitchen work, others, better trained and more specialized, served as cooks, seamstresses, laundresses, nurse-maids, or even housekeepers and virtual ladies-in-waiting to wealthy women. Among poorer families, female slaves performed all household duties and often worked outside the home as well. Street vendors sometimes sold their wares during parts of the day, when they were not engaged in household work. Female slaves seemed to monopolize the marketing of fruits and vegetables and prepared foods like confectioneries, while male slaves sold meat and fish.[26]

According to the 1872 Brazilian census, the number of slave women performing domestic service (129,816) far exceeded men (45,561). Among nonagricultural occupations, domestic service surpassed all others in employment of female slaves, followed by dressmaking (40,766), a profession no male slaves followed, and then textile manufacturing (12,354), another overwhelmingly female field.[27]

Whether slave or free, the majority of female urban workers in 1872 were domestic servants. In Rio de Janeiro they outnumbered seamstresses, the next most common occupation, 38,462 to 11,592. Domestic service, an overwhelmingly female field—70 percent of all domestics were women—employed 63 percent of the city's total female labor force. Little change would occur in the next half century, so that in 1920, when 82 percent of all domestic servants were women, 50 percent of Rio's female labor force would be employed in domestic service.[28]

Wealth continued to bring privileges. The elite, with their family connections, controlled access to status and political power in Brazil. However, even though education was largely the prerogative of those entitled to its benefits by birth or position, far fewer women than men, no matter what their class, received any schooling. According to the census of 1872, Brazil had a total population of 10,112,061. But only 1,012,097 free men, 550,981 free women, 958 slave men, and 445 slave women were able to read and write.[29]

Improvements in literacy and schooling could help open the way into the modern world for both men and women. Literacy, after all, is more than a technical skill; it makes possible new kinds of competencies and can weaken continuities in traditional behavior. It facilitates the maintenance of a communications network wider than one's own locality and can promote skepticism about local opinions by providing access to other viewpoints. For women, a lessening of the disparity between female and male literacy rates can have tremendous implications, helping them enter a larger world. Increased dependence on writing rather than on oral communication might ultimately help to bridge the gap between male and female experience, since the spoken word, tied to the speaker's physical presence, conveys the speaker's gender in a way that the written word cannot.

In Brazil, girls' education remained backward compared with boys'. Women's reading, as British merchant John Luccock reported in 1808, "was not to extend beyond the prayerbooks, because it would be useless to a woman, nor were they to write lest, as was sagely remarked, they should make a bad use of the art."[30] Two decades later, an upper-class Brazilian traveling widely in the interior of the country noted even more resistance to educating women among the general populace, for they considered it a virtual crime for a woman to be literate; "if a woman knew how to read, she would be able to receive love letters."[31] According to a popular saying that clearly demonstrates what women were expected to learn or not learn in order to function in society as well as what was seen as their principal role in that society:

> A girl who knows a lot
> Is a mixed-up girl,
> To be a good mother,
> One should know little or nothing.[32]

The idea of schooling for girls was slowly added to the older idea of domestic education, although it was not schooling identical to that given to boys. No longer would foreign visitors like the Frenchman Charles Expilly see as applicable to the Brazilian upper class the Portuguese proverb that "a woman is sufficiently educated when she can read her prayer book properly and knows how to write the recipe for guava jam; more than this poses a peril for the home."[33] With time, rich girls not only learned to prepare cakes and sweets and to sew, embroider, and make lace, but they also could study French, piano, and dancing so as to provide more charming and agreeable company on social occasions. Herman Burmeister, a Prussian zoologist visiting Rio de Janeiro in 1850, noted that "parents prefer to learn that their daughter is the best dancer in school rather than that she is the pupil who best knows how to read and write and to translate from English or French."[34] While the two American missionaries, Kidder and Fletcher, believed that the number of schools for girls was increasing, they held that "in eight cases of ten, the Brazilian father thinks that he has done his duty when he has sent his daughter for a few years to a fashionable school kept by some foreigner: at thirteen or fourteen he withdraws her, believing that her education is finished."[35] Elizabeth Agassiz reported how teachers complained that those girls were "taken away from school just at a time when their minds begin to develop." As she observed with dismay, "the next step in their life is marriage."[36]

In the mid-nineteenth century few comfortably situated Brazilians protested the social and economic conditions under which the vast majority of the population, both male and female, lived, or opposed specific institutions like slavery. Nor did many signs of women's rights activities or thought appear among Brazil's women during the first half of the nineteenth century. Nísia Floresta Brasileira Augusta, perhaps the most outstanding Brazilian woman intellectual of the period and one of the country's first women's rights advocates, proved the marked exception. Born in Rio Grande do Norte in 1809, Nísia Floresta, like so many other upper-class Brazilian girls, was forced to marry young. But she soon separated herself from her husband and moved to the city of Olinda, where she formed a new personal alliance. The death of her companion left her alone in Porto Alegre at the age of twenty-four with two children and an aged mother to support. Like some later feminists and a variety of other Brazilian women, she turned to school-teaching and settled in Rio de Janeiro, where she founded a school that endured seventeen years. Her free translation of Mary Wollstonecraft's *A Vindication of the Rights of Woman* first appeared in 1832.

While we cannot easily measure the direct impact of this translation, the spirited heroine of *A moreninha* (The little brunette), the popular romantic novel written in 1844 by Joaquim Manuel de Macedo, had read Mary Wollstonecraft. This lively and mischievous fourteen-year-old girl became irritated with a suitor who jokingly requested "a sinecure when she became a minister of state and a commission as army surgeon should she become a general," only forgiving him when he promised to introduce a women's rights bill into the provincial assembly should he ever be elected.[37]

Nísia Floresta continued to advocate increased education and a higher social position for women, as well as freedom of religion and the abolition of slavery. She also published a book of moral prescriptions and advice for girls in 1843 and a collection of articles on female education in 1853, as well as writing for various newspapers. In 1856 she moved to Europe, where she met French intellectuals, impressed Auguste Comte and others with her brilliant mind, converted to positivism, traveled extensively, and published several more books. Except for the period from 1872 to 1875, she remained in the Old World, enjoying its more congenial intellectual atmosphere, until her death in 1885 at the age of seventy-six.[38]

Changes of all kinds, including some that would affect the lives of upper-class urban women and bring increasing opportunities for less exceptional women than Nísia Floresta to expand their horizons, would come more quickly in the second half of the century. In the cities, more women could secure some education, and a few upper-class individuals would call for female emancipation. But little change occurred in the harsh lives of poor women. In this highly stratified society a small elite of ever better educated women would continue to coexist with a large mass of women at the bottom of the economic and social ladder.

Chapter 1

Pioneers for Women's Rights

During the second half of the nineteenth century Brazil's cities grew in size and in economic and social complexity. Increasing commercial activity, the beginnings of industrialization, improved communications and transportation, and rising literacy in major urban centers facilitated the appearance of new ideas and ideologies. In the relative proximity of urban life, some members of the growing minority of literate women attempted to move in new directions. Out of their ranks rose both the early advocates of the emancipation of women in Brazil and the audience for these pioneers' published efforts and exhortations.

European technological advances such as the railroad, the steamboat, and the telegraph stimulated the rapid growth of many urban centers, both in physical area and in population. Submarine cables rather than slow boats provided the urban elites with the latest news from Europe. Regional disequilibrium within Brazil increased. By the 1850s and 1860s, at the height of the reign of Emperor Pedro II, João VI's grandson, the rising coffee exports of south-central Brazil overshadowed the relatively inefficient sugar cultivation and processing in the Northeast, which was struggling to meet the competition of European beet sugar. The balance of income and population shifted more decisively to the south. The principal coffee-growing provinces of Rio de Janeiro, São Paulo, and Minas Gerais drained slaves from the Northeast after the international slave trade ended in 1850 and attracted increasing quantities of European immigrants and capital after 1880. Social organization in the south underwent rapid changes, with increasing numbers of wage-earning laborers both on the coffee plantations and in the cities, growing European immigration, and agriculture based on small farms in the southernmost states.[1]

Planters and their families increasingly deserted the somnolent rural towns for the greater excitement and amenities of urban life. Improvements in communication and transportation led many landless rural workers and townsmen living hard lives in weakly organized communities in the interior to become aware of the attractions of city life, and they also migrated to the cities. Urban centers likewise provided shelter for some runaway and former slaves. During the late empire, as throughout the colonial period, the Brazilian economy depended on a slave labor system, but this was coming under increasing criticism, especially in the cities, following the end of the Paraguayan War in 1870.

Rio de Janeiro, and later São Paulo, served as commercial, financial, administrative, and transportation centers based on the cultivation and exportation of coffee and the importation and distribution of both necessities and luxury items, including the latest European fads and notions. They benefited financially and politically, as well in size and population, from the growing coffee economy. By the third quarter of the nineteenth century, these and other major Brazilian cities had shed many of their colonial airs and could boast improvements in public transportation, lighting, and water supply, as well as numerous paved streets, more elegant public buildings, and ever-increasing populations. Such developments claimed the attention of foreign travelers, especially those visiting Rio de Janeiro, the imperial capital.[2]

After first exclaiming over the natural beauties of Guanabara Bay, foreign travelers then inspected downtown Rio de Janeiro, the old colonial central city, where only the red-tiled roofs struck them as "essentially tropical."[3] In the 1870s the Primeiro de Março (First of March) remained the city's principal artery. Once called the Rua Direita (Straight Street), it ran the length of the colonial city from the Morro do Castelo, site of the oldest settlement, to São Bento hill, and paralleled the waterfront where the visitors had landed. Approximately midway along this wide street, which was filled with a "noisy multitude"[4] and lined with wholesale merchants' establishments, banks, warehouses, offices, three- and four-story houses, and various public buildings such as the customs house, exchange, and post office, the visitor came to the Largo do Paço, with the government palace and the church and convent of Carmo.

House slaves pounding coffee beans on a *fazenda* in the
province of Rio de Janeiro, ca. 1860. (Lithography from
photograph by Victor Frond in Charles Ribeyrolles,
O Brazil pittoresco)

Many foreigners preferred to stroll along fashionable Ouvidor Street,
one of the transversals of the Primeiro de Março, which was lined with
the city's best shops, including numerous jewelry stores. But even here
some visitors experienced dirt and discomfort. In this older portion of
Rio they found the sidewalks "scarcely wide enough for two to go
abreast," and they fled from coffee carts and ships' cargoes moving
through the streets "at reckless speed" on mule-drawn wagons "with
yelling excited drivers." During a heavy shower Ouvidor Street became impassable for pedestrians unless a street porter fixed a "temporary foot-bridge." Otherwise, "a too confident jumper" might "land

in the water, much to the amusement of the by-standers."[5] While foreigners acquainted with the city a decade or two earlier noted improvements in drainage, sewerage, and lighting, others connected the still-faulty sanitation with feared diseases.[6]

Despite some visitors' complaints, Rio's boosters could cite a series of municipal improvements in the third quarter of the nineteenth century. Public lighting first appeared in Rio in 1854, substituting for fish oil on a few downtown streets. By the 1870s even the most critical foreigners agreed that the city was well lighted, and its main thoroughfares well paved, although their appraisals of the sewer system, begun in 1862, differed. The 1860s also witnessed the planting of trees on city streets and the improvement of public gardens and squares. Communications and transportation advanced. The telegraph arrived in 1854; submarine cable services linked north to south in 1873, and Brazil to Europe the following year. In 1856 the omnibus, a large carriage driven over fixed routes on a rough schedule, made its appearance, followed in 1868 by the *bondes*, mule-drawn cars on rails. New railroads edged northward from Rio, beginning with the Estrada de Ferro Dom Pedro Segundo, later called the Central do Brasil, whose first section was completed in 1858. These improvements in urban transportation accelerated Rio's growth, both in physical area and in population size.[7]

The new residential districts made possible by the improvements in urban mass transportation during the second half of the nineteenth century were more stratified by income and social level than the colonial and early-nineteenth-century cities. By the 1860s Rio's merchants were abandoning residences above their downtown business establishments for suburbs and evening rush hours.[8] Rather than continuing to live in the closely packed buildings edging the streets of Rio's old mixed commercial and residential center, the wealthy constructed impressive separate houses with "avenues of royal palms, and gorgeous flowering shrubs, and dark-tinted trees" in newer neighborhoods.[9] At the same time, some urban workers moved to more distant and dismal suburbs built along the railroad lines stretching north of the city center. There they found slightly less congested housing than in the disease-ridden downtown tenements. By the early twentieth century ever more skilled workers—those best able to afford the transportation costs— would spend long hours commuting to small houses

Table 1. Population of Brazil and Its Principal Cities, 1872–1920

	Brazil	Rio de Janeiro	São Paulo	Salvador	Recife	Belém	Porto Alegre
1872	10,112,061	274,972	31,385	129,109	116,671	61,997	43,998
	(100%)	(100%)	(100%)	(100%)	(100%)	(100%)	(100%)
1890	14,333,915	522,651	64,934	174,412	111,556[a]	50,064[a]	52,421
	(142%)	(190%)	(207%)	(135%)	(96%)	(81%)	(119%)
1900	17,318,556	811,443[b]	239,820	205,813	113,106	96,560	73,674
	(171%)	(295%)	(764%)	(159%)	(97%)	(156%)	(167%)
1920	30,635,605	1,157,873	579,093	283,422	238,843	236,402	179,263
	(303%)	(419%)	(1,845%)	(216%)	(205%)	(381%)	(407%)

Source: Adapted from Brazil, Directoria Geral de Estatística, *Recenseamento do Brazil realizado em 1 de setembro de 1920*, vol. 4, pt. 1, p. x. All data are for *municípios*. Rio's population is that of the former Município Neutro, then the Federal District.

[a]The 1890 results for Recife and Belém are generally considered erroneous and extremely low.
[b]The 1900 census results for Rio were set aside. The results given here are from a census conducted in 1906.

lining the dirt streets of districts lacking most municipal services rather than live in the costly, unsanitary, but conveniently located downtown tenements.[10]

As the seat of national power and by far the biggest city in Brazil, Rio de Janeiro remained the country's economic, cultural, and intellectual leader. By 1872 this socially and racially diverse city contained well over a quarter of a million inhabitants, making it one of the largest cities in the Western Hemisphere (see table 1). More than other Brazilian cities, Rio served as a center for the early manifestations of protests concerning female subordination voiced by upper- and middle-class women.

Schools and Schoolteachers

The Brazilian school system expressed the social consensus on the role of women. Women were taught only what they were expected to need for functioning in society. The relatively few schools found in nineteenth-century Brazil emphasized activities that would complement women's roles as mothers and wives. Differences in the education

Table 2.   Literacy Rates in Brazil, 1872–1920

	Literate		Illiterate		Literates among total male population (%)	Literates among total female population (%)
	Men	Women	Men	Women		
1872	1,013,055	551,426	4,110,814	4,255,183	19.8	11.5
1890	1,385,854	734,705	5,852,078	6,361,278	19.1	10.4
1920	4,470,068	3,023,289	10,973,750	12,168,498	28.9	19.9

Sources: Brazil, Directoria Geral de Estatística, *Recenseamento da população do Império do Brazil a que se procedeu no dia 1° de agosto de 1872*, Município Neutro, 21:102; Brazil, Directoria Geral de Estatística, *Recenseamento do Brazil realizado em 1 de setembro de 1920*, vol. 4, pt. 4, pp. xii, xvi.

men and women received reinforced the sense of distinct male and female worlds.

While educational opportunities for girls generally remained limited even in the cities, some improvements occurred during the last half of the nineteenth century.[11] But few Brazilians had access to schools. Education remained largely limited to those entitled to its benefits by birth or position. According to the census of 1872, only 19.8 percent of the nation's men and 11.5 percent of its women could read and write (see table 2). In 1873 the empire contained only 5,077 primary schools, public and private. These schools had a total of 114,014 male and 46,246 female pupils, while Brazil's population exceeded 10 million people.[12] However, in Rio de Janeiro, with over 275,000 inhabitants, 6,589 boys and 4,872 girls attended the capital's 123 public and private primary schools.[13] Only in the twentieth century would the percentage of literates among the nation's total population rise, long after the literacy rate among the urban population had increased. In major cities like Rio de Janeiro and São Paulo the percentage of literate women was not only higher than in the nation as a whole but also much closer to male literacy rates (see tables 3 and 4). Although illiteracy among urban women remained higher than among urban men, the gap between male and female rates progressively narrowed. That gap always remained greater among the nation's entire population than among urban dwellers.

The first legislation concerning women's education came in 1827,

Table 3. Literacy Rates in Rio de Janeiro, 1872–1920

	Literate		Illiterate		Literates among total male population (%)	Literates among total female population (%)
	Men	Women	Men	Women		
1872	65,384	34,101	93,382	82,105	41.2	29.3
1890	169,960	100,370	123,697	128,624	57.9	43.8
1906	260,941	160,131	202,512	187,859	56.3	46.0
1920	398,144	312,108	200,163	247,458	66.5	55.8

Sources: Recenseamento do Brasil . . . 1920, vol. 2, pt. 1, pp. cvi, 414–15; vol. 4, pt. 4, p. xiii; Brazil, Directoria Geral de Estatística, Recenseamento do Rio de Janeiro (Districto Federal) realizado em 20 de setembro de 1906, 1:108–9.

Table 4. Literacy Rates in São Paulo (City), 1872–1920

	Literate		Illiterate		Literates among total male population (%)	Literates among total female population (%)
	Men	Women	Men	Women		
1872	5,055	2,673	10,672	12,984	32.1	17.1
1890	12,040	6,774	22,196	23,924	35.2	22.1
1920	189,097	148,605	104,910	136,421	64.3	52.1

Source: Recenseamento do Brasil . . . 1920, vol. 4, pt. 4, pp. xxvi–xxvii.

but the law admitted girls only to elementary schools, not to institutes of advanced learning. The emphasis remained on the needle, not the pen. Even the arithmetic required in girls' schools was less advanced than that mandated for boys. The law ordered, and parents desired, that girls' schools stress domestic skills, subjects never taught to boys. Relatively few public schools for girls were ever set up, and the low salaries offered to teachers proved generally unattractive. An 1834 constitutional amendment (part of a decentralizing process) which conferred on the provincial assemblies the power to establish and regulate public primary schools, while leaving legislation on higher education to the central government, indirectly led to lower-paid and less-trained women to teach girls. Public education in this agrarian, slavocrat society received little support from impoverished provincial treasuries.[14]

The inadequacies of both public and private school teachers prompted the creation of normal schools to train primary school teachers. Although the first school appeared in Niterói in 1835, followed by Minas Gerais in 1840 and Bahia in 1841, normal schools remained few in number, small in enrollment, and precarious in position until the last years of the empire. For example, the normal school decreed for São Paulo in 1846, for boys only, disappeared in 1867 (after having graduated just 4 students), to be reinstalled in 1875, with a separate section for girls added the following year. Then the school, which lacked its own building, furniture, and permanent professors, closed for want of funding in 1878 (having produced 39 male and 7 female graduates). But in 1880 it was definitely established, and that same year 12 female and 16 male first-year students passed their final examinations. Enrollments rose rapidly, with courses frequently oversubscribed and classrooms overflowing. Between 1881 and 1889 alone 158 women and 199 men received their degrees from São Paulo's normal school. By the end of the nineteenth century these professional schools, which were generally coeducational, not only prepared girls for teaching careers but also provided one of the few available opportunities for them to continue their education.[15]

Many girls still received their scanty education at home or in private schools, some religiously oriented and some run by foreign women. Among the elite, children were often educated at home. The "best families" employed private tutors or sent their daughters to convent schools, especially those run by the Sisters of Charity of Saint Vincent de Paul, who had arrived in Brazil in the mid-nineteenth century. Children from less wealthy families attended other private schools, while poorer children frequented public primary schools, as a Rio school inspection commission admitted in 1873.[16] But the majority of Brazilians received no instruction.

In the mid-nineteenth century few "respectable" jobs other than schoolteaching were open to women, and few "proper" women engaged in any money-making activities, let alone worked for wages. To be sure, some exceptional widowed women in the cities took charge of their husbands' businesses, just as forceful widows had long run *fazendas* in the interior. The ranks of widows directing family enterprises not only included those operating printing shops or other modest establishments but also female merchants and entrepreneurs controlling large sums of money. In the early 1860s, Ana Joaquina da Silva Cajueiro took full responsibility for major street and quay construction begun by her husband and carried out the extensive project to the satisfaction of the imperial government. However, such women were extremely rare.[17]

For women without powerful families and large resources who had acquired some education, schoolteaching provided one of the few genteel means of earning a living. The normal schools did not attract women from the most privileged strata of society, for the wealthy never wished to become primary school teachers; nor did they lack access to private schooling. But for middle-sector women obliged to support themselves, few acceptable alternatives like office work existed before the twentieth century. With education, they could avoid lower-class jobs like domestic service, the most common occupation for urban women.

Despite some male disapproval of women entering the classroom, by the end of the nineteenth century teaching was generally accepted as an extension of the traditional nurturing role of women—motherhood on a larger scale. Moreover, female schoolteachers could be hired at lower salaries than their male counterparts, as men well knew. In his first speech in the Rio de Janeiro provincial legislature in 1874, Alberto Brandão argued that women should become elementary school teachers, even instructing coeducational classes, ostensibly because they would "guarantee more the principles of morality." But he clearly implied that women could be paid less, and he envisioned the teaching profession as one presenting opportunities for poorer women.[18] And as one educator recognized several years later, the increasing numbers of women entering this field definitely led to declining salaries.[19]

The replacement of men by lower-paid women in the nation's primary school classrooms was well under way by the end of the nineteenth century. Until late in the century virtually no jobs other than teaching existed for women with some education and status. Hence there were women willing to teach for lower salaries than men received. In Rio de Janeiro in 1872, women already comprised a third of the city's teachers. By the early twentieth century more than two-thirds were women, and by 1920 more than three-fourths. Similar growth could be seen in other cities (see tables 5 and 6). By the last

Table 5. Primary and Secondary School Teachers in Rio de Janeiro, 1872–1920

		Men				Women			
	Total	Brazilian	Foreign	Unknown	Total	Brazilian	Foreign	Unknown	Total
1872	897[a]	396	188	—	584 (65.1%)	269	44	—	313 (34.9%)
1890	2,057	1,106	161	—	1,215 (61.6%)	666	124	—	790 (38.4%)
1906	2,842	693	189	1	883 (31.1%)	1,740	216	3	1,959 (68.9%)
1920	7,363	1,014	370	—	1,384 (18.8%)	5,391	586	2	5,979 (81.2%)

Sources: Recenseamento da População . . . 1872, Município Neutro, 21:61; Recenseamento do Rio de Janeiro . . . 1906, 1:104, 180–389; Brazil, Directoria Geral de Estatística, Recenseamento geral da República dos Estados Unidos do Brazil em 31 de Dezembro de 1890. Districto Federal (Cidade do Rio de Janeiro), pp. 408–11; Recenseamento do Brazil . . . 1920, vol. 4, pt. 5, tomo 1, pp. 24–27.

[a] 1872 figures include "teachers and men of letters."

quarter of the nineteenth century ever more girls were entering normal schools, sometimes forming a majority of those in attendance. Not only did the number of female primary school teachers increase, but some women even taught at the normal schools or directed schools for boys.[20]

Despite meager wages and difficult working conditions,[21] school-teaching gave some women more economic independence than they otherwise would have had. In her diary of life in a town in the old diamond-mining district of Minas Gerais in the 1890s, Alice Brant, a lively, outspoken schoolgirl, recounted how several of her aunts entered normal school late in life when one finally opened in Diamantina in 1879, became schoolteachers, and were able to live frugally on their limited income as well as help their families.[22] Moreover, schoolteachers could serve as agents of social change. Such women not only helped to increase female literacy but sometimes also consciously sought to disseminate new ideas on women's roles and rights. A few teachers even numbered among the earliest opponents of the subordination of women in Brazil, who, through the printed word, sought a wider audience for those new views. Out of the ranks of the nation's growing

Table 6. Primary and Secondary School Teachers in São Paulo, 1872–1920

		Men			Women		
	Total	Brazilian	Foreign	Total	Brazilian	Foreign	Total
1872	57[a]	29	10	39 (68.4%)	17	1	18 (31.6%)
1893	396	121	65	186 (47.0%)	146	64	210 (53.0%)
1920	4,439	673	433	1,106 (24.9%)	2,878	455	3,333 (75.1%)

Sources: Recenseamento da População . . . 1872, São Paulo, 19:1–17; São Paulo (State), Repartição de Estatística e Arquivo, Relatório, 1894, map 6A; Recenseamento do Brazil . . . 1920, vol. 4, pt. 5, tomo 1, pp. 170–73.

[a]1872 figures include "teachers and men of letters."

minority of literate women came both the early advocates of the emancipation of women in Brazil and the audience for these pioneers' published efforts and exhortations.

The Women's Rights Press

Newspapers served as a major medium for the exchange of ideas and information among Brazil's literate classes. In the nineteenth century, and into the twentieth, both ephemeral and longer-lived periodicals proliferated. Numerous Brazilians in urban areas resorted to journalism for the propagation of a wide range of beliefs and activities.[23] Like their male compatriots, advocates of female emancipation also considered the press a major means of diffusing knowledge, and they urged women to read newspapers to learn their rights and obligations.[24] Periodicals provided women with a means for initiating the discussion of their own interests.

During the second half of the nineteenth century a few daring women published their own newspapers, beginning with O Jornal das Senhoras, whose first issue appeared in Rio de Janeiro on January 1, 1852. This journal was edited by Joana Paula Manso de Noronha, an Argentine whose family had fled the Rosas regime years before. In Rio, where she married a Portuguese violinist and composer in 1844, she taught school, collaborated on Brazilian newspapers, and published several literary works. In the introductory editorial to *O Jornal das Senhoras* Joana Paula Manso stated her intention to work for "social betterment and the moral emancipation of women." She recognized what a novelty it was for a woman to edit a newspaper in Brazil. People would inquire as to "what kind of a Hydra-headed monster it would be." She knew that to speak of women's rights, their mission, and their education would cause others to say, "this is not the kind of reading matter that should be permitted inside a family's home." But God gave woman a soul and made her "equal to man," and "his companion." Women were not inferior to men in intelligence. Moreover, the nineteenth century was the "century of knowledge," and South America should not remain apart and stationary. Like later feminist newspaper editors in Brazil, Joana Paula Manso believed strongly in progress and looked to the examples set by European nations and by the United States, which she visited in 1846. Since many members of the Brazilian elite favored progress in theory and responded to foreign leadership in other matters, she argued that Brazil must not remain apart "when the entire world marches toward progress and moves toward the moral and material improvement of society."[25] (See appendix A for the complete text of Joana Paula Manso's introductory editorial from the first issue of *O Jornal das Senhoras*.)

The picture that emerges from the pages of *O Jornal das Senhoras* as to how Brazilian men regarded women is not dissimilar to that painted by foreign travelers. Decades earlier, John Luccock had described Brazilian women as "regarded by the men as dolls, or spoiled children."[26] Like women in other countries during the nineteenth century, including the United States and Great Britain, Brazilian women might resent the so-called Victorian image of themselves as doll-like, one-dimensional figures and complain that they were not taken seriously. A Brazilian woman was considered modest and proper only when "always looking at the ground and responding in monosyllables." Many Brazilian men thought women came into the world "only to serve as a *propagation machine*." For *O Jornal das Senhoras*, the moral emancipation of women must include "the just enjoyment of their rights, of which they have been robbed and disinherited by *brutal male egoism*, because men have physical force and because they are still not convinced that an angel will be more useful to them than a doll."[27]

Men and women viewed marriage very differently. According to *O*

Jornal das Senhoras, for a woman, marriage was "the goal, the purpose of her life," since love was the only hope for her existence. But love, the greatest thing in the world, could not exist between master and slave. In marriage women always found deception, unbearable tyranny, or abandonment. In contrast, for most men, marriage was just a "means for satisfying a desire, a whim, or simply a way to alter their civil status. Or to assure their fortune." Hence, a man would say "my wife—with the same vocal intonation that he uses to say—*my horse, my boots,* etc.," for all were "household instruments he used," unworthy of his attention. *O Jornal das Senhoras* held that until men ceased to "consider women as their property, we will not have accomplished anything."[28]

Through its entreaties and arguments, *O Jornal das Senhoras* attempted to persuade Brazilian men of the mid-nineteenth century to elevate their women to the position that later writers often stated they had actually occupied. The image of the secluded, passive female has often been accompanied by the glorification of the woman as the mother of Brazil's sons; and it has been argued that even though she was denied economic and political influence outside the home, she was very influential within the confines of the family circle. The fervent pleas of the outspoken, determined editor of *O Jornal das Senhoras* that men see their wives as the focal personality around whom all the members of the family should group themselves spiritually, bound by sentiment, are evidence that their "unknown mission" often did go unrecognized.[29] Again, image did not match reality.

The pathway up to the pedestal, to becoming an angel rather than a doll, led through the family, with an assist from Jesus of Nazareth. He "was the first who raised you from your ignominy! He was the first who revealed your mission to the world." While some later women might think the Virgin Mary cast too deep a shadow across their lives, *O Jornal das Senhoras* attempted to enlist her assistance and that of her Son in its efforts to improve women's lot. But perhaps of more immediate importance was the continued appeal to male self-interest as a means of ameliorating the position of women. After all, men were concerned for the future of their sons, and that must include their education. The way in which women could "have any influence other than that over pots" or "a mission beyond needlework" was through "the education of their children," who learned their first lessons and their morality from their mothers. This noble task of educating children gave women value. Moreover, one way to change men's minds was by molding those of boys. Mothers could help all women by "eradicating this fatal prejudice in their sons' souls, this idea of an unwarranted superiority." Women had to be educated and treated with respect if they were to fulfill their duties.[30]

Although impossible to gauge fully, the response to the fervent pleas and entreaties of *O Jornal das Senhoras* seems to have included both male hostility and female timidity and indifference. Collaborators had to be promised anonymity in publication. One reader, who had learned of the journal through an announcement in a major Rio newspaper and who had to ask her father to order the paper, expressed her gratitude to the editor. It was as if "I were very thirsty and hot, and you offered me ice cream." She complained that women in Brazil were "almost passive," but *O Jornal das Senhoras* "came to open a field of activity" in which women could exercise their talents and "escape our state of vegetation." However, like other readers who offered to contribute to the journal, she wished to remain anonymous. Even the author of the section on fashions showed herself very much afraid of possible ridicule, and, admitting she lacked the editor's courage, requested that her anonymity be maintained.[31] Within four years some changes came, and a few women signed their initials to their contributions. Male contributors who gave their full names also appeared.

The weaknesses of this early effort at female emancipation were also demonstrated by the financial problems faced by *O Jornal das Senhoras*. Its first editor, Joana Paula Manso, lacked a private fortune and felt obliged to leave the editorship six months after she began. In order to save the newspaper, she turned it over to Violante Atabalipa Ximenes de Bivar e Vellasco, the widow of João Antonio Boaventure and the daughter of Diogo Soares da Silva de Bivar, member of the Imperial Council and founder and director of the Brazilian Dramatic Conservatory in Rio de Janeiro. Before collaborating on *O Jornal das Senhoras* Violante Ximenes de Bivar e Vellasco had translated French and Italian comedies, only one of which appeared in print, and had reviewed some plays for the Dramatic Conservatory, which had the power to license and censor them. Moreover, she probably was the hesitant author of the section on fashions in *O Jornal das Senhoras* mentioned above.[32] As editor, Dona Violante stressed the emotional superiority of women and their numerous spiritual qualities. She also appealed to male self-interest, arguing that when men deny women education, they are endangering society and their own existence. A "well-educated woman replete with the religiosity that is always natural to her" would better exercise "her sacred functions as wife and mother." But Dona Violante left the editorship after one year, turning it over to Gervasia Nunezia Pires dos Santos, a contributor who had been signing herself "Gervasia P.," and whose husband was able to aid the newspaper. *O Jornal das Senhoras* could not survive on exhortations or feminine literary attempts alone.[33]

As ideas such as those advocated by *O Jornal das Senhoras* gained wider acceptance, they could be used to help improve the position of women. Subsequent editors of feminist newspapers did not call so insistently for a place on the pedestal. They assumed that womanhood, especially motherhood, was already a respected and somewhat elevated position. They employed such esteem in their efforts to help women move beyond a restricted family circle and improve their position in the outer world. Perhaps it would be easier for an angel than for a doll to become an active, equal human being. But the pathway remained a difficult one for either to tread.

Although the contributors to *O Jornal das Senhoras* had demonstrated great timidity, they had taken a small step along the road toward overcoming their fears and had become more conscious of the problems they faced. A further awakening, and a different method for facilitating it, became evident with the publication of *O Bello Sexo* in Rio de Janeiro in 1862, less than a decade after the demise of *O Jornal das Senhoras*. No longer would contributors, mostly women who had acquired a secondary education, feel the need for complete anonymity, although they seemed reluctant to sign their full names to their contributions despite the insistence of the editor, Júlia de Albuquerque Sandy Aguiar, that no unsigned articles would be published. And, more important, they actively sought out each other. In fact, a group of women met once a week to discuss items to print in *O Bello Sexo*. Their numbers increased steadily, from ten at the first session to thirty-seven by the fifth. Through their discussions, new viewpoints and ideas emerged that allowed women to express themselves more freely.[34]

In the 1870s, new journals founded by women appeared in Brazil's growing cities, where educational opportunities for women surpassed those in rural areas and small towns. The proportion of literates among the women of Rio de Janeiro stood at 29.3 percent in 1872, as compared with 11.5 percent for Brazil's entire female population.[35] In 1873 a forthright and outspoken schoolteacher, Francisca Senhorinha da Motta Diniz, published her first newspaper, *O Sexo Feminino*, in Campanha da Princeza, Minas Gerais. The next year both *O Domingo*, edited and owned by Violante Ximenes de Bivar e Vellasco, and *Jornal das Damas* appeared in Rio de Janeiro, followed by Maria Heraclia's *Myosotis* in Recife in 1875 and Amélia Carolina da Silva Couto's incisive *Echo das Damas* in Rio de Janeiro in 1879. Although several women were now publishing journals, they remained relatively isolated. While each newspaper might have its own circle of like-minded women, the editors often lacked not only personal contact with one another but also knowledge of all their predecessors and contemporaries.[36]

These female newspaper publishers advocating the emancipation of women stood apart from the more numerous male editors of newspapers also directed toward women. While several of those journals, which emphasized fashions or literature, endured for decades, others lasted only a few weeks. Most relied on male contributors, although some published female literary efforts. Few attempted to provide more than entertainment, let alone question the established order. One newspaper even sought to explain how "the emancipation of women should not be, as some insist, the same as the emancipation of men, because for women religion is everything and women's influence is manifested in all their deeds and acts." Other journals just compared women to flowers or lauded them as "the smile of the world."[37] But most preferred to limit their opinions to matters of fashion, balls, and the theater. Many literate Brazilian women no doubt found such journals less challenging or upsetting and more enjoyable than those advocating women's rights.

From the beginning, newspaper publishers like Francisca Diniz stressed the importance of basic education for women, both to benefit them and to improve the world. Francisca Diniz dedicated *O Sexo Feminino* to the education, instruction, and emancipation of women; in it she would "continually fight for the rights of our sex, which up to now have been trampled underfoot by the opposite sex." Instead of directing herself to men, pleading with them to change their attitudes and behavior toward women in their own interests, or repeatedly appealing to the image of the Virgin Mary, as had *O Jornal das Senhoras* two decades earlier, she strove to awaken women to their conditions, needs, and potential. She saw that the enemy they were fighting was hiding in women's ignorance, which "is determined by the body of

Anno 1.   Cidade da Campanha, 7 de Setembro de 1873.   Num. 1.

O SEXO FEMININO

SEMANARIO DEDICADO AOS INTERESSES DA MULHER.

Assignaturas.

Por anno. . . . . 5$000
Por semestre . . . 2$500
Publica-se 1 vez por semana.

« E' pelo intermedio da mulher que a
natureza escreve no coração do homem »

(AIMÉ' MARTIN.)

Observação.

Toda correspondencia será
dirigida á D. Francisca Senhorinha da Motta Diniz.

PROPRIETARIA E REDACTORA—*D. FRANCISCA S. DA M. DINIZ.*—COLLABORADORAS, DIVERSAS.

O Sexo Feminino.

A educação da mulher.

Zombem muito embora os *pessimistas* do apparecimento de um novo orgão na imprensa—O *Sexo Feminino*; tapem os olhos os *indifferentes* para não verem a luz do progresso, que, qual pedra desprendida do rochedo alcantilado, rola violentamente sem poder ser impedida em seu curso; rião os *curiosos* seu riso sardonico de reprovação á idéa que ora surge brilhante no horizonte da cidade da Campanha; agourem bem ou mal o nascimento, vida e morte do *Sexo Feminino*; persigão os *retrogrados* com seus diterios de chufa e mofa nossas conterraneas, chamando-as de *utopistas*: O *Sexo Feminino* apparece, hade luctar, e luctar até morrer: morrêrá talvez, mas sua morte será gloriosa e a posteridade julgará o perseguidor e o perseguido.

O seculo XIX, seculo das luzes, não se findará sem que os homens se convenção de que mais de metade dos males que os opprimem é devida ao descuido, que elles tem tido da educação das mulheres. e ao falso supposto de pensarem que a mulher não passa de *um traste de casa*, grosseiro e brusco gracejo que infelizmente alguns individuos menos delicados ousão atirar a face da mulher, e o que é mais as vezes, em plena sociedade familiar ! ! !

Em vez de paes de familia mandarem ensinar suas filhas a coser, engomar, lavar, cosinhar, varrer a casa etc., etc., mandem-lhes ensinar a ler, escrever, contar, grammatica da lingua nacional *perfeitamente*, e depois, *economia e medicina domestica*, a *puericultura*, a *litteratura* (ao menos a nacional e portugueza), a *philosophia*, a *historia*, a *geographia*, a *physica*, a *chimica*, a *historia natural*, para coroar esses estudos a *instrucção moral e religiosa*; que *estas meninas assim educadas* não dirão quando moças estas tristes palavras:

« Si meu pai, minha mãi, meu irmão, meu marido morrerem o que será de mim ! ! »

Não sirva de cuidado aos paes que suas filhas, assim educadas e instruidas, não saibão coser, levar, engomar, cortar uma camisa, etc. etc.

A riqueza intellectual produzirá o dinheiro, e com este se satisfarão as necessidades.

O dinheiro, Deos o dá e o diabo póde tirar; mas a sabedoria que Deos dá—o diabo não a roubará.

First number of *O Sexo Feminino*, published in Campanha, Minas Gerais, September 7, 1873.

knowledge of men." Now these "meek lambs" must "cease being sub-jugated" and "always manacled, oppressed, and dominated" by men. They must open their eyes "to the injustices, the control, and the neglect of their rights." With education they could recuperate lost rights, raise their children properly, understand their families' business and finances, and be their husbands' companions, not slaves. "With instruction we will attain everything, and we will also break the chains that have choked us since the remote centuries of obscurantism."[38] (For the complete text of Francisca Senhorinha da Motta Diniz's Oc-tober 25, 1873, article in *O Sexo Feminino* stating feminine needs and demands, see appendix B.)

Francisca Diniz, one of the most outspoken female newspaper pub-lishers, expressed no doubts as to the abilities and potential achieve-ments of women. They were "endowed with the same mental powers as men, with intellects and minds apt for the cultivation of the arts and sciences, so that they could be useful to the nation and fulfill their mission in society."[39] Francisca Diniz utilized the old notion of separate spheres of activities for men and women—long employed to keep upper- and middle-class women in the home—to carve out additional realms for them. The nurturing and maternal functions could easily be ex-tended beyond the home into the classroom. She not only declared that women made superior primary school teachers but also that this field should be exclusively theirs, thus opening the door to more jobs for women. In turn, some fields, especially those involving brute force or violence, like soldiering, would be left exclusively to men. But Fran-cisca Diniz insisted that all other careers should be open to women. Through work and the right education, girls could "acquire the ways and means of obtaining what was necessary for their subsistence and even for their fortune," and could be "independent of men."[40]

Francisca Diniz's commitment to the emancipation of women ex-tended far beyond the ideal of self-determination, and also far beyond that of some other Brazilian women's rights advocates in the 1870s. Her personal experiences and observations had convinced her of the need to provide women with basic skills because so many of them, as in her own case, became the sole support of themselves and their families. She knew full well that economic dependence promoted fe-male subjugation and that improved education could help raise wom-en's status.

Francisca Diniz's faith in the power of education was closely related to her belief in progress. Continually affirming her century to be one of knowledge, as had Joana Paula Manso decades earlier, she noted "gigantic steps of progress." Thanks to these, a Brazilian father would no longer "dare declare with impunity that *it is not necessary, I do not want my daughter to learn to read,* as our ancestors once used to say." Those opposed to the "rational emancipation of women" would find themselves isolated and left behind. Seeing "a new era of prosperity and justice for our humiliated sex" dawning in different countries, Francisca Diniz eagerly reported specific examples of female achievements in *O Sexo Feminino*. In the United States, which had "sounded the cry of the independence of women," females were "free from the ridiculous prejudices that vex[ed] them in older societies, and [were] an active element of progress, zealous coparticipants in social improvement and prosperity."[41] While Brazil's women faced a more difficult struggle for their freedom, Francisca Diniz remained confident of eventual success. Violante Ximenes de Bivar e Vellasco (*O Domingo*) and Amélia Carolina da Silva Couto (*Echo das Damas*) also drew inspiration and evidence of women's capacities from female accomplishments in other countries, as well as from famous women in history. The United States, the *Echo das Damas* asserted, provided "examples of the moral and material improvements" reaped by a nation which not only progressed in technology and industry but also cultivated women's intelligence.[42]

Judging the nature of the response to these newspapers and their message is no easier than measuring the direct influence of other new ideas. Some readers wrote in to express their agreement with the mind-expanding notions presented in periodicals like *O Sexo Feminino*, as they had to *O Jornal das Senhoras* two decades earlier, and to urge others to publish their thoughts, for it was time for Brazilian women to imitate, if not exceed, women in other countries. Francisca Diniz expressed satisfaction and pride when important personages like Emperor Pedro II and his daughter Princess Isabel were subscribers. Perhaps some members of the elite who wished to keep abreast of the latest intellectual developments—such as the emperor with his cherished reputation as a scholar—felt obliged to purchase and possibly read *O Sexo Feminino* and other newspapers calling for the emancipation of women. At other times, however, Francisca Diniz felt discouraged, for most women in Rio de Janeiro seemed never to have heard of her journal.[43]

In 1875 she moved *O Sexo Feminino* from the small city of Campanha,

Minas Gerais, where it had proved successful, to the nation's capital, with high hopes of extending her work among the people of Rio, who were "always enthusiastic for ideas of progress." During its year in Campanha, *O Sexo Feminino* had attained a circulation of eight hundred, with subscribers from various parts of the Brazilian empire.[44] Since only 1,458 women out of a total population of 20,071 in Campanha could read and write in 1872,[45] *O Sexo Feminino* probably reached a sizable percentage of the local literate female population, as well as an audience beyond the town's limits. In fact, reader response led Francisca Diniz to reprint four thousand copies of the first ten issues to satisfy new subscribers and to sell in Rio de Janeiro. But publishing in Rio proved more costly and difficult than in Campanha. Only by increasing the number of subscriptions could her journal survive, for she lacked a private fortune and refused to go to the "extreme of depriving my family of bread" to propagate her ideas and aid women. Indifference, as she knew, can be more deadly than hostility. Not all women responded to ideas of "liberty" or "emancipation"; many preferred to spend their time on their physical appearance rather than cultivate their minds.[46]

For almost three years *O Sexo Feminino* survived, without diluting its message or compromising its standards, in a Brazil replete with ephemeral newspapers often enduring through only one or two issues. Then a yellow fever epidemic forced Francisca Diniz to leave Rio de Janeiro and suspend publishing in 1876. Four years passed before she could begin another journal in Rio de Janeiro. *Primaveira* appeared in 1880 but did not survive the year, and was followed by the short-lived *Voz da Verdade* in 1885. In 1889 *O Sexo Feminino* reappeared and encountered more success than before, achieving a circulation of 2,400.[47]

By 1890 the number of women editing or writing for women's rights newspapers was sufficiently large for mutual support and intellectual interchange. The increase in literate women in major cities as urban growth intensified provided a larger audience for this and other journals advocating the emancipation of women, but it was an audience still limited to upper- and middle-class women. The proportion of literates among the total female population in Rio de Janeiro rose from 29.3 percent in 1872 to 43.8 percent in 1890 while at the same time the capital's total population nearly doubled.[48] In the 1880s and 1890s more newspapers defending women's rights appeared. *O Domingo* had ceased publication in 1875 when Violante Ximenes de Bivar e Vellasco died at the age of fifty-seven. The number of subscriptions had not been sufficient to cover expenses.[49] But Amélia Carolina da Silva Couto's *Echo das Damas,* suspended in 1880, returned in 1885, defending women's equality and right to education more strongly than before. New journals appeared: Idalina d'Alcanatara Costa's *O Direito das Damas* in Rio de Janeiro in 1882; Josefina Alvares de Azevedo's *A Família,* begun in São Paulo in late 1888 and moved to Rio de Janeiro six months later in search of greater opportunities; and *A Mensageira,* directed by Preciliana Duarte de Almeida in São Paulo in 1897. Rio, the nation's largest city and political and intellectual center, continued to provide the most fertile ground for newspapers calling for female emancipation; very few appeared elsewhere. Through the journals they published in tiny but increasing numbers during the second half of the nineteenth century, Brazilian women's rights advocates demonstrated concern with a number of major issues, including the legal status of women, family relationships, access to higher education and careers, and, finally, political questions such as the abolition of slavery and the vote for women.

Women's Associations and the Abolition Movement

Women's associations can play a large role in creating feminist ideology and sparking a demand for women's rights, as in the United States during the 1830s. Unlike urban men, who could pursue community and personal fulfillment through a variety of ways, middle-class women in the United States had virtually no alternatives other than joining voluntary associations. Boredom, loneliness, and a craving for identity all helped lead to a network of women's organizations.[50]

While the female voluntary associations of the second quarter of the nineteenth century found no exact parallel in Brazil, some upper-class Brazilian women in the 1860s also proposed benevolence as an antidote for a tedious, useless existence. Among the Brazilian elite, slaves and servants carried out domestic chores, including much of the work of child raising. While some upper-class women liked being idle, others abhorred it and voiced their discontent. As one contributor to the short-lived *O Bello Sexo* stated in 1862, women wanted to become useful members of society. They opposed a world that kept them busy inventing new fashions, or provided them "with so many gatherings to tire us out gossiping instead of working for others," or expelled them from secondary schools when they had "barely begun to read, scribble, add, subtract, and multiply" in order to attend parties and look out windows and sleep until ten or eleven o'clock in the morning. Such women did not want to let society "always distract us from what is more useful, though more difficult." While they still wished to marry well and be happy, they also saw the need to "regenerate" their sex and ensure "moral and physical liberty" to all its members. They could help remedy society's imperfections—a slow, difficult task necessitating patience and goodness, not excesses.[51] Boredom helped stimulate a desire for change in at least a few Brazilian women, as it had in the United States several decades earlier. For these women, charity work outside the home would constitute a step forward. Choosing the motto Religion, Work, Literature, and Charity, the women publishing *O Bello Sexo* assigned the hoped-for profits from their newspaper to be given in the name of their sex to the Imperial Sociedade Amante da Instruc-ção, a charity for orphans.[52]

While increasing numbers of voluntary associations appeared in Brazilian cities during the nineteenth century, they were never as pervasive as in the United States.[53] Nor did Brazilian women's groups attract public attention. Only a few small female abolitionist societies received brief and sporadic notice in the press.

The gradual elimination of slavery elsewhere in the Western Hemisphere left Brazil as the institution's largest and last bastion, to the

Josefina Alvares de Azevedo, editor
of *A Família*. (Special number of
A Família, 1889)

chagrin of many foreign-oriented members of the elite.[54] Pressure from abroad had helped lead to the suppression of the African slave trade in the mid-nineteenth century. Within Brazil, slavery declined in importance in the impoverished Northeast while concentrating within the prosperous southern coffee provinces. In 1864 one-fifth of the inhabitants of the northeastern sugar province of Pernambuco were slaves, while they comprised only one-tenth of the population of São Paulo. By the early 1870s approximately one-fifth of the inhabitants of the prosperous coffee-exporting province of São Paulo were enslaved, as compared with one-tenth of the people of Pernambuco. During this period the proportion of slave to freeman within the nation as a whole declined only slightly, to approximately 15 percent.[55] Emancipation sentiment proved strongest in the cities and in those regions with the fewest slaves. A year before the final abolition of slavery in May 1888, the city of Rio de Janeiro, an abolitionist stronghold with a total population of approximately 500,000, contained fewer than 7,500 slaves, while the province of São Paulo, with well over 1 million inhabitants, had 107,329 slaves.[56]

As the abolitionist campaign gathered strength in the 1880s, the handful of active urban-based abolitionists skillfully mounted their verbal attacks on the institution of slavery. Military officers, engineers, bureaucrats, journalists, and businessmen all participated. Some abolitionist societies also sent agents into the countryside to provoke slaves to flee, as well as aiding the escapees arriving in the cities. However, many slaves needed no persuasion to abandon the plantations, especially by the late 1880s.

Although their assistance has since been largely forgotten, some Brazilian women contributed to the movement for the abolition of slavery, but not in policy-making positions. By the 1880s abolition had become a praiseworthy goal, the object of a broad-based movement in various urban circles. Like charity work, this noble cause could safely evoke female efforts, which were seen as an extension of traditional female benevolence.

Women's roles and activities in the abolition campaign reflected their subordinate situation in society. They helped raise funds to free slaves rather than participating in public debate over emancipation. Piano performances or arias by daughters and wives of male abolition leaders graced abolition meetings. Since elite women had long entertained at private social gatherings, few Brazilians could think it improper for talented Luiza Regadas of Rio de Janeiro to lend her lovely voice to numerous abolitionist fund-raising meetings. Like other abolitionist women, she also sold flowers and dainty handmade objects for the cause. Some women were sent by male members of abolitionist clubs to collect funds at the entrances to cemeteries and churches.[57] While these activities necessitated a certain resolve and a determination to undergo such physical discomfort as standing in the rain all day, they also served to reinforce the noble, self-sacrificing female image.

Some women established their own abolitionist societies, often sponsored or suggested by male abolitionists. The female organizations founded in different Brazilian cities included the Sociedade da Libertação installed in Rio de Janeiro on March 27, 1870, following its suggestion at a Masonic meeting; the Sociedade Redemptora, established in São Paulo on July 10, 1870, under the inspiration of Martim Francisco Ribeiro de Andrade, whose wife served as the society's president; the Associação Protetora dos Escravos, formed in São Paulo in December 1882 to raise funds to purchase slaves' freedom; Avé Libertas, set up in Recife on April 20, 1884; and the short-lived Club José do Patrocínio in Rio, centered in the home of Patrocínio's father-in-law. The experiences these women gained increased their ability to deal with the outside world and improved their organizational skills.[58]

Few abolitionist women, however, moved beyond philanthropic activities. Those like Luiza Regadas in Rio or Leonor Pôrto, president of Avé Libertas in Recife, who sheltered runaway slaves in their homes, learned more lessons in courage and resourcefulness. Furthermore, very few Brazilian women ever spoke out publicly on the issues involved in abolition, although Leonor Pôrto published newspaper articles and pamphlets. Women's rights advocates like newspaper editors Amélia da Silva Couto and Francisca Diniz printed abolitionist statements in their journals; in fact, Francisca Diniz devoted more attention in *Voz da Verdade* in 1885 to abolition than to women's rights. But only rare women like Maria Amélia de Queiroz of Pernambuco confronted public ridicule and gave public lectures on abolition in 1887. Later, she became a leading collaborator on the outspoken newspaper *A Família* as well as continuing to travel and lecture.[59]

Unlike participants in the women's rights movement in the United States, often said to have been virtually born into the abolition movement, Brazil's nineteenth-century advocates of female emancipation did not receive their early training and stimulation from the struggle to free the slaves. They began their work long before abolitionism gathered strength in Brazil. Moreover, women remained in subordinate and auxiliary positions in that movement. While some Brazilian women aided the abolition campaign in their country, their contributions proved far less significant than those of their sisters in the United States. Not only did major Brazilian abolition associations remain male dominated, but their membership also included only the exceptional women like Leonor Pôrto, who formed part of the semi-clandestine Club do Cupim (Termites' Club) under the leadership of José Mariano in Recife. Although male abolitionists in the United States had not welcomed women into their newly formed organizations in the 1830s and suggested the formation of auxiliary ladies' societies, after much dissension and debate some of the major societies did accept women members. Women even served on the executive committees of such leading bodies as the American Anti-Slavery Society and the Philadelphia Anti-Slavery Society. However, women in the United States probably made greater contributions to the abolitionist cause through the numerous vigorous female antislavery societies that they themselves organized.[60] Unlike the United States, Brazil never served as a home for major nonhierarchical and egalitarian religious groups like the Quakers, who helped shape and carry on the American abolition movement, or Protestant evangelical groups, with their perfectionist aspirations and activist creed. Brazil's advocates of the emancipation of women remained isolated for many years and never benefited from full participation in anything like the ferment of social movements found in the mid-nineteenth-century United States.

The women who participated in the Brazilian abolition movement took another step beyond the home. Although most stopped with philanthropic activities, a few spoke out publicly on the issues involved in abolition, thereby asserting women's right to participate in political debate. Like the handful of female newspaper editors calling for the emancipation of women while also advocating the abolition of slavery, they displayed faith in the efficacy of the printed word.

During the second half of the nineteenth century, as urban society in Brazil became more complex and diversified, a small band of pioneer advocates of women's rights voiced their dissatisfaction with the traditional male-determined roles assigned to women. Largely through their newspapers, they endeavored to awaken other women to their potential for self-advancement and to raise their level of aspirations. They sought to spur changes in women's economic, social, and legal status. Members of the growing minority of literate females, the early women's rights advocates emphasized education for women as a source both of increased options for economic independence and of societal improvement.

Chapter 2

The Quest for Education, Employment, and Suffrage

Brazil's early women's rights advocates saw education as a key to female emancipation and improved status. By the 1870s some even sought higher education for women to enable them to move on to more prestigious occupations. Like many male members of the urban upper classes who pursued the material manifestations of progress, these women responded strongly to new ideas from abroad and placed their hopes in future achievements. By the end of the nineteenth century some outspoken women wanted more than mere respect and favorable treatment for females within the family and the right to education, even university education, which became possible with the educational reform law of 1879; they wanted the full development of all women's abilities, both within and outside the home. Several finally advocated the right to vote, a demand that shocked or surprised many men but which was debated, and denied, in the Constituent Congress of 1891.

Urban society in Brazil became more complex and diversified during the last quarter of the nineteenth century. The balance of income and population shifted more decisively from the Northeast to the south, whose rapidly expanding urban centers were swelled by waves of European immigrants as well as by internal migrants. Increasing industrialization and commercial activity together with improved communications and transportation contributed to an intensification of intellectual and political life among the urban upper classes. Not only did the abolitionist movement command the attention and dedication of numerous Brazilian men and women, but republicanism also reasserted itself amid increasing calls for reform of various aspects of the

imperial political and socioeconomic structure, including the education system.

Politics in Brazil produced heated debate in Parliament and the
press, but little turmoil in the streets. Although sectors of the national
elites competed among themselves for political and economic advantage, they preferred to resolve their disputes peacefully, through compromise, during the last four decades of the monarchy. Even major
political changes like the fall of the empire and the establishment of a
republic in 1889 did not involve bloodshed or mark a sharp break in
Brazilian history. The use of force was generally limited to dealings
with the poor; and here threats usually proved sufficient. Segmented
and divided by ethnicity, nationality, occupation, and workplace, the
poor and powerless had little means of articulating their common interests. The failure of virtually all movements of social protest in Brazil
since the colonial period attests to the resilience and effectiveness of
the political order.

Politics during the late empire proved highly personal in nature and
were marked by shifting coalitions of factions and individuals within
the upper classes. Personalism and clientelism marked relations among
members of the upper strata of society just as it did their dealings with
the lower orders. Within the small political community, personal relationships, distinctions, and interests rather than ideologies guided
decision making. The parties lacked national organization and popularity as well as political philosophies. Their major concern remained
the control of local patronage and power so as to secure their places
in the central government.[1] The vast authority of the emperor, Pedro II,
further personalized imperial politics. He could veto legislation, dis-
solve the Chamber of Deputies at will, and make war or peace, as well
as appoint ministers of state, presidents of the provinces, magistrates,
and other major officials. Generally conservative and lacking in imag-
ination, Pedro II had helped provide the elite with efficient government
reflective of their needs during his early reign. But his decreasing energies and powers of concentration in his later years contributed to the
decline in efficiency and effectiveness of the imperial government in
the 1880s and to his overthrow in 1889.[2]

Challenges to the existing political and economic structures mounted
in the 1880s, accompanied by the ebbing of the monarchy, the decline
of coffee cultivation in the Paraíba Valley, the successful campaign for
the abolition of slavery, and the beginnings of mass European immi-

gration to south-central Brazil. The republican movement, strongest in the coffee-rich province of São Paulo, provided one of the earliest visible, if long ineffective, sources of opposition.

With the crumbling of the coffee economy in the Paraíba Valley of the province of Rio de Janeiro by the 1870s and the expansion of production in São Paulo, *paulista* planters assumed a position of economic importance. But they did not exercise commensurate political power. The sugar barons of the Northeast and the coffee planters of the Paraíba Valley retained the ear of the imperial court and remained principal pillars of support for the existing political structure. The central government showed little sympathy for administrative and other reforms required by the social and economic transformations occurring in southern Brazil. *Paulistas* complained of neglect by the central government, unfair revenue allocations to their province, and under-representation in Parliament. A federal regime with greater local autonomy would best serve their expanding export economy.

Abolitionists saw slavery not only as an evil corrupting the nation's moral character but also as an obstacle to material progress and national self-respect. Liberation somehow would advance industry and agriculture and stimulate immigration, besides raising Brazil's status in the international community. Many abolitionists believed abolition meant merely replacing slavery with a free-labor system; freedmen would continue to work for their former masters. But to some of the movement's leaders abolition represented more than liberation. Leaders like Joaquim Nabuco, a brilliant orator and well-educated patrician planter from Pernambuco, and André Reboucas, a mulatto engineer and teacher, called for agrarian reform, compulsory education, broader political representation, and readjustment programs for ex-slaves.[3] Not only abolitionists and republicans but also the more numerous liberal monarchists proposed changes in the imperial structure. While some just sought to diffuse power, giving greater strength to the provinces, others called for an expanded suffrage, greater limitations on the emperor's power, an independent judiciary, and other reforms that would lead to federalization and decentralization.

More Brazilians pursued material growth based on technological improvements, placing their faith in a combination of science, industry, and progress. Many male members of the elite traveled abroad, exposing themselves directly to innovations in Europe. Ever more aware of the material progress made in the United States and northern Europe,

Passport photo of an Italian family emigrating to São Paulo. *(Courtesy of the Arquivo Edgard Leuenroth, Universidade de Campinas)*

Passport photo of a Spanish immigrant woman, 1921. *(Courtesy of the Arquivo Edgard Leuenroth, Universidade de Campinas)*

Immigrant families harvesting coffee on a plantation in São Paulo, ca. 1905.
(Photograph by Guilherme William Gaensly, courtesy of the Biblioteca Nacional do Rio de Janeiro)

Brazilians constructed railways, roads, and telegraph lines, and established banks, manufacturing enterprises, and insurance companies. Businessmen responded to ideas of industrial capitalism, the gospel of work, and laissez-faire, as well as to the general belief in progress and trust in science. Increasing numbers of Europeans settled in southern Brazil, where the climate most resembled that of Europe and where entrepreneurial-minded coffee planters sought them as slave substitutes. Relying on monoculture and the export of coffee to finance most of the progress they pursued, the nation's leaders tied modernization to neocolonial practices which did not benefit the majority of Brazilians and which increased dependence. Brazil remained a society with severely limited educational opportunities, restricted political participation, and large land-holdings. Admirers of the latest European ideas, inventions, and trends, the governing elites sought to modernize their nation, even to transform the cities into copies of admired European centers, but not to drastically restructure society.

Some modernizers argued, although unsuccessfully, for an improved educational system, seeing education as a key to progress in Brazil. Diffusing education, like raising the level of technology, would promote economic advancement and material growth. In a critique of Brazil's public education system widely praised by contemporaries, Antonio de Almeida Oliveira, a republican from Maranhão, deplored the ignorance and misery in which the majority of Brazilians vegetated, and advocated general education and work as means of ensuring the nation's development. Only through "enlightening the populace" would the nation "advance along the pathway of progress."[4] Statesmen like José Liberato Barroso of Ceará contended that the greatness of Brazil's future and the "achievement of its elevated destiny" depended largely on improving public education. As in the United States, universal primary education might produce not only prosperity but also political stability and unity.[5]

In 1879 the imperial Parliament passed legislation designed to improve primary and secondary education in Rio de Janeiro as well as the nation's institutions of higher education. The U.S. consul in Rio, who bemoaned the "deplorable" state of primary instruction in Brazil, welcomed this law as a major reform.[6] But primary education outside the nation's capital remained the responsibility of the penurious provinces. And even in Rio, the recipient of more governmental attention and funds than any other city, the obligatory primary education mandated by the new law never became a fact. Education remained the privilege of a few, even if the size of that minority slowly expanded in the urban areas.

Proper Female Education

Education for women centered on preparation for their ultimate destiny as wives and mothers. Even Brazilian men who considered themselves progressive and who approved of "the universal equality proclaimed by Christianity" believed the goal of women's education to be preparation for motherhood.[7] Girls should be taught to run homes well, for their destiny was to provide some man's happiness. Some education could help them become better mothers to their children and better companions to their husbands. Although traditionalists and modernizers alike assumed that women belonged in the home, modernizers enlarged the significance of the female familial role by emphasizing women's power to direct their children's moral development and furnish the nation with good male citizens. Such arguments provided a justification for increased education for women, but it was instruction that would still equip women only to fulfill familial responsibilities.

As José Joaquim da Cunha de Azeredo Coutinho, the bishop of Pernambuco, had declared at the turn of the nineteenth century, women's education, like that of men, should correspond to their duties and activities. Echoing the ideas of the seventeenth-century French churchman and writer François de Salignac de la Mothe Fénelon, he opposed those who saw no need to educate women or who condemned reading itself on the grounds that it diverted women from their proper household tasks. As guardians of the home and mentors to their children, women had a great impact on society. A sound education would better enable them to undertake their prime functions in life.[8]

As the nineteenth century progressed, more Brazilian men opposed the traditional view that motherhood did not demand learning, frequently citing Louis Aimé-Martin's 1834 book *Education des mères de famille ou De la civilisation du genre humain par les femmes* on the importance of instructing women, in whose hands reposed the "destiny of humanity." Since mothers mold tomorrow's men, girls must receive an ample education. Only well-trained and moral mothers could serve as guarantors of their children's character. By linking motherhood with progress and patriotism, Brazil's modernizers provided women with a more significant role in the life of the nation, but one they were to play only in the home. These men still believed that women's energies were properly fully devoted to the service of their families. The family circle remained a woman's state.

In his weighty critique of public education in Brazil, Antonio de Almeida Oliveira contended that women could contribute to national progress and educational reform through the moral training and early instruction they gave their children. But the great neglect of women's education left them ill-prepared to fulfill this mission. Only through enlightening future generations of women could "instruction and love become universal and Brazilian society be freed from most of its sufferings." To meet their familial, and therefore societal, obligations, girls needed a basic education equal to boys', plus sewing and embroidery. Even physical education for girls could be justified in these terms.[9]

For José Liberto Barroso, a distinguished statesman and jurist from northeastern Brazil, preparation for motherhood was the prime requirement of popular instruction, because mothers constituted the "principal source of individual happiness and public prosperity."[10] He argued that in order for Brazil to achieve greatness and "fulfill its elevated destiny, it is necessary to educate children; and to educate children it is necessary to instruct women and educate mothers" both intellectually and morally. Unlike other men who only acknowledged women's familial roles, he recognized women as "daughters, wives, mothers, and *citizens*," (emphasis mine) and praised John Stuart Mill's writings on women's rights. But he deemed premature a discussion of women's political rights in Brazil. "A man is destined to live an external life," while "a woman is destined to live an internal life, one as great and glorious as the other's. . . . The title of wife and mother is the highest honor" women can attain.[11]

The books women were to read, like the subjects they studied in school, reflected male perceptions of female roles and activities. Just as they enacted legislation regulating public education and debated theories of education in Parliament or in the press, men wrote the texts and approved the books women read. This prescriptive literature embodied the values upheld by nineteenth-century Brazilian society for the socialization of women and reflected the cultural attitudes and preferences emanating from the perception of gender roles within that society.

Brazil's literary culture was bifurcated. Upper-class men might read works on politics or philosophy, but the women of that class should exercise their weaker intellects on the less demanding fare of devotional and moralistic literature. In the schools, as in the homes, girls read books of moral sayings or the life stories of model women, which were to make them better mothers. Novels, as everyone knew, could be dangerous. Such attitudes and restrictions were encountered and condemned by Elizabeth Agassiz on a visit to a Brazilian plantation in the 1860s. When the "master of the house" saw her turning the pages of a romance found on the piano, he

> came up, and remarked that the book was not suitable reading for ladies, but that here (putting into my hand a small volume) was a work

adapted to the use of women and children, which he had provided for the senhoras of his family. I opened it, and found it to be a sort of textbook of morals, filled with commonplace sentiments, copybook phrases, written in a tone of condescending indulgence for the feminine intellect, women being, after all, the mothers of men, and understood to have some little influence on their education. I could hardly wonder, after seeing this specimen of their intellectual food, that the wife and daughters of our host were not greatly addicted to reading.[12]

Such nineteenth-century educational material can serve as an index to the behavioral norms sought for women. In 1879 Félix Ferreira, a writer and journalist critical of existing textbooks, published two works for use in Brazilian schools, one written for girls and the other for boys. *Noções da vida doméstica* stressed the "domestic" aspect of female lives, while *Noções da vida prática* highlighted the "practical" tenor of male lives. Women, he argued, needed better preparation to "fulfill their double and magnificent mission on earth," as mothers and as the "inseparable companions of men."[13]

A similar approach predominates in the collection of biographies of eminent women by Joaquim Manuel de Macedo, a writer, history teacher, and educator perhaps best known for his first novel, *A moreninha*, which featured a high-spirited young woman who had read Mary Wollstonecraft. In a book adopted by the imperial government for use in female public primary schools in Rio de Janeiro, Macedo set forth a series of "excellent examples" for Brazilian girls to emulate: charitable ladies; pious, long-suffering maidens; dutiful daughters; and virtuous, self-sacrificing wives and mothers, such as Cornelia, mother of the Gracchi, or patient Griselda. Macedo might have connected motherhood with patriotism, for as mothers, women served as the principal determinants of the nation's future, but he preferred them passive and nonintellectual. Only one writer, Madame de Sévigné, whose letters to her daughter were praised, and a few forceful women enter the pages of this book. Joan of Arc was "exceptional, beyond ordinary circumstances," and vain Elizabeth of England, "one of the greatest *men* of her day," suffered from "typical female weaknesses" and decapitated Mary Stuart out of jealousy of her reputation for beauty.[14]

Through their writings and activities, women's rights advocates such as newspaper publisher Josefina Alvares de Azevedo sought to counter the effects of such books and provide young Brazilian women with more forceful role models. She too would teach by example, while also encouraging women and proving their capacities. As part of her "propaganda" for the emancipation of women, this outspoken newspaper editor published a collection of biographies demonstrating the active, individualized roles she envisioned for Brazil's women. She offered them historical examples of women demonstrating intellect and courage as well as moral virtue as an assurance that women could indeed be people of accomplishment in their own right. Not only queens and political figures, from Joan of Arc to Isabel of Spain, but also less proper women like Cleopatra and George Sand served as heroines.[15] Such a collection of biographies, obviously, was never adopted by the Brazilian school system.

Only the rare man in Brazil would approve of the aspirations of a Josefina Alvares de Azevedo or welcome the entrance of women into elite professions like medicine and law. But the possibility of women pursuing higher education had become a topic worthy of debate in certain circles. In 1875 professors at the medical school in Rio de Janeiro, one of only two in the entire empire, considered the possibility of female students. Again, both foreign examples and traditional views of women's nature played a large part in the debate. Those who favored the "emancipation of women" pointed to the numbers of female doctors in Europe and the United States and urged that Brazil "proceed in the vanguard of civilization," while those who "believed that female aspirations should not extend beyond matters of the heart" wanted women's "world . . . limited to that of *daughter, wife, and mother.*"[16] Even after higher education for women became a legal possibility in Brazil, most educated men still assumed that women's energies should be fully devoted to the service of their families.

A work commissioned to celebrate the opening of the Liceu de Artes e Ofícios in Rio de Janeiro to women affords us an opportunity to examine the views of a large group of Brazil's leading men of letters and other distinguished citizens concerning female education.[17] With the exception of the normal school, the capital had no public institution that provided women with secondary education. In 1881 the Liceu de Artes e Ofícios, founded in 1856 to furnish technical training for working-class men, inaugurated special classes for women in drawing, music, and Portuguese. One hundred and twenty-four men and four women accepted invitations to write twenty lines to commemorate the occasion. Some sent more, and a few less, including almost two dozen poems to mark this milestone. Several ignored the stated topic, instead submitting odes to Francisco Joaquim Bethencourt da Silva, founder of the Liceu, and even a lyrical description of the "Last Day of Homer." Félix Ferreira, author of several books on women's education and one of the editors of this commemorative volume, lauded artisans and work without mentioning women or their education. Others uttered patriotic sentiments or invocations to progress. Several hailed women as angels, saints, or roses, and one viewed them as both angels and devils. With awkward images, Ignácio de Moura, an engineer and sometime poet from Pará, declared:

> Go forth, miners of the Future
> From woman's cranium extract gold![18]

Like Brazil's educators, the vast majority of the contributors to this commemorative volume who addressed themselves directly to the topic of women's education viewed it as preparation for motherhood. Most expressed the belief that better educated women could better educate their children. Through their offspring, home-bound women might influence humanity, regenerate society, or contribute to "national greatness," a phrase employed by over a dozen writers. Women's mission lay mainly in the realm of morality, transmitting "true principles" to their children. Moral virtues remained the most frequently cited subject that women should be taught.[19] For Inocêncio Serzedelo Corrêa, a positivist and political-minded army officer, women's education should be directed "more to the heart than to the brain, more to sentiments than to intelligence." "There is no question," *paulista* B. Gurgel do Amaral categorically stated, that "women do not need abstract or concrete sciences . . . since these are applied . . . in a larger sphere, outside the home." In his modernized reformulation of the old separate spheres doctrine, Senna Campos Júnior declared that "the law of the division of labor entrusts the world to men and the home to women."[20]

Over a dozen contributors hailed women in terms of an apparently sacred trinity of mother, wife, and daughter, although others added such roles as sister and grandmother. Only a few, like lawyer and dramatist Rodrigo Octavio de Oliveira Menezes, who quoted at length from a Wyoming judge's commendation of women performing jury duty, implied a concept of woman as citizen. Rather, women were destined to serve as the companions, instructors, and inspiration of citizens. Of all the patriotic models or historical examples cited, Cornelia, mother of the Gracchi, proved by far the most popular. Two contributors, however, mentioned Joan of Arc, one adding the name of Catherine the Great. Only abolitionist André Reboucas wished to educate women to become Harriet Beecher Stowes, not just Cornelias. Far more typical was the view of leading folklorist Alexandre José de Melo Moraes Filho:

> To be mother, wife and virgin
> This is woman's purpose, nothing more![21]

Even though the Liceu de Artes e Ofícios had been established to aid the working class, almost all the men of letters celebrating women's entrance into this educational institution disregarded lower-class women's need for occupational training and improved earning capacity. Some, like Brazil's leading positivists Raimundo Teixeira Mendes and Miguel Lemos, even denounced the "monstrous idea" of letting women compete with men in the job market; they wanted to see women, somehow, freed from workshops and outside work. Giving women occupational training resembling men's would contravene the laws of society, according to public official Rubem Tavares. Only a half dozen contributors, like Octávio Hudson, a typographer and republican who helped form one of Brazil's earliest labor associations, recognized that working-class families could not survive without the income women produced, or realized that work could make women independent. As Antonio Pinheiro Guedes, the army's chief surgeon, acknowledged, elementary education and professional training "constitute female emancipation, giving women the capacity to subsist on their own." But abolitionist Joaquim Nabuco stood alone in urging that women be made aware of "their abilities to pursue many different occupations which they had never thought of entering," as well as be "prepared to compete, and not be forsaken, in the struggle for life."[22]

Advanced Education and Careers for Women

Both younger and older advocates of female emancipation agreed in their emphasis on instruction for women. With improved education Brazilian women might secure better forms of paid employment. A few might even attempt to enter the professions, which provided not only forms of livelihood but also sources of influence and power.

In Brazil, higher education traditionally served to prepare young men for the prestigious professions, especially law and medicine. Few connections existed between such training and the primary school system directed (and not even successfully) at the mass of the population, for most Brazilians remained illiterate. Possession of a post-secondary degree constituted a major condition for entrance into the elite group dominating political life in Brazil during the nineteenth century. A woman could not enter the academy because it offered not disembodied knowledge but a classical curriculum intended to equip men for survival in the political world of the governing elite. Serious learning was an exclusively male puberty rite largely limited to those entitled to its benefits by birth or wealth.

Although writers and educators like Félix Ferreira approved of women studying to become schoolteachers, they opposed the idea of advanced female education. Women obliged to support themselves or contribute to family income might be trained to revise literary proofs, color fashion plates and maps, decorate hats, and make artificial flowers.[23] But in no case, Ferreira declared, should girls "proceed contrary to the laws of society" and dream of securing a university degree or becoming "literati or freethinkers."[24]

Since the early fifteenth century and the writings of Christine de Pizan, the primary demand of opponents of female subordination had been that women be permitted to obtain a serious education.[25] In the mid-1870s Brazilian advocates of female emancipation raised a similar cry, protesting the barring of women from Brazilian institutions of higher education. Not only in the capital but also in smaller cities a few women demanded equal educational opportunities. In Brazil's southernmost province of Rio Grande do Sul, schoolteacher Luciana de Abreu mounted a public platform in 1873 to denounce the injustice with which men treated women. A foundling raised by a bookkeeper's family, Luciana de Abreu married a municipal worker and, as a young mother, entered Porto Alegre's newly established normal school in 1869. Soon she was directing her own elementary school and participating in the literary and political debates of the Parthenon Society. Unlike other women who just sang, played the piano, or recited poetry at the society's meetings, she advocated equal opportunities for women, including access to advanced instruction and the freedom to follow whatever occupations they could master. Her public defense of women's rights earned her a degree of local fame prior to her death of tuberculosis at the age of thirty-two in 1880.[26]

In their defense of women's rights to advanced education, such women employed arguments similar to those advanced by their country's progress-minded men. Using the rhetoric of patriotism and the desire for economic development, they argued that a country's progress depended on its women. As Violante Ximenes de Bivar e Vellasco contended in *O Domingo,* those peoples not according women their rightful place "would always deserve the epithet of barbarians."[27] The United States, Amélia da Silva Couto claimed in *Echo das Damas,* provided "useful examples of the moral and material improvements" occurring in a country which cultivated women's intelligence.[28] In *O Sexo Feminino* Francisca Diniz depicted women in the United States as "zealous coparticipants in societal improvement and prosperity," for the nations in which women received the most complete education were the most developed and civilized. Women could be citizens "in the fullest and loftiest sense of the word," not just daughters, wives, and mothers.[29]

At the same time, some of the older advocates of female emancipation, such as Violante Ximenes de Bivar e Vellasco, never stopped using the concept of motherhood in justifying increased education for women. Like many male writers, she contended that women needed an education equal to that given men in order to educate their children properly and be good wives.

When a group of young Brazilians studying at Cornell University defended women's right to advanced education in their student newspaper, Violante Ximenes de Bivar e Vellasco hastened to reprint their article in *O Domingo.*[30] These young Brazilian students had left their homeland to struggle for the "triumph of the cause of science, which is the cause of progress, which is the cause of humanity!" Believing that Brazil needed their dedication more than ever in the age of engineering now dawning, they hastened to the United States "in order to study that science, nourished by their conviction as to the great benefits they could bestow on their country." They had observed the people of the United States "advance with giant strides toward their perfectibility, as they have an inexhaustible treasure of benefits in their women." These engineering students opposed the ignorance, pride, and egoism that led men to consider women "inferior in intelligence and discernment." As believers in progress and the work ethic, they claimed that "the light of civilization" would now vanquish "the prejudices of the past," calling everyone to work, and that "the century's progressive spirit" would demand that women share in "the monopoly of rights, the prerogatives denied them, the suppressed liberties to which they were entitled by reason and by justice." Like women in the United States, who could attend major universities like Cornell, their Brazilian counterparts should also have access to higher education.[31] Such male support for the "intellectual emancipation of women" might well please and encourage women such as Violante Ximenes de Bivar e Vellasco, who stressed the need to persuade men as well as to awaken women, and might give them more hope for the future, when such young men would play leading roles in Brazil.

Like later women's rights advocates, Francisca Diniz argued that if women in other countries could attend institutions of higher education, they should be permitted to do the same in Brazil. She rhetorically questioned "why our Brazilian empire, which prides itself in being the submissive imitator of Europe and the United States in every advancement, does not pass legislation permitting women to graduate in the fields of knowledge most indispensable in life?" "Can it be," she sarcastically inquired, "that the government fears some revolution resulting from feminine knowledge?" Francisca Diniz stressed the economic and moral benefits accruing to a country whose women became active participants in national life, an argument that might interest those Brazilians hoping to modernize and develop their homeland.[32] Nevertheless, until the 1880s, any Brazilian girl who wanted medical training had to go abroad to pursue her studies. And several did.

In 1875 a fourteen-year-old Brazilian girl, Maria Augusta Generosa Estrela, left Rio de Janeiro to study medicine in the United States. The next year, following some preparatory work in Oswego, New York, she secured special permission—she was underage—to enter the New York Medical College and Hospital for Women. According to a contemporary biographer, she had resolved to attend medical school in the United States after reading an article in *O Novo Mundo*, a Brazilian newspaper published in New York, about an American woman who earned a medical degree. Maria Estrela had already achieved a measure of fame in Brazil for her decisive behavior two years earlier when the ship carrying her and her father, a Rio merchant, home from a European business trip struck another vessel and began to sink. When her father later suffered financial reverses, his friends contributed to his daughter's education expenses in New York. The emperor also granted her financial assistance. During the course of his long reign, Pedro II bestowed educational awards on 151 of his subjects, paying their expenses in Brazil or abroad. While the male grantees devoted themselves to a variety of fields, from painting to engineering, the dozen female beneficiaries, except for Maria Estrela, were music or secondary school students.[33]

Maria Estrela's progress in medical school in New York did not go unrecorded in the Brazilian press. Some newspapers even published excerpts from her cheerful letters home, including one describing the "lovely" 1877 graduation ceremony at the New York Medical College and Hospital for Women. Not only did the new doctors receive their diplomas, but the first- and second-year students also filed by for certificates, with Maria Estrela last as she was "the shortest one of all." She anticipated how happy she would be on the day she too would climb the platform to receive her diploma: "I hope to God that you will be here, Papa, on that occasion to be the first to embrace and congratulate me on becoming the first Brazilian woman medical graduate. . . . Afterward, I shall return to our beloved and never forgotten Brazil—to cure, for free, all the poor, sick individuals of my sex. . . . Never for a moment have I regretted having embraced this profession: the more I study, the greater desire I have to learn."[34]

Like the serialized novels published by the nineteenth-century Brazilian press, biographies of this "future physician" appeared in various newspapers, including the *Echo das Damas*, praising her as an example worthy of emulation by other Brazilian women. Her successful completion of medical studies in the United States also received ample attention in the Brazilian press, ever eager to report Brazilians' accomplishments abroad, and stirred patriotic pride. Valedictorian of her graduating class of four at the New York Medical College and Hospital for Women in 1881, Maria Estrela returned to Brazil the next year, following postgraduate work in American hospitals. In 1884 she married Antonio da Costa Moraes, proprietor of the Farmacia Normal in Rio, where she carried on a practice specializing in the treatment of women and children.[35]

Maria Estrela did more than help pave the way for the provision in the 1879 educational reform legislation opening Brazil's medical schools to women. She also inspired other Brazilian women to seek a medical education. Even before she obtained her degree in 1881 and became the first Brazilian woman physician, she was joined by a second young Brazilian girl, Josefa Águeda Felisbela Mercedes de Oliveira. In 1878 Josefa de Oliveira's father, a combative journalist, lawyer, and republican from Pernambuco, had introduced a petition into the provincial legislature to send her abroad for medical training. This request led to a legislative debate illustrative of the tensions produced by attempts to widen women's sphere of action. In March 1878 Pernambuco's provincial assembly debated women's capacity for scientific activity, with the well-known surgeon Malaquias Gonçalves opposed by Tobias Barreto, a distinguished jurist who helped spread the ideas of German materialist philosophy in Brazil. Malaquias Gonçalves claimed that women's physical weaknesses and anatomically inferior brains precluded their undertaking abstract, serious study and entering such professions as medicine. In his erudite reply Tobias Barreto not only contested those physiological theories based on brain size but also cited examples of European women successfully completing medical school during the previous decade, as well as the achievements of earlier female intellectuals. During the debate Josefa de Oliveira made a personal appeal to the legislators, imploring them: "Give me a scholarship for I wish to be useful to my province." Although the legislature granted her request, the provincial president vetoed the bill. In the end, several influential and wealthy men helped her begin medical studies in New York. In 1882, during the administration of José Liberto Barroso, who, as we have seen, had long advocated improved education for women, the provincial government finally awarded financial assistance to Josefa de Oliveira.[36]

While studying medicine in New York, Josefa de Oliveira and Maria Estrela demonstrated their concern with women's rights in Brazil. Employing the language of patriotism and progress so dear to the hearts of male modernizers, they described themselves as "two Brazilians who abandoned our homeland and left the bosom of our dear families to make the great sacrifice of coming to study medicine in order to be useful to our country and to serve suffering humanity." Two "great ideas" burned in their hearts: "love of country and defense of our sex, so attacked as incapable of receiving higher education."[37]

These two medical students, "fervent partisans of human progress," published a newspaper, *A Mulher,* designed to convince Brazilian women of their latent abilities and to show that "women, like men, can dedicate themselves to the study of the sciences." Women must "acknowledge that men treat them unjustly, judging them incapable of sublime ideas and scientific undertakings" when only their lack of education kept them from being on a level with men. They cited evidence from history and science and the evolution of modern civilization to prove that "women are intelligent and capable of great undertakings." But for them, as for other Brazilian women's rights advocates, the United States, the "country favored by God to be the cradle of female emancipation," provided the best examples. Through *A Mulher* they attempted to inform their compatriots of American women's achievements and activities in fields ranging from law to medicine to philanthropy to the temperance movement. And they managed, but only briefly, to continue publishing their paper after their return to Brazil.[38]

Although a number of Brazilian newspapers cordially and briefly noted the appearance of *A Mulher,* as they did other new newspapers, the *America Illustrada* of Recife devoted four pages of rambling prose to disparaging the journal for pompously and illogically claiming to defend the rights of Brazilian women, for women should remain "timid, weak, small, but great in heart and in sentiment." These small-brained beings "should limit themselves to motherhood, making their children the alpha and omega, the beginning and end, of their lives." Otherwise, the family and society would suffer. Despite such attacks, including a two-page cartoon depicting mourners by a tombstone inscribed "Here lie the rights of man," Maria Estrela and Josefa de Oliveira persisted.[39]

Like the older Brazilian advocates of female emancipation, these two women were "convinced that without working one does not achieve a more or less independent life." Any "woman who believes that because she is a woman she has no need to study, learn, and work commits an irreparable error." Through "work, the perennial source of human well-being," women could support themselves and live free and independent lives.[40]

In arguing the urgent need for women doctors in Brazil, older women's rights advocates like Amélia Couto had contended that innumerable female "victims of cruel infirmities . . . preferred death to revealing their bodies to a man."[41] Similarly, some male physicians favoring women's entrance into Brazil's medical schools maintained that excessively modest women concealed certain illnesses from their doctors because they feared being examined by men.[42] Maria Estrela and Josefa de Oliveira also employed traditional beliefs about the distinct needs and behavior of men and women to expand occupational opportunities for some women. Citing the advantages of their chosen field for both women and society, they asserted that gentle female doctors would inspire the necessary confidence in women patients, who, in Brazil, were often reluctant to bare their bodies and their ills to male doctors. Men should "cure men, and women, women," they claimed in the name of "morality" and the "laws of equality." They hoped other Brazilian women would follow their example and demand higher education, and they expected to be followed by a phalanx of women doctors in Brazil.[43]

Even after the Brazilian government opened the nation's institutions of higher learning to women in 1879, thereby enabling them to enter the professions, only a small number of women could follow this path to prestigious employment. In addition to overcoming social pressures and disapproval, girls had to secure the necessary and frequently costly secondary education enabling them to proceed. In Brazil secondary education served essentially to prepare a limited number of male pupils for higher education. Never easy for nonmembers of the elite to obtain, it remained elusive even for women with influential parents.

Some Brazilian elementary and normal schools enrolled both boys and girls, but such mixed schools generally gained acceptance only in cases of economic necessity, particularly in smaller towns where separate facilities for both sexes proved too expensive. In these less-prestigious institutions, as in all-girl schools, women might be employed as schoolteachers; they were willing to teach for markedly lower salaries than men received, as virtually no other jobs existed for women with some education and status. But coeducation remained suspect, or at least distasteful, to Brazil's elite, as in other predominantly Roman Catholic countries. In his critique of Brazil's public education system, Antonio de Almeida Oliveira proposed coeducation, but he recognized the depth of opposition to it. Even the progress-minded Brazilian students at Cornell University in the mid 1870s who favored the emancipation of women equivocated on this subject, although they described the success of coeducation in the United States. Some educators, like Joaquim Manuel de Macedo, favored coeducational classes at the primary level, for these could be entrusted to women, who were generally "more virtuous than men"; but he did not even consider the idea of advanced education for women.[44]

It would prove very difficult for girls to pry open the doors of the best schools, such as the Colégio Dom Pedro II in Rio de Janeiro, the nation's model public secondary school, although a few girls did briefly gain admittance in the mid 1880s. That elite school received almost as much government funding as all the capital's other public secondary and primary schools combined, or, converted into dollar amounts by the U.S. consul in Rio de Janeiro, $173,095 for the Colégio Dom Pedro II as compared with $230,436 for the others in 1885.[45]

In 1883 Cândido Barata Ribeiro, a professor at Rio's medical school, enrolled his two daughters in the Colégio Dom Pedro II, a step authorized by Pedro Leão Veloso, minister of the interior, whose proposals for a female public secondary school in Rio had not met with success. An additional dozen girls also entered that prestigious institution. However, two years later, another minister of the interior, the baron of Mamoré, refused to appropriate funds for the woman engaged to accompany the girls to class and chaperon them in an otherwise all-male institution.[46] As an opposition newspaper, the *Gazeta da Tarde*, lamented, this was the equivalent of expelling these girls, who had done well in their examinations. However, this journal did not disagree with the government contention that female students, "as all authorities on education have recognized, could not remain except under appropriate vigilance." Although the government suggested that the girls could go to "suitably organized schools in which they could continue their education," none equivalent to the Colégio Dom Pedro II existed.[47]

Private secondary schools for girls remained costly and frequently inadequate, and their choice of free or public education in Rio de Janeiro was limited to the normal school and the Liceu de Artes e Ofícios. When the Liceu added specialized courses for girls in 1881, the pent-up force of female demand for education surprised the school's directors, who had allocated 200 places for women, a limit few expected to be reached. But 120 women and girls enrolled within the first two hours, and registration was closed at 600. Yet the Liceu only offered women courses in music, drawing, and Portuguese, far fewer subjects than those given the school's 1,042 male pupils, and nothing like the philosophy, algebra, geometry, Latin, Greek, English, and rhetoric taught at the Colégio Dom Pedro II. The normal school's largely female student body, in accord with the 1880 regulations, studied Portuguese, French, mathematics, geography, history, elementary sciences, and the principles of law and economics, as well as religion, music, calligraphy, drawing, gymnastics, and, of course, pedagogy. However, boys also took shop, and girls studied needlework.[48] According to an observant European journalist, Brazil's normal schools were still attended "only by the daughters of less wealthy families. . . . In

Brazil, there are no public secondary schools or institutes of advanced education for women functioning with the requisite rigor . . . as in Europe. The private girls' schools here are very far from filling this gap."[49] Rio's Liceu Santa Isabel, established by the experienced schoolteacher and newspaper publisher Francisca Diniz and her daughters, did offer girls courses in geometry, calculus, natural science, philosophy, and such foreign languages as French, German, English, and Latin, but for extra charges. And this school's financial position proved shaky in the 1880s.[50] Not until the twentieth century would coeducation come to the tuition-free Colégio Dom Pedro II, several decades after women had breached the walls of institutions of higher education in Brazil.

Despite the obstacles, a few Brazilian women followed Maria Augusta Generosa Estrela's lead and pursued a medical education. Throughout the 1880s women enrolled in Brazil's two medical schools, although, like their male classmates, not all obtained their degrees. In 1887 Rita Lobato Velho Lopes of Rio Grande do Sul transferred from Rio's to Bahia's medical school, where she was then the only woman in attendance.[51] While we cannot tell exactly how Rita Lobato was received by her professors and fellow students, her presence apparently provoked the discussion which soon ensued in the pages of a Bahian medical journal as to whether women should study medicine. One side to this debate in the *Gazeta Academica* employed physiological arguments that women's small brain size precluded their retaining the "intricate jewels" of medical truths; "women were created by Nature" just for home, family, and motherhood. As a fifth-year medical student contended, no one would want to marry a female physician, "corrupted by her continual habit of going out on the streets"; therefore, such doctors must either abandon their medical careers or remain single, "shirking their duty to provide the nation with more citizens and society with more members." The other side to the debate, stressing the wide differences in brain weight and volume among individuals of both sexes, argued that some women could master scientific subjects which smaller-brained men could not, and that women could and should study medicine.[52]

Rita Lobato graduated from Bahia's medical school in 1887, becoming the first women to receive a medical degree in Brazil. Only in the previous year had two Chileans earned medical degrees, the first women in Latin America to do so, followed by the first Mexican female doctor,

Matilde P. Montoya, who received her degree several months prior to Rita Lobato's graduation. Two Brazilian women received law degrees in 1888, while the first Chileans followed in 1892.[53] The *Echo das Damas* jubilantly proclaimed Rita Lobato an "example for young Brazilian girls, who only through education can hope to aspire to independence and personal dignity."[54] Rita Lobato married and practiced medicine for many years. In 1888 Ermelinda Lopes de Vasconcelos, a normal school graduate, earned her degree from Rio's medical faculty. She too married, in her case a classmate, Alberto Xavier de Sá, with whom she had two children, and for almost fifty years she carried on a practice specializing in the treatment of women and children.[55] More women obtained medical degrees shortly after her. Just as *Echo das Damas* praised Maria Estrela's and Rita Lobato's accomplishments as living proof of Brazilian women's capabilities, so did *A Família*, one of the most vocal women's rights advocates in the late 1880s and early 1890s, claim Antonieta Dias's graduation from the Rio medical school in 1889 as "one more victory for the sex she represents over the brutal prejudices of a limited education, still unfortunately in effect." Her accomplishment reinforced "the most vehement protests against opinions contrary to our emancipation."[56] But such opinions persisted, as did overt male hostility to women's practicing medicine.

Many male members of the elite expected lower-class women, unlike their own relatives, to enter the work force. Whether Brazilian-born or newly arrived immigrants, "every man and woman, of whatever color or nationality," should have "an honest means of livelihood by which they can obtain their daily bread." For lower-class women, this "honest work" would be performed within the homes of wealthier Brazilians.[57] Upper-class women should remain in their own houses, supervising the work of these poorer women, and should not attempt to enter the professions pursued by men of their own class.

The field of health services illustrates some of these male attitudes and illuminates problems different groups of women faced. For years, the so-called profession of nursing had been open to women, and its ranks were laden with low-paid women with limited training. Only a nurse like Ana Justina Ferreira Neri, a volunteer during the Paraguayan War clothed with the aura of patriotism, received recognition. Most women who earned their living by their nursing skills did not. Their lives of renunciation were not chosen voluntarily. While the position of midwives may have been somewhat better, only an exceptional woman like the French-born Maria Josefina Matilde Durocher, mid-wife to the imperial family and author of several works on obstetrics as well as a tract on the abolition of slavery, with her distinctive dress and sixty years of service in Rio de Janeiro, could command any re-spect from the medical profession.[58] Her severe and comfortable cos-tume also served to set her apart from other midwives, who, as she lamented, often lacked even elementary education and yet received municipal permission to practice in Rio.[59] But upper-class women who wanted to become doctors met with opposition from men of their class. While one might conceive of medicine as an extension of the traditional nurturing role, many male Brazilians did not. Opposition to women entering this profession was far greater than had been true with less prestigious and skilled fields like nursing and education.

Brazil's pioneer women doctors encountered hostility and ridicule. A challenge to exclusive male control of a prominent profession like medicine might well elicit more vocal criticism than would novel fe-male activities that posed no direct threat to male dominance, as was generally the case. Male self-interest helped determine male attitudes and behavior.

Some of the most visible manifestations of this male opposition occurred on the stage. In his 1889 comedy *As Doutoras,* Joaquim José da França Júnior, a lawyer, government official, and leading playwright of the late empire, voiced some of the more measured opposition to women in medicine. This play's plot concerns two medical classmates who marry on graduation day and set up a joint practice. But the wife's insistence on equality within the marriage and her successful com-petition with her husband for patients endangers their union. Both she and her father, a believer in progress and a pursuer of crackpot money-making schemes, argue for women's individuality and emancipation. Like some other opponents of female subjugation, she specifically ob-jects to women being transformed through love into mere "procreation machines" (act 2, scene 2). Her mother far prefers the old days when women did not think of being doctors and "limited themselves to their noble and true role as the mothers of families" (act 1, scene 2). Finally, this woman doctor succumbs, not to argument but to jealousy of an-other woman and to love for her husband who has insisted on being the "head of the family"—"or else." She renounces her career and has a baby. As her mother says, the laws of nature must win out. The play ends with the former doctor proclaiming that the child is sufficient to fill her life.[60]

The successful run—fifty performances—of *As Doutoras* no doubt helped generate an imitation even less sympathetic to women practicing medicine, penned by a lesser-known author, L. T. da Silves Nunes. Later that year, he felt obliged to defend his comedy, *A Doutora*, which depicted a female physician unknowingly entering a brothel to treat a dying woman, against charges in the women's rights press that he had intentionally "disparaged the dignity and virtue of all educated women," insulting half of humanity, and had arrived at the "absurd conclusion that the medical profession is incompatible with a girl's honor."[61] He explained that he merely sought to demonstrate that "a girl ought not to get a university degree because the very profession of medicine at times can place her in situations inappropriate for an honest woman."

Medicine remained an improper profession for the female sex.[62] As the *Revista Ilustrada*, a leading magazine of political satire, observed that same year: while some men might concede "social equality" to women, "others combated this point of view by every means and with every possible weapon, including ridicule."[63] But the question of female emancipation did not disappear, and more women attempted to enter prestigious fields of activity, finally raising the issue of political equality as well.

Women's Suffrage and the Constituent Congress of 1891

The further women moved from their traditional domestic, non-assertive roles, stepping out of the home in ways not easily viewed as extensions of their maternal functions, the more male opposition they encountered. If some men objected to female schoolteachers and doctors, they found the thought of female lawyers and politicians much more upsetting. Women performing charitable tasks outside the home were more easily accepted than women breaching the male preserve of public affairs.

The first women law graduates in the late 1880s encountered difficulties in practicing law, to the chagrin of newspapers like *O Sexo Feminino* and *A Família*. However, by the end of the century a woman had gained admission to the bar, to the applause and rejoicing of a less fervent advocate of women's rights like *A Mensageira*. This São Paulo–

based journal, published by Presciliana Duarte de Almeida, a poet and the first woman elected to the *paulista* Academy of Letters, followed the events in Rio de Janeiro with great interest. After consideration of the question by various legal bodies and decisive action by Judge Francisco José Viveiros de Castro, Mirtes de Campos, the first woman to attend the new law school in Rio de Janeiro, was permitted to defend a client in court. The trial, of a man accused of knifing another, was attended by several hundred spectators, including some fifty upper-class women. Mirtes de Campos's 1899 victory followed by just two years the admission of a woman to the bar in Ontario—the first woman lawyer in the entire British Empire. *A Mensageira* expressed great satisfaction with the events in Brazil: "Brazilian women had obtained a great triumph in the struggle for their undeniable and just demands." But only in 1906 would Mirtes de Campos succeed in gaining admission to Brazil's national legal association, the Instituto da Ordem dos Advogados Brasileiros.[64]

In the late 1880s some advocates of female emancipation carried their desire for equal rights to the point of demanding the vote, horrifying many other Brazilians, male and female. Suffrage did not lie within women's world of sentiments and the home; it marked a definite breach of the active male sphere. Many feared that if the purest and noblest of the sexes stepped down from the pedestal and out of the isolation of the home, she might be soiled or corrupted, and society would be disrupted. Like Luís Guimarães Júnior, writing in Rio's *Gazeta de Noticias,* such men recoiled from the very idea of a woman casting a ballot. Even though Guimarães Júnior cited approvingly the praises which another newspaper columnist, Alceste of *O Cruzeiro*, heaped upon women in the United States, who followed "all civil and professional careers" and served as one of the main "stimuli" for American "aggrandizement," he preferred patriotic Brazilian women to follow in the well-trod footsteps of Cornelia, mother of the Gracchi. Guimarães Júnior shrank from the very thought of "an army of female novelists, philologists, pamphleteers, and—voters. My God, no." His fervent desire that Brazilian mothers occupy themselves with "a little more than the needle, a little more than crochet, a little more than playing polkas on the piano" was reduced to a request that women inspire or stimulate male activities and accomplishments. As Guimarães Júnior declared, "a book leafed through by your hands, gentle and potent, will be read with more love, will be memorized with more desire, will be understood with more enthusiasm." His condescending words served to conclude the volume of contributions celebrating the opening of Rio's Liceu de Artes e Ofícios to women in 1881.[65]

In an 1886 article entitled "The Eternally Feminine," the *Revista Ilustrada*, Brazil's leading satirical journal, advocated a slight expansion in women's activities outside the home while deriding any move toward female political participation. Not long ago, it complacently noted, "fathers, full of prejudice and aversion to the written word, opposed their daughters' learning to read under the pretext that thus they would be prevented from corresponding with lovers." But now the press even discussed the "better half of humanity's aptitude for the liberal professions, for a wider circle of activity and work." The article concluded that "the gentle sex's sphere of action should be expanded," but that circle of activities "should not have a large radius." Without even considering the possibility of women voting, the magazine opposed the very idea of their "meddling in political struggles, . . . forming committees, or supporting candidates," for that might lead them to "sacrifice the tastiness of their husbands' supper and even [ignore] their youngest children's despondent crying."[66]

The specter of female politicians soon joined the troubling thought of women voters to rouse men's imaginations. França Júnior's play *As Doutoras* also featured a well-dressed woman lawyer who attracted newspaper attention and secured triumphs in court, proclaiming that everywhere women could "gradually conquer masculine redoubts" (act 1, scene 6). She even ran for federal deputy so as to reform the nation's legislation and further the cause of feminine emancipation. But she too succumbed to marriage and motherhood, gladly giving up her career.

Women were expected to have personal commitments to their families, but none to the public world. With the exception of Princess Imperial Isabel, designated successor and legitimate heir to Pedro II, no women occupied positions in the formal political structure. And part of the republican opposition to the monarchy during the emperor's declining years centered on Isabel and her supposedly female weaknesses, for she was widely regarded as excessively religious and under clerical influence as well as dominated by her foreign-born husband, the Conde d'Eu.[67] Moreover, the overthrow of the empire in 1889 precluded the possibility of a woman reigning over Brazil.

Brazil's early advocates of female emancipation had not sought the

vote for women even though a few exceptional women had long demonstrated interest in political questions. Years before female newspaper
editors made their appearance in Brazil, Ana Eurídice Eufrosina de
Barandas had defended women's right to participate in political discussions. During the Farrouphilha Rebellion (1835–45) in her native
Rio Grande do Sul, the principal regional revolt under the empire, she
penned a justification of women's right to voice opinions and take
political stands rather than just attend to their sewing. Women, she
insisted in a dialogue published in 1845, have the "same attributes,
the same sentiments" as men; whatever defects women demonstrated
stemmed only from masculine oppression.[68] Abolitionist women, as
we saw in chapter 1, contributed to the suppression of slavery in Brazil,
one of the few successful popular movements in the nation's history.
But voting remained a forbidden form of political activity for women
in this land of severely limited male suffrage. Since the franchise for
all literate males became a theoretical possibility only after the abolition of slavery in 1888 and the advent of a republic the following year,
it is not surprising that in the mid 1870s Violante Ximenes de Bivar e
Vellasco opposed women's admittance to either government or the
army.[69] Like *O Domingo, Echo das Damas* denied wishing to provoke
"pernicious aspirations to triumphs in politics" in women through
education, although she approved of their studying political affairs.[70]
Even *O Sexo Feminino* did not demand the vote in the mid 1870s. However, unlike the other two journals, *O Sexo Feminino* demonstrated sympathy for this proposal and expressed hope for its eventual achievement
in Brazil.

At first, *O Sexo Feminino* saw little benefit to women's suffrage and
less possibility of achieving it. Few men voted in Brazil, and an expanded suffrage was not a major issue. Changes in forms of government
scarcely affected women. To opponents of the Brazilian monarchy
Francisca Diniz retorted that in no "great republic or so-called republic
did women cease being slaves and enjoy *political rights*." But even before
she moved from Campanha to the nation's capital, she responded favorably to the idea of women voting in municipal elections, for which
foreign precedents could be cited.[71] In Brazil, as elsewhere, municipal
concerns might be viewed as an extension of the domestic sphere.
Francisca Diniz had seen the connection between complete equal
rights and the vote. Although she did not stress suffrage as an immediate goal, she viewed it as a logical extension of women's rights.

The ferment of the republican agitation of the late 1880s strengthened feminist desires for political rights and indirectly furnished women with additional prosuffrage arguments and opportunities to seek the vote. As a small minority, the republicans sought support among various segments of the population. Like other dissident politicians, they addressed the concerns not only of established political and economic entities but also of groups outside the generally closed and narrow imperial power structure, in the process helping to raise political aspirations among some of them. In São Paulo the republicans appealed to local economic interests, attracting some prosperous planters into their fold. Others attempted to make converts among the armed forces, championing demands of army officers during the "military question," the series of incidents between the imperial government and sectors of the armed forces during the 1880s. Some republicans also sought to assure skilled urban workers of their support, mingling general declarations of sympathy, expressions of concern over high food prices and rents, and promises of protection for labor with their attacks on the monarchy. But republicans, like monarchists, never directly considered the question of women's suffrage.

On November 15, 1889, a military conspiracy culminated in the overthrow of the empire and the unexpected declaration of a republic. The establishment of this republic at first provided the possibility of a slightly more open, fluid political structure. Especially in Rio de Janeiro, much of the urban population became more politicized during the early republic. With the extension of the vote in theory to all literate men, the suffrage question might well become a more vital issue to well-educated women's rights advocates experiencing a sense of political frustration and deprivation. Various groups such as the skilled urban workers, whose self-confidence and assertiveness had been stimulated by the abolition campaign and whose hopes for a better life the republicans had raised, attempted to mobilize and unify themselves and entered the political arena. Would the establishment of a republic open a new world of possibilities for women also?

Immediately after the declaration of the republic, Francisca Diniz changed the title of *O Sexo Feminino* to *O Quinze de Novembro do Sexo Feminino* (The fifteenth of November of the female sex), symbolizing her determination to gain full political rights and freedom for women as well as her hope for success. Now her newspaper devoted its columns to the women's suffrage issue above all others. No longer would a limited vote, as advocated by many in England or as once envisioned by Francisca Diniz herself, be sufficient. Women had the right to a voice on the national scene, including election to congress, although nowhere in the world had they yet achieved this.[72] (For the complete text of Francisca Diniz's editorial in the April 6, 1890, issue of *O Quinze de Novembro do Sexo Feminino* linking suffrage with women's emancipation, see appendix B, "What Do We Want?")

The emancipation of women was acquiring an ever-broader significance. By the late nineteenth century some women no longer wanted merely respect and favorable treatment within the family, or the right to education, even university education; they wanted the full development of all women's abilities, both within and outside the home. Like Josefina Alvares de Azevedo, a member of a well-placed family and the most forceful women's rights advocate of the late 1880s and early 1890s, they envisioned women working on an equal footing with men in all spheres, occupying "all positions, performing all functions; in everything we should compete with men—in governing the family as in directing the nation."[73] They tied the case for suffrage to women's equality and general human rights.

Older women's rights advocates such as Francisca Diniz no longer placed the same emphasis on educating and freeing women so that they could serve their families or even society. Now self-fulfillment was important. Women could not continue being "mutilated in our personalities." When men treated them as queens, it was only to give them "the scepter of the kitchen, or the procreation machine."[74] Now they must have full freedom and equality of rights, of which the right to vote formed an intrinsic part. Without suffrage women could not be truly equal.

Unlike other women's rights advocates, even before the fall of the monarchy, Josefina de Azevedo claimed that women's right to vote was a "latent necessity." She bitterly opposed "the ancient, stupid prejudices" which ruled Brazilian society and kept women "always in such an atrophied state that we were not even permitted to have aspirations." She urged Brazilian women to escape "the restricted sphere in which they were maintained," and to act "as complete human beings, intellectually, morally, and materially." Beyond the domestic hearth they would find "a vast field of opportunities which ha[d] been forbidden them up to now," including those in the political arena. Both in print and in public discourse, in Rio de Janeiro and on an 1889

speaking tour of northern Brazil, Josefina de Azevedo blamed the "natural egoism of the so-called stronger sex" for preventing women from
"entering directly into our titanic political battles." Women had rights
to defend, too, and with the vote they could improve their position
within and beyond the home. Aware that she could not cite foreign
precedents for full women's suffrage, she appealed to Brazilian patriotism, contending that "some nation will have to be the first to initiate
this great improvement; why not Brazil?" Following the establishment
of the republic, Josefina de Azevedo redoubled her efforts for women's
suffrage, envisioning female political participation as extending beyond
the largely passive act of casting a ballot: "We want the right to participate in elections, to vote and *to be elected* (emphasis mine), like men,
under conditions of equality."[75] (For the complete text of the December
31, 1889, editorial summarizing Josefina de Azevedo's views and arguments on the first anniversary of *A Família,* see appendix C.)

Hoping to take advantage of the vagueness of various electoral regulations, some Brazilian women strove to enter their names on voters'
lists. Under the empire, Isabel de Matos Dilon, a law graduate, attempted to vote. Later, she collaborated with Josefina de Azevedo on
A Família. When the republic was declared, five women in the far
western state of Goiás requested inclusion on the electoral lists but
were refused. In Minas Gerais two other women attempted to register
and vote.[76] Josefina de Azevedo saw their actions as a sign that women
now intended to "affect social destinies, to escape from the complete
nothingness in which we hitherto have lived." Despite setbacks, she
affirmed that "with resolution and constancy we will obtain everything that society owes us."[77]

Both Josefina de Azevedo and Francisca Diniz directed many of
their arguments to the nation's male leaders. Since the new Brazilian
republic was attempting to reconstruct government and society on a
basis of "full liberty and fraternal equality," men should not work
against the emancipation of women. Francisca Diniz charged "men
who proclaim equality" to "put it into practice."[78] As Josefina de Azevedo reminded men, since women have to obey the law, they should
have a voice in making it. No longer should men "with impunity deny
women one of the most sacred individual rights." Josefina de Azevedo
considered the vote crucial for women; on it depended their "elevation
in society."[79]

Male resistance to women's suffrage proved difficult to counter.

Much of the opposition centered on men's conception of the family and female duties. As Maria Clara Vilhena da Cunha, one of Josefina de Azevedo's collaborators on *A Família*, recognized, many men believed a woman should not deal with public affairs or even show interest in them because "she has the domestic hearth, where she is queen, able to exercise her domain there." But as Maria Clara retorted, not only was this a limited domain, but men also ruled there, making all the basic decisions.[80] Even though Josefina de Azevedo praised motherhood, employing the need to improve women's preparation for that state as an argument for increased female education, she saw no conflict between women's activities within and without the home; women did not have to choose between the two. In response to male arguments that women should dedicate themselves to motherhood alone, she contended that "a woman who is a mother does not forfeit anything in being a citizen"; she can both "educate her children and fulfill civil duties, just as a man assumes family duties and those of a citizen."[81]

Like some male opponents of female emancipation, Josefina de Azevedo turned playwright to present her views, publishing and staging at the Recreio Dramático theater in Rio de Janeiro a comedy entitled *O Voto Feminino* to help persuade the nation's leaders to act. But her play would be far more coolly received than França Júnior's *As Doutoras*.[82] In Josefina de Azevedo's rather serious one-act comedy, set in the home of a wealthy ex-minister of the empire, the women, who have all the best lines, argue strongly for the right to vote and to be elected, while the men, with the exception of a congressman who introduced a suffrage bill, oppose them. When the ex-minister berates his wife over a few cents unaccounted for in the household budget, she retorts that "we no longer live in the age of woman as household object, slave to masculine insolence," for "each person is an individual equally fit for the struggles of life." Although he replies that "women were made for household tasks and nothing more!" and tells her not to become involved in politics, we learn that she used to write his official reports and rulings for him. Their daughter follows in her mother's footsteps, arguing for female equality as well as instructing her less intelligent congressman husband "each night as to what he must say." Should women's suffrage legislation be approved, the mother envisions a glorious future for her daughter; rather than just supporting her husband's ambitions, the daughter should run for deputy, and then become a "senator, afterwards a minister, and perhaps even achieve the position of president of the republic." She can be both a good mother and a distinguished politician. After all, as her mother declares, "we are equal to men, with just some sexual differences and added virtues." In this play, as in her newspaper editorials, Josefina de Azevedo pinned her hopes for women's suffrage on a new republican constitution. The last scene finds both sides confidently awaiting the coming of the constituent congress and its decision on the issue.[83]

A year after the overthrow of the monarchy, the provisional republican regime headed by Marshal Manuel Deodoro da Fonseca called a constituent congress to reestablish the nation on a legal basis by framing a republican constitution for Brazil and electing a president and vice president. In that constituent assembly, which met early in 1891, men debated women's suffrage as well as other political issues that most thought far more important. Congressional halls heard but did not reverberate endlessly with the Spencerian arguments of Tito Lívio de Castro on women's child-size brains, mental inferiority, and evolutionary retardation.[84] Few congressmen admitted believing, as did José Candido Lacerda Coutinho of Santa Catarina, that women were physically and mentally incapable of withstanding the excitement of struggles in the outside world. For this practicing physician, even education could not change women's nature; women "have functions which men do not; these functions are so sensitive, so delicate that the slightest nervous agitation, a fright, a moment of excitement, is sufficient to disturb them with consequences which many times are disastrous."[85] Rather than agree with Lacerda Coutinho on women's weaknesses, other congressmen conceded women's intellectual capacities but opposed suffrage in the name of the conservation of the family. For José de Mello Carvalho Moniz Freire of Espírito Santo, women's suffrage was "immoral and anarchic." He held that "the day Congress passes such a law we will have decreed the dissolution of the Brazilian family."[86]

In Brazil, as elsewhere, a sentimental vision of home and mother lay close to the heart of antisuffrage orators. They viewed each woman's vocation as determined not by her individual capacities, requirements, or wishes but by her sex. And the entire sex was one whose duties, privileges, and needs never changed, because they flowed from an interior and particular feminine nature. While men might expect to have a variety of ambitions and skills, women were destined from birth to be full-time wives and mothers. Many men, however, seemed to need the concept of a peaceful, stable abode providing a respite from their varied activities more than they did the actual dwelling, for they spent far less time in the home than did women. Marriage and the home were glorified for women, not for men.[87]

The opposition to women's suffrage in Brazil based on the supposed nobility, purity, and domesticity of women was carried to its extremes by the positivists, both within and without Congress, who had elevated the old belief in separate spheres of male and female activities to the level of religious dogma. Unlike man, woman lived primarily through sentiments. Her unique nature determined her activities, which should be limited to home and family. Woman should be a comforting angel, man's loving companion, and the goddess of the home, but never his adversary or rival in life's daily struggle. For the positivists, the woman formed the moral part of society, the basis of the family, which in turn was the cornerstone of the nation. Womankind as a whole was to be worshipped and set apart from an evil world.[88] In Congress, Major Lauro Sodré of Pará, proclaiming his adherence to positivist doctrine, denounced women's suffrage as an "anarchic, disastrous, fatal" idea. While Sodré advocated giving women "complete, solid, encyclopedic, and integral education" for the sake of increased morality,[89] another positivist and member of the provisional republican government, General Benjamin Constant Botelho de Magalhães, the minister of public instruction, mail, and telegraphs, closed Brazil's institutions of higher education to women. In her angry and scornful denunciation of this temporary restriction on women, Josefina de Azevedo attacked the "wild and tormented positivist philosophy" for viewing women as "brainless beings, underdeveloped animals."[90]

Foreign examples, which served many purposes among the elite, as feminist newspaper publishers had long recognized, could also be employed to limit Brazilian women to a subservient position. Congressmen like Lacerda Coutinho cited the lack of foreign precedents for suffrage. Without regard to complete accuracy, he proclaimed that "in no part of the world does one find women enjoying voting rights." But César Zama, an outspoken politician from Bahia who also held a medical degree and chastised his colleagues for not always taking the subject seriously, knew "it will be sufficient that any important European country confer political rights on [women] and we will imitate this," without weakening the family.[91]

Despite support from some radical republicans in Congress, such as José Lopes da Silva Trovão, who favored divorce, not just legal separation, as well as women's suffrage, the advocates of the vote for women remained a decided minority. Even a proposal in favor of limited suffrage for highly qualified women with university or teaching degrees or property, who were not under a husband's or parent's authority, failed. Congress also refused to enfranchise illiterate men, a proposal favored by the positivists but opposed by most of the political elite. The constitutional article on voter eligibility stood as originally drafted. Electors were citizens over twenty-one years of age and properly registered, except for paupers, illiterates, soldiers, and members of religious orders.[92] For decades to come this article would be interpreted as excluding women because they were not specifically included.

The rising expectations of the small band of Brazilian women's rights advocates had met with frustration at the Constituent Congress of 1891. But the issue of women's suffrage could no longer be ignored. It surfaced in newspapers, books, public discussion, and even during carnival, inscribed in 1891 on the float of one of Rio's leading carnival societies shortly after the constituent congress had debated the matter.[93] In coming years the question of votes for women would not be forgotten. More and more men and women would view suffrage as part of women's rights.

In a nation undergoing significant economic and social changes during the late nineteenth century, women as a group seemed to represent moral stability to most articulate Brazilian men. Women could influence society in the context of the household, but not in the context of the public sector. Brazil's modernizers, however, enlarged the significance of what women did in their homes. Through their power to direct the moral development and behavior of male citizens, women might determine the destiny of the nation. Advocates of female emancipation also employed such arguments to justify additional instruction for women. But they wished women educated for independence, not dependence. They saw that improved education could lead to greater economic and social opportunities for women, and even to political rights, and women's emancipation assumed an ever-broader significance.

Brazil's nineteenth-century women's rights advocates believed in progress, and they drew inspiration and promises of future success from women's achievements in other countries. Well aware of male opposition, female indifference, and the limited acceptance of their own ideas, they remained convinced of the importance of their cause and its eventual success. Unlike many of their male detractors, who assumed women to be easily corruptible should they step outside the home, and the family to be weak and in need of defense, they displayed confidence in women and their abilities.

As the nineteenth century proceeded, increasing numbers of Brazilian women received some education, and the doors of the nation's institutions of higher learning finally opened to them, as the early women's rights advocates had demanded. Only a few women gained admittance and succeeded in entering traditional, prestigious professions like law and medicine, but from their ranks came most of that minority of Brazilian women consciously working to change their social and political status in the twentieth century, including the leadership for the successful suffrage campaign. The majority of women, however, like most men, remained uneducated. Questions of the vote, legally limited to literates, did not assume the same importance for them as for the educated minority. In this highly stratified society, different groups of women continued to lead very different lives.

Chapter 3

Contrasting Women's Worlds in the Early Twentieth Century

In the early twentieth century foreign visitors not only praised the physical transformations occurring in Brazil's major cities, which were being modernized and beautified by progress-minded governments concerned with their country's commerce and image abroad, but they also noted approvingly the appearance of increasing numbers of upper-class women on the newly built boulevards, shopping, promenading, taking tea, and attending movie theaters without male escorts. More and more well-off women entered the universities and elite professions, and works by women writers appeared in print more frequently. But fewer signs of change could be detected in the lives of poor women struggling to survive in dark, damp tenements or toiling in airless workshops and unsafe factories far from foreigners' view. Like the men of their class, urban lower-class women endured not only job insecurity and miserable working conditions but also crowded, unsanitary housing, disease, and poor food and nourishment, problems ignored by Brazil's governments. Yet these women received even less than the pittance paid to men.

During the first decade of the twentieth century Brazil's governing elites sought to sanitize, beautify, and modernize the nation's major cities. Responding to the demands of an export-oriented economy, they improved transportation, constructed new port works, and mounted campaigns against diseases like yellow fever that posed the greatest threat to their own health and to the nation's reputation abroad. Admirers of the latest European ideas, inventions, and trends, they remodeled city centers, lavishing the most money and attention on Rio de Janeiro, the nation's political center and principal port. For the elite, hoping to emulate Hausman's success in Paris, progress more often meant ornate buildings and wide, tree-lined avenues than adequate water supplies, lighting, or sewage disposal for all city districts.[1] Public services did not keep pace with urban growth, and poor neighborhoods lagged furthest behind. The new thoroughfares which sliced through settled areas of Rio de Janeiro led to higher rents, housing shortages, and economic distress for the laboring poor. But the capital, which once possessed "not a single street worthy of showing to foreigners," according to one Brazilian writer, now had a broad boulevard extending from "sea to sea," the Avenida Central (later named Rio Branco).[2]

As Rio's remodeling continued, increasing numbers of both rich and poor moved farther from the city's center, but generally in opposite directions. While workers went northward and inland, the wealthy settled along the southern beaches. Improved transportation facilitated suburban growth. Soon foreign visitors would describe the pleasures of trolley rides along the "magnificent beaches" of Leme, Copacabana, and Ipanema, "pretty Atlantic suburbs" where "cool breezes always blow and excellent bathing may be had," and where the elite erected their elegant new homes.[3] Rio's northern districts also benefited from streetcar lines linking them to downtown Rio. But far more members of the urban poor spent long hours riding the crowded trains carrying them to distant suburbs and outlying towns strung along rail lines branching northward from Rio. Unlike the south zone, the northern suburbs lacked not only paved streets and decent roads linking them to one another or to the central city but also most urban services like sewage disposal and mail delivery.[4]

Housing proved ever more difficult for those of the urban poor unable to afford a move to distant suburbs. Less likely than the elite to promenade along wide new avenues or enter elegant new downtown buildings, they suffered from the resultant housing scarcities. Perhaps one-fourth of the capital's population lived in some form of crowded collective housing rather than in the small, damp, one-story houses that had sheltered uncounted numbers of Brazilians for generations. While this slum housing took different forms, the most common were the tenements termed *cortiços* (literally, beehives) and the *casas de cómodos*. As one reporter described the older tenements, *cortiços* were "flimsy wooden structures consolidated by time through clandestine repairs." These two-story buildings were commonly erected around a cramped interior patio where women tenants often toiled as laundresses. Sanitation in *cortiços* compared unfavorably with that in newer, and scarcer, collective dwellings, where family units contained individual cooking and sanitary facilities. In the *cortiços* the "sleeping alcoves [were] hotter, smaller, and darker; there [was] far less separation of families; life, day or night, [was], therefore, more promiscuous. You can only enter some *cortiços* with a handkerchief held to your nose, and you still leave nauseated."[5]

The *casas de cómodos,* which had appeared by the end of the nineteenth century, were even worse. Old multistoried mansions whose owners had moved from the city center to newer residential areas had been turned into warrens of rented rooms and cubicles. Landlords' efforts to "create the largest possible number of inhabitable spaces" resulted in sleeping rooms of any shape, even three feet wide and thirty feet long, carved from "beneath stairs, from storerooms, areaways, kitchens, and even from bathrooms." Such rooms received only "secondhand air and light." And basement quarters received neither. Each communal latrine generally had to serve dozens of people, and bathing facilities were even scarcer. Families or groups of individuals of either sex slept, cooked their food on tiny gas or kerosene stoves, and washed their clothes all in the same room, which they sometimes shared with dogs, cats, parrots, rabbits, or chickens. In these crowded chambers, separated by flimsy wooden partitions or even burlap curtains, privacy was virtually nonexistent, night or day.[6]

The massive remodeling of Rio de Janeiro during the first decade of the twentieth century led to worsening housing conditions in the city center, as rents rose and crowding increased in the *casas de cómodos.* Although many of those forced from their homes joined the trek to the suburbs, slum dwellers who could not afford or find housing elsewhere had to remain downtown. Some took to the hillsides and unoccupied, undesirable land within Rio and erected *favelas,* or shantytowns. In future decades these *favelas,* rather than the Avenida Central, centerpiece of the government's beautification and modernization program, would symbolize Rio de Janeiro to many visiting foreigners.

Female Life and Labor among the Upper and Middle Classes

In the early twentieth century, foreign visitors noted certain changes occurring in the lives of upper-class women. Even at the turn of the century, prior to the remodeling of Rio de Janeiro, travelers had remarked over the increasing freedom these women enjoyed. An American, Alice R. Humphrey, recalled how when she "went to Rio first in 1884 it was not proper for a woman to go into the street without some man to take care of her. She certainly could not go to shop alone in the Ouvidor [Rio's principal shopping and socializing street prior to the construction of the Avenida Central] as she sometimes does now. . . . Now she is verily a new woman, being far less restricted."[7] Elite women benefited from the growth in commerce, technology, and transportation, most noticeably the improved streetcar system enabling them to venture downtown more easily and take tea or shop for imported luxury goods.

Like wealthy Brazilians, foreigners visiting Rio de Janeiro during the first two decades of the twentieth century paid far more attention to the capital's modern districts than to the slums. They exclaimed over the metamorphosis of the metropolis, with its "splendid" new boulevard.[8] All of society promenaded along the Avenida Central, the city's most fashionable thoroughfare.[9] *Fazendo a Avenida,* as this parading was called, became a daily afternoon pleasure and activity of upper-class women. Soon the "Carioca girl" was "stepping off the Rio Branco Avenue [the retitled Avenida Central] in the course of her afternoon promenade with mother or sister, into a cinema hall for an hour. After that, or before, she trip[ped] into one of several pleasant teahouses" before returning home in "her latest Paris frock."[10]

Foreign visitors invited into elite homes noted the signs of wealth and Europeanized culture, with their "collections of rare bric-a-brac, choice paintings, [and] well-modulated arrangements of flowers."[11] As one American woman related, "the interior of the dwelling is furnished to suit the climate, heavy carpets and draperies being avoided in favor of more appropriate materials. The big lounging chairs and rockers scattered about with a disregard for 'arrangement' in the parlors of North America are not often seen in Brazilian *salas,* which always have a sofa at one side, with two parallel rows of chairs facing each other and extending from each end of it toward the center of the room. . . . The furniture of the *sala* is often quite costly, and, in many of the more beautiful residences, the halls, dining-room, staircases, music-room, and even the *patio* are filled with souvenirs of foreign travel."[12]

Social life among the elite still centered on the family, which was often a far-flung network of kin. As foreigners noted, "the custom of

Leading literary lights and other fashionable men and women taking tea in Rio de Janeiro, 1910. *(Caricature by E. Ayres, courtesy of the Biblioteca Nacional do Rio de Janeiro)*

afternoon calling is not so popular in Brazil as in some other countries, and there are not so many dinners, luncheons, and receptions to pay social debts, as among the English and American people." Rather, family members socialized with each other, often at big birthday celebrations including even remote relatives.[13] Confined mainly to this family circle, an elite woman led "a circumscribed life that would seem tame enough to her North American sisters. Mothers [were] known chiefly through their children." "Their domestic existence" provided upperclass women with their only "sphere of action and influence."[14] Promenades along the Avenida Central did not imply a drastic shift in family relationships within the home.

The husband remained the legally designated head of the family. Like the Philippine Code compiled in Portugal in 1603, the republican Civil Code of 1916 recognized and legitimized masculine privileges and supremacy, limiting women's access to employment and property.

Married women were still legally incapacitated. Only in the legal absence of the husband could the wife assume the leadership of the family. Without her husband's authorization a wife could not accept or refuse an inheritance, exercise a profession, serve as a legal guardian, undertake litigation except to protect the family's communal property, or contract obligations which might lead to the alienation of that property. Similar restrictions, obviously, were never imposed on husbands. While the wife might receive a pension or open a bank account without her husband's formal permission, he retained the right to prohibit these actions. Within the home, in contrast, much of the wife's legal incapacity ceased, for the Civil Code of 1916 authorized her to make necessary purchases for domestic consumption. Hence the code clearly implied that the home was her proper sphere of action, although one in which the husband still exercised legal control.[15]

Like the sheltered and naïve central figure in *Clara dos Anjos*, Afonso Henriques de Lima Barreto's novel of Rio's lower-middle-class suburbs, many urban women still lived in virtual seclusion in the early twentieth century. Not only did Clara's mother rarely leave their home, but she also refused to allow her daughter to shop or go to the movies unescorted. This constant vigilance increased Clara's curiosity about the outside world, which she knew chiefly through *modinhas*, songs conveying a simple-minded, amorous sentimentalism. With her lack of experience, her penchant for daydreaming fostered by her cloistering, and her taste for *modinhas*, this mulatta became easy prey for a higher-class white seducer whose superior social position and color protected him from punishment while ensuring her ruin.[16]

Women in the countryside often endured even more restricted lives. In rural areas well into the twentieth century both foreign visitors and Brazilians from big coastal cities affirmed that women continued to be segregated at social functions, unable to go where they pleased and expected to obey their husbands.[17] For José Pacheco, a popular poet from the Northeast, the most traditional region of Brazil, poor

> Women's work
> About which people don't need to speak,
> Is tying up a goat,
> Giving milk to a kitten,
> Caring for a piglet,
> Scattering corn for the chickens
> And looking around for eggs.

There are household duties
Each one well known,
Sweeping the house and sewing,
Searching clothing for fleas,
Taking care of their children,
And also picking bugs
Out of their husband's beard.

Women could not sell goods in stores or local markets, let alone dance or wear stylish clothing. But the poet's longing for days past when women knew their place no doubt indicates that change came to the countryside and to agricultural laborers also, though far more slowly than to urban areas and to the upper classes.[18]

In the cities the largely bifurcated class structure long characteristic of Brazil had begun to evolve into something more complex by the beginning of the twentieth century. Among the emerging urban middle sectors, as among the elite, some signs of change in women's lives could be detected. The expansion of the cities, industry, and government bureaucracy had facilitated the growth of the poorly defined, diverse Brazilian middle sectors, comprised of members of the civil and military bureaucracies, commercial workers, store and workshop owners, and professionals such as pharmacists. Rather than forming a distinct group, they proved heterogeneous socially, culturally, ideologically, and economically, but they were still a group marked off from the mass of manual laborers. Those members of the most prestigious liberal professions, medicine and law, who depended on fixed wages or fees as a principal source of income might be considered upper-middle class. But they were often related to large landowning families, and they preferred to avoid social intimacy with petty bureaucrats, poorly paid primary school teachers, bookkeepers, and shop clerks, who comprised what might be termed the lower-middle classes. Whether salaried or self-employed, the middle sectors aspired to gentility. They would never soil their hands with manual labor. The lower level of the middle sectors lacked the upper level's kinship ties and family connections that facilitated access to government employment, but they still attempted to emulate the upper classes' life-style and appearance whenever possible. As among the upper classes, domestic servants performed essential household duties in middle-class homes.

Maria Lacerda de Moura, a feminist and anarchist whose activities we shall examine in chapter 4, claimed as typical the idle middle-class housewife's existence she had enjoyed as a young bride in the 1910s prior to her own intellectual awakening. This normal school graduate and, later, normal school teacher from Minas Gerais spent the first ten years of her marriage "leading the life which every recently married woman leads: embroidering, sewing, painting decorations for the house, playing piano, strolling about, carrying on useless conversations, sleeping well and eating better, reading romantic novels, enjoying relative good health."[19] Critical of well-off women, she claimed that they were intelligent but careful to hide that intelligence in order to please men and secure a comfortable position in life.

Like Maria Lacerda de Moura, increasing numbers of urban women entered Brazil's normal schools, unique institutions providing nonelite women with opportunities for education and social advancement. Even Brazil's anarchists, who advocated women's equality but opposed most government actions, considered the normal schools public institutions worthy of support. As an anarchist newspaper in Rio de Janeiro declared in 1915, "the Normal School is the only institution we have where women, to a degree, can emancipate themselves from the harmful prejudices of present-day society. . . . On a basis of equality, rich and poor, whites and nonwhites rub shoulders every day on the school's benches, receiving the same education and instruction."[20] The normal schools helped widen women's horizons as well as foster the slow rise in literacy in Brazil. But very few normal school graduates ever entered elite professions.

By the beginning of the twentieth century, professional women had made their appearance in Brazil. An American woman who spent almost two years in Brazil at the turn of the twentieth century, impressed with the country and its progress, reported their existence:

> There are several women in the professions, who, without any ostentatious display of "advanced views," are quietly making their way to the front rank. São Paulo has a successful woman physician, and there are two who have good practices in Rio de Janeiro. In the law, there are women attorneys who enjoy an assured standing among the best. There are also women students of pharmacy and of architecture. The representatives of the "new woman" in Brazil are not so aggressive as in some other countries, and there are no Suffrage Societies or Women's Rights Leagues; the Brazilian feminine authority on "home rule" is not, however, the meek little creature that fiction portrays her, forever subject to the sovereign will of her lord and master.[21]

The first day of classes at São Paulo's Normal School, 1917. (*A Carreta*, March 31, 1917)

It would take two additional decades for an organized suffrage movement, led by these women, to appear.

Professional women, although members of the Brazilian elite, continued to encounter discrimination, which undoubtedly stimulated their awareness of women's rights issues. Contributors to the *paulista* women's newspaper *A Mensageira* at the close of the nineteenth century admitted that Brazil possessed few female doctors, and these had to "struggle against . . . stupidity and prejudice."[22] As the Pernambuco-born writer Inéz Sabino Pinho Maia complained in Rio Grande do Sul's *Escrínio* at the beginning of the twentieth century, women doctors were "considered shameless and indecent."[23] The editor of *Escrínio*, Andradina América Andrada de Oliveira, asserted that even while studying at the universities, women encountered male hostility and comments that "cut like knives."[24] In the 1920s Maria Lacerda de Moura still lamented that "it is the general opinion that woman cannot, that they should not, practice male professions, which are incompatible with their sensibilities and even their honor. Men criticize women doctors, lawyers, and writers, their competitors, after all."[25] Even men who supported women's theoretical right to enter "masculine professions" argued that female employment was necessary only because some women failed to pursue the "best feminine career, marriage." As one such man added, with insult, when "women do not marry, in most cases, it is not that they do not wish to, but rather that men have rejected them."[26]

The opposition encountered by the lonely few seeking to win entry into male-dominated liberal professions could act to increase their commitment to women's rights. According to a sympathetic biographer, such was the case with Mirtes de Campos, the first woman admitted to the bar in Brazil.[27] Long before the appearance of formal suffrage associations in Brazil in the early 1920s, women like Mirtes de Campos pressed for women's suffrage in print and through the Association of Brazilian Lawyers.

While a handful of women sought admission to the nation's medical and law schools in the early twentieth century, more concentrated on pharmacy, perhaps because of the latter profession's loss of social prestige. Only in small communities lacking physicians or patients able to pay high fees did apothecaries retain their traditional roles. As the proportion of men seeking medical rather than pharmaceutical careers increased, so did the number of female graduates in pharmacy grow.

Dentistry, which women could practice without leaving offices attached to their homes, also attracted a relatively higher proportion of women. In 1907, according to the newly reorganized federal bureau of statistics, just 6 women were studying law, 1 studied architecture, and 1 studied engineering, while 6 devoted themselves to medicine, 9 to obstetrics, 22 to dentistry, and 56 to pharmacy. Yet less than half as many men studied pharmacy (670) as medicine (1,769). And even more men (2,475) enrolled in the nation's law schools.[28]

That same year less than 40 percent of the school-age children in the federal capital were enrolled in public or private elementary schools. Nationwide, only 15 percent of the boys and less than 13 percent of the girls were registered in Brazil's primary schools, for a total of 638,379 pupils. And far fewer actually attended school. At the secondary level three-fourths of the students were male. While women dominated primary education in Brazil, outnumbering male elementary school teachers by three to two—and by almost six to one in the Federal District of Rio de Janeiro—no women taught in the nation's medical, law, or polytechnic schools. The few women who succeeded in gaining entrance to the professional schools encountered institutions whose male members held a monopoly over instruction and administration.[29]

For women without advanced degrees but with some education, schoolteaching had long supplied a socially acceptable form of paid employment, and the normal schools turned out ever-greater numbers of female teachers. Lower-paid women had largely replaced men in Brazil's primary school classrooms by the beginning of the twentieth century (see tables 5 and 6). Newer fields of employment provided additional sources of employment not associated with the working class and women of lower social status. As government, commerce, finance, and communications grew, more women with some skills and education secured positions. Perhaps women found it easier to enter such areas and hold their own precisely because these were expanding fields.

By the late nineteenth century, women had begun to work in mail, railroad, and telegraph offices. Government bureaus that once employed no women came to include a small but growing female contingent. In 1872, according to Brazil's first national census, no women were employed by the government in Rio de Janeiro. But in 1906 women comprised 0.7 percent of the capital's government employees.

Between that year and 1920, the date of the next census, the total number of government employees in Rio more than doubled, and the percentage of women in the bureaucracy rose to 4.3 percent, a sixfold increase.[30] According to one of Rio's leading newspapers, the total number of female government employees almost doubled between 1920 and 1930, with most of them continuing to work in post office, telegraph, and railroad offices. But in small cities, especially outside the more prosperous south-central portion of Brazil, little increase in government employment for women could be detected.[31]

When the rebellious Malvina in *Gabriela, Clove and Cinnamon*, Jorge Amado's novel of life and love in the booming cacao port of Ilhéus in southern Bahia in the mid 1920s, sought to escape her restricted life, she fled southward. As in the nineteenth century, wealthy girls in her hometown could only attend parochial school and learn embroidery and piano, not acquire a thorough education or take a job; their brief adolescence ended with an arranged marriage. But the determined and intelligent Malvina defied not only the town gossips but also her authoritarian and brutal father. She refused to lead a submissive life like her mother or other married women, for in Ilhéus "the husbands were absolute masters and the wives were reduced to passive obedience. Worse than being a nun. . . . Her school chums, daughters of rich fathers, chattered away, while their brothers, in high school or college in Bahia, could do as they pleased and had monthly allowances to help them do it." After a girl married, her husband "was her master, he owned her. He had all the rights and was to be obeyed and respected. She was the guardian of the family's honor and of her husband's name, the keeper of the house, the caretaker of the children." Through her books Malvina "discovered another world, far beyond Ilhéus, where life was beautiful and women were not slaves. Big cities were where she could earn her own living and her freedom."[32] Seizing her opportunity, she fled to São Paulo, where she worked in an office, studied at night, and lived alone.

With the expansion of large banking, insurance, and commercial establishments in major urban centers, more women sought and secured white-collar positions and, for some, a degree of economic and social freedom. One typing school in Rio de Janeiro registered an increase in female enrollments from 24 in 1911 to 452 in 1919. By 1930 typists clearly comprised one of the largest groups of female office workers, in both government and private concerns. Telephone companies employed large numbers of women as operators, just as in the United States.[33]

While some women worked behind store counters in the mid-nineteenth century, their numbers increased markedly in the twentieth. However, even though clerking might offer an attractive alternative to factory work, shop girls, like industrial workers, put in a long day, generally eleven hours, for a meager return. As in factories, women working in commercial establishments received less pay than men for the same work. During the first decade of the twentieth century some of Rio's ever-growing contingent of female sales clerks and employees in retail commerce sought to safeguard their occupational interests by joining the powerful Associação dos Empregados no Comércio do Rio de Janeiro, a combined mutual benefit society and commercial association founded by store clerks in 1880 but increasingly dominated by businessmen. Although refused several times, women gained admittance in 1913 after a reinterpretation of membership restrictions. Three years later, a woman sought election to the association's general council on a platform of equal wages for women. The white-collar positions that provided employment for increasing numbers of women undoubtedly had a greater impact on women's lives than did occasional but limited breakthroughs into areas where few would follow, such as barber shops.[34] The growth in middle-class jobs not only affected women's long-range economic situation but could also help provide the basis for future social and political changes, as in the United States and England.

Unlike the lower classes, these women's wages were calculated on a monthly, not daily, basis. According to the English author of a frequently updated, fact-filled businessman's handbook on Brazil, typists in Rio de Janeiro earned 200 milreis a month in 1916, or as much as the average schoolteacher (100$00 for junior teachers to 250$00 for senior teachers), and more than double the wages paid closely supervised young telephone operators (80$00 per month for a six-hour day). A typist with a knowledge of shorthand received a higher salary, but still nowhere near that of male bookkeepers and cashiers. Nursing, still considered menial work, paid only 15$00 to 40$00 monthly, as compared with a postmistress's salary of 250$00 in 1916.[35]

Women earned higher wages in their new middle-sector jobs than did working-class women, but they still received less than men for comparable work. They provided a labor pool easily channeled into performing routine white-collar chores under male supervision. With fewer job options available to them, they had little choice but to work for less pay at tasks considered compatible with their sex. Their low wages could be rationalized as appropriate for women employed only temporarily, prior to marriage or just supplementing their parents' or husband's wages. Office managers found female labor "more convenient and economical than male labor," as long as the work did not require "innovations" or the "assumption of responsibilities." These women had "limited" aspirations, were "patient, docile, and conscientious," and did "not smoke."[36] Very few continued to work after marriage. Office work rarely paid enough for a woman to live independently on her own income, and it provided little opportunity for advancement. Only after a half dozen years with the same firm, according to a Department of Labor official, might a woman earn a decent living wage.[37] But office work did give younger unmarried women some cash and personal freedom. By the 1920s even a few daughters of well-off families sought employment as cashiers or typists, claiming it was "fashionable for women to work, earn money, become free from the paternal yoke, and be independent."[38]

The far smaller number of well-educated women who achieved entry into elite professions like law and medicine obviously enjoyed greater opportunities to achieve a higher income and a more independent life than could office workers. These professional women would supply the leadership for the successful suffrage campaign of the 1920s and early 1930s, while primary school teachers and other middle-class women entered the ranks.

Women's Work among the Urban Lower Classes

Unlike outspoken women of the elite, who eventually would gain much of what they wanted and secure entrance to the professions without losing social prestige, poor women had no choice but to work for pay. During the early twentieth century, as in the nineteenth, Brazil's working-class women toiled long and hard for petty returns. Work for pay remained an overwhelming feature in the lives of most poor women, whether they lived in crowded, dank downtown tenements, in distant, dusty suburbs, or in the growing hilltop shantytowns like those soon to become one of the most prominent features of Rio de Janeiro. Some took in laundry or served as maids in the homes of the middle and upper classes, and some labored as street vendors. Others plied their needles as seamstresses at home or in airless workshops, or toiled in unsanitary and unsafe factories. In Rio's distant suburbs, amid the small houses lining unpaved, treeless streets, married women could plant gardens or raise animals to help sustain their families.

Black women continued to labor at some of the least skilled jobs and endured some of the worst treatment. Although the final abolition of slavery in Brazil in 1888 supposedly substituted wage labor for unpaid servile labor, working conditions and jobs performed by black women in the cities remained largely unaltered. Even in the days of slavery, few freemen experienced a marked change in their material condition because of manumission.[39] After 1888, black women continued to work as maids, cooks, nursemaids, laundresses, street vendors, and sometimes prostitutes. The employment opportunities available to them were the most modest and least remunerative. In a society of rigid class lines, black women remained on the lowest rung of the social ladder. To be both black and female continued a double disadvantage. Many worked far from their homes, departing early in the morning and returning late in the day. They had to leave their children with relatives or friends, or to their own devices. Weak marital bonds and the frequent absence of husbands or fathers among this struggling,

Lace maker in the Amazon, ca. 1880. (Smith, *Brazil. The Amazons and the Coast*)

A street vendor with her
basket of small wares in
Rio de Janeiro, ca. 1898.
(Photograph by Marc
Ferrez in Gilberto Ferrez,
*O Rio antigo do fotografo
Marc Ferrez*)

unstable, disorganized group increased the burden on black women.
Although they maintained their position in domestic service, they did
not rise into better-paying and more prestigious occupations in stores
and offices, except in periods of great economic expansion.[40]

Most fields of employment, whether skilled or unskilled, were either
predominantly male or female. While women generally toiled at jobs
which could be seen as extensions of traditional household or familial
tasks, like the preparation of food and clothing, men labored at a larger
variety of jobs. Skilled craftsmen worked as carpenters, plasterers, masons, cabinetmakers, printers, glassblowers, coopers, and tailors—occupations closed to women. Such men ranked well above porters,
dishwashers, and day laborers, as did streetcar conductors and teams-
ters, and even semiskilled mill hands. Some unskilled men, like women,

found temporary employment in the service sector, working as street vendors or performing odd jobs. But domestic service, an overwhelmingly female field, constituted the major source of employment for women in urban areas.

Unlike carpentry or construction, which were entirely male occupations, some skilled handwork remained women's work. Women not only toiled in factories producing textiles, stockings, ties, pants, slippers, cord, string, and oakum, but also in innumerable dressmaking shops and shops producing embroideries, clasps, hats, and gloves.[41] They labored in repair shops and laundries. A dozen women might spend their days hunched over long tables in dark, airless rooms, producing the luxury garments in which elite ladies promenaded on the Avenida Central, attended receptions, or frequented theaters and tea salons.[42] The few activists among São Paulo's seamstresses complained of toiling up to sixteen hours a day; the remaining eight hours provided "insufficient time to recuperate our strength and to overcome our exhaustion through sleep."[43] Even when forced to work Sundays also, they earned only 50 to 60 milreis a month, or 1$500 to 2$000 a day— less than most female factory hands, let alone skilled male workers earning up to 10$000 daily.[44] (For the complete text of these seamstresses' appeal for support and denunciation of their working conditions and colleagues' apathy, see appendix D.)

As in the nineteenth century, seamstresses with individual clients still plied their needles at home. But the growth of the putting-out system increasingly turned tenement rooms into sweatshops, with women now performing piecework for industrial purposes up to eighteen hours a day. Thus industrialists cut costs and wages while escaping taxes and public notice. In Rio's early-twentieth-century *cortiços* outsiders observed "poor but modest girls" sewing heavy cloth goods for the arsenals in their tiny, clean rooms decorated with beloved family pictures. The production of lingerie, canvas, slippers, and openwork fabric all lay in the hands of women laboring at home.[45]

Like other lower-class women, seamstresses were in a weak position to resist the sexual advances of upper-class men, and some resorted to occasional prostitution to meet economic hardships. Prostitution never appears among occupational categories in Brazilian censuses, but one wonders how many of the seamstresses enumerated also followed this pursuit. Some dressmakers, particularly Frenchwomen, won renown as luxury prostitutes, or *cocotes*. The upper ranks of prostitution, but not the lower, provided an attractive alternative to sweatshop labor for some women.[46]

Unlike various European or Latin American countries, including neighboring Argentina, which had licensed municipal bordellos from 1875 to 1936, prostitution was never legalized in Brazil.[47] Neither the imperial nor the republican governments attempted to control prostitution or require prostitutes to register, thus depriving future researchers of types of data found in some other countries. But foreign travelers as well as physicians and police officials reported the presence in large port cities like Rio de Janeiro of a variety of prostitutes ranked in a hierarchy reflecting the class divisions of this stratified society.

The top rungs of Brazilian prostitution included well-dressed, self-employed women, many of them foreigners, who circulated freely but discreetly in public places. According to one police official in late-nineteenth-century Rio, these women "dressed in silk, with expensive feathers and costly jewels and diamonds; they attended the theater and other public events, and had elegant carriages at their disposal."[48] If not French, these first-class prostitutes often pretended to have come from that country of high cultural achievements so beloved by Brazil's elite.

Far more numerous were prostitutes of different colors and nationalities serving the range of less-wealthy sectors of society. Prior to the abolition of slavery in Brazil in 1888, slaves comprised a large but uncertain percentage of Rio's prostitutes, many apparently ordered by their owners into prostitution.[49] Their blatant exploitation, although not clearly illegal, at times aroused moral indignation as well as concern for public health and decorum. Whether slave or free, the poorest prostitutes were seen as disorderly and disease-ridden, and as living in squalor and filth.

The precarious economic situation of many poor women, who faced uncertain and limited employment opportunities, drove some to occasional as well as long-term prostitution. In bustling seaports and rapidly growing commercial centers like Rio de Janeiro, full of unmarried males, some prostitutes earned more than domestic servants, seamstresses, or factory workers. Writing for Brazil's male-controlled labor press, which often portrayed women as fragile, submissive, and in need of protection, an anarchist poet in early-twentieth-century Rio depicted a frail "little seamstress, meek and gentle," facing the choice between "tuberculosis or the brothel."[50] A woman who lost her job or was sexually assaulted by her employer might also turn to prostitution. Half a century later, a woman textile worker recalled how one of the foremen in Rio's huge Bangú factory "shut girls up in his office in order to force them to have sex with him. Many of the mill hands became prostitutes because of that scoundrel! He even suspended women for ten or fifteen days for the slightest shortcomings, or even for no reason, in order to make them submit to his desires."[51] (The complete text of the recollections of this former textile worker, Luiza Ferreira de Medeiros, recorded in 1970, are in appendix E.)

Due to the clandestine nature of much prostitution, efforts to estimate the total number of prostitutes in Brazil remain exercises in frustration. Poor women working out of their own homes, just like luxury *cocotes,* never received the public attention accorded full-time prostitutes lodged in hotels or brothels, especially when those prostitutes were foreigners or were controlled by pimps.

The frequency with which men of different classes in cities like Rio de Janeiro turned to prostitutes cannot be determined either. But we have an occasional indication that steady, and expected, visits were paid them by some skilled workers. Among the unions sending a variety of reports and resolutions to the anarcho-syndicalist–dominated Second Brazilian Labor Congress of 1913 was Rio's General Union of Painters, which submitted a list of members' expenses. Bachelors' monthly expenditures, no doubt theoretical rather than completely realistic, since they totaled 165 milreis as compared with an average monthly wage of 110$000, included not only food (65$000; by far the major component in working-class budgets), room rent (20$000), and carfare (12$000), but also 15$000 per month for "extraordinary expenses that only someone who is a monk made of stone can avoid." This sum far exceeded the amounts allotted to medical care (3$000) or even to tobacco, matches, and kerosene (9$000).[52]

Although rowdy behavior or brazen solicitations on the part of individual prostitutes certainly led to public complaints, only a few police chiefs, moralizers, or physicians advocated the regulation of prostitution. Nineteenth-century hygienists reflecting the work of French physician Alexandre Parent-Duchâtelet proposed controlling prostitution by limiting it to licensed brothels under police surveillance. These Brazilian medical reformers viewed prostitutes as lazy, greedy, and highly sexed women who transmitted venereal disease into the "bosom of families." But they still considered prostitution a "necessary evil," a not uncommon Catholic belief. By the end of the nineteenth century, however, new medical views arrived from Europe—those of abolitionists seeking to end reglemented prostitution, which subjected prostitutes to police brutality without improving public health.

Prostitution in Brazil only occasionally became a "police matter." Understaffed, underfunded, and poorly trained police forces just arrested some women for disturbing the peace. Police officials generally maintained that suppression of prostitution was impossible. Most nineteenth-century police reports that even mentioned prostitution treated it much the same as they did gambling: an immoral activity, but one that could never be stopped completely. Even in the early twentieth century, any foreigner walking through Rio's downtown zone of prostitution saw "a hundred shameless hussies flaunt their faded charms in broad daylight before his eye without the slightest regard for the policeman at the corner."[53] Pimps no doubt paid off the police, too.

The foreign presence in prostitution commanded more public attention. In the nineteenth century some Brazilians contended that foreign prostitutes were invading, and corrupting, their country. By the beginning of the twentieth century European Jews would be accused of engaging in the "white slave trade," the international trade in women and children, and of running bordellos in Brazil where they forced prostitutes to live like slaves.[54] While coffee planters and other prosperous Brazilians might seek and benefit from increases in immigrant "manpower," they also feared a rise in crime and other disruptive social effects. They could easily blame foreigners for prostitution, just as they blamed foreign anarchists for provoking labor unrest, and deportations of alleged pimps and procurers did occur.[55]

Despite occasional public outcries, Brazilians demonstrated lower levels of outrage over prostitution than were seen in some other countries. No great campaigns against prostitution were mounted in Brazil, unlike those seen in the United States and Uruguay.[56] Luxury prostitutes who interacted only with the Brazilian upper classes and caused no public scandal never aroused widespread public opposition. Brazil's opinion makers proved more likely to protest the presence of foreign pimps or too obvious displays by poorer prostitutes. Prostitution reflected class, not just gender, relationships. Under the new republic's penal code, produced in the late nineteenth century, only procuring, not prostitution, was illegal. And the law remained unconcerned with

Table 7.   Domestic Service, Rio de Janeiro, 1872–1920

	Women in labor force	Domestic servants			Female component of domestic service (%)	Percentage of total female labor force employed in domestic service
		Male	Female	Total		
1872	60,961	16,549	38,462	55,011	70.0	63.1
1906	124,181	23,174	94,730	117,904[a]	80.3	76.3
1920	117,327	12,852	58,895	71,752	82.1	50.2

Sources: Adapted from *Recenseamento da População . . . 1872*, Município Neutro, 21:61; Brazil, Directoria Geral de Estatística, 1:100, 104; *Recenseamento do Rio de Janeiro* (Districto Federal) realizada em 2° de setembro de 1906, *Recenseamento do Brazil . . . 1920*, vol. 2, pt. 1, p. 514.

[a]According to the 1920 census, the 1906 figures on domestic servants are far too high because many women doing housework without remuneration were inadvertently included in this category.

the prostitutes' clients. In commercial sex, too, a moral double standard continued to prevail.

Domestic service, another traditional female field, provided more employment for urban lower-class women than factories, workshops, or any other sector of the economy. According to the 1920 census, 80.7 percent of those employed in this sector were women, and these women comprised 19.3 percent of Brazil's total female population and 35.6 percent of nonagricultural women workers.[57] In Rio de Janeiro 50.2 percent of the female labor force was employed in domestic service (see table 7). These women lacked much personal freedom or privacy. Almost all lived under close supervision in the homes of their employers, who regulated their working conditions. Except when sleeping, domestic servants were on call, generally every day of the week. Although in theory they worked for pay as well as receiving room and board, often their wages were merely symbolic. The prejudice against women working outside the home and the need for someone to perform domestic tasks helped keep women in these poorly paid and dreary jobs.

No government bureaus investigated domestic service. Unlike factory inspections, inquiries into these traditional female tasks would be viewed as an invasion of privacy. Not only the elite but also the amorphous middle classes, including bureaucrats, employed maids. Any inquiries into domestic service would constitute a violation of the sanctity of their homes.

Closely related to the domestic duties servants performed within their employers' homes were the menial activities of laundresses working outside their "patrons'" houses. Public fountains and streams served as prime centers for laundering in the mid-nineteenth century. During the late nineteenth and early twentieth centuries, the disease-ridden, congested *cortiços* which "sheltered" much of the urban lower class, both Brazilian and foreign born, provided another location for this activity.[58] Units of the *cortiços* were often grouped about an interior patio, where the laundresses spent their days. As one foreign observer noted, "the workman leaves his house for his work, and the wife passes the whole day washing and ironing. The health of these women often breaks down from overwork."[59]

The expansion of Brazilian industry in the early twentieth century drew more women, and men, into the factories, although industrial laborers remained a minority of the urban lower classes.[60] Centered in the south, especially the cities of São Paulo and Rio de Janeiro, industrial production in Brazil increased in conjunction with the rise in Brazilian exports, particularly coffee. Those two cities offered large regional markets for industrial products as well as capital, labor, transportation facilities, and government connections.

In Brazil's large industrial enterprises men, women, and children exchanged long hours of weary work in unsanitary and often unsafe factories for meager wages. Many of the poorly lit and ventilated structures housing machinery had not been designed for manufacturing. With machines crowded together and gears and belts unshielded, accidents were frequent. As in other countries during initial stages of industrial capitalism, a general climate of job insecurity prevailed. In most industries job turnover was rapid. Accident or unemployment compensation was unknown. Reigning laissez-faire attitudes impeded passage of legislation regulating working conditions, not to mention salaries and hours. The only federal labor legislation enacted during the first two decades of the republic—the provisional republican regime's decree controlling child labor in Rio's factories—was not enforced.

While male and female industrial workers endured many of the same kinds of harsh treatment, some abuses were sex specific. Both male and female workers were subject to speedups and fines. They complained about terrible conditions in the textile factories, citing closed windows to prevent them from looking out, air loaded with lint, rarely washed factory walls and floors, and a lack of toilets. Textile workers had to suck the shuttles in order to thread their looms, increasing the spread of infectious diseases like tuberculosis, a scourge of Brazil's industrial laborers. The gruesome accidents workers witnessed heightened their distress. They claimed that foremen humiliated, cursed, insulted, and capriciously dismissed them. But women and children received the worst treatment. While children suffered beatings, women were subject to sexual exploitation by foremen and supervisors. Female workers complained of the jokes, insults, and abuse they received when they had no lovers, and therefore no protectors, present. If they protested, they received no redress and were fired.[61]

Since the days of slavery, large numbers of unskilled women had labored in the Brazilian textile industry, just as they did in many other countries. Textiles represented the main source of industrial employment in Brazil, and the proportion of female and child labor in textiles exceeded that in other manufactures.[62] The major mills, which possessed the highest degree of mechanization, utilization of electricity, and concentration of workers per unit of machinery among Brazil's industries, surpassed almost all other factories in size. Textile manufacture demanded neither brute force nor slowly acquired skills, but rather vigilance and manual dexterity. Unskilled labor of both sexes and all ages, literate or not, could be profitably employed in the mills and paid lower wages than in less mechanized industries.

Some industrialists created a system of social services that assisted and regulated factory workers' lives. At times they provided not only company stores and housing, or medical care and schools, but also child-care facilities. Few of these services were free, and some were granted in lieu of higher wages. They were apparently considered necessary, and sometimes profitable, arrangements for maintaining the work process and facilitating the close supervision of workers, who remained dependent on mill owners and vulnerable to manipulation through paternalism.[63]

The child-care facilities sometimes provided by large factories enabled the mill owners to utilize lower-paid female labor more efficiently. According to various observers, textiles employed a larger proportion of married women than did other industries. In Bahia and

Recife, as in the south, these observers found married women continuing to toil in the textile mills up to the last days of pregnancy and recommencing factory work shortly after childbirth. Most mothers could not afford to pay other women to take care of their young offspring. Unless they could find willing friends or relatives to tend children too young for school or factory, they could not work a full day in the mills. Relatively few children began mill work before the age of ten, and not all the younger ones attended factory or outside schools. Nurseries and kindergartens thus enabled factory owners to extract larger quantities of low-cost female labor.[64]

Concentrated in a handful of industries, women labored at some of the most demanding and least desirable factory jobs for even lower wages than the pittance paid to men. The textiles, food-processing, and clothing industries, which fabricated goods once produced by women in their own homes, remained their major employers. According to the 1920 census, textiles employed an overwhelming majority of all female factory workers: 70.0 percent, as compared with 33.4 percent of male workers in factories with eight or more laborers. While women may have clustered by chance in industries with low wage scales, it seems more likely that those industries paid such poor salaries because of the concentration of women. These sectors of the economy could be seen as more appropriate for women, therefore justifying lower wages, even for men. Textiles ranked ninth in male industrial salary level, and food processing ranked eleventh. In these, as in all major manufacturing fields, women's wages stayed well below men's, as the 1920 census shows. While one-third of Brazil's male factory workers earned 4$000 to 8$000 per day, only one-tenth of the women were within this range.[65] In Rio de Janeiro, the highest-paying region of the country, where approximately one-fourth of all Brazil's industrial workers found employment, adult women received an average wage of 4$600 while men earned 6$900, over 50 percent more (see table 8). As in other countries, certain jobs were frequently known as men's jobs or women's jobs, the latter requiring less skill and providing lower pay and fewer chances for advancement. But even when women did the same work as men, they were paid less. According to Rio's textile workers union, the Sindicato dos Trabalhadores em Fabricas de Tecidos do Rio de Janeiro, in 1913 men and women worked under equal conditions in the factories, but in the woolen textiles division men generally earned 3$000 per day while women earned only 2$000. Men producing

Table 8. Analysis of Salaries of Adult Workers, Rio de Janeiro, 1920

Daily Wage	Workers[a]			Total workers (%)	Total male workers (%)	Total female workers (%)
	Total	Male	Female			
2$900 or less	5,397	2,129	3,268	10.9	6.1	22.2
3$000–3$900	3,896	1,101	2,795	7.8	3.1	19.0
4$000–5$900	14,916	9,619	5,297	30.0	27.4	36.0
6$000–7$900	11,899	9,893	2,006	23.9	28.2	13.7
8$000 and over	13,670	12,339	1,331	27.4	35.2	9.1
Total	49,778	35,081	14,697	100.0	100.0	100.0

Source: Recenseamento do Brazil . . . 1920, vol. 2, pt. 2, p. xciii.

[a]Includes only enterprises with 8 or more workers.

linen and cotton cloth received an average of 4$000 daily, while women earned just 2$500. In burlap, men averaged 3$000 daily, and women only 2$000.[66] Women's industrial wages would continue to lag far behind men's.

While Brazil's factories grew in size and numbers in the early twentieth century, relatively few workers in "manufacturing" found employment in them. Many more women, and men, apparently labored in smaller, less mechanized shops or in repair shops. In 1920 the apparel industry engaged just 9,116 female factory workers, as compared with 331,115 female workers, or over 36 times as many, in the entire clothing sector.[67] We cannot tell whether most of those women engaged in piecework for industrial purposes or whether they were seamstresses working in small shops or for individual clients. The 1872 census had recorded 506,450 seamstresses in Brazil.[68] Their numbers must have declined by 1920, when seamstresses no longer comprised a census category. As O Sexo Feminino had accurately predicted in 1875, the introduction of sewing and weaving machines, while beneficial "to humanity," would cost thousands of women their jobs.[69] A drop in the number of seamstresses may also help to explain the apparent absolute decline in the number of women in the total manufacturing sector between 1872 and 1920 (table 9). Relatively few appear to have been absorbed into factory work, certainly as compared with men. Is this what occurs with the development of industrial capitalism and the

Table 9. Occupations, Brazil, 1872–1920

Occupations	1872		
	Men	Women	Female component %
Agriculture[a]	2,318,718	964,325	29.4
Manufacturing[b]	180,948	653,970	78.3
Capitalists	23,140	9,723	29.6
Commerce	93,577	8,556	8.4
Transportation	—	—	—
Armed forces and police	27,716	—	—
Religious	2,332	286	10.9
Liberal professions[c]	11,674	3,365	22.4
Government employment, administration	10,710	—	—
Private administration	—	—	—
Domestic service	196,784	848,831	81.2
Day laborers	274,217	90,162	24.7
Poorly defined or unknown	—	—	—
Without profession[d]	1,984,053	2,171,663	52.3

Sources: Adapted from *Recenseamento da População . . . 1872*, Quadros Gerais, 19:5; *Recenseamento do Brazil . . . 1920*, vol. 4, pt. 5, tomo 1, pp. xii–xiii.

[a]Includes pastoral, mining, and fishing.

decline of the family as a productive unit, as some who write about non-Western nations maintain?[70]

According to Brazilian censuses, the percentage of women in the labor force declined markedly between 1872 and 1920. In 1872 54.8 percent of the female population was employed, while in 1920 only 9.7 percent had occupations. The drop in male employment was far less severe—from 61.3 percent of the total male population in 1872 to 52.6 percent in 1920. It is difficult, however, to believe that the absolute number of women working could decline by over a million during the same half century in which Brazil's population more than tripled. Nor is it easy to understand how the proportion of women in agriculture and related activities, which, according to the censuses, declined from 29.4 percent of agricultural workers in 1872 to 9.4 percent in 1920, could then rise to the former figure by 1940 and remain at that level

| | 1920 | |
Men	Women	Female component %
5,843,665	607,865	9.4
758,757	429,600	36.2
27,384	13,406	32.9
474,707	22,841	4.6
249,879	3,708	1.5
	—	—
88,363		
6,059	2,944	32.7
107,634	51,474	32.4
	3,225	3.3
94,487		
37,303	2,864	7.1
70,335	293,544	80.7
—	—	—
	46,657	11.2
369,911		
7,314,334	13,713,659	65.2

[b]Includes artisans and seamstresses.
[c]Includes midwives and schoolteachers.
[d]Includes those who did not declare a profession and those underage.

in subsequent decades.[71] Yet the Brazilian censuses show a marked decrease between 1872 and 1920 in both agricultural and nonagricultural employment for women, notably in the poorest-paying fields.

How can we account for this apparent decline? One possibility involves a massive increase in the prosperity of the bulk of the population, which would permit large numbers of lower-class women to stay at home and not contribute to family income. But there is little evidence of this. A more likely possibility is that women assumed less steady or visible jobs, or that only male heads of household were counted by census takers, as was the case on São Paulo's coffee plantations, despite the fact that entire immigrant families provided the actual work force. With rising urbanization came the growth of the informal sector of the economy, which is highly concentrated on women. But census takers were generally unable to envision women

Table 10. Occupations, Rio de Janeiro, 1872–1920

| | 1872 | | |
Occupations	Men	Women	Female component %
Agriculture[a]	18,445	7,831	29.8
Manufacturing[b]	28,108	11,825	29.6
Capitalists	984	1,023	51.0
Commerce	23,045	436	1.9
Transportation	—	—	—
Armed forces and police	5,474	—	—
Religious	214	50	18.9
Liberal professions[c]	2,016	367	15.4
Government employment, administration	2,351	—	—
Private administration	—	—	—
Domestic service	16,549	38,462	70.0
Day laborers	23,696	1,990	7.7
Poorly defined or unknown	—	—	—
Without profession[d]	37,884	54,222	58.9

Sources: Adapted from *Recenseamento da População . . . 1872,* Município Neutro, 21:61; *Recenseamento do Rio de Janeiro . . . 1906,* vol. 1, p. 104; *Recenseamento do Brazil . . . 1920,* vol. 4, pt. 5, tomo 1, pp. 24–27.

[a]Includes pastoral, mining, and fishing.

working in any but highly structured contexts like textile factories. And one form of women's work in the informal sector which they could recognize, prostitution, never appeared among occupational categories in Brazilian censuses. The 1920 census undercounted women working part time, irregularly, or as unpaid workers in family enterprises. Better-paid workers in more prestigious fields were more accurately tallied. In the nineteenth century members of the elite expected the daughters as well as the sons of the poor to work. But during the twentieth century the view spread that employment outside the home was improper for women. Brazilian census takers then classified people as "working" or "inactive" depending on what they considered their principal activity to be, and it was assumed that the principal activity of women was to run the home and socialize the children.

When we examine the situation in Rio de Janeiro, we do not see

| | 1906 | | | 1920 | |
Men	Women	Female component %	Men	Women	Female component %
22,753	2,822	11.0	29,105	1,559	5.1
93,503	22,276	19.2	112,962	41,435	26.8
2,183	1,339	38.0	3,593	2,317	39.2
61,732	1,043	1.7	85,212	3,094	3.5
22,702	105	0.5	43,053	1,054	2.4
16,484	—	—	24,835	—	—
346	280	44.7	616	562	47.7
9,005	2,419	21.2	16,953	9,088	34.9
12,350	87	0.7	24,466	1,097	4.3
—	—	—	9,249	543	5.5
23,174	94,730	80.3	12,857	58,895	82.1
29,514	419	1.4	—	—	—
32,069	40,018	55.5	31,801	3,858	1.1
137,638	182,452	57.0	203,605	436,064	68.2

[b]Includes artisans and seamstresses.
[c]Includes midwives and schoolteachers.
[d]Includes those who did not declare a profession and those underage.

nearly as severe a decline in female employment figures. Perhaps it was easier for census takers to assess work roles in the nation's capital than in the hinterland. The percentage of employed women in Rio increased slightly from 53.5 percent in 1872 to 59.3 percent in 1906, and then declined sharply to 22.1 percent in 1920. Yet that 1920 figure is still more than double the national average of 9.7 percent. Male employment in Rio declined far less—at approximately the same rate as in the nation as a whole—from 76.1 percent in 1872 to 70.3 percent in 1906, and to 66.0 percent in 1920.[72] In Rio's manufacturing sector we find no great drop in female employment between 1872 and 1920. On the contrary, at the same time that national census figures indicate an absolute decline in the number of female workers in this sector, a three-and-a-half-fold increase occurred in Rio. Their ranks expanded almost as quickly as did the total population of this major industrial center and almost as rapidly as male employment in manufacturing, both of which quadrupled during this period (tables 9 and 10).

Statistics on total female employment, even if accurate, cannot tell us many things about the status of women. The extent of women's participation in the labor force is at best an ambiguous indicator of gender equality. For example, in mid-twentieth-century Europe the proportion of women who worked was nearly identical in Spain and the Netherlands. For years, both Italy and France had rates of female employment double that of the United States.[73] A high rate of employment may denote women's large-scale relegation to low-paying, unskilled, and dead-end positions whose major social function is to supplement low family incomes or to support female-headed households. This certainly was the case with domestic service in Brazil.

While national census figures demonstrate a decline of almost two-thirds in the number of men and women engaged in domestic service—the major nonagricultural female employment category—between 1872 and 1920, data for Rio de Janeiro indicate an increase in female servants (see tables 9 and 10). The absolute number of women in domestic service in Rio more than doubled between 1872 and 1906. While the 1920 figure represents a decline from 1906, it still exceeds the 1872 figure by some 30 percent. Census officials claimed that the 1906 figures on domestic servants were far too high because many women doing housework without remuneration were inadvertently included in this category. Yet the 1906 figure for men also exceeds that for either 1872 or 1920; presumably few Brazilian house husbands existed in 1906 who could be inadvertently included in the domestic service category. Moreover, the proportion of male to female domestic servants remained virtually unchanged in Rio from 1906 to 1920, just as in the nation as a whole. Despite the difficulty determining the exact number of domestic servants, it is clear that this sector, whose feminine component averaged 80 percent, still constituted the major source of jobs for women in urban areas, although declining somewhat in importance (table 7).

Most lower-class families could not survive without female and child labor. In 1913 Rio's major textile union calculated that a single male worker's average monthly expenses totaled 110$000, while a family with two children generally required 210$000. Even if he managed to obtain work every day but Sundays and holidays, an adult male factory worker earning 4$000 a day, the highest average wage among workers in different textile divisions, could only earn 90$000 a month. That adult male daily wage was not sufficient to purchase a kilo each of rice, beans, lard, sugar, and coffee.[74]

Although the percentage of female-headed households among the urban lower classes cannot be accurately determined, available evidence indicates the existence of a number of families supported by women working as seamstresses or doing piecework. These households apparently greatly outnumbered those supported by female shop clerks or mill hands. Traditional female activities like sewing permitted women to work at home, put in longer hours, and, no doubt, also utilize the labor of their children. Factory employment required twelve or more hours a day away from home and apparently paid even less. A woman alone found it extremely difficult to support or care for her family through factory work, and female factory wages generally served to supplement male earnings.

Not untypical among steadily employed lower-income groups may be the high percentage of female-headed households found in the government-subsidized *vilas operárias* of the Companhia de Saneamento do Rio de Janeiro, by far the least crowded and least common form of worker housing, whose attached family units contained individual cooking and sanitary facilities. In response to charges of rent gouging in the mid 1890s, the company published lists of tenants in their five projects in Rio. Not only laborers but also clerks, students, and low-level public functionaries and military officers lived in the biggest and best *vila,* the centrally located Vila Rui Barbosa. Of the 81 families there, 20, or 24.7 percent, were headed by women: 13 women doing piecework, 5 seamstresses, and 2 schoolteachers. In contrast, of the *vila's* 174 single inhabitants, only one, a schoolteacher, was female. Apparently, respectable women rarely lived alone, unlike men. Perhaps, too, child labor was often needed to supplement female earnings and pay the rent. Of the 32 families living in Vila Sampaio, near the main railroad station, 12, or 37.5 percent, were headed by women: 11 pieceworkers and 1 schoolteacher. Only in Vila Arthur Sauer in Jardim Botânico near the Carioca textile factory did any female factory workers support families. Two factory workers, a laundress, a nurse, and 2 pieceworkers paid the rent for 12.8 percent of the *vila's* 47 households. In addition, 2 widows, or 12.5 percent of the *vila's* 16 single inhabitants, lived alone doing piecework. No women factory workers headed households in Vila Maxwell or Vila Senador Soares, both located in Rio's suburban Vila Isabel district near the Confiança Industrial textile factory. Of Vila Maxwell's 15 families, 2 were headed by women doing piecework and 1 by a seamstress. In Vila Senador Soares 20.8 percent, or 11 of 53 households, had female heads: 11 pieceworkers, 2 schoolteachers, and 1 woman pensioner. No male head of household ever listed piecework as his employment. Opportunities for lower-class men, though limited, generally exceeded those for women.[75]

Life for urban workers, never easy, could suddenly worsen. When illness, accidents, fines, or layoffs reduced wages, individual and family suffering increased. In some fields of male employment, like the construction trades, bad weather and shortages of materials further decreased the numbers of workdays per month. Sometimes the deficit between family income and necessary expenditures was met by reducing individual food consumption. As the representatives of Rio's textile workers union sadly recounted, "in order to pay their expenses, workers are obliged to deprive themselves of absolute necessities, . . . working more than their strength allows and eating less than their bodies require to function normally."[76] Female family members' food consumption suffered most. Housewives deprived themselves of food to feed children and husbands. Female factory and shop workers living in Rio's suburbs who rose early to commute long distances by trolley or train to their workplaces breakfasted on "a cup of coffee, a crust of bread." For women with special expenses, like ladies' hat makers, "obliged" by their employers to dress "elegantly, even sumptuously," nothing remained of their wages to purchase proper food.[77]

While some women openly reacted against their treatment in industry, as a group they proved even slower to organize than did men. During the first two decades of the twentieth century only small sectors of Brazil's working poor protested their poverty by forming a variety of generally short-lived labor organizations. Unions remained a means of resistance largely limited to skilled male workers. Craftsmen like printers, shoemakers, construction and transportation workers, stevedores, waiters, and eventually some textile workers (but never day laborers, pieceworkers, or domestic servants) organized separate local unions, reflecting the structure of the Brazilian economy. Effective labor organization proved very difficult when the government sought to silence labor militants' voices. Moreover, the relative lack of both industry in Brazil and literacy among workers in this vast country hindered communications and organization efforts. A crowded labor market, chronic unemployment, government and employer hostility, ethnic, racial, and regional divisions among the lower classes, and the barriers separating skilled and unskilled workers severely limited unionization among men and women alike.[78]

The world of organized labor in early-twentieth-century Brazil, like the world of elite politics, remained overwhelmingly male. Most of the trades organized into unions employed men only, while women worked at traditionally hard-to-organize semiskilled jobs in textiles, food processing, and apparel, or labored as pieceworkers and domestic servants. Women's double burden of family responsibilities and unpaid work at home and paid work in the labor force limited their participation in union activity. The frequent turnover in many women's jobs also hindered the establishment of a sense of collective membership or grievance. As in Rio's América Fabril factory, women textile workers tended to be concentrated in spinning, not weaving, where they were paid by the hour and had even less security than day laborers.[79]

While many unions did accept women as members, they almost never chose them for leadership positions. As demonstrated by available lists and photographs of participants, delegates to labor conferences of various ideological hues were almost entirely male.[80] A perusal of dozens of labor newspapers from Rio de Janeiro and São Paulo in the late nineteenth and early twentieth centuries, all edited by men, reveals no female labor leaders among anarchists and socialists. While a few women contributed articles to these periodicals, or signed manifestos—generally directed toward other women—or even spoke at public meetings, they did not participate in decision making. In neighboring Argentina, with its stronger labor movement and proportionally larger immigrant population, anarchist feminists managed to publish their own newspaper, *La Voz de la Mujer,* in 1896. But the passionate rejection by these largely Spanish anarchists of women's traditional lot and their stress on the multiple nature of women's oppression, by male authority as well as by society, met with more male opposition than encouragement.[81]

Brazilian labor leaders and representatives demonstrated an ambivalent attitude toward female remunerative labor not dissimilar to that seen in other industrializing countries. Male workers or their spokesmen lamented the need for the income female family members provided. Some even echoed the middle-class ideal of a male breadwinner and a female housekeeper, an arrangement which often did not necessarily respond to traditional lower-class patterns. As one moderate socialist declared, "to remove a woman from the home where she comforts her children and watches over the household represents a frightful cruelty."[82] However, some female socialists complained not only about "companions," who, like bourgeois males, "consider women luxury objects," but also about those who "thought that women exist only to bear children and carry out household duties"; women workers were "enslaved and humiliated by men and by industry."[83]

Although many union leaders thought that women should be restricted to the domestic sphere, economic necessity, they admitted, forced women into the job market where they were miserably exploited. At a 1912 congress of reformist labor unions, delegates concluded that ideally, "in the interests of humanity, it would be best if women did not pursue tasks other than those of the home and a few limited occupations appropriate to the female sex." But industrialization reduced men's salaries to the point where they could not support their families, and "forced women to leave home, compelling them to perform arduous labor for a ridiculously low salary that, nonetheless, [was] indispensable for meeting urgent family needs."[84] In an effort to end the exploitation of female and child labor, these delegates demanded protective legislation, especially that stipulating minimum wages and maximum hours, but not equal pay for equal work.

Some unions and groups, however, especially among the anarchists and socialists, did call for the equality of women. The program of the Second Socialist Congress in 1902, for example, demanded equal wages for women, together with political and judicial equality, including the vote.[85] But problems ensued in the pursuit of some socialist and anarchist ideals. For instance, when the companion of one member of the first anarchist circle in Rio de Janeiro in the 1890s put the doctrine of "free love" into practice by switching her affections to another member of the circle, her action caused the disintegration of the group.[86] On other occasions this doctrine did not appeal to women, leading some anarchists, such as Giovanni Rossi, founder of the Cecília Colony, to suggest measures not in keeping with their stated beliefs. In a confidential letter proposing a new colony in Mato Grosso, Rossi admitted that the main problem with such ventures was that few women accepted the anarchist principles of free love. He proposed buying Indian girls from tribes in the interior and initiating them into these principles free from the corrupting influence of bourgeois society.[87]

A few women workers responded to the anarchist or socialist doctrines beginning to spread among the nascent Brazilian labor movement and published urgent, often despairing, appeals in labor newspapers for others to join their struggle for better wages and working conditions.[88] Seamstresses in São Paulo chastised their coworkers for their apathy and for not joining unions although they had "to work up to sixteen hours a day, double that of the stronger sex!"[89] In 1907, the year after three seamstresses issued this anguished plea for solidarity, both among their mistreated colleagues and between seamstresses and other workers, that "most ignorant and backward group among the working classes" struck their employers. The strike was broken, however, according to the city's labor federation, by pressures brought against many strikers by male members of their families anxious to receive the women's pitiful wages.[90]

The ambivalent attitude of male labor leadership toward female workers is evident in the report of Rio's syndicalist-oriented União dos Alfaiates (Tailors' Union) sent to the 1913 Second Brazilian Labor Congress. Demonstrating both pity for female suffering and fear of female competition, the leaders of a union losing members maintained that "women are by far the most exploited people in our profession, and, although we regret saying so, at this time they are our most dangerous competitors, contributing mightily to our distress."[91] The anarcho-syndicalist-dominated 1906 labor congress also termed women "terrible competitors with men" and blamed them for their own victimization, claiming that the exploitation of women was largely due to their "lack of cohesion and solidarity."[92] When Rio's printers suffered massive unemployment following the introduction of linotype machines, their representatives opposed companies' hiring of women.[93] Certainly labor organizations were far more inclined to advocate the "protection" of female labor than to demand equal pay for women. Such protection, in the form of restrictions on female workers and the prohibition of night work, reinforced stereotypes of women as weak and dependent and of men as breadwinners. Furthermore, should protection be combined with equal wages, as some urged, female workers would be placed at a marked disadvantage when seeking employment. Catholic jurist Augusto Olympio Viveiros de Castro accused unions of "masculine hypocrisy" when they advocated equal salaries for women, claiming this was just a maneuver to get lower-paid women out of the job market; if owners were ever obliged to grant women equal wages, they would employ only men.[94] Among urban workers, values and attitudes as to women's place persisted and often resembled, and perhaps reflected, those found among the dominant classes.

By the second decade of the twentieth century, Brazil's governing elite demonstrated mounting concern over protests by the poor. Rather than taking the form of spontaneous outbursts, urban lower-class resentments erupted in mass demonstrations or strikes, culminating in the general strikes of the World War I years. With urban unrest assuming more visible and alarming forms, the dominant elites turned to more elaborate and effective forms of repression. But the Brazilian government also employed more subtle means of control, taking a few tentative steps toward the paternalistic and protective policies elaborated after 1930, in an attempt to control urban discontent and channel class conflicts by guiding or forcing them into institutional forms administered by the state.

Although the danger of anarchism preoccupied conservative politicians, certain members of the elite hoped to integrate the lower class into the existing social and political structure. These comfortably situated Brazilians now expressed concern with workers' welfare. Without wishing to overturn the structure of Brazilian society, they sought solutions to the "social question," a phrase widely used in Europe and Latin America to describe problems of poverty, illiteracy, illness, and discontent among the urban populace. In late-nineteenth-century Europe concern with the social question prompted Pope Leo XIII's encyclical *Rerum novarum* on the condition of the workers, Bismarck's social security system, and other efforts to improve the living and working conditions of the lower classes. Brazilians followed suit, discussing, if not attempting to solve, the social question.

Alarmed by the possibility of conflict between labor and capital and fearful of anarchism and socialism, some educated Brazilians not only lamented the low salaries paid workers during a period of rising living costs but also condemned the exploitation of women and children.[95] Unlike their nineteenth-century predecessors, some denied women's right to work for pay at all, although they found no practical alternative to family dependence on the paltry wages women and children contributed. Catholic writers like Augusto Olympio Viveiros de Castro, a law professor in Rio de Janeiro, declared it was evident that "work performed by women outside the home is unnatural, antisocial, and uneconomic." Moreover, women's physical weaknesses prevented them from performing long hours of factory work, and factory noises led to "multiple displays of hysteria." He cited the encyclical *Rerum novarum*, in which Leo XIII argued that women's employment was regrettable and insisted on men's responsibility to provide for their families, as well as "common knowledge," to prove that nature had destined women for domestic tasks and that they were "born exclusively for the home." As in other Catholic countries, however, papal condemnation of women's outside employment did not lessen the need for that income nor the number of women seeking it. Low though their wages were, these meager allotments remained essential for family survival. Even if male relatives wished to support these women, their earnings alone were insufficient. Viveiros de Castro himself had to admit that the "complete withdrawal of women and children from all outside work," the "highest ideal of Christian civilization," remained "a lovely dream." Sadly he acknowledged that even such measures as the establishment of a minimum family salary for men would not resolve the problem, since many women headed households. Hence, given the impossibility of eradicating this "social evil of work," all governments could do was prevent some abuses through providing such protective measures as a few months' maternity leave.[96] And not even this was done. Views such as Viveiros de Castro's that women should not work outside the home and that they were incapable of hard labor, although in fact they performed it, could only contribute to low wage levels.

Socialism and anarchism appeared much more revolutionary to male members of the elite than did questions of women's rights. While a few of these men regretted poor families' dependence on female wages, far more viewed as inevitable and unavoidable the entrance of lower-class women, unlike their own female relatives, into the work force. In comparison to the social question, the "woman question," largely limited to women of their own class, seemed far less alarming to upper-class men.

Changing Views of Proper Female Pursuits

In the early twentieth century, writings by and about women appeared in print more frequently, and the "woman question" became a fit subject for serious discussion within the elite. But the strongest demands for both female emancipation and female subordination tended to be obscured by more moderate expressions.

Since the days of that outspoken intellectual and pioneer women's rights advocate Nísia Floresta, a few Brazilian women had produced an occasional piece of prose or poetry for publication. But for many years only extraordinary women like Narcisa Amália de Campos could achieve renown as poets and literary figures. In addition to writing for the general press in Rio de Janeiro, she also contributed to *O Sexo Feminino* in the 1870s, advocating a higher status for Brazil's women.[97]

During the second half of the nineteenth century, periodicals directed toward women and journals edited by women provided an outlet for some of the creations of well-educated women in Brazil. By the end of the century the ranks of both women's rights advocates and literary ladies had grown, and some women could be found among both groups. No longer isolated, clusters of women writers could be found in Brazil's major cities; they maintained contact with similar groups in the different urban centers and often contributed to each other's newspapers and literary endeavors at opposite ends of the country. A number of women from prominent families, like Júlia Lopes de Almeida, Inéz Sabino Pinho Maia, and Maria Clara Vilhena da Cuna contributed to various female-oriented periodicals with different positions on emancipation. Some women overcame prejudices against writing for the general press as well, no doubt aided by French examples.[98]

Júlia Lopes de Almeida became one of the best-known female authors and novelists in Brazil, combining her intellectual endeavors with a conventional domestic life. The daughter of the possessor of a Portuguese title of nobility and the wife of a Portuguese poet, both of whom supported her career, she achieved recognition as a member of the period's literary elite, becoming the first woman to seek entrance into Brazil's newly established Academy of Letters, and the first to be refused. Her career demonstrates both the possibilities open to women in her position and the limits imposed on them by a male-dominated society. No fervent women's rights advocate, this very popular and prolific author tended to stress the need for women to be good housewives in addition to being well educated. Writing at home, "in a warm corner of her garden," surrounded by her loving children, she placed the family at the center of her arguments and subordinated her own literary career to her role as mother and wife. Once more, the need for well-educated mothers who could awaken the intellectual curiosity of their children justified feminine endeavors.[99] Unlike earlier advocates of female emancipation such as Francisca Diniz, women like Júlia Lopes de Almeida were not obliged to support themselves and their families, which no doubt influenced their views on women's rightful place and pursuits.

Literary activities which could be pursued at home provided an acceptable outlet for female energies, and it was one increasingly used by some upper-class women. The less controversial women writers who praised home and family could be viewed as proof of female intellectual abilities by men sympathetic to moderate female emancipation. Furthermore, neither their persons nor their views made men of their own class very uncomfortable. Unlike lower-class women, they could still be seen as delicate and gentle creatures. Their benign literary manifestations caused no one great concern.

The cultural and technological innovations coming to Brazil's urban centers in the early twentieth century affected women as well as men. Like their male kin, women of the "finest families" met and passed their time at teahouses and theaters. Soon they were traveling in automobiles and attending movie houses, which exposed them to new attitudes and modes of female behavior. Women of the elite had long visited Europe, making "frequent voyages with their husbands, bringing home the latest thing in styles, both for dress and the ornamentation of their homes."[100] Rather than returning with just the physical accoutrements of modernity and fashion, some women also acquired new ideas about women's activities and rights.

Novel attitudes and images of female behavior arrived in Brazil from Europe and the United States in easily assimilated form through the movies. Films portrayed women as independent working girls, modern heroines, and even as sexual temptresses, not just as models of resignation and self-sacrifice. Like the theater and the popular press, the movies helped elite women to acquire new ideas and aspirations and to escape the narrow physical and mental confines of the household. Although the urban working class was less likely to purchase glossy illustrated magazines chronicling the activities of foreign film stars or to frequent first-class cinemas on the broad new boulevards, they could attend lower-priced suburban theaters. Admission to São Paulo's suburban movie "palaces" cost no more than the equivalent of a trolley ride. Entire families attended, bringing baskets full of sandwiches, sweets, and beverages to consume while watching new worlds flickering in front of them.[101]

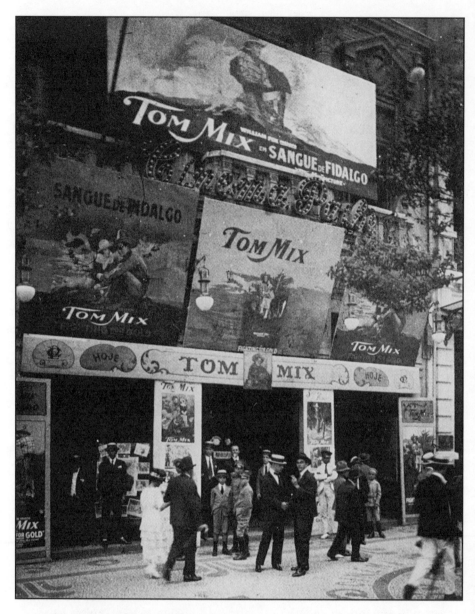

Pathé Cinema, which opened in 1907, on the Avenida Central in Rio de Janeiro, 1918. (Photograph by Marc Ferrez in Gilberto Ferrez and Weston J. Naef, *Pioneer Photographers of Brazil, 1840–1920*)

As in Western Europe and the United States, the "woman question" became a fit subject for discussion by the nation's opinion makers. And the term *feminism* began to come into very loose use by the first decade of the twentieth century. Even in distant Terezinha, capital of the poverty-stricken northeastern state of Piauí, some men viewed the "cause of feminism" as "noble and appealing," for "free, emancipated" women would be "dedicated companions" and "collaborators" in the "struggle for progress."[102] But "radical feminism," which sought to "disorganize society," only offended men seeking to "calmly analyze" the "woman question."[103]

In glossy fashionable reviews and magazines like Rio's *Kosmos*, Brazilian men pondered solutions to this problem. For positivists it ranked in importance with the "proletarian question." They continued to argue women's moral superiority, intellectual equality, but physical inferiority, and advocated a purely domestic existence for women. Women should function as the "soul of the family," which was the keystone of civilization, and as the educators of men, but not as their equals.[104] Another magazine contributor stressed the improvements Christianity had brought to "the amiable sex." In a patronizing fashion he questioned whether women had ever meditated on the role they had played during the course of human evolution and progress. And he reassured his readers that women would serve as "faithful and dedicated priestesses" of "modern liberty" when they turned their attention to politics, the only area to which they had not yet contributed.[105]

Some members of the Brazilian elite might view an incipient women's rights movement as another worthy activity or charity, a fashionable cause to champion. As Maria Amália Vaz de Carvalho, a popular Portuguese writer and longtime contributor to Brazilian newspapers advocating female emancipation, had shrewdly noted in the general press at the turn of the century, feminism was no longer déclassé. Women's rights movements had become stronger and more respectable in many countries, with ladies of high social standing participating in international women's congresses. The upper classes liked novelties as long as these did "not dislodge them from the comfortable position" in which they were solidly established.[106]

Nor did women's rights activities seem to threaten, or be threatened by, the Roman Catholic church in Brazil. The church did not occupy as central a position in Brazilian society as it did in many other Latin American countries. And the legal separation of church and state effected by the republican Constitution of 1891 following the fall of the empire in 1889 removed the church from the formal political system, providing new possibilities for reform. The Brazilian church mounted no effective opposition to increasing rights for women. But it did firmly oppose legalizing divorce.

Divorce never became a major issue in Brazilian feminist circles during the early twentieth century, for legal separation satisfied many of the nation's women, and men. As long as Roman Catholicism had remained the official state religion of Brazil, divorce had not been a possible option. Even in the 1890s, following the promulgation of the new republican constitution, only a few women like the outspoken newspaper publisher Josefina de Azevedo favored divorce laws that permitted the dissolution of marriage ties already broken by mutual consent. Otherwise, she said, the law was tyrannical. If a woman "could repudiate the husband whom her parents chose without consulting her desire," she would control her destiny more than the woman who "sacrifices her entire existence so as not to disobey parental authority."[107] But by the early twentieth century, women like Mirtes de Campos, Brazil's first practicing female lawyer, Inéz Sabino Pinho Maia, a Pernambucan writer educated in Paris and living in Rio de Janeiro, Emília Moncorvo Bandeira de Melo (pseud. Carmen Dolores), one of Brazil's first female newspaper columnists, and Andradina América Andrada de Oliveira, a newspaper publisher in Rio Grande do Sul, publicly advocated divorce legislation and defended their stand in the name of the family and morality. At the beginning of the century Inéz Sabino declared legal separation (which did not permit remarriage) insufficient; only a true divorce law could right existing wrongs.[108] Carmen Dolores contended that legal separation, not divorce, involved immorality, for divorce provided an "honest, straightforward, and decisive solution without hypocritical ambiguities."[109] Even Júlia Lopes de Almeida accepted divorce as a necessity, pointing out that the government would never compel anyone to get divorced and that good Catholics could "continue to regard marriage as eternal and indissoluble."[110] In 1912 Andradina de Oliveira, a normal school graduate and teacher, published her plea for legalized divorce in the form of a book of fictitious letters from male and female victims of unfortunate marriages. For her, not divorce but adultery dissolved families. Not divorce but legal separation led to depravity, concubinage, and prostitution, and prevented people in love from becoming legally and morally joined. Not divorce but indissoluble marriage induced hypocrisy and desperation. Well aware of the depth of church opposition to divorce, Andradina de Oliveira still needled the clergy, asking if they feared Catholic beliefs to be so shallow that these could not withstand "matrimonial disillusionment." Divorce served as an "extremely painful, bitter remedy" only for those in dire need, those "with a noose around their throats—the indissoluble bond—and almost strangled by it."[111]

For years, Andradina de Oliveira had emphasized emancipation through work, defending women's right to employment outside the home in her newspaper *Escrínio*. After all, she had to work to help support her own family. But Andradina had felt obliged to assure her audience that women could "work side by side with men, struggling for their daily bread, . . . without losing their sex's special virtues or neglecting the sacred duties of wife and mother." In the most theoretical letter in her 1912 book on divorce, a happily married feminist, proud to use that term, not only advocated divorce legislation but also stressed the "necessity of work which gives one independence." Women should study and "acquire a profession, a means of subsistence." Like her nineteenth-century predecessors, this alter ego of Andradina argued that through work and education women could become free, strong, and equal to men. Feminism would "open all women's eyes," and they would "cease to be slaves, servants, beasts of burden, objects of pleasure for men, *bibelots* for the drawing room" and become "men's true companions, their sisters, their equals." However, just as she had in the pages of *Escrínio* a decade earlier, Andradina de Oliveira also justified increased education for women as preparation for motherhood. A woman might leave her home to work, but she should still be "the true queen of the home."[112]

By the second decade of the twentieth century, more women were trespassing on terrain long culturally understood as male, from stores and offices to the medical schools and even the courtroom, where they proved almost as much a novelty as did female barbers. Ever more upper-class women promenaded along the principal avenues of major urban centers like Rio de Janeiro, taking tea or shopping in stylish stores where they were attended by members of a growing female labor force. Although large segments of the population remained illiterate, increasing numbers of women secured education and could enter occupations requiring some instruction. More middle-class women found employment outside the home, especially in classrooms, government offices, and commercial establishments. But even the far smaller minority of well-educated women who achieved entry into prestigious professions like law and medicine encountered job discrimination. However, lower-class women, who had no choice but to work for survival, endured far harsher treatment. Few joined unions or participated in the incipient feminist movement, which would increasingly focus on suffrage. The franchise, legally limited to literates, meant little to most members of the lower classes, male or female. The Brazilian women's suffrage movement would be largely confined to urban upper- and middle-class women. The small minority of well-educated professional women would supply the leadership while primary school teachers and other middle-class women entered the ranks. Although some feminists in the 1920s and 1930s would tackle problems of concern to working-class women such as long hours, low wages, and miserable working conditions, interclass linkages proved difficult.

Chapter 4

The Women's Suffrage Movement

By the beginning of the 1920s, feminist activities in Brazil had proliferated at an increasingly rapid pace. Sustained efforts would now be mounted to improve women's social, civil, and political status. More women explored and debated their own problems, defining their own grievances and their own hopes. Women's achievement of the vote in several major European countries following the conclusion of World War I aided the cause in Brazil, and advocacy of female suffrage became acceptable in some elite circles. Not only the examples given by certain "advanced" nations but also the personal links established between Brazilian feminists and international suffrage leaders spurred the formation of formal women's rights organizations in Brazil. Led by well-educated urban women who had benefited from the improvements in female education during the late nineteenth century, the new associations provided increasing numbers of Brazilian women with a channel of expression while helping to create a political arena for women.

The years marking the First World War witnessed a series of changes in Brazil, from accelerating national consciousness to increasing industrial production and the end of the century-old dependence on Great Britain. Although Brazil was the only South American country to declare war on Germany, its participation in the conflict was largely limited to furnishing supplies to the Allies, who reduced their intake of nonessentials like coffee but purchased increasing quantities of sugar, meat, rice, and beans, reducing the supply available to Brazil's urban population. Food shortages, lagging wage levels, and the government's inflationary policy placed many members of the middle classes in a precarious economic position while producing severe hardships and growing unrest among the urban workers. As their fears of anarchism, socialism, and "foreign agitators" increased, more people paid attention to the social question, which had surfaced as a political issue during the 1910 presidential campaign. A wave of wartime strikes and protests by the poor forced the question into the halls of Congress. But the Brazilian government was slow to see how social legislation could help pacify and control segments of the laboring poor, preferring to use force and suppress autonomous labor organizations.

In the 1920s Brazil faced a series of upheavals and challenges on both the political and cultural fronts from other elements of the population. Modern art and military uprisings shocked and perturbed the nation's cultural and political establishments. Junior officers rose in rebellion against the federal government, calling for an end to oligarchy and corruption, while the intellectual avant-garde articulated a challenge to established order and practice, proclaiming their artistic iconoclasm in poetry, painting, novels, sculpture, and music, as well as sometimes displaying a disregard for the conventional morality of the family. At the same time, elements of the urban middle classes voiced their growing nationalism and desire for development and reform. As political discontent and protests against the entrenched oligarchy mounted, it was more likely that female enfranchisement might find a place among middle-class demands for electoral reform.

Concerned with Brazilian themes as well as preoccupied with new styles, a small group of young and adventurous intellectuals experimented with new forms and subjects, seeking to define and encourage national culture and to concentrate on the present and the future, not on the past. In 1922, the centenary of Brazilian independence, a group of writers and artists in the rapidly growing industrial center of São Paulo organized the Semana de Arte Moderna, a week-long series of public meetings, performances, and exhibits. These young men and women, with diverse media and outlooks, had found a common cause in trying to render into form the flux of modern art and life. While their iconoclasm was ill-received by the general public and the academicians, it would finally help bring Brazilians to a new awareness of their country. The Modern Art Week was a major milestone in the awakening of Brazilian intellectuals to the themes and idiom of their own country and of the twentieth century.[1]

In the changing cultural climate of the 1920s, some avant-garde intellectuals led by the poet Oswald de Andrade, a leader of the modernists, attacked the Brazilian conception of relationships between the sexes. But few Brazilians were prepared to follow them. While physicians and educators called for the introduction of sex education into the schools, no such courses were instituted. Advocates of sex education did not seek to upset traditional gender roles. Instead, they claimed, sex education would lessen the incidence of female neuroses and prevent moral perversion while ensuring healthier offspring.[2] The late 1920s and 1930s saw the translation and publication in Brazil of several dozen foreign texts treating various aspects of sexuality, but the Brazilian physicians promoting such works justified them as instruments for preserving conjugal happiness.[3] Even avant-garde intellectuals whose personal behavior might offend public proprieties took care not to display their disregard for conventional morality.

Tarsila do Amaral, the most prominent woman among the modernists and the companion and wife of Oswald de Andrade for several years, pursued an independent personal and artistic course, escaping the confines of academic art as well as the limitations of the traditional upper-class female role. Born into a wealthy landed *paulista* family, she experimented with poetry, music, and art following the disintegration of her arranged marriage. At the age of thirty she began a serious career as a painter, and her distinctive and colorful works brought her fame and recognition in Europe as well as in Brazil. Her wealth and social position facilitated her artistic and intellectual emancipation. Unlike many others, Tarsila do Amaral possessed abundant financial resources and an elevated social background that allowed her to travel extensively, receive lessons from prestigious Brazilian and European artists, and set up ateliers in Paris and São Paulo that became popular gathering places for artists and intellectuals. She never flaunted her unorthodox private life; her open rebellion was limited to the aesthetic realm. Although she sympathized with the plight of the proletariat, admired the early achievements of the Russian Revolution, and disdained many of society's conventions, Tarsila refrained from political activities and attacks on marriage and traditional female roles. Nor did she demonstrate interest in questions of women's political or civil status.[4] But Brazilian feminists in the 1920s cited her among those outstanding Brazilian women whose accomplishments gave proof of their sex's abilities.[5]

Technological innovations such as movies and motorcars no doubt exerted greater direct influence on female behavior in Brazil's major urban centers than did the views and behavior of the avant-garde. Young Brazilian women of "good families" became more conspicuous, appearing on beaches rather than just promenading along the avenues, playing tennis, riding bicycles, and being photographed by newspaper reporters. In vain did conservative school officials bemoan the effects of the abundant diversions found in "this feverish age"; not only movies and automobile rides but also "the three fascinating *f*'s—*football, footing* [promenading], and *flirting*" (these English words are the terms employed in the original Portuguese quotation)—beguiled students.[6]

Newspapers of the 1920s reported new female activities and achievements, including the exploits of Brazil's best-known female aviator, Anésia Pinheiro Machado. When this nineteen-year-old *paulista* received her license in 1922, she declared to a local reporter that since childhood she had wanted to overcome "restrictions inherent to my condition as a woman" and to distinguish herself. And she criticized the São Paulo authorities for putting obstacles in her way. That same year she joined the newly formed Federação Brasileira pelo Progresso Feminino, which would become Brazil's leading suffrage organization, and she gave a major address on new careers for women at its first national conference.[7]

Political events earned the biggest newspaper headlines. Beneath the excitement of individual exploits and the iconoclastic proclamations of avant-garde intellectuals swirled powerful political currents. Many of the contributors to the intellectual ferment of the 1920s became deeply involved in politics. While some moved to the far left, like Oswald de Andrade, who briefly flirted with communism, others ventured to the far right or stayed someplace in between. Elements of the growing middle classes and young army officers alike voiced dissatisfaction with the existing oligarchical form of government and the dominance of the coffee interests.

Under the Old Republic (1889–1930), coalitions of political leaders from major states like coffee-rich São Paulo and Minas Gerais, backed by the army, controlled national political affairs and chose the president. Rarely were those elections disputed. National politics in Brazil remained largely a game of patronage and economic privilege, with the president of the republic dispensing the major prizes. Elections were little more than a formality. Even with literate male citizens over

Homage to the flapper, who was considered independent but still
attractive and feminine, in the form of traditional hand kissing, as
depicted by one of Brazil's leading illustrators, J. Carlos, on the cover
of the stylish magazine *Para Todos*, 1929. An automobile, the symbol of
modernity, is seen in the background. (*J. Carlos, 100 anos*)

the age of twenty-one allowed to vote, less than 3 percent of the nation's population participated in presidential elections.[8]

In 1922, the same year that the elite celebrated the centenary of Brazilian independence and young avant-garde intellectuals organized the Semana de Arte Moderna, junior officers staged the first of a series of unsuccessful revolts against the federal government. The contested presidential elections of that year had exposed a growing rift between the officer corps and the ruling politicians, who represented the coffee elite. While senior officers proved reluctant to take up arms against the government, a small group of junior officers did not. Rather than just proclaim the need to reform, regenerate, and modernize the nation and end the corruption, inefficiency, and pettiness of the politicians, they turned to physical protest. On July 5, 1922, a poorly planned and badly coordinated revolt broke out in Rio de Janeiro. Although most of the rebels at the fort in Copacabana quickly surrendered to government forces, a handful won national fame by storming the beach and dramatically giving their lives for their vaguely defined cause. Other unsuccessful military moves followed, ending with the overthrow of the Old Republic in 1930.

Elements of the urban middle classes with backgrounds and beliefs similar to those of the young officers also sought reform and change. The growth in the size and importance of that urban sector had not been reflected in national elections. Pressures for political and electoral change grew during the 1920s, and more attempts were made to broaden the nation's narrow political base and loosen the grip of the coffee oligarchy. Despite military revolts, oligarchical government, and suppression of strikes, Brazil still offered fewer obstacles to organized political and social action than did some other Latin American countries where dictatorships completely negated the value of the ballot box. Whether in its actual or potential form, the vote was important to many men in Brazil, and therefore might also be important to women of the same class.

Some women sought to be included in the political mobilization of the 1920s. During this decade of political unrest, most of the feminists' efforts would be channeled toward increasing women's civil and political rights. Women's moralizing mission in society could be extended from the home to the political arena, and they could present their desire for the franchise within the context of needed reforms.

Organizing for Women's Rights

By the second decade of the twentieth century, a moderate women's rights movement had become acceptable in Brazil. New but never radical women's newspapers appeared in major urban centers, as did ever more women's organizations. The franchise received more sympathetic discussion and could now be freely contested, both informally and formally, as at a debate held at the YMCA in São Paulo in 1912. In theoretical discourse, and perhaps in reality also, the cult of womanhood could be combined with suffrage. The "angel who prays for our peace and happiness" might yet cast her ballot. Even some Brazilian men argued that this superior individual should be permitted to vote and run for office.[9] Motherhood might be incompatible with the exercise of masculine professions, according to some male writers, but not the franchise; after all, voting would not remove women from their homes for lengthy periods of time.[10]

Events abroad could reassure upper-class Brazilians that an increase in women's rights, especially suffrage, would not upset or alter societal or familial structures. As the press noted, women in New Zealand had not abused their suffrage victory, and no great changes had occurred in the composition of the legislature.[11] What women voters might be expected to do was clean up government in keeping with their image of nobility and purity.

Like other urban groups in Brazil, educated women sought to gain a measure of participation and authority. They requested rights similar to those exercised by their husbands and brothers, concentrating on access to professional positions and on the vote. Few openly defied public proprieties or conventional morality. Unlike several earlier proponents of female emancipation, they advocated no major changes in family relations. Neither ballot nor university degree would hinder a woman from attending to her household duties. A male physician and educator sympathetic to some feminist concerns approvingly noted in 1923 that Brazilian women had managed to achieve liberties and prerogatives over the past dozen years that "surprised all of us," and this occurred without "any scandal, struggle, or radical alterations within the family or in proper public behavior in Brazil's large cities."[12] The nation's rulers felt more comfortable with the energetic but polite women leading the new women's rights associations than they had with the outspoken nineteenth-century advocates of female emancipation.

Suffragists on the cover of the popular magazine *Fon Fon*, 1914.

In the process of broadening its appeal and widening its basis of support among the upper classes, the women's rights movement in Brazil grew more conservative. As had occurred in the United States by the early twentieth century, the movement in Brazil tended to stress legal and constitutional reform rather than more radical changes. During the 1920s and 1930s, Brazilian feminists channeled most of their efforts toward increasing their civil and political rights. The relatively muted ideological character of the Brazilian movement, like the U.S. movement, may well have stemmed from the leadership's concern for retaining respectability in order to enhance their chances of success. Their movement's moderation might secure support among male politicians favoring reform without social or political upset.

In Brazil, as in the United States, professional women supplied much of the leadership for the twentieth-century suffrage movement, which would attain its stated goal in 1932. Although daughters of both the elite and the emerging middle sectors enjoyed increased opportunities for social contacts and employment outside the home by the second decade of the twentieth century, those opportunities were far from equal. Well-educated and well-connected women might secure entrance to the liberal professions, but those with limited training looked for employment in expanding fields like primary education, commerce, banking, and government service. Between 1906 and 1920 the number of female schoolteachers in Rio de Janeiro alone more than tripled (see table 5). These women comprised a new audience for the advocates of women's suffrage. Some schoolteachers and other members of the growing urban middle classes felt a definite need for the vote. Closely linked to the government bureaucracy, either as primary school teachers or as the wives of public functionaries, and even in a few cases as civil servants themselves, they feared that the economic difficulties and inflation of the World War I period might lead to cuts in public expenditures and government positions.

This was the audience addressed by Leolinda de Figuereido Daltro, a Bahia-born schoolteacher, journalist, and president of the Partido Republicano Feminino founded in 1910. The party sought to carry the suffrage issue into congress, which had not taken it up since the Constituent Congress of 1891. Besides the vote, Leolinda Daltro called for the emancipation of Brazilian women in general terms, and she specifically advocated that public service positions be open to all Brazilians regardless of sex. Economic need and women's rights had combined with middle-class patriotism and national politics to give rise to a party tied to the family of President Hermes da Fonseca, a hearty career officer who served as president of Brazil from 1910 to 1914. His first wife, Orsina da Fonseca, served as the party's honorary president.[13]

The increasing patriotism of the urban middle class and the campaign for a well-trained modern army, supported by Marshal Hermes da Fonseca, led to a new draft law in 1908 and to the creation of shooting clubs, or *linhas de tiro*, whose members would form the army's reserve. The war in Europe only added to Brazilian patriotic fervor, and prominent Brazilian statesmen and writers aided the prodefense campaign. While women's contributions to the national effort were generally expected to be limited to nursing and Red Cross work, a token female shooting club also received official patronage. Leolinda de Figuereido Daltro helped create the Linha de Tiro Feminino Rosa da Fonseca as well as a school of nursing.[14]

Unlike the social question, which commanded more attention and engendered more alarm among Brazilians fearful of anarchism and socialism, the woman question apparently posed little danger for the existing structure of the nation. The Hermes government had sponsored a moderate workers' congress in 1912 and sought to capture sections of the emerging labor movement. Hermes recognized that potential political profit might be reaped from organizing women as well. Such actions might also suggest that the inclusion of women was now needed to demonstrate national unity on some issues.

With many members of the middle classes in a precarious economic position during the inflation-ridden World War I years, the income contributed by unmarried daughters, widows, or, in cases of severe distress, wives, often proved essential to family maintenance. Unmarried women might win praise for their diligence at work or in school and their avoidance of frivolity or idleness, but wives needed economic excuses for their employment. Even some professional women whose families did not depend on their earnings used economic arguments to justify their employment outside the home. Few but the staunchest feminists would defend an unconditional female right to paid employment or encourage women to seek work in order to fulfill personal ambitions or emancipate themselves.

The Brazilian women who achieved high-level government service positions possessed the necessary organizational skills and determination—as well as the personal contacts—to lead a successful women's suffrage campaign. By 1920 a few women had not only managed to enter the professions but also had secured important public positions. In 1917 Maria José de Castro Rebelo Mendes obtained a legal ruling permitting women to compete for government positions, for neither the Constitution nor the civil code contained any provisions to the contrary. Claiming the need for more secure employment than tutoring in order to support her widowed mother, this daughter of a prominent politician sought to enter the competition for a position in the Foreign Ministry, and she won first place. Citing her example, other women sought to enter different ministries. In 1919 Bertha Lutz, a biologist who had recently returned to Brazil with a degree from the Sorbonne, successfully competed for a high position in the national museum in Rio de Janeiro. She became the leader of the Brazilian women's suffrage movement. Other women were nominated to such positions as inspector of municipal schools in Rio de Janeiro. Mirtes de Campos, the first woman lawyer admitted to the Brazilian bar and the second woman to hold that inspectorship, would continue to press for women's right to vote, in print and through the association of Brazilian lawyers. Women secured prominent civil service positions not only in the nation's capital but also in other Brazilian cities. Ever more women obtained higher education. And in 1924 the first woman received appointment to a permanent faculty position at a professional school, Rio's medical college. Besides law and medicine, women moved into civil engineering, pharmacy, and dentistry. In the 1920s and 1930s Lutz's lieutenants included lawyers, doctors, and engineers, both inside and outside government service.[15]

These professional women, tied to the governing elites, advocated less drastic changes in women's roles and attitudes than had schoolteachers like Francisca Diniz in the late nineteenth century.[16] Francisca Diniz and her daughters had to supplement schoolteaching and newspaper publishing with the proceeds from everything from giving piano lessons to doing translations just to survive economically.[17] Unlike sheltered literary ladies, they needed the income derived from writing for newspapers.

In contrast, twentieth-century women's newspaper publishers like Cassilda Martins, widow of politician and diplomat Enéas Martins and president of the Associação Protectora do Recolhimento de Desvalidos de Petrópolis, a charitable society, did not fear economic hardship, any more than did her collaborator, the noted novelist Júlia Lopes de Al-

NOSSO·JORNAL

N. 6 — **ANNO I**
Directora **CASSILDA MARTINS**
(Viuva Enéas Martins)
— Rio de Janeiro, 30 de Abril de 1920 —
Para a mulher — Pela mulher

A mulher brasileira na burocracia e no magisterio

NOSSO JORNAL desvanece-se de render, hoje, a homenagem do seu apreço a duas illustres senhoras brasileiras, que acabam de ser chamadas a desempenhar importantes funcções na administração publica.

São as Exmas. Sras. D. Esther Pedreira de Mello, professora, inspectora escolar, nomeada para dirigir a Escola Normal desta capital, e Dra. Myrtes de Campos, talentosa advogada, nomeada inspectora das escolas municipaes.

Nesta mesma occasião apraz-nos tributar o preito da nossa admiração a uma jovem e

Professora D. Esther Pedreira de Mello, inspectora escolar, que acaba de ser nomeada para dirigir a Escola Normal do Districto Federal

distincta patricia, Dra. Evangelina de Carvalho, que acaba de fazer, com tanto brilho, a sua estréa na tribuna do Jury, defendendo a ré Malvina de Sousa Lima, que foi absolvida.

Pedimos venia, a proposito, ao brilhante vespertino *A Tribuna*, para reproduzir o interessante editorial em que se occupou de á *evolução do feminismo no Brasil*.

Eil-o:

"Depois de um incidente grave, e por todos os motivos deploravel, occorrido na Escola Normal, demittindo-se o director deste estabelecimento, foi nomeada, em sua substituição, D. Esther Pedreira de Mello, inspectora escolar. Ao mesmo tempo, dava-se a

nomeação da Dra. Myrthes de Campos para exercer as funcções do cargo de que se afastava a primeira destas senhoras.

Pode-se chamar a isto mais uma victoria do feminismo em nosso paiz? E, em ultima analyse, que é, na realidade, o feminismo? A tendencia emancipada de um sexo? A luta pelo conseguimento de reivindicações contra o egoismo dos homens? A demonstração pratica de que a mulher possue qualidades identicas ou superiores ás do homem, susceptiveis de se revelarem por entre as exigencias do progresso e da civilização?

O feminismo é tudo isso e alguma coisa mais difficil de precisar, e tão indefinivel como a mulher. Mas, seja qual fôr o ponto de vista por que o encaremos, já considerando-o um ideal universal em marcha victoriosamente, já tomando-o com a restricção de um programma de partido agitando determinada sociedade, o certo é que, no Brasil, seja como tendencia emancipativa do sexo, seja como objectivo de reivindicações sobre o nosso egoismo, seja como evidenciação de qualidades eguaes ou superiores ás nossas na luta da civilização, seja por que fôr, o feminismo está realizando uma evolução triumphal, absolutamente serena, pacifica e symphatica.

Comparativamente com os mais adeantados paizes da terra, o Brazil pode orgulhar-se de ter um feminismo que está vencendo, tão só, pela projecção da cultura mental. Parece que não ha mesmo, presentemente, no mundo, nação alguma que possa disputar-nos a primazia nesse terreno. A Inglaterra e os Estados Unidos onde a questão da emancipação civil da mulher irrompeu com violenta acuidade, pondo á face das nações mais um problema social de solução delicada e imperativa, o feminismo tomou logo o caracter demagogico de uma hostilidade libertaria de sexo contra sexo. Muitas das conquistas do feminismo inglez foram alcançadas pela violencia, muitas vezes selvagem, de verdadeiros viragos, munidos de bombas, petroleo, mechas, todo um arsenal depredativo e incendiario, em que as mulheres britannicas revelaram qualidade de virulencia tão aggressiva e intolerante, que surprehenderam e penalizaram o mundo culto.

Esse movimento barbaro tomou o nome de suffragismo, porque o que a mulher ingleza pleiteava era o direito de votar e ser votada, era a sua inclusão nas actividades da politica, com a perspectiva de uma influencia real nos conselhos do governo.

Lastrado da Inglaterra, o rastilho communicou-se, com maior força explosiva, aos Estados Unidos, onde tambem o feminismo tomou essa fórma suffragiaria, que faz depender da politica activa o successo ulterior das suas idéas geraes.

Ora, no Brazil, não sómente o feminismo

apenas se manifesta sob o aspecto de generosa assistencia social ao sexo e o de um simples torneio de cultura intellectual, como as suas reivindicações estão longe, remotissimamente longe de revestir mesmo um caracter de impertinencia hostil. Muito ao contrario, não ha ninguem que não louve, com espontaneo prazer, o empenho da mulher brazileira, já procurando a defesa moral e social para as creaturas infelizes do seu sexo, já buscando occupar, por meios absolutamente honrosos e brilhantes, os postos que na burocracia e no magisterio têm sido tradicionalmente servidos pelos homens.

Ha 10 annos atraz o feminismo era, entre nós, uma coisa vaga, brumosa, impenetravel,

A distincta advogada doutora Myrthes de Campos, nomeada inspectora escolar no Rio de Janeiro

de que muita gente, não podendo devassar-lhe o futuro, deve ter sorrido com deleite.

Quando precisamente a actual directora da Escola Normal foi nomeada inspectora escolar no Districto, essa nomeação foi, mesmo recebida sem applausos e, em certos circulos, com reprovação. Ninguem confiava no exito da capacidade femnina no serviço da administração publica.

Vieram, depois, as provas admiraveis de competencia, dadas pela senhorita Maria José de Castro Rebello, no rumoroso concurso do Itamaraty, e pela senhorita Bertha Lutz, no notavel concurso do Museu Nacional. As provas da primeira e da segunda foram tão concludentes, o seu preparo, a sua intelligencia, a sua capacidade ficaram de tal modo paten-

meida. Their newspaper, *Nosso Jornal,* begun in Rio de Janeiro late in 1919, resembled a stylish society magazine like *Kosmos* far more than it did the nineteenth-century *O Sexo Feminino.* In the glossy pages of *Nosso Jornal* the wife of President Epitácio Pessoa expressed her views about how Brazilian women could reconcile their social duties with those as daughters, wives, and mothers. Articles appeared on everything from Lady Nancy Astor's activities in the British Parliament to how American film star Mary Pickford fixed her hair. While *Nosso Jornal* lauded many of the opportunities opening to Brazil's women and favored women's suffrage, it sought to harmonize the old with the new. *Nosso Jornal* opposed the "radical feminism" found in other countries, which subverted the "classical molds of women's existence."[18] Like much of the regular press, these women expressed pride in a Brazilian feminist movement achieving its goals without the violence and anti-male hostility seen in the United States and Great Britain, and they felt superior to "aggressive and intolerant" bomb-throwing English suffragettes.[19]

Revista Feminina, published in São Paulo between 1915 and 1927, also preached moderation. Founded by Virgilina de Souza Sales, daughter of a well-respected *paulista* family and mother of playwright Claúdio de Souza, *Revista Feminina* became the most popular women's magazine in early-twentieth-century Brazil. In just two years this resourceful businesswoman turned her four-page biweekly periodical into a hundred-page, abundantly illustrated, glossy monthly publication. By 1918 it had achieved a circulation of over twenty thousand. Largely directed to middle-class urban housewives, a sufficiently numerous group able to afford an annual subscription price of 10$000 (roughly the cost of eight kilos of beef, or more than double the daily wage of a female textile worker), the magazine carried advertisements for health and beauty aids, household appliances, furniture, automobiles, and clothing, tips on running a household economically, advice on making decorative paper boxes and other items to earn pin money, and stories with moral messages in addition to articles on world history and politics, scientific advances, and cultural events.[20] It reinforced traditional gender roles while seeking simultaneously to foster women's social activism.

Revista Feminina consciously served as a forum for discussing women's roles and activities, issuing appeals to feminine organizations throughout Brazil to contribute information on their programs and achievements. The magazine considered itself an indispensable "organ for intellectual communication" as well as the "first great work" of women, arguments also used to attract new subscribers.[21] It provided women who belonged to neither the upper nor the urban working classes with a vehicle for exploring and debating their problems. Through its pages women who possessed some education but generally not jobs outside the home could learn about a larger world and receive encouragement to enter that world. Yet *Revista Feminina* always contained far more pages of advertisements and tips on household management than news of the feminist movement at home and abroad, or of women's achievements in countries around the globe. It focused on the home, not the political arena. The need to preserve family life and Christian morality provided the justification for women's entry into the political sphere and even into the work force. Women's roles as wives and mothers remained paramount. While churchmen and Roman Catholic–oriented women's organizations piled compliments on the magazine or sent in news of their activities, the major Brazilian feminist organization, the Federação Brasileira pelo Progresso Feminino, led by Bertha Lutz, would not contribute.

In 1918 Bertha Maria Júlia Lutz returned to Brazil after seven years of study in Europe, where she had closely followed the English suffrage campaign. Born in São Paulo in 1894 to a Swiss-Brazilian father, Adolfo Lutz, a pioneer of tropical medicine in Brazil, and an English mother, Amy Fowler, a former volunteer nurse of lepers in Hawaii, Bertha Lutz was educated first in Brazil and then in Europe. In 1918 she received her Licenciée dès Sciences from the Sorbonne. Later, she earned a degree from the Faculty of Law in Rio de Janeiro.[22]

Shortly after her return home in 1918, Bertha Lutz published a seminal article which helped initiate a formal women's suffrage movement in Brazil. In response to a Rio newspaper columnist's contention that recent feminist achievements in the United States and Great Britain would exercise little influence on Brazil, she issued a formal call for the establishment of a league of Brazilian women—not "an association of suffragettes who would break windows along the street," but rather of Brazilians, who understood that "women ought not to live parasitically based on their sex," but instead should be useful and capable of assuming future political responsibilities. Thus women would "become valuable instruments in the progress of Brazil." Like earlier Brazilian women's rights advocates, she objected to the indulgent treatment of

Bertha Lutz. *(Courtesy of the Biblioteca Nacional do Rio de Janeiro)*

Maria Lacerda de Moura, ca. 1930. (Moura, *Religião do amor e da belleza*)

women as toys or spoiled children and expressed her faith in the power of education to remedy this, for Brazil still lagged far behind the dominant countries of the world.[23] (For the complete text of this article see appendix F.)

Although the projected organization could not be formed immediately, several women's associations appeared in the next few years. The Legião da Mulher Brasileira, a social service organization created in Rio de Janeiro in 1919 with the motto Aid and Elevate Women, viewed women's interests and rights as best served through mutual self-help and improved organization. This society, headed by Alice Rego Monteiro, with Júlia Lopes as honorary president and ties to Nosso Jornal, reflected a not uncommon paternalistic attitude toward lower-class women. While Bertha Lutz served as director of the legion's administrative commission, her own priorities would be better advanced by the Liga para a Emancipação Intelectual da Mulher, which she established in Rio in 1920 together with Maria Lacerda de Moura, a schoolteacher and author from Minas Gerais.[24] They displayed a secular orientation that marked them off from the women of the Revista Feminina, with their self-proclaimed Christian morality, as well as rejecting the charitable approach characteristic of other women's groups.

The Liga para a Emancipação Intelectual da Mulher, really just a study group, sought women's "intellectual emancipation." As Maria Lacerda de Moura wrote Bertha Lutz at the time of the league's organization, they had agreed on the need for "something more than Christian Associations or the Legião da Mulher [Brasileira]." Like Bertha Lutz, Maria Lacerda de Moura wished to push beyond the limited scope of previous undertakings like "domestic schools or philanthropic establishments or any other local matters," which never solve basic problems. She wanted to leave "charitable concerns, day nurseries, and so on to other associations" and advocated the formation of "a small army of propagandists—using the spoken word, the press, and direct action—for women's rational and scientific education so as to achieve their complete intellectual emancipation."[25] However, the ideas of the two women did not always coincide, and they eventually parted ways. More and more, Maria Lacerda de Moura drew apart from formal feminist organizations, apparently feeling that the franchise would chiefly benefit middle-class women rather than aid the bulk of Brazil's population or alter the country's social structure. Very few Brazilian feminists of the period took her radical positions opposing the church, capitalism, and militarism.[26]

Bertha Lutz concentrated on increasing women's political and legal rights and improving their economic position within Brazilian society rather than radically restructuring that society. As she wrote to a foreign friend, she had "been wanting to found some kind of association meant to help the feminist movement in this country by stimulating, consolidating, and unifying individual efforts," and she envisioned the newly formed Liga para a Emancipação Intelectual da Mulher as a study and support group that would promote intellectual progress among women. She cited the successful competition of women for important government service positions, as contrasted with the accomplishments of distinguished musicians, painters, or authors like Júlia Lopes, who acted "individually quite apart from any feminist cause," together with the "writings of Maria Lacerda de Moura . . . and the periodic proposals of political rights for women" made in Congress as providing a basis for the feminist campaign.[27] Located in the nation's capital, Bertha Lutz showed her preference for a political course of action. The next year the league would be called simply the Liga para a Emancipação da Mulher. Lutz preferred to discuss women's political and legal rights or specific economic and educational issues rather than intellectual or sexual emancipation. The vote would serve not only as a tool for achieving feminine progress but also as a symbol of the rights of citizenship.

In various newspaper interviews Bertha Lutz expanded upon the goals of the movement. These ranged from such highly generalized concerns as world peace to specific issues such as equal pay for equal work and equal educational opportunities. But to achieve such goals, she contended, women must have access to the political process as full and equal citizens; they must have direct and legitimate political participation. Bertha Lutz and other suffragists saw the vote as a means of action, an instrument for overcoming the barriers to a more complete liberal society. It would serve as the necessary instrument to progress, and not merely as an end in itself.[28]

This early burst of organized feminist activity in Brazil brought few tangible results, although the women developed the political and publicity tactics they would employ for years to come. For example, as head of the Liga para a Emancipação da Mulher, Bertha Lutz wrote letters congratulating supporters of women's suffrage like Maurício de Lacerda for the legislative amendment he presented, while also appealing to key congressmen to support such suffrage projects. Nor did she neglect questions of women's work and education in dealing with others in authority. At the same time Lutz began the interchange and correspondence with feminists abroad, such as Dr. Paulina Luisi, Uruguay's most outstanding feminist, that would prove basic to the development of the Brazilian suffrage movement.[29] But as Bertha Lutz, with her perennial high expectations, recalled a decade later, "it was possible to do very little. Our efforts could be summarized as consisting of interviews, newspaper articles, and cooperation with those few legislators aware of women's rights."[30] A noticeable change came in 1922, with her participation in the first Pan American Conference of Women, held in Baltimore, and the subsequent establishment of the Federação Brasileira pelo Progresso Feminino.

International Linkages

Brazilian feminists participated in the international intellectual ferment surrounding the cause of women. The Brazilian suffrage movement established close ties with foreign suffragists and organizations, which would serve as additional sources of support and legitimacy. In the nineteenth century, foreign influences on Brazilian feminists had taken the form of useful ideas and examples. Now, the international movement would provide organizational techniques and personal contacts as well. In 1920 *Nosso Jornal* reported overtures by the International Woman Suffrage Alliance to its director, Cassilda Martins. And in 1923 the International League of Iberian and Latin American Women, a moderate feminist organization founded by Elena Arizmendi, a Mexican then living in New York, and apparently the only attempt made in the 1920s to unite all Spanish-speaking feminists, selected Virgilina de Souza Sales, publisher of *Revista Feminina*, as the league's representative in Brazil. However, the firmest connections between the Brazilian and international struggles would be established by Bertha Lutz several years later.[31]

The women's suffrage movement in the United States had long demonstrated its concern with the status of women elsewhere. In 1883 Susan B. Anthony proposed an international suffrage conference and visited England to invite the British suffragists' cooperation, but the

conference was never held. Five years later, she sponsored the formation of the International Council of Women, a collection of women's
groups, not a suffrage association like the National American Woman
Suffrage Association (NAWSA). After Carrie Chapman Catt assumed
the presidency of the NAWSA, she sponsored an international conference in Washington in 1902. That conference voted to form a permanent
organization, the International Woman Suffrage Alliance, launched at
a congress in Berlin in 1904. Following her resignation from the presidency of the NAWSA in 1904, in part due to her role in the growing
international suffrage struggle, Carrie Chapman Catt devoted herself
to that cause for ten years. Even after she resumed leadership of the
U.S. movement in 1916, she continued to serve as president of the
Alliance.[32]

During its first ten years the International Woman Suffrage Alliance
grew from the original eight affiliates—seven European plus the United
States—to twenty-five. One Chilean woman had traveled to the 1902
Washington conference, attending as a visitor, as had over a dozen
Latin American women residing in the United States. But the first Latin
American branches, Argentina and Uruguay, did not enter the alliance
until the post–World War I congress at Geneva in 1920, by which time
women had achieved the franchise in twenty-two countries.[33]

For far more years, Latin American women had attended international conferences dealing with scientific and social questions. Professional women, mainly from Argentina, Chile, Uruguay, and Brazil,
played a noticeable role in the series of Latin American scientific conferences held from 1895 to 1916 concentrating on questions of hygiene,
maternity, and child care, which coincided with traditional female concerns. When no women were invited to the Second Pan American
Scientific Congress, a wartime meeting held in Washington, D.C., in
1915–16 that resembled a diplomatic conference more than a scientific
gathering, various relatives of Latin American and U.S. diplomats res-
ident in the United States laid plans for the First Pan American Wom-
en's Auxiliary Conference, which in turn led to the formation of the
Pan American Women's International Committee. Nearly all the women
active in Pan American affairs were members of the International
Council for Women.[34] Far fewer would welcome ties with the International Woman Suffrage Alliance.

The link between the Brazilian and international suffrage movements was forged at the first Pan American Conference of Women, held

in Baltimore in April 1922 under the sponsorship of the National League of Women Voters working with the Pan American Women's International Committee, and held in conjunction with the league's national convention. Here Bertha Lutz made her debut on the international suffrage scene, as Brazil's official delegate; she was chosen, like other such delegates, by her country's government. (Women's organizations could also send representatives, but the League of Women Voters did not contribute to their expenses.)[35] However, this was not Lutz's first experience as a delegate to an international conference. In 1919, together with Olga de Paiva Meira, she represented Brazil at the International Labor Organization's conference on women's working conditions, for international organizations had decided to deal with the status of women, and Brazil was a member of these organizations.[36] Lutz's position in government service provided her with opportunities to establish international ties as well as facilitate organizational activities within Brazil.

Bertha Lutz's visit to the United States in 1922 altered her vision of the women's movement. The U.S. model seemed more appropriate to Brazil than some of the violent European activities. And denunciations of the English suffragettes might lend respectability to the Brazilian movement. In an extensive interview given upon her return to Brazil she expressed her belief that the conference she had just attended would help Latin American women avoid tactical errors and would give their movement "a very salutary orientation since the movement in the United States has always been very respectable and completely removed from the violent methods employed in some European countries." She preferred the Americans' "completely calm processes, without any violence like that employed by the English suffragists." For Bertha Lutz, the first Pan American Conference of Women demonstrated a "friendly approximation of women from all countries in the Americas, who displayed an extraordinary unanimity in their thinking" on a wide range of issues dealing with children, working women, education, women's political and legal rights, and the "betterment . . . of humanity."[37]

The Pan American Conference of Women in Baltimore led to the formation of a Pan American Association for the Advancement of Women by the Latin American delegates, as proposed by Olga Capurro de Varela, an official delegate from Uruguay and representative of the Uruguayan Alliance for Women's Suffrage, as well to the establishment of additional national branches of that association. Late in 1922, Carrie Chapman Catt, a veteran of years of world tours and international congresses, embarked on a visit to South America to encourage the movement for equal suffrage. Her first stop was Brazil, where she found encouraging activity.[38]

Several months earlier, immediately following the return of Bertha Lutz from the United States, the Liga para a Emancipação da Mulher had been transformed from a small local group into a national organization, the Federação Brasileira pelo Progresso Feminino (FBPF), an affiliate of the International Woman Suffrage Alliance. A few days after the creation of the federation in August 1922, the Liga Paulista pelo Progresso Feminino, later called the Conselho Paulista de Senhoras, was founded, and then the Liga Mineira pelo Progresso Feminino. Additional branches would be established in other states.[39] The constitution of the FBPF, drawn up during a weekend visit by Bertha Lutz to Carrie Chapman Catt's home following the Baltimore conference, proclaimed the federation's goals, which echoed those of the Pan American Association for the Advancement of Women: to promote the education of women and raise the level of their formal schooling, to protect mothers and children, to obtain labor legislation for women, to increase women's political and social awareness, to ensure the political rights the constitution grants women and to instruct them in the intelligent exercise of those rights, and to strengthen bonds of friendship with other countries in the Americas so as to guarantee the perpetual maintenance of peace and justice in the Western Hemisphere.[40]

The FBPF now scheduled a well-publicized women's congress in Rio de Janeiro to coincide with Carrie Chapman Catt's visit in December 1922, and also, as the federation's leaders noted, with the centenary of Brazilian independence. Since the participation of prominent men could enhance the conference's legitimacy as well as increase publicity, invitations were extended to statesmen such as Senator Lauro Muller of Santa Catarina. Muller addressed and presided over the final session, devoted to women's suffrage, a cause he now supported. The governors of nine states sent official delegates to the conference, which dealt not only with the franchise but also with child welfare, education, organizational methods, and work, hearing testimony from associations of teachers, shop clerks, the YMCA, and others who protested women's limited opportunities to enter the labor force and detailed the problems of long hours, low pay, unsanitary work places, sexual harassment,

Carrie Chapman Catt addressing the First Congress of the Federação
Brasileira pelo Progresso Feminino in 1922. Bertha Lutz is on her immediate
left, followed by the writer Júlia Lopes de Almeida. *(Courtesy of the Arquivo
Nacional)*

and lack of legal guarantees which working women faced. An Aliança
Brasileira pelo Suffragio Feminino was inaugurated, with Bertha Lutz
as general secretary, and as president the wife of Senator Justo Chermont, who had introduced a women's suffrage bill into the federal
Senate in 1919.[41]

After addressing the conference in Rio de Janeiro, Carrie Chapman
Catt traveled to São Paulo in January 1923 with Bertha Lutz and several other women for another meeting. Paulista society turned out to
hear her. In São Paulo such women as Diva Nolf Nazario, a writer, law
student, and feminist propagandist, and Wakyria Moreira da Silva, a
lawyer and the daughter of a women's suffrage supporter in the Constituent Congress of 1891, formed their own suffrage association,
which affiliated with the national suffrage alliance. Cassilda Martins,
who had edited *Nosso Jornal*, headed the Petrópolis branch.[42] While the
Federação Brasileira pelo Progresso Feminino and Bertha Lutz dominated the suffrage movement, other individuals and associations, now
forgotten, also contributed. As with male organizations, the Brazilian
women's suffrage movement was not immune to problems of individual differences and rivalries.

After her return to the United States, Carrie Chapman Catt published her impressions of women and conditions encountered on her South American tour. Aware of cultural differences between countries and of class differences within them, she pointed out to her U.S. audience that Latin American elections at times were almost meaningless, and that the vote was less important to Latin American women than were changes in laws and society. While very sympathetic to the suffrage cause in Latin America and desirous of cooperation and interchange between women in the Americas, she called attention to the dangers of misunderstandings and warned her countrywomen not to patronize, act superior, or insist that theirs was the only way, as American men had done; Latin American women "must build their own [road] and travel on it alone."[43] At the same time she spoke out in opposition to general U.S. intervention in Latin American affairs, giving speeches in the United States decrying the Monroe Doctrine as "false in theory and pernicious in its application."[44]

Carrie Chapman Catt had been much impressed with the state of the Brazilian women's suffrage movement. She noted that although some women hesitated to go on the streets alone, Brazil had "many practicing women physicians, dentists, and lawyers; many able women writers, sculptors, poets, and painters; a famous young aviatrix; six civil engineers; several women engaged in the chemical service of the Department of Agriculture; and several who [were] very notable in science." She regarded Bertha Lutz, who would continue to lead the FBPF, Brazil's major suffrage organization, as the propulsive force of the movement, and found her "fearless and perennially optimistic."[45] In coming years the two women would continue to correspond, with Bertha Lutz even referring to the American leader, her senior by many years, as "my dear (step) mother" or even "dear mother."[46]

Few among the leading Brazilian suffragists enjoyed Bertha Lutz's degree and depth of foreign contacts and experience. Nor did they have European-born parents as she did. (This was far more frequently the case among feminists in Argentina and Uruguay than in Brazil.)[47] As Carmen Velasco Portinho, one of her closest associates in the suffrage movement and a founding member of the FBPF (at the age of eighteen) explained decades later, Bertha Lutz had the most experience and international contacts and the greatest access to information, as well as excellent foreign language skills.[48] Her fluent English enabled her to conduct an extensive and far-ranging foreign correspondence. She was elected vice president of the newly formed Pan American Association for the Advancement of Women in 1922 and president of the Inter-American Union of Women three years later. While Lutz's international suffrage activities generated favorable domestic publicity for the Brazilian suffrage movement and enhanced her authority on feminist issues, as well as increasing her personal prestige and strengthening her leadership of that movement, they also marked her off from other Brazilian suffragists. Sometimes she seemed a bit of a foreigner.[49]

Not all women's rights advocates were upper-middle-class professional women. Some female relatives of the political and social elites also played prominent roles in the Brazilian women's rights movement. Although professional women conducted much of the actual campaigning through the FBPF, upper-class women also helped. Wives of leading politicians like Justo Chermont, Félix Pacheco, and Enéas Martins supported the cause, as did distinguished writers like Júlia Lopes and Maria Eugenia Afonso Celso, granddaughter of the viscount of Ouro Preto.[50] In Brazil, more than in some Latin American countries, various members of the elite, especially in Rio and São Paulo, sent their daughters to the university and into the professions, and a number of those women became suffragists. It may well be that the Brazilian suffragists enjoyed closer ties to the political elite, facilitating the enfranchisement of women in Brazil sooner than in most other Latin American countries. Before 1945, women had gained national voting rights only in Uruguay, Cuba, El Salvador, the Dominican Republic, Brazil, and Ecuador. Paraguay, the last Latin American country to extend the franchise to women, did so only in 1962.

Campaigning for Women's Suffrage

The franchise provided the focus for feminist activity in the 1920s. Brazil's feminists mounted an effective and well-publicized suffrage campaign which attained its stated goal in 1932, only a decade after the founding of the Federação Brasileira pelo Progresso Feminino. The vote, they believed, would provide the key to future feminine advances. As Carmen Portinho firmly asserted decades later, "without political rights one can do nothing."[51]

Throughout the 1920s Bertha Lutz and the FBPF employed tactics suitable to the position of the persistent upper-middle- and upper-class women leading a suffrage campaign designed to influence political leaders and educated public opinion. As women, they had no direct access to the political process. Publicity together with the judicious use of personal contacts within governing circles served as their major political tools while they expanded their network of organizations into most of the states, mobilizing ever more women.

The press provided some of the most effective publicity for the suffrage cause. Bertha Lutz and other suffrage leaders gave frequent interviews and were adept at the use of press releases. In their interviews they used reasoned argumentation, believing that this could and would sway opinion, thereby changing minds and votes. Besides stressing potential female contributions to the social and political needs of the nation, they also employed arguments based on justice and on constitutional law and interpretation. At the same time they sent well-publicized telegrams of praise to politicians who took favorable public stands on women's suffrage as well as messages supporting state efforts favoring a local vote for women. In the early 1930s, the FBPF even sponsored a short-lived radio program entitled "Five Minutes of Feminism." Manifestos, letter campaigns, petitions, and public forums provided more publicity, as did the attempts by several women to register to vote. Like a handful of late-nineteenth-century feminist pioneers and like Leolinda Daltro during World War I, Diva Nolf Nazario, general secretary of the Aliança Paulista pelo Suffragio Feminino, and several other women unsuccessfully sought to inscribe their names on the electoral rolls.[52]

The suffragists cultivated congressmen just as they did the press, even seeking, according to Carmen Portinho, to "catechize individual legislators."[53] They concentrated on the national Congress, where no bill for women's suffrage had ever gone beyond its first reading. (Three readings were necessary for approval.) In 1917 Deputy Maurício de Lacerda presented a women's suffrage bill to the Lower House's Committee on the Constitution and Justice, but it never reached even the discussion stage. Two years later, Senator Justo Chermont introduced a project into the federal Senate advocating the vote for women who had attained their twenty-first birthday. He argued that Brazil should follow the lead of other civilized nations that had granted women equal rights in order to repair past injustices and to complete "civilization's and humanity's conquests," especially when Brazilian women had already given ample demonstrations of their capacities and abilities. Nevertheless, he did not fail to reaffirm that the "mysteries of maternity" comprised "women's principal mission on earth."[54] His bill, sent to the Senate's Committee on the Constitution and Diplomacy on December 19, 1919, emerged with a favorable opinion on May 14, 1921. The Senate received the bill and passed it in its first reading on July 8, 1921. Then the bill was sent to the Committee on Legislation and Justice, which took more than six years to report out a substitute bill on November 12, 1927. In the Chamber of Deputies even less action occurred. A project paralleling the Justo Chermont project had been introduced there in 1921 by Nogueira Penido and Bittencourt Filho. Although approved by the Committee on the Constitution and Justice on September 16, 1922, nothing ever came of it. Nor did the 1927 project presented in the Chamber of Deputies achieve success, although leaders of the FBPF increased their publicity campaign and actively attended congressional sessions. Nevertheless, the existence of the bills did provide legitimacy for the debate over suffrage as well as a symbol about which the movement could organize.[55]

Press coverage of Brazilians' activities on the international suffrage scene provided additional publicity. Bertha Lutz continued to attend international women's conferences, maintaining close ties with the international movement as well as a good press abroad.[56] She served as the official Brazilian representative to the Ninth Congress of the International Woman Suffrage Alliance in Rome in 1923 and as delegate to the 1925 Inter-American Congress in Washington, where she was chosen as the first president of the Inter-American Union of Women. In 1929 she was elected to another leadership position at the Eleventh Congress of the International Woman Suffrage Alliance. In fact, Bertha Lutz continued her international activities long after Brazilian women achieved the vote; she even attended the United Nations–sponsored International Women's Year conference in Mexico City the year prior to her death in 1976 at the age of eighty-two. Nor did she cease her far less publicized scientific work. Even on her 1922 trip to the United States, to attend the first Pan American Conference of Women, she pursued one of her special interests, frogs, to the surprise of the American suffragists. While walking by a stream with Carrie Chapman Catt on her farm, she astonished her host by crouching down on the bank, freezing, and then plunging her hand into the water and bringing out "a frog which she explained with absorbed scrutiny. It proved to be a specimen new to her and for the rest of the day she devoted herself to catching frogs to take back" to Brazil.[57]

Brazil's suffragists created a national network of personal contacts

Bertha Lutz on her eightieth birthday in 1974.
(Courtesy of the Arquivo Nacional)

Carmen Portinho, one of Bertha
Lutz's closest associates in the
suffrage movement, in 1984,
when she was director of
Rio's Escola Superior de
Desenho Industrial. *(Photograph
by the author)*

which served to recruit more activists as well as to spread their ideas. In the 1920s the leadership of the FBPF successfully sought out younger professional women. As Carmen Portinho explained, "whenever we heard of a woman university graduate, we wrote her and tried to get her into the movement."[58] Even women who worked in distant states would be found and enlisted, as was Maria Rita Soares de Andrade, a lawyer in the small northeastern state of Sergipe; she claimed that most of her contemporaries among the small band of Brazilian professional women also entered the suffrage movement.[59] In the capital, Carmen Portinho, a civil engineer, went directly to Rio's engineering school to contact and convince future female engineers. As Elisa Pinho Osborne recounted, Carmen Portinho "tracked me down" at the school and "caught me."[60] Carmen Portinho actively pursued recruits even outside Rio. While serving on an engineering inspection commission in the Northeast, she sought out Lylia Guedes, a law graduate and school teacher in Rio Grande do Norte, and persuaded her to found a local branch of the FBPF. Lylia Guedes also provided Carmen Portinho with names of women in the neighboring state of Paraíba, where another feminist organization was soon created.[61] No doubt the need these relatively few pioneering professional women felt for mutual support in an often hostile masculine world led them not only to seek each other out but also to join in a struggle for women's rights. Collective rather than individual action, concentrating on political and legal rights, would best enable them to confront career obstacles and overcome gender inequalities.

In the 1920s and 1930s the FBPF remained Brazil's preeminent suffragist and feminist organization. Although new groups would form and splinter, especially during the final years of the suffrage campaign as the enfranchisement of women came closer to becoming a reality, none would approach the FBPF in size, geographic range, or extensive network of personal contacts. Moreover, the proliferation of organizations not only demonstrates the vitality of feminist activity but also indicates a consensus as to these women's goal of suffrage and political participation despite the fragmentation in organization.

The leaders of the Brazilian suffrage movement wished to reform rather than radically restructure the nation's political system and society. They sought to join the system as equal participants and improve it, not upset it. Like their predecessors they stressed potential female contributions to the social and public needs of the nation. An ethos of service and participation pervaded the movement. In confronting anti-suffragists' fears, especially over the fate of the family, they had to argue that a woman's political obligations would not pose a serious threat to home life, or even take much time. The vote, they claimed, would actually enhance the role of women as mothers. Just as they argued that a woman's biological status should not affect her ability to act in a political capacity, so did they accept—as did male supporters of women's suffrage—the basic definition of a woman's sphere of interest as revolving about the home, the family, and issues concerning education, health, and welfare. What they did was to redefine the home to include new and far broader areas of concern. In a 1921 interview Bertha Lutz specifically declared that "it is neither accurate nor logical to assert that when women acquire electoral rights they will abandon the place conferred on them by nature. . . . Women's domain, all feminists agree, is the home. But . . . nowadays the home no longer is just the space encompassed within four walls." Factories and offices where women earned money to feed their children, like legislative halls where child protection laws were debated, were "nothing but appurtenances of the home."[62] At the same time, however, the leaders of the FBPF also reminded men that "married women are not the only ones living for their homes and families, for husbands should do the same, if they have a clear concept of their duties to society."[63]

The FBPF brought together a diverse group of women's suffrage, professional, charitable, and civic associations. While the breadth of its program encouraged collaboration between career women and housewives, the need to accommodate the concerns of such diverse women meant, in effect, that the FBPF would avoid confronting conflicts between women's public and private roles. In their pronouncements the federation's leaders took care not to criticize the family or the domestic identity on which many women depended, even if they themselves rejected the traditional role of wife and mother as a sufficient source of self-fulfillment and economic security.

More moderate feminists who were not active members of organizations such as the FBPF placed a greater emphasis on women's moralizing mission, linking feminism more closely to motherhood. Employing nineteenth-century rhetoric concerning the "fair sex" while also citing centuries of female accomplishments, they too sought to project home, motherhood, and female superiority into the national arena. Women's place of honor was the home, through which they could, and should, contribute to "the elevation of morality in the world in which we live." Women had the "right to vote because we work [hard] and because we are the guardians of Brazilian homes where the future leaders of the nation are formed."[64] Thus they could justify the female franchise on the grounds of morality and altruism, linking maternal sentiments to social purposes. With the vote and "with the same civil rights [as men] we will work for the good of humanity."[65]

Just as suffrage served as a unifying goal for many women of divergent views, so did opposition to the moral double standard. Even moderate feminists like educator Else Nascimento Machado called for equal standards of morality for men and for women.[66] When newspapers reported a proliferation in the number of husbands murdering their wives and then being exonerated as acting in legitimate defense of their honor, Revista Feminina mounted a campaign against such so-called crimes of passion.[67] And leaders of the FBPF like Maria Eugenia Celso denounced uxoricide.[68] Without the vote women could not change the laws, and husbands would retain the right to "maltreat, sell, exchange, or even kill their wives!"[69] Brazilian feminists also took stands against pornography and the legalization of lotteries, gambling, and prostitution. Unlike feminists in Argentina or Uruguay, they did not have to campaign actively against legalized prostitution, as prostitution had never been regulated in Brazil. Rather, they repeated the demands to end the white slave trade voiced at international feminist congresses. And they favored sex education. Prostitution, like sexuality or sexual emancipation, was not a major subject of discussion for organized feminism in Brazil. Only a rare woman like Ercília Nogueira Cobra violently attacked the cult of virginity in her forceful novels Virginidade anti-higiénica (1924) and Virginidade inútil (1927), not only denouncing the moral double standard but also defending sexual liberty and the right of women, like men, to sexual pleasure. Patrícia Galvão, popularly known as Pagú, also publicly proclaimed her right to express her sexuality. An irreverent teenager who delighted in shocking polite society and who found a place within São Paulo's modernist literary and artistic circles, she later took up the cause of proletarian revolution in a tumultuous relationship with the Brazilian Communist party while simultaneously attacking the feminist movement as bourgeois. Not until the 1970s would questions of abortion or birth control generate public discussion among middle-class feminists. In the 1920s and 1930s, political, educational, and economic concerns loomed larger.[70]

The women's suffrage campaign in Brazil was not tied to any political party or other social movement. Coherent national parties occupied no prominent position on the contemporary political landscape. Hence women could not be relegated to women's sections of competing parties, as in Chile, or form a branch of an inclusive national party, as in Mexico. Moreover, in Brazil, which lacked strong parties able to oppose or favor enfranchising women, the parliamentary supporters of women's suffrage followed no one political orientation and ranged from Senator Adolfo Gordo, a *paulista* businessman and archconservative formulator of the Gordo Laws expelling troublesome foreigners, to Congressman Maurício de Lacerda, long associated with various labor and unpopular causes.[71] However, the goodwill of other politicians remained untranslated into action, for, as Carmen Portinho recounted decades later, the female vote was a politician unknown.[72] Politicians could not be sure for whom women would vote, and while some may have expected or hoped for female support, others did not.

Some prestigious bodies joined weaker socialist or worker associations in taking public stands on the female franchise. After years of dedicated labor by lawyers like Mirtes de Campos, the Brazilian Association of Lawyers at a 1922 judicial congress commemorating the centenary of Brazilian independence officially declared that the Constitution did not prohibit women from exercising political rights and that they should be permitted to vote.[73] But when individual women sought to register to vote, they met with refusal. While the women might present constitutional arguments, the judges rendered denials set in social custom and the "nature of women."[74] The resistance to feminist demands ran deeper than some women realized.

Open opposition to women's suffrage was expressed not only in the courtroom but also in the press, in books, through satirical cartoons, on the streets, and in endless conversations among people of all classes and backgrounds. Seen as a threat to traditional gender roles, feminist desires and activities provoked a strong reaction. In fear and anger, some antifeminists attacked what they perceived to be a dangerous tide of social disorganization and a growing threat to masculine authority. They accused feminists of wishing to turn the world upside down and induce anarchy.[75] Like nineteenth-century positivists, other antifeminists, averring that they considered women "different," not "inferior," claimed that women's moral superiority required their isolation at home, far from the world of corrupt politics.[76]

Women who protested their subordination or dared assume male roles could be subjected to both physical and verbal harassment. Late in 1927 Eulina Thomé de Souza, a teacher, journalist, and feminist activist for over a decade, scheduled a public meeting on women's rights in one of the main squares of Rio de Janeiro. Despite prior police permission to conduct the meeting and the abundant publicity it had received, she was arrested a few minutes after she began speaking and kept in jail for hours.[77] But verbal hostility to feminism remained more common.

Ridicule proved one of the most powerful weapons used to intimidate women. Suffragists were portrayed as ugly man haters who, "when they meddled in politics, became hysterical."[78] Seen as sexual aberrants devoid of feminine charms, independent, educated women faced repeated humiliations and mockery. As in Europe and the United States, such women were labeled a "third sex," one men did not wish to marry.[79] Popular magazines like *A Cigarra* printed cartoons and satires such as "Feminism in 1990," depicting a large, hatchet-faced professional woman coming home to her beribboned house husband. Behaving in ways the magazine no doubt considered appropriate for housewives, that able cook and baby tender kept dutifully quiet at the breakfast table while his wife studied congressional debates in the morning newspaper, and, after she left for work, he relaxed with romantic novels.[80]

Feminist intellectuals like Maria Lacerda de Moura could be deeply hurt by ridicule and insults. She characterized her "critics, with their monocles or eyeglasses with tortoiseshell frames," as "authors of weepy, sensual little verses who pretend to be critics of serious works when their own 'serious' life is spent listening to jazz bands, going to the movies, or attending dances in elegant hotels." They had "never produced anything except poetry that does not scan or nonsense for an undemanding public," and yet they "detest female intellectuals."[81]

Afonso Henriques de Lima Barreto (1881–1922), one of Brazil's best novelists but an author frustrated by a lack of recognition during his lifetime, also opposed the ascent of professional women and the growth of feminism in Brazil. This Rio-born writer, who used ridicule and caricature to point out his country's foibles, satirized the feminist movement as a mere imitation of English or American models. A dark-skinned Brazilian for whom society offered limited opportunities, Lima Barreto had to earn his living as a minor public employee in the War

Ministry. He opposed the entrance of women into the civil service, complaining about "self-seeking and bureaucratic feminism" and well-connected women attempting to "invade government offices with their delicious smiles and well-cut dresses." Women only did well on civil service examinations because they had "little capacity for invention and creation," and therefore could retain and repeat information.[82] Acknowledging his position as an antifeminist, Lima Barreto satirized activities of women like Leolinda Daltro, who also worked with Indians, and especially Bertha Lutz, labeling her first small feminist organization the "League for the Manumission of White Women."[83] Yet his novels, such as *Clara dos Anjos,* demonstrate the disasters awaiting overly protected women like the young mulatta Clara who never learned to work and support themselves. In that novel he praised the strong-minded, self-sufficient Dona Margarida, who worked hard to maintain herself and her small son—and her respectability—under difficult circumstances. However, this lower-middle-class woman never sought traditional male employment.

The mockery and humiliation to which outspoken women could be subjected may well have helped keep their feminism within acceptable bounds. Certainly the fear of masculinization pervaded the pronouncements of those who called only for feminine progress. Educator Else Nascimento Machado considered "masculinization to be contrary to our advancement and, far worse, to be the cause of the antipathy felt by those who ridicule us." She even criticized those professional women who adopted a "manly bearing" for failing to please their male colleagues with their charms.[84]

Brazilian feminists made persistent attempts to disassociate themselves from the image of feminists as violent, aggressive, English-style suffragettes who slashed paintings or broke windowpanes, for, as Carmen Portinho recounted, that image damaged the Brazilian movement.[85] Maria Rita Soares de Andrade, a lawyer and suffragist from Sergipe, contended that "many men feared the word *feminist* because of the English suffragists."[86] Brazilian feminists denied any desire to compete with men. In its inaugural manifesto in 1931, São Paulo's Federação Internacional Feminina declared that in demanding women's rights, it entertained "absolutely no thought whatsoever of conflicts with the stronger sex; on the contrary, it ardently desires that sex's collaboration in the task of feminine education and aspires to mutual concessions, accord, and harmony."[87]

Not only did Brazilians praise motherhood and morality, but many also claimed that women could be feminists and still be feminine.[88] Even Maria Lacerda de Moura, who strenuously sought to redefine the role of motherhood in women's lives by advocating the bearing and rearing of children outside marriage, continued to celebrate motherhood as women's mission.[89]

Both men and women in Brazil often used the term *feminism* very loosely, thereby helping to trivialize the feminist movement. Some who praised Brazilian feminism refused to connect it with female emancipation or self-determination. Instead, like psychiatrist Antonio Austregesilo Lima, they considered the proper goal of feminism to be the mobilization of women's energies and aptitudes for the good of society, as had some nineteenth-century believers in progress and improved female education.[90] The press tended to link any endeavor undertaken by women with feminism, thereby restricting the public's understanding of feminism. Protesting the common "corruption" of the term *feminist*, Maria Lacerda de Moura sarcastically but accurately observed that in newspapers "we continually see the expression 'victories of feminism' referring at times just to what is in fashion. To hold a prominent position in any government department, to travel alone, to attend institutions of higher education, to publish a book of verse, . . . to get divorced three times, . . . to swim the English Channel, to be a champion in any sport—all this constitutes 'victories of feminism.'"[91]

The pervasive influence of the Roman Catholic church also helped to keep the feminist movement within acceptable bounds, preventing feminist attempts to link the oppression of women to motherhood, family, or religion. While disestablishment in 1889 and the denial of state funds by the Constitution of 1891 had left the church institutionally weak, it developed close ties to Rome, benefiting from the importation of both foreign priests and monies, and underwent an intellectual and political revival in the 1920s. Although it never occupied as strong a position as in some Spanish American countries, by the 1920s the church in Brazil had become a well-run institution under the leadership of Sebastião Cardinal Leme, working to increase its political power and regain its former influence within the nation. Dom Leme encouraged the establishment of associations to advance church interests, such as the Centro Dom Vital established in 1921 by Jackson de Figueiredo, a reactionary intellectual who denounced liberalism, positivism, and socialism while praising order and hierarchy. And right-wing Catholicism gained strength.[92] But even suffragists like lawyer Zéia Pinho Rezende, who viewed the church as a "relentless opponent of women's rights," and Carmen Portinho, who considered the "Catholic religion to be against everything which could give women some liberty," admitted that the Brazilian church did not block the suffrage campaign.[93] The suffragists, however, generally refrained from public discussions of the divorce issue, although many personally favored legislation permitting legal divorce in Brazil. They sought to avoid conflict with the church as well as divisions within their own ranks, for many suffragists were practicing Catholics.[94] Legal divorce would not come to Brazil until 1977.

Except for a few individual feminists like Maria Lacerda de Moura, who disassociated herself from the movement led by the FBPF, Brazilian feminists did not demonstrate the influence of such radical European ideas as anticlericalism. Nor did they take an openly anticlerical stand, as she did. And, although she was a prolific writer and energetic lecturer and teacher, Maria Lacerda de Moura remained largely isolated and alone in her intellectual journeys and experimentation. Brazilian feminists generally avoided attacking those aspects of Roman Catholic church dogma that fostered women's subordination, and the church refrained from publicly attacking the feminist movement.

While the ranks of Brazil's feminists included agnostics, freethinkers, anarchists, and socialists, far more practicing Catholics seem to have participated than was the case with the feminist movement in Mexico. In that nation, unlike Brazil during the same period, the church hierarchy discouraged even the most moderate forms of feminism and refused to countenance the establishment of any feminine organizations not under clerical control. Thus relatively few pious women were found among Mexico's feminists.[95] Brazilian women educated in exclusive schools run by nuns, such as Nossa Senhora de Sion, joined the FBPF, and the clergy offered no objections. Nor did Brazilian feminists encounter nearly the same degree of public opposition and ridicule as in Mexico. The attitudes and behavior of the nation's politicians also differed markedly. While agreement among feminists on issues, tactics, and programs could never be complete in Brazil or any other country, the Brazilian movement did not suffer from the same exhausting battles fought among Mexican feminists. The Brazilian movement displayed a greater degree of organization, coherence, and continuity. And the FBPF provided leadership with noticeable political acumen. Encountering less overt opposition, the better-organized Brazilians secured the franchise some twenty years before their sisters in Mexico received the vote in 1953.

No Brazilian suffragists had to suffer the fate of María Jesús Alvarado Rivera of Peru, leader of her nation's tiny suffrage movement in the early 1920s. This young, largely self-taught woman, a schoolteacher who actively sought justice for Peru's Indians and workers and who opposed the Leguía dictatorship, succeeded in founding Peru's first women's rights organization, Evolución Feminina, in 1915. But few women joined her association. Even in the early 1920s some women attending one of María Alvarado's lectures on women's social condition used their hats to shield their faces from newspaper photographers, in striking contrast with the behavior of their Brazilian feminist contemporaries, who always seemed pleased to appear in the press and gain favorable publicity. Members of the National Council of Women in Peru, founded shortly after Carrie Chapman Catt's 1923 visit to that country, could not agree to press for any rights beyond the vote; many opposed María Alvarado's proposal that the civil code be reformed and women, including married women, be given equality before the law, an idea which also met with much press and church hostility. In 1924 María Alvarado was arrested, imprisoned in solitary confinement for three months, and then banished to Argentina. Only in 1955, more than two decades after women in Brazil gained the vote, would Peru's women be given the franchise by the nation's president, General Manuel Odría, who hoped to secure their support.[96]

Attaining the Vote

In 1927 women in the small, poor northeastern state of Rio Grande do Norte became the first in Brazil to obtain the franchise. This breakthrough not only animated Brazil's suffragists but also provided them with additional publicity and arguments, although it would be several more years before women secured the vote nationwide.

In April 1927 Juvenal Lamartine de Faria, a longtime supporter of women's suffrage, announced the platform for his candidacy for governor of Rio Grande do Norte. He promised full political rights for women, including the right to be elected, declaring that the federal Constitution did not prohibit women from the full enjoyment of their immutable political rights, and opposing as absurd the automatic deprivation of half of the Brazilian population of the exercise of those political rights. Even before he assumed office, Juvenal Lamartine secured the necessary changes in the electoral code of Rio Grande do Norte.[97]

Following this success, the FBPF stepped up its campaign, using arguments based on the proven capacity and contributions of women in other areas of endeavor, the substantial increase in the number of literate citizens contributing to governance which female enfranchisement would provide, and events in Rio Grande do Norte as well as international precedents. When the Senate once again debated women's suffrage, members of the FBPF not only attended sessions and bombarded senators with postcards and pamphlets, but they also presented the legislators with a petition signed by two thousand women— a large number of politically active individuals in contemporary Brazilian terms—demanding passage of the suffrage bill. Besides employing the usual arguments based on universal principles of democratic government and foreign examples, these women drew a close connection between work and suffrage. Defensively asserting that "not politics . . . but necessity tore mothers from their homes," they went on to proclaim that "once women were forced into the workplace by economic pressures, their political emancipation was an inevitable corollary, impossible to avoid."[98]

When a Senate committee met the following year to determine whether or not female participation had invalidated recent federal elections in Rio Grande do Norte, the leaders of the FBPF sought to focus the pressure of public opinion on the legislators. Besides the usual interviews and letters, they employed more dramatic measures. Early on the morning of May 11, 1928, Bertha Lutz, president of the FBPF, Maria Amália Bastos, the first secretary, and treasurer Carmen Portinho flew over the capital dropping leaflets appealing to the press, the Senate, and the citizenry to support women's rights.[99] But the senators were not persuaded.

Although the Committee on the Powers of the Senate voided the women's ballots in the 1928 senatorial election in Rio Grande do Norte, subtracting them from the total awarded the sole candidate, women could still vote in local elections in that state. The following year Alzira Teixeira Soriano, daughter of a local political chieftain, was elected mayor of the municipality of Lages with the support of Juvenal Lamartine. In several other states individual women sought to vote; some judges permitted the women to inscribe their names on the electoral rolls, while others still refused them.[100]

The FBPF responded to the setback delivered by the Committee on the Powers of the Senate with a manifesto to the nation in May 1928 couched in terms of a "Declaration of the Rights of Women." In addition to the signatures of Bertha Lutz's close collaborators Gerônima Mesquita and Maria Eugenia Celso, as well as Lutz herself, the manifesto bore the names of several other women belonging to influential political families, including Clotilde de Mello Viana, wife of the vice president of Brazil. They placed their advocacy of women's suffrage on a fundamental human rights basis: "Women, like men, are born free and independent members of the human race, endowed with equal faculties and called upon equally to exercise, without impediments, their individual rights and duties." But they also argued that suppression of women's rights would be detrimental to the nation and impede general progress. They attacked false beliefs in subordination and reminded their opponents that those who pay taxes and obey laws should have a voice in making them. The vote was "the only legitimate means for defending those rights of life and liberty."[101] This manifesto made it clear that political rights were not mere privileges to be conferred through a whim of those in power but were inalienable rights whose denial did Brazilian women a grave injustice.

While the 1928 Senate debates on the franchise had generated temporary optimism, legislation granting political rights to women still languished in both houses of Congress. Then, in October 1930, the Old Republic came to an abrupt end, and Getúlio Vargas assumed power (1930–45, 1950–54). Mounting dissatisfaction with the course the republic had taken and with the domination of the coffee elite had erupted into open and swiftly successful rebellion. Throughout the 1920s, disgruntled groups, centered in the cities, had demonstrated their discontent. Leaders of other large states resented the dominance of public office and the presidency exercised by the major coffee producers, São Paulo and Minas Gerais. A split between those two powerful states over the presidential succession of 1930 afforded the noncoffee states the opportunity to capture the presidency, especially as the deepening world depression caused the collapse of the coffee market, weakening São Paulo's position. United by their dissatisfaction with the existing regime much more than by their goals, a coalition of disappointed or ambitious politicians, resentful middle-class elements, restive young military officers, disaffected intellectuals, and anxious nationalists supported Getúlio Vargas, the capable and clever governor of Brazil's southernmost state of Rio Grande do Sul, for president. The assassination of Vargas's running mate, the governor of the tiny, poor northeastern state of Paraíba, set off the far-reaching rebellion that ended the Old Republic and elevated the pragmatic *gaúcho* politician to the presidency.[102]

With Getúlio Vargas's ascension to power, Brazil's political structure was altered, facilitating female enfranchisement. Vargas implemented some of the programs the dissidents had favored. His new regime sought to present the appearance of reform and proved willing to listen to groups long neglected or repressed by government, such as urban workers. Women too might appeal to the president, and women's suffrage could be presented as another electoral reform. Oligarchical politics and the role of São Paulo and coffee in the nation would change after 1930, but no immediate modification in the suffragists' tactics was required. Persuasion of leading political figures remained basic, even if different individuals now had to be approached.

As in most Latin American countries, no marked government opposition to women's suffrage existed, and some politicians were favorably inclined. Brazilian suffragists claimed that the federal government was indifferent to bills providing for a female franchise.[103] Even some former opponents of women's suffrage, like José Francisco Assis Brasil, a veteran politician from Rio Grande do Sul, now believed that its time had come. Assis Brasil had voted against women's suffrage in the Constituent Congress of 1891. Women did not yet possess a proper civic education, he claimed, and would just vote in accord with their husbands' or fathers' wishes. But by 1930 Assis Brasil acknowledged women's suffrage to be a "victorious idea of the civilization to which we belong," a mark of the progress so appealing to him and to other nineteenth-century statesmen. As head of the government commission charged with reforming the electoral code in 1931, he favored an unrestricted female franchise.[104]

In Brazil, as in neighboring countries, the actual legal changes enfranchising women depended to a large extent on conclusive action being taken by the nation's chief executive. Male allies, and decisive support, remained essential. Even if it had wished to, the FBPF could not afford the position at which the militant Women's Social and Political Union of Great Britain had arrived by mid 1913: not to seek aid from male supporters. The Brazilian suffragists lacked the English suffragettes' numbers and discipline and could not exert the same pressure on their government. Nor did they believe that women would become conscious of their worth only through independence from men and male movements.[105] Surviving Brazilian suffragists are still quick to assert that they did not oppose men. Latin American feminists in general have rarely expressed a sense of competition with men, and they tend to pride themselves on this.

The drafting of a new Brazilian electoral code following the establishment of the Vargas regime provided the opportunity to secure the franchise for women. The provisional government had publicly committed itself to electoral reform and had proclaimed its intention to reexamine and change the political practices of the past. Neither Getúlio Vargas nor his close aide Oswaldo Aranha were champions of women's suffrage, and the new war minister, General Leite de Castro, even sought to prevent three women from competing for positions in his ministry, despite the authorization they had received from his predecessor.[106] But some members of the new regime, like Baptista Luzardo, chief of police of the Federal District of Rio de Janeiro, and General Juarez Távora, publicly favored women's suffrage. And Vargas himself, according to his daughter, who would soon enter law school, was moving ever further from his earlier "provincial prejudices" and views of women's place. While he had formerly been in the habit of declaring emphatically that "women do not need to study much. They should just know how to cook, play piano and sew," he now abandoned his "patriarchal" views.[107]

In February 1931 the directorate of the FBPF, sensing the timely possibilities, decided to organize a second international feminist congress in Rio de Janeiro. Set for June of that year, the conference could serve to expand their organization and generate more publicity. Representatives came from fifteen states plus the nation's capital, as well as from eight other countries. In late August the government released a provisional electoral code which provided a restricted franchise for women. Much to the displeasure and perhaps surprise of the FBPF, only certain groups of women, including single women, widows with their own income, and married women with their husbands' permission, would be permitted to vote. Protesting this provisional code as insufficient, the FBPF and other feminist groups such as the Aliança Cívica das Brasileiras and the Aliança Nacional de Mulheres quickly mounted a campaign to remove the restrictions from the code before it was adopted. Again, publicity and lobbying of public officials seemed their most effective tactics. The FBPF took the lead, for no other suffrage organization had achieved a similar size, geographical range, or network of personal contacts. Bertha Lutz and several other women met with Getúlio Vargas, and his agreement to full women's suffrage proved decisive. The new code, decreed on February 24, 1932, enfranchised women under the same conditions as men.[108] (Illiterates of both sexes were still denied the vote.) Brazil became the fourth country in the Western Hemisphere to grant women the vote, following Canada, the United States, and tiny Ecuador, a country far removed from Brazilian concerns.

While the women's suffrage campaign in Brazil never became a mass movement—few can be found in Brazilian history—it proved larger and better organized than most subsequent ones in Latin America. The enfranchisement of women in Brazil may have depended on men, as it did to one degree or another in all countries, but Brazilian women, unlike their sisters in some Spanish American countries, were not simply handed the vote by conservative male leaders viewing them as a force for the preservation of the status quo.

Social Class and Social Reform

Rather than limit themselves to political and civil rights, Brazil's feminists tackled problems of concern to working-class women such as long hours, low wages, and miserable working conditions. Like feminists elsewhere, the largely middle-class leadership of the FBPF sought protection for children and improvements in the conditions of working women. But interclass linkages proved extremely difficult to establish. The feminist movement, like male movements, could not overcome the class divisions prevailing in Brazil.

Few cross-class organizations ever existed in Brazil. And relatively few comfortably situated Brazilians concerned themselves deeply with their poorer compatriots. In the early twentieth century Anália Franco, a *paulista* public school teacher, won praise from the moderate labor press for her efforts on behalf of poor women and children. This normal school graduate, who had written for late nineteenth-century women's rights newspapers such as *Echo das Damas*, *A Família*, and *A Mensageira*, founded a series of orphanages in her home state. Citing the free schools for mothers, asylums for poor women and children, and day-care centers she had established, Anália Franco described herself as a fighter for the proletarian cause.[109]

Those men who spoke in the name of the proletariat in Brazil, which numbered few industrial workers in the early twentieth century, exhibited far more concern for male than for female workers. As we saw in chapter 3, male labor leaders and representatives demonstrated an ambivalent attitude toward female remunerative labor. Many union leaders thought women should be restricted to the domestic sphere and lamented the need for the income female family members provided. Often fearful of female competition, some blamed women for their own victimization and exploitation in the job market. Even among anarchists and socialists, whose egalitarian ideals made them the most likely to call for the equality of women, few demanded equal wages for female workers. And if ideas of gender equality in the workplace posed problems, such equality in the intimate realm of the home could not even be considered. Anarchist intellectuals, like bourgeois writers, often depicted women as the companions of men and the teachers of their children. As São Paulo's anarchist-inspired review *Renascença* urged in 1923, women should contribute to the "new era" in civilization, preparing "our daughters for the advent of a future society, to be the guardian angels of the generations to come."[110] Anarchist fathers who believed in equality and liberty in the abstract sense might even prevent their daughters from securing paid employment outside their homes, as did Zélia Gattai's Italian-born father, a mechanic and garage owner, in the late 1920s. When his seventeen-year-old eldest daughter, who had finished her formal schooling, sought to assist her family, which was caught in difficult financial circumstances, he refused permission, declaring that "a woman's place is at home, learning to cook."[111]

In nineteenth-century Europe the "woman question" had proved central not only to the conflict between the proponents of capitalism and its socialist critics but also to the disputes among those critics. Since the 1830s, when the Saint Simonians and Fourierists in France linked the cause of women to that of the proletariat, the "woman question" had served as an obstacle to doctrinal unity.[112] But in Brazil, where the relative lack of industry, a crowded labor market, chronic unemployment, government and employer hostility, massive illiteracy, and ethnic, racial, and regional divisions severely limited unionization, the "woman question" did not loom nearly as large for the country's relatively few anarchists and socialists, who spent little time on doctrinal matters. While Europe developed a strong feminist socialist tradition, this could not occur in Brazil, where only a handful of female socialists or anarchists spoke out publicly on women's issues.[113] There was no rivalry in Brazil, as there was in Europe prior to the outbreak of World War I, between socialists and liberals vying for the political support of women.

Few links were possible between the Brazilian suffrage movement and the nation's anarchists or socialists. Each group wished to change the condition of women and to benefit society as well as women themselves, but each pursued a different path. After all, anarchists rejected the idea of the vote and political participation. They strove to modify the structure of society through direct economic action and ideological struggle, not political struggle. While socialists did employ the ballot in their fight for institutional change, advocating, as in the program adopted by the Second Socialist Congress in 1907, both universal suffrage and divorce laws, their movement made little headway in Brazil, where no enduring national socialist party took form.[114] As believers in political participation, socialists encountered problems in areas of high immigrant concentration like São Paulo, for European-born workers showed little inclination to acquire Brazilian citizenship and participate in electoral politics. In other areas of Brazil, reformist unions of skilled workers following traditions of political patronage and compromise gained more adherents than proponents of what appeared to be a foreign doctrine. Like organized labor itself, the socialist movement proved far weaker in Brazil than in neighboring Argentina, where the Socialist party endured for decades, always claiming to support working women's rights.[115]

More than most men seeking to lead Brazil's urban workers, the well-educated suffragist leadership addressed specific concerns of the nation's working women. Feminists linked women's emancipation to their ability to achieve economic independence. Economic issues were central to the development of the feminist movement in Brazil and appealed to women of different social classes and backgrounds. To be sure, the professional concerns of upper-middle-class feminists remained distinct from those of lower-class women struggling for economic survival. But working women of different classes were attracted to the FBPF and the suffrage campaign from its inception.

Membership in the FBPF stretched across class lines. While the same kinds of well-educated women who had long provided the impulse for changes in women's roles in Brazil ran the federation, women with low-paying jobs as well as those with prestigious occupations filled the membership rolls, which reveal the variety of women who joined the FBPF as well as the predominance of employed women in the federation. Founding members of the organization ranged from experienced and dedicated fighters for women's rights like Mirtes de Campos, the first woman admitted to the Brazilian bar more than twenty years before, to members of illustrious families like Gerônima Mesquita, daughter of the baron of Bomfim, who would become one of Bertha Lutz's close associates and head of the Brazilian Girl Scout movement, to the more numerous primary school teachers and typists. Of the 170 women who entered the FBPF in 1922, the year it was founded, 121, or 71 percent, listed a profession. And no doubt more women held paid positions outside their homes without listing them, for Bertha Lutz herself did not declare a profession. The professional women like engineers (3), lawyers (1), and pharmacists (1) who joined the FBPF in 1922 were far outnumbered by typists (9), elementary school teachers (17), civil service employees (17), typesetters (19), and bookbinders (44).[116]

Urban working women with economic as well as political concerns would continue to be attracted to the federation. Although surviving records and membership lists of the federation and its state affiliates rarely indicate occupations, the August 1934 list for the Federação Mattogrossense pelo Progresso Feminino, the affiliate in the far western state of Mato Grosso, does do so. In a state lacking large cities or industry and with an economy based on agriculture and stock raising, female university graduates and professional women were rare. But 64, or 77 percent, of the 83 members of the Federação Mattogrossense pelo Progresso Feminino in 1934 listed an occupation. While elementary school teachers (28) and civil service employees (16) predominated, seamstresses (5), shop clerks (3), typists (2), piano teachers (2), a landowner, a merchant, a dressmaker, a confectioner, and 4 students also belonged.[117] In addition to the state affiliates, separate associations of public employees, typists, and nurses also joined the FBPF, but no factory workers' groups joined.

The leadership of the FBPF remained far less broadly based than the membership. Rather than lead the women's rights movement, primary school teachers entered the ranks. And bookbinders or typists were much less likely to sign petitions or demonstrate than were school-teachers. While upper- and middle-class women could see the advantages men of their class derived from the vote, lower-class women no doubt realized that the theoretical extension of the franchise to all literate males in the late nineteenth century had not benefited even urban craftsmen. Lower-class women lacked the skills as well as the time needed to participate fully in the FBPF's campaigns. While the federation was not an exclusively upper- or middle-class organization, few poor members could attend meetings. And as the federation's long-time secretary Carmen Portinho later explained, key decisions were made at the directorate's sessions.[118] Even the series of feminist congresses held from 1922 to 1936, which tackled problems of concern to the urban poor such as working conditions and maternity leaves, were held at times and in places difficult of access for most workers, and few lower-class women ever appeared.

While the FBPF experienced dissension and factionalization due to personal and policy differences, some incidents revealed class overtones. Late in 1924, Valentina Biosca, the federation's first secretary and one of the feminists most closely linked to lower-class concerns, openly broke with the FBPF. Well acquainted with the world of working women from her investigations into factory conditions, she had sought to organize those women to defend their own interests. However, minutes of the federation's executive committee reveal a non-publicized parting of the ways some months earlier over monetary matters, including insinuations of financial mismanagement. Although acknowledging the needs of "a woman obliged to work in order to support herself," the FBPF directorate had found the services of its only paid associate too costly for the financially strapped federation.[119] In a published declaration following an interview Valentina Biosca gave in November of that year, not only did the FBPF leadership display umbrage because she had claimed to be initiating feminism in Brazil, but they also demonstrated an attitude of superiority regarding less well-off women, pointing out that she had held the only paid position in the federation as well as being a foreigner who had not sought naturalization.

Brazil's organized feminists felt that class conflict should be avoided. Implicitly rejecting conflictual tactics like strikes, they asserted that the FBPF would "continue to act within the law."[120] Unlike São Paulo's self-proclaimed "feminist weekly," *A Reacção,* edited by Vicentina Soares and affiliated with the Aliança Cívica das Brasileiras, few feminist newspapers would even publish articles dealing with labor union issues and the defense of revolutionary principles of class struggle.[121] The FBPF's publications never did.

At the FBPF's 1931 congress another internal conflict made the newspapers. When Conceição Andrade de Arroxellas Galvão, a school-teacher from Minas Gerais, resigned as secretary of the congress, the federation first learned of her intentions from the press. She had sent a letter of explanation to Ilka Labarthe, a representative from Rio Grando do Sul who also challenged FBPF priorities and had succeeded in inserting the issue of abandoned children who sold newspapers into the congress's debates. But that letter arrived after the copy sent to a major Rio daily. Conceição Arroxellas Galvão complained that the congress was too rigidly controlled by the chair and that no meeting should "deal with problems concerning the working class without closely consulting the true leaders of that class."[122]

The FBPF's leaders worked for rather than with lower-class women. They could not overcome the approaches inherent in their social and economic backgrounds. While their attitudes appeared less paternalistic than those of many members, male and female, of the old upper class, theirs was still a guiding and counseling approach similar to that of male reformers. Feminists wanted all women to organize, but these professional women expected to take the lead in organizing women in Brazil. Rather than adapt themselves to poor women's behavior and speech, they expected those women to adapt to their patterns. Even differences of dress kept them apart. Very few feminists sought to upset the social system or even realized the radical implications of some of their views.

More than other leaders of the FBPF, Bertha Lutz linked women's economic emancipation with their political and social emancipation. She warned women that the franchise was no end in itself, and she clearly understood that without access to education and work, political rights would remain mere abstractions. In the 1930s she saw feminism as more than a peaceful reform movement, for it sought a "permanent revolution" in customs and laws. Economic emancipation remained the key precondition for all other forms of female emancipation.[123]

In print and in public Bertha Lutz spoke out against the exploitation of the working class, especially lower-class women. She recognized that "proletarian women pay a *double penalty* [emphasis mine], for added to their factory shifts are the unmeasured hours spent on work they do at home."[124] (Not until the 1970s would the phrase "the double day" be frequently employed by feminists in Latin America to describe the double burden of women's unpaid work at home and paid work in the labor force.) As head of the Liga para a Emancipação da Mulher before the founding of the FBPF in 1922, Bertha Lutz had protested the unequal treatment of female workers at the national press, for, despite their years of service, they were not treated and classified as regular workers like men. In 1922 she worked with the Union of Commercial Employees in Rio de Janeiro to obtain a reduction in the working day for shop clerks. (This union sent representatives to the 1922 feminist congress in Rio.) At the same time, the FBPF secured the entrance of girls to the prestigious Colégio Dom Pedro II. Under her leadership the federation sought to develop extension programs stressing health and income-generating activities for rural women in the states of São Paulo and Rio de Janeiro and became involved in programs for abandoned children. The federation continued to lobby for labor legislation to benefit working women as well as pressing for educational opportunities for women, political rights, and reforms in the civil code to end the relative incapacity of married women.[125]

Many of Rio's female shop clerks, factory workers, and even waitresses evidently viewed the FBPF as a vehicle for voicing and supporting their demands. In 1924 seven hundred women employed in stores, workshops, and factories petitioned the federal government through the intermediation of the FBPF to place women on the newly created National Labor Council, which was charged with studying female and child as well as male labor but included only representatives of the male labor force, capital, and government.[126] Other working-class women continued to view the FBPF as an instrument for exerting pressure on government or employers on their behalf. In 1933 a group of waitresses sought out FBPF support in opposing new labor regulations that would cost them their jobs. A government decree the previous year had prohibited women from working between 10:00 p.m. and 5:00 a.m. in industrial or commercial establishments. According to the bulletin of the FBPF, which no doubt tidied up their words and arguments, the waitresses opposing this "false protectionism" based their case not just on the claims of motherhood, always an appealing image, but also on their having been denied professional education, contending that "since the government has no obligation to support the children of mothers whose livelihood depends on their labor alone, and since the government has demonstrated no obligation to help women acquire a profession that our society considers suitable for their sex, the government is not entitled to prohibit women, whose education and training it disregards, from supporting themselves by this or that kind of work."[127] But the waitresses were fired despite the FBPF's efforts.

The series of resolutions passed at Brazilian feminist congresses between 1922 and 1936 demonstrate the range of issues the FBPF confronted as well as the emphasis given economic concerns. At its second international convention, held in Rio de Janeiro in 1931, before the franchise was won, the FBPF "proclaimed women's economic emancipation to be one of the basic problems of the feminist movement," and urged that all women be properly prepared to exercise a profession. The delegates not only called for equal pay for equal work but also for such measures as the creation of a women's and children's bureau to deal with child and female labor, the establishment of a corps of inspectors for factories and businesses employing women and children, and paid maternity leaves, as well as insisting on general labor provisions like a living wage and paid holidays for the working class. Aware of the potential conflict between protective regulations and economic independence, the congress urged that "laws concerning working women in their roles as mothers be written in ways that would not hurt them as economic agents." The civil service, which commonly received special attention in Brazilian legislation, and which by the 1930s was employing ever more women with varying degrees of education, would be prohibited from sex discrimination in hiring. The delegates also sought to aid domestic servants, a group of workers ignored by the government as well as by private agencies, but only by convincing employers to give maids Sundays off rather than by promoting legislation on their behalf. Housewives also received attention. Despite their emphasis on wage labor, the delegates did not neglect the economic activities of women outside the paid labor force, and they sought to win acknowledgment that housewives' contributions were as valuable as other productive activities.[128]

Subsequent congresses endorsed similar resolutions. The 1936 national congress proposed a statute on women which focused on economic issues. The government should guarantee all women, regardless of civil status, the freedom to pursue, without anyone's permission, whatever profession or economic activity they chose, as well as prohibiting all restrictions based on sex or civil status, especially those regarding hiring and firing. To prevent the principle of equal pay for equal work from being undermined, "work should be distributed independent of sex, and the withholding of better-paid jobs from women should be prohibited." The statute even included a proposal of salaries for housewives as part of the minimum wage. The FBPF sought "equality of opportunity in economic, juridical, political, social, and cultural matters" for both sexes, and a "minimum of comfort and well-being" for all Brazilians.[129]

Brazilian women, like men, remained classbound. But, to their credit, Brazil's feminists demonstrated greater concern with the problems facing the lower classes than did most men of their class. Questions of work, health, and education, not just political rights, preoccupied them. And the FBPF paid increasing attention to obtaining protective legislation once the franchise was achieved. But class differences could never be overcome by their efforts alone. Lower-class women, like lower-class men, derived far less benefit from such guarantees than did the urban upper and middle classes. For many Brazilians, neither ballot boxes nor legal codes meant much.

After the Vote

In the days immediately following the promulgation of the 1932 civil code granting women the franchise, the suffragists sought to secure that vote, for it would serve as a key instrument to improve women's status. After that they could fight to implement the full FBPF program. They saw the necessity of getting women to register to vote and making sure that the new constitution of the republic would include a provision guaranteeing women their equal political rights.

One obvious way to influence the outcome of the new constitution was to participate in writing it. But personal rivalries within the suffrage movement surfaced during the efforts to place a woman on the drafting committee. The two major competitors for the position were Bertha Lutz, who was strongly supported by the FBPF, and Natércia da Silveira, a lawyer and the leader of the Aliança Nacional de Mulheres based in Minas Gerais. An excellent speaker, Natércia da Silveira had publicly proclaimed her support for her fellow *gaúcho* Getúlio Vargas prior to the revolution of 1930, while Bertha Lutz and the FBPF had pursued a policy of political neutrality. Like Lutz, Silveira had lobbied politicians on behalf of women's suffrage. The Vargas government asked both of them to join the committee, and the Constitution of 1934 would confirm the women's 1932 victory by specifically guaranteeing women the vote.[130]

The new constitution guaranteed women equal political rights and citizenship as well as equal nationality rights with men. Not only would women married to foreigners retain their nationality—a major issue for feminists in many countries—but that nationality could be transmitted equally by the father or mother to his or her child. Civil servants received special attention in the Brazilian Constitution of 1934, with both sexes equally entitled to hold government positions, but with female civil servants allowed three months' pregnancy leave with pay. Nor could married women be dismissed from the civil service simply because they were married. Women were expressly exempted from military service, as women's organizations had demanded when the war minister sought to include them. Bertha Lutz and her allies fought attempts to discriminate between men and women in other areas, avoiding all prohibitive measures except some on work. At the same time they managed to introduce into the Constitution of 1934 articles providing for the key feminist demands of equal pay for equal work and an equal right to work for both sexes, as well as some social welfare measures for pregnant women and mothers. However, like many other articles in the Constitution, including that establishing the eight-hour day, these provisions remained statements of aspirations more than facts. And many fundamental feminist demands voiced by Bertha Lutz during the drafting of the Constitution of 1934, such as the abolition of all restrictions on women's juridical capacity, notably the juridical incapacity of married women, embedded in the Civil Code of 1916, would not be written into the fundamental law of the land. It was far easier to secure a constitutional reaffirmation of their major political victory, the female franchise.[131]

With the achievement of the vote the suffragists lost the major symbol around which they had coalesced. Factionalization and fragmentation increased. Some women withdrew from sustained political activity, believing that their goal, the franchise, had been obtained. Personal conflicts also loomed larger. According to Carmen Portinho, some found Bertha Lutz too authoritarian, brusque, and impatient, and preferred to transfer their energies from the FBPF to other women's associations, as Portinho did.[132] Even some women remaining with the FBPF, like Maria Rita Soares de Andrade, contended that if Bertha Lutz's temperament had been amiable rather than difficult, she might have accomplished more.[133]

Relatively few women registered to vote during the first months after their enfranchisement, despite the efforts of the FBPF. In Rio de Janeiro, the major scene of suffragist activity, only 15 percent of those registered to vote by January 1933 were women. But the FBPF persisted. On January 1, 1933, the federation formed the Independent Electoral League, which would not only promote political education but also present feminist candidates. However, none of the FBPF candidates for national office won election in 1933.[134]

Also unsuccessful in the 1933 congressional elections was pioneer suffragist Leolinda Daltro. A persistent feminist who headed Rio's small Partido Republicano Feminino, founded in 1910, and who attempted to register to vote and then organized a public demonstration in favor of the female franchise in 1917, she continued to try for public office, even running for city council in 1919. Her narrowly based party was comprised largely of schoolteachers (nonvoters like other women) concerned with the status of government employees like themselves. But this served as a potential political constituency of interest to others as well. In 1925 Julieta Monteiro Soares da Gama and some two dozen public school teachers founded the prosuffrage, profamily, probureaucrat Partido Liberal Feminino, also limited to the nation's capital but based in the city's neglected northern worker suburbs. While Leolinda Daltro's dedication to such causes as the education of Brazil's surviving Indians brought her a measure of fame, attracting the barbed pen of the antifeminist author Lima Barreto, she had found no real political support following Marshal Hermes da Fonseca's presidency (1910–14).[135] In her campaign fliers for the 1933 elections, this determined retired public school teacher, with perhaps a note of resentment, described herself as "the Brazilian woman who had begun the campaign for the vote some eighteen years ago. . . . Her feminist campaign preceded that of all the ladies who present themselves as feminist leaders. It was she who long ago in Brazil raised the idea of women's political rights." Unlike the far younger Bertha Lutz, though, Leolinda Daltro had never succeeded in creating an effective feminist organization.[136]

Only one woman, Carlota Pereira de Queiroz, a member of one of

Carlota Pereira de Queiroz, the only woman elected to the Constituent
Congress of 1933, seated amid the male deputies during a 1934 session.
(*Mulher e Constituente*)

the most influential families among São Paulo's traditional political
elite, won a national office in the 1933 elections, the first with female
participation. A medical school graduate and an educator who had
served as a delegate to the 1922 FBPF conference and continued to
favor women's suffrage, she became the first woman member of a
national legislative body in Brazil, aided by the family connections that
remained essential to her political career. (Later, she would become
the first female member of the National Academy of Medicine.) Unlike
Bertha Lutz and the FBPF's other unsuccessful congressional candidate, Carlota Pereira de Queiroz received major political party support
in the elections for the Constituent Assembly. The previous year, the
state of São Paulo, whose virtual autonomy the Vargas regime had
restricted, had risen in revolt against the federal government, demanding an immediate return to constitutional procedures. During this brief

rebellion, upper-class *paulista* women raised money for their state's military effort, organized medical services, ran kitchens for the troops, and sewed uniforms. Following the defeat of the regional revolt, the major political parties in São Paulo agreed on a single slate of candidates which would include one woman. Carlota de Queiroz, who had coordinated women's volunteer work during the revolt, emerged as that female candidate. Unlike the FBPF, which had sought to cooperate with the Vargas regime, the *paulista* women's organizations which urged Carlota de Queiroz's candidacy had supported Vargas's opposition, thereby reducing the potential political effectiveness of Brazil's first congresswoman. When the Constituent Assembly elected Getúlio Vargas to the presidency in 1934—there were no other candidates—the *paulista* bloc cast blank ballots. This, no doubt, diminished the impact of the first female participation in presidential elections (albeit indirect elections) in Brazil.[137]

Despite its failure to elect legislative representatives in May 1933, the FBPF prepared to run candidates for the congressional elections of October 1934. Shortly before those elections, the federation held a national convention in Bahia which sought to launch a broad women's political education campaign as well as to elaborate a detailed program dealing with women's legal rights, social status, and political role. In the October 1934 elections Bertha Lutz, again a FBPF-supported candidate in the Federal District of Rio de Janeiro, managed to become an alternate, while Carlota Pereira de Queiroz secured reelection from São Paulo. The elections for state assemblies held at the same time produced several female legislators: a veteran schoolteacher in Sergipe, a member of the FBPF's affiliate in Amazonas, two *paulistas*, and two leading feminist activists—Lily Lages, a twenty-five-year-old physician who founded and headed the federation's branch in Alagoas, and lawyer Maria Luiza Bittencourt, founder of the federation in Bahia. The 1935 elections raised to ten the total number of women in state legislatures.[138]

Late in 1936 Betha Lutz, who had been elected an alternate, entered the Chamber of Deputies to fill the vacancy created by the death of the incumbent. During her year in Congress she helped create the Commission on the Code for Women, which she headed. Through the commission she pushed vigorously for the enactment of a statute on women, a comprehensive law concerning women's legal status and social rights, which included specific work rules for women. Just as she had during the drafting of the Constitution of 1934, Bertha Lutz also proposed a national women's department charged with supervision of services relating to such paramount feminine concerns as child protection, women's work, and the home. However, Deputy Carlota Pereira de Queiroz disagreed. She claimed that such a virtually autonomous department would infringe on the work of at least three existing ministries, besides smacking of sex segregation, and she suggested that it be subordinated to an existing ministry, preferably Education and Health. Carlota de Queiroz found Bertha Lutz's actions too combative. She preferred "cooperation" instead, and she also placed far less emphasis on women's economic roles and the need to enable women to become economically independent. Carlota de Queiroz proposed protection and social aid for women, while Bertha Lutz objected to making them the passive beneficiaries of the state. Bertha Lutz's activities, consistent with middle-class ideals regarding social advancement, were directed toward opening up new paths toward women's economic emancipation. A women's bureau would have also provided increased legitimacy for the feminist movement as well as financial support and employment for female social workers and administrators, for women would be given preference for such positions. In any case, the proposed women's department, like the statute on women, did not win final approval prior to the forced closing of Congress on November 10, 1937.[139]

The establishment of the Estado Novo in 1937 ended electoral politics and women's participation in them until 1945. During the 1930s, extremist forces emerged in Brazil on both left and right. Communist and fascist doctrines attracted more and more followers who posed political threats to Getúlio Vargas's regime. But Vargas proved the more astute, playing off different groups and politicians against one another.

In 1935 the small Brazilian Communist party encouraged the formation of the National Liberation Alliance (Aliança Nacional Libertadora) as an antifascist, anti-imperialist popular front organization designed to unite all liberal Brazilians under the banner of Bread, Land, and Liberty. Only a minority of the nationalistic alliance's founding fathers were Communist party members, and the new group's program, reflecting views common among the Brazilian Left, stressed the country's semicolonial status and subservience to the international capitalist system as well as emphasizing civil liberties and the interests of the working classes. During its brief legal phase the alliance frightened conservatives with its effort to fight the growing fascist threat in Brazil and with its concern with social reform. As had the Communist party, the National Liberation Alliance created a variety of special-purpose front organizations in the cities, including a national women's auxiliary, the Brazilian Women's Union (União Feminina Brasileira), which favored female emancipation and addressed matters of immediate concern to its largely middle-class membership, such as the high cost of living, while seeking to mobilize female support for the alliance's program.[140] Female activists spoke at alliance rallies, including those held in the factory districts outside São Paulo. There these middle-and working-class women not only employed the general language of morality and anti-imperialism in their appeals for women to join the alliance and struggle shoulder to shoulder with their male companions, but some also called on their coworkers to form a united front under the alliance's banner to secure, in the words of one factory worker and leader in the local women's union, "our emancipation and the well-being of working women." She vigorously asserted their right to participate in political activities as well as their right, like "the daughters of the rich," to obtain advanced education. Although women now had the franchise, female factory workers' votes "belonged to our bosses who threaten us if we do not vote for their candidates," or, in the case of housewives, to their husbands' bosses.[141] However, any challenges, political or personal, mounted by the National Liberation Alliance and its women's union were short-lived, for Getúlio Vargas outlawed the alliance after its honorary president, Luís Carlos Prestes, the romantic revolutionary who had led a march across Brazil in the 1920s and who later became leader of the Brazilian Communist party, issued a manifesto calling for an end to the Vargas government and the creation of a popular front revolutionary government.

Following abortive communist uprisings in 1935, Vargas mounted a vigorous anticommunist campaign and then turned to meet the challenge on the far right from the green-shirted Integralists. The vehemently nationalistic Integralist party (Ação Integralista Brasileira) stood at the opposite end of the ideological spectrum from the National Liberation Alliance. Founded in 1932 with the support of conservative elements and in frank imitation of contemporary European fascist parties, complete with its own symbol, salute, and flag as well as colored shirts, the Integralist party issued appeals to morality, traditionalism, and hierarchical order while also attacking foreign economic domination. God, Country, Family was its motto.

The Integralist party's leader, Plínio Salgado, a *paulista* intellectual, evidently feared feminism sufficiently to mount an attack on it. In his book on women's place in the twentieth century, Plínio Salgado insisted on their absolute adherence to Catholic dogma and morality. Without a strict religious education these impulsive creatures could easily be led astray. Equality between the sexes would bring not liberation but degradation and enslavement. Women must preserve their purity and piety and embrace their "natural" role as wives and mothers, avoiding all competition with men and maintaining a strict separation of male and female spheres of action.[142]

In 1937 Plínio Salgado ran for president, as did a government-backed army officer and a former governor of São Paulo. Getúlio Vargas ended the general agitation accompanying the presidential campaign by carrying out a coup d'etat against his own government on November 10, 1937. Claiming that the democracy of political parties only endangered the nation in this time of crisis, he canceled the presidential elections, closed Congress, and assumed all political power for himself. The Estado Novo, or New State, had begun. Vargas now ruled by decree, imposed press censorship, disbanded all political parties, and created a special police force to suppress any resistance to his regime. But only the Integralistas mounted an armed, and unsuccessful, attack on the newly established dictatorship. The armed forces, nationalists, and many in the urban middle sectors welcomed the new government. Getúlio Vargas retained his immense popularity even as earlier authoritarian tendencies within his regime surfaced. The Estado Novo, which lasted until 1945, would be marked by accelerating industrialization and increasing nationalism. Under Vargas, the urban middle classes and elements of the urban working classes were incorporated into the political system. Through paternalistic and protective policies the government attempted to control urban discontent and channel class conflicts by guiding or forcing them into institutional forms administered by the state. But women occupied a very subordinate position within Vargas's vision of the corporate state. That view of social harmony required hierarchy and the subordination of wives to husbands. The gender hierarchy would help maintain the social and political hierarchies.[143]

The advent of the Estado Novo put an end to the modest feminist movement of the 1920s and 1930s. The new regime's leaders, with their beliefs in strongly differentiated gender roles, proved hostile toward women's quest for greater equality. Despite later denials by close female relatives, Getúlio Vargas, a supreme political pragmatist, had not been committed to women's rights. He had opposed divorce legislation and had freely granted presidential pardons to men who had committed "crimes of passion" in defense of their "honor." With the arrival of the Estado Novo the antifeminist reaction gathered force. Not only were women (and men) denied the opportunity to participate in electoral politics, but they also found major areas of government service closed to them. Earlier, the Vargas regime had nominated women to various important government positions and facilitated their entrance into government service. In 1932, the year Getúlio Vargas appointed Bertha Lutz and Natércia da Silveira to the committee drafting a new constitution for Brazil, he also chose Carmen Portinho, a civil engineer and one of Lutz's long-term associates, to sit on a commission inspecting public works in the drought-ridden Northeast. The following year Rosalina Coelho Lisboa, a writer and political activist, was nominated to the commission regulating educational broadcasting in Brazil. Other women secured places in the consular service and on delegations sent abroad. But after 1937 the regime removed women from the consular service and barred them from various civil service positions.[144]

The right of women to hold posts in the prestigious Foreign Ministry had long helped to determine their position elsewhere in government service. And the treatment accorded them by the Foreign Ministry illuminates male attitudes and behavior toward active, independent women. As we have seen, Maria José de Castro Rebelo Mendes's successful suit to enter a job competition in that ministry in 1917 led to the legal ruling permitting women to compete for prominent civil service positions. Until 1931, however, the consular and diplomatic corps, based abroad, remained separate from the Foreign Ministry's secretariat, which she had joined, whose members served only in Brazil. That year the government decreed that high-level members of the secretariat should also serve abroad as part of the consular and diplomatic corps, but added that the female officials integrated into the consular service could spend no more than twelve months abroad. This proviso, according to Bertha Lutz, who vehemently protested such discriminatory treatment, was designed to deny women the additional compensation given officials stationed more than two years at a foreign post. She also chastised Foreign Minister Afranio de Melo Franco for expressly prohibiting a female official with the requisite seniority from transferring into the diplomatic corps and ordering her into the consular service instead.[145]

Despite the obstacles and discriminatory treatment they faced, women persisted in seeking positions in the Foreign Ministry. In 1934 Beata Vettori, an administrative functionary, became the first woman to win a consular competition. (She became an ambassador in 1968.) And a few other women followed her. In 1937 the eighty-five candidates completing registration requirements for the competition for third-class consul included fifteen women. But in 1938, in a general reorganization of the Foreign Ministry, the government fused the consular and diplomatic corps and expressly limited the competition for the diplomatic service to male candidates. The twelve women already registered for the 1938 consular competition were summarily dismissed. The Brazilian diplomatic service would remain an exclusively male preserve for almost twenty more years, and a white one for even longer. Not until 1954 would a woman once again be permitted to pursue a diplomatic career.[146]

Even during World War II, when the increase in army size presaged a shortage of male civil servants, some officials fought to exclude women from governmental service. In 1942 the finance minister, Artur de Souza Costa, ordered that a competition for Class H auditors be limited to male candidates. He claimed that "experience has shown that women should not be assigned inspection duties owing to the special conditions under which these are carried out," for tax audits were conducted in large, busy commercial establishments. Such prohibitions had already been imposed on a number of other job categories within the Finance Ministry. When a civil service commissioner, citing wartime needs, sought to circumvent the exclusion of women from the auditors' competition, the finance minister quickly secured an order from President Getúlio Vargas mandating that exclusion.[147] In other government departments, too, lesser officials proclaimed their opposition to hiring women. Not only should women be denied auditors' positions because these involved travel, but also because the government needed "calm, capable, discreet, discerning civil servants who understood something about business transactions," and that meant no women or men under twenty-five years of age.[148] Only a very determined woman, such as Iracema Ferreira Campos, who sought to enter a competition for police clerk, would directly challenge such prohibitions. This typist cited the constitutional provision that civil service positions were open to all Brazilians, as well as arguing that the position of police clerk involved "absolutely no police functions, just bureaucratic and administrative duties." But her petition was denied.[149]

The hostility toward women's quest for greater equality and the attempt to force them back into more traditional patterns of behavior extended beyond government service. The government even decreed the separation of boys and girls in coeducational secondary schools. While the Constitution of 1934 had affirmed that all were equal before the law without distinction of sex, the 1937 Constitution promulgated by Getúlio Vargas eliminated that reference to sex.

As Bertha Lutz sadly wrote Carrie Chapman Catt in 1940, Brazil's women were "unable to hold all that was conquered."[150] Having worked hard for years to achieve the right to participate in the political system, and then having spent several additional years attempting to accommodate to that system, the suffragists found that it had crumbled beneath them. Arguments based on liberal democratic precepts were now useless. No organized political activity by women could take place in Brazil until after Getúlio Vargas's removal from office in 1945. Whatever the suffragists might have accomplished remained problematic. The Federação Brasileira pelo Progresso Feminino never again was able to regain its organizational strength or its preeminent position as a voice for Brazilian women.

The call for women's rights, voiced by only a handful of dedicated and determined women in the mid-nineteenth century, grew ever louder over the decades as Brazilian society became increasingly complex and diversified. By the end of the century greater numbers of women were receiving education, although large segments of the population remained illiterate. The doors of Brazil's institutions of higher learning finally opened to women, as the early advocates of female emancipation had demanded. And more women trespassed on terrain culturally understood as masculine, from stores and offices to medical colleges and courtrooms. Achievement of even token access to new areas undermined sweeping claims about the limitations placed on the female sex.

Centered in the cities, with their greater educational opportunities, the Brazilian women's rights movement increasingly focused on suffrage in the twentieth century. Although they represented only a tiny fraction of the labor force, the women who succeeded in entering prestigious professions like law and medicine provided the leadership of the suffrage movement as well as most of that minority of Brazilian women consciously working to change their social and political status in the twentieth century. The majority of women remained uneducated. Change came far more slowly to members of the lower classes in this highly stratified society.

By the 1930s Brazil's educated women had achieved the measure of participation and authority they sought. They had gained access to professional positions as well as obtaining the vote. Neither radical in their goals nor militant in their tactics, the women who led the suffrage campaign to victory in 1932 wanted some of the rights exercised by men of their own class. They did not wish to revolutionize society or restructure the family. The vote would only enhance the role of women as mothers. The Brazilian women's rights movement grew more conservative as it became more respectable and acceptable to the ruling elites. But it did help to raise the level of consciousness of middle-class women concerning their problems in a changing world, as well as legitimating many female activities beyond the home. And it prepared the way for other women's organizations formed after the fall of Getúlio Vargas's Estado Novo in 1945.

With the vote, women could no longer be excluded from the political process. At the same time their ground of expected domesticity remained firm. The franchise might eventually threaten other aspects of gender relationships, but for women, unlike men, family concerns were expected to rank above all others. Hesitant or indifferent, many women did not attempt to traverse the long, painful road to equality and independence. The franchise proved useful to some, but not to others, and many of the hopes once embodied in the promise of the franchise were not fulfilled. Only in the late 1970s and early 1980s, as Brazil slowly emerged from the military dictatorship installed in 1964, would gender again serve as the basis for large-scale political and social mobilization in Brazil, small feminist organizations form, and gender inequality once more become a serious subject for political debate.

Epilogue

Fifty Years Later

In the mid 1970s a new feminist movement emerged in Brazil. Both similar and dissimilar to earlier feminist efforts, this movement grew in size and prominence as the nation began a protracted retreat from military rule. New issues and problems, as well as old, would confront those striving for a more equitable society during a period of political uncertainty and economic instability. By the late 1980s, increasing numbers of gender-conscious political and social movements, not just small, specifically feminist groups, had made their appearance, and certain women's concerns such as health and child care had secured limited institutional support. Brazil's feminist movement had become an acknowledged part of the political scene.

As in the nineteenth century, women's issues achieved the greatest recognition among the modernizing urban sectors of society. Elements of the nineteenth-century Brazilian elite, ever desirous of "progress," had accepted limited improvements in such areas as women's education. The suffrage campaign also benefited from the examples of the more "advanced" nations they admired. The economically privileged sectors, concentrated in the large urban centers, continued to demonstrate far more openness to change than did the majority of the population, both rural and urban, who were denied the benefits of the highly concentrated economic growth Brazil experienced during the late twentieth century. Ever increasing in size and importance, the urban-based modernizing segment of society provided a responsive climate for some feminist demands as well as a field for limited feminist activities. The late 1970s and early 1980s witnessed a ferment of feminist activity surpassing that found elsewhere in Latin America. Like their predecessors, these feminists sought to broaden female political participation and address social issues. But Brazil remained a society marked by severe inequalities in the distribution of wealth and resources. Brazilian women, like men, were separated by class and racial divisions, and conscious feminists still comprised only a small segment of the female population despite their efforts to reach ever more women across class barriers and build successful interclass coalitions.

While the feminist movement of the late 1970s could not have arisen without the foundation laid by the suffragists of the early 1930s, the intervening decades demonstrated far less organized feminist activity. With the establishment of Getúlio Vargas's Estado Novo in 1937, the elimination of elections and congresses, and the suppression of all forms of popular protest, the first small wave of feminine political activism in Brazil was smashed. The entire feminist movement passed from public view.

Women's organizations such as the Brazilian Federation of Women and the Women's Committee for Amnesty, formed after the end of World War II and the demise of the Estado Novo in 1945, lacked a specifically feminist orientation. Such leftist gender-based organizations focused on political issues and the high cost of living rather than on women's rights. Women participated in campaigns for a state monopoly on petroleum and for world peace, and housewives' associations addressed neighborhood problems. In the factory districts of Santo André and São Caetano outside São Paulo, the Communist party, during its brief postwar period of legality, formed numerous neighborhood Democratic Progressive Committees "designed to serve as the community analogue of the workplace-based trade union mobilizations of the day." Those committees, aimed largely at housewives, not only dealt with problems of living costs and scarcities but also sought to improve schools and other neighborhood services; some even attempted to register voters.[1] However, only an exceptional woman like Zuleika Alambert in São Paulo State overcame resistance to rise to a position on the Communist party's Central Committee. In Brazil, as elsewhere in Latin America, women remained largely absent from leadership and policy positions in movements or parties working for basic reforms, just as they lacked directing roles in conservative political organizations. Women's activities beyond the home still were to parallel those performed within the walls of their homes, from domestic service to those government service positions relating to public morality and the family, health, and education. While such virtual segregation also meant that women could obtain the top positions in certain fields—and avoid confrontation, and even competition, with men—they were still overwhelmingly excluded from areas of prime male interest like party politics.[2]

Political parties largely limited women to sex-segregated branches which often served as women's auxiliaries. As in other Latin American countries, such special sections frequently focused on fund-raising and social activities, reproducing and reinforcing traditional gender roles rather than advocating women's issues or attempting to advance women within party structures.[3] Relatively few women ran for office, and even fewer were elected. Women might achieve local office, but they found it far more difficult to enter the realm of political elites and national institutions. From 1946 and the return to legislative government following the end of the Estado Novo until the 1964 military coup d'etat, only two women secured election to the national Congress.[4]

In a 1950 letter defending the old feminist leadership from charges that they had retired from political conflict, diminutive but indefatigable veteran suffragist and political activist Maria Rita Soares de Andrade acknowledged their powerlessness within party structures. She admitted that "the feminists were really gone from newspaper headlines and columns" but claimed that they "had penetrated deep into the life of the nation." And she complained sharply about the attitudes and behavior of male politicians. Except for a few female relatives of important personages, women were still barred from political and administrative posts. While experienced leaders like suffragist Natércia da Silveira in Rio de Janeiro and former congresswoman Carlota de Queiroz in São Paulo met defeat, Getúlio Vargas's grandniece, Ivette Vargas, secured election to Congress in São Paulo. Women could be found "in medical consultation rooms, hospitals, laboratories, the courts, the offices of lawyers, and as engineers and journalists, but rarely in political parties. While we worked with them when battles [were] fought, we [were] always pushed out when the benefits [were] distributed."[5]

The same kinds of well-educated upper-middle-class professionals who once had fought for women's suffrage continued to lead most of the organizations concerned with women's status, both before and after the 1964 military movement that toppled the civilian government headed by President João Goulart. In 1962, after a decade-long struggle led by lawyer Romy Medeiros da Fonseca and her colleagues, they secured a major modification of the civil code that ended the husband's virtually complete control over decisions affecting the family, although he remained "head of the marital union." Married women would no longer be considered permanent minors under the law, and they could control their own earnings and property gained before marriage. Activists struggled to force government compliance with legal changes permitting married women to exercise any profession without their husbands' prior permission, and they worked for 1968 legislation prohibiting discrimination against women in hiring.[6]

Far more numerous than the professional women seeking changes in the civil code or in women's legal status were the conservative middle-class women who marched against the João Goulart government in 1964. In Latin America the Right has often recognized a political potential in women when the Left has not. During Salvador Allende's presidency in Chile, the rightists mobilized working-class women as well as urban middle-class women for protest demonstrations contributing to the 1973 fall of the democratic regime; relatively few women had been included in Chile's strong tradition of working-class politics.[7]

During the early 1960s, politics in Brazil became increasingly polarized. Following the sudden resignation of charismatic but erratic President Jânio Quadros, his constitutional successor, Vice President João Goulart, ascended to the presidency only after popular pressure secured the grudging compliance of the armed forces. Since their decisive action in ousting Getúlio Vargas and ending the Estado Novo in 1945, thereby opening the way for an experiment in political democracy, Brazil's armed forces remained close to centers of power, intervening briefly at key moments but then returning to the barracks. Like conservative civilian elements, many army officers feared and distrusted Goulart and his promised reforms. Building on the populist ideology of his mentor, Vargas, Goulart pursued a highly nationalistic policy, attempting to loosen ties to the United States and to limit profit remittances abroad by foreign companies while also seeking to reform the landholding structure in Brazil. Labor unrest and rampant inflation frightened the middle and upper classes, which felt their security and well-being endangered. Political conflict in Brazil became increasingly radicalized and unstable.[8]

Conservative women's organizations like CAMDE (Women's Campaign for Democracy) contributed to the destabilization of the Goulart regime. In 1962 Amélia Molina Bastos, a retired Rio primary school teacher, strong Catholic, and the "granddaughter, niece, sister, and wife of generals," as she aptly termed herself, founded CAMDE in Rio de Janeiro with the aid of her brother in the army secret service and with the support of several conservative churchmen.[9] Traditional symbols of feminine piety, morality, and motherhood, as well as individual women themselves, would be successfully mobilized by the Right against the threat of radical change; they served to legitimize attacks on the Goulart government. Under slogans calling for the preservation of the Brazilian family and declaring opposition to communism, the women in CAMDE and similar organizations engaged in letter-writing campaigns and then sit-ins and antigovernment demonstrations, drowning out speakers by praying and rattling their rosaries. Finally, they conducted mass marches "of the Family with God for Liberty" in Brazil's major cities early in 1964.[10] These women did not view their militancy as an independent activity, and most would return to more traditional female endeavors like charity work following Goulart's overthrow. Unlike the suffrage movement, theirs was not a sustained political act.

On March 31, 1964, alienated army officers executed a bloodless coup d'etat, sending President João Goulart into exile the following day. While the far Left had found Goulart's measures halfhearted, the far Right, a markedly more united force, had successfully conspired to depose him. But the officers refused to relinquish power to their civilian coconspirators following Goulart's ouster, and they imposed an increasingly harsh rule on the nation.

Like other popular groups, women's organizations largely disappeared following the military takeover. The political party system which had taken shape after World War II and the end of the Estado Novo was effectively reshaped and controlled by Brazil's military masters, who ruled by decree and by force, purging their political adversaries and imposing censorship. Attempting to curb inflation and accelerate economic growth, they sought to promote industrialization at almost any cost. In the 1960s and early 1970s newspapers spoke of the "Brazilian miracle," for Brazil then boasted the largest gross domestic product in the developing world, increasing some 10 percent per annum. By the early 1970s Brazil had become a major exporter of manufactured goods, and coffee comprised only a quarter of the country's exports by value. Volkswagens jammed city streets as ever more consumer goods became available to the expanding middle classes. But as annual growth rates soared, health and living standards for much of the population deteriorated, and income disparities between the classes and the regions increased. The country was dependent on foreign investment, technology, and markets and would accumulate the largest foreign debt in the developing world. When Brazil experienced the first world oil shock in 1973, the "Brazilian miracle" began to collapse. With the second oil shock in 1979 the country entered a deep recession marked by tremendous unemployment and underemployment. Even the middle classes were badly hurt. The social cost of Brazil's economic growth and debt-led development could no longer be ignored.

While women in Brazil shared with men the effects of military dictatorship, underdevelopment, an oppressive class structure, and the decline in minimum salaries, they also bore special burdens. And Brazil's least visible and vocal women suffered most. So-called economic development frequently undermines women's roles in agriculture and trade.[11] While men are pulled into capital-intensive occupations, women are left with jobs in the lower-paid service sector. Census figures, which should be approached with caution since they tend to exclude from the active population those women working part time or irregularly, indicate that the structure of female employment in Brazil underwent little basic change in the period up to 1970.[12] Although industrialization and urbanization dramatically lowered the percentage of both women and men in agriculture over the course of the twentieth century, industry provided few new jobs for women in the 1950s and 1960s. In 1960, 13.1 percent of the male labor force worked in industry, while just 6.9 percent of women workers held industrial jobs. By 1970 the percentage of male workers occupied in industry had increased to 19.3 percent, while that of female workers had declined to 6.0 percent.[13] Expanding industrial sectors, such as capital-intensive heavy goods industries, employed far fewer women than such older and lower-paying manufacturers as textiles and clothing, where women continued to be concentrated. While female industrial employment, especially in São Paulo, grew during the economic surges of the 1970s, the sexual division of labor remained strong. Economic development in Brazil created few new opportunities for lower-class female workers as compared with the rising number of women absorbed into the urban population, thus contributing both to female unemployment and underemployment and to the continuance of domestic service as the major source of employment for women. The 1970 census listed 32 percent of all employed women as domestic servants.[14] Although the percentage, but not the absolute number, of women working as maids declined during the subsequent decade, domestic service still provided the largest number of jobs.

Most working women in Brazil remained in traditional female low-productivity occupations, the least rewarding, most unpleasant, unskilled jobs, with black women clustered in the worst positions and earning the lowest wages.[15] Black women and men, concentrated in Brazil's poorer northern states, as opposed to whites, who were found in far greater numbers in the more developed south-central portion of the country, suffered from strong inequalities not only in income but also in years of formal education, basic literacy, and other measures of attainment. But the widespread, officially endorsed myth of racial democracy hindered recognition of the reality of racial discrimination.

Equal pay for equal work, even for white women, tended to be a statement of aspiration, not of fact, despite the law. Many employers still believed lower salaries to be sufficient for women. Buyers of labor power derived clear benefits from the traditional view of working women as mothers, wives, or daughters contributing to family income rather than as coworkers. In 1973 54.8 percent of all working women earned only the minimum wage or below, as compared with 39.4 percent of working men.[16] With the fall in real minimum wages after 1964, additional members of families, particularly wives, in such cities as São Paulo had to take jobs outside the home, apparently further depressing already low wage levels in female fields of employment.

In contrast with these lower-class women, many middle- and upper-class women in the cities benefited from the economic "miracle" of the 1970s, which created new educational and job opportunities for them. From the early 1960s to the early 1970s the number of women attending universities in Brazil increased tenfold, while the number of male university students only quadrupled, so that women came to comprise close to half the nation's university students by 1980.[17] Even today, though, only 1 percent of Brazil's total female population hold university degrees. The majority of women, like most men, remain uneducated, and female illiteracy rates surpass those of men in both rural and urban areas.

Even though women holding professional positions also suffer from inequities in salary and treatment, they enjoy many benefits denied that mass of urban women living in slums or performing menial tasks. The "liberation" of upper- and middle-class women, with their growing interests outside the family and home, is partly based on the labor of the lower class, generally darker-skinned women who cook for their families, clean their homes, run their errands, and take care of their children. Very few comfortably situated Brazilian women, whether or not they pursue careers outside their homes, can imagine life without their maids. Even feminists generally avoid discussion of maid-mistress relationships or their racial component. By their presence, domestic servants help to attenuate tensions over household responsibilities, thereby lessening the possibility of challenges to a gendered division of labor.[18]

The small group of dedicated professional women pressing for changes in women's legal status had to tread cautiously during the worst years of Brazil's military dictatorship. The nation's military masters looked with suspicion even on public meetings held by these "respectable" women. Family planning remained a sensitive subject, for nationalists on both the left and the right claimed that this was a foreign plot to weaken Brazil by keeping the population down. Although some small women's organizations favored family planning as responsible parenthood, they could not advocate the legalization of abortion at that time. The 1972 national women's congress called by Romy Medeiros da Fonseca's tiny National Council of Brazilian Women avoided the abortion issue, but the professional women and intellectuals of various political persuasions attracted by the unusual initiative of this presumed political conservative did come out strongly for planned parenthood as well as for more day-care centers. They spoke of participating in the development of their country rather than of emancipation.[19]

In the early 1970s neither the old term *feminist* nor the new foreign phrase *women's liberation* found much favor in Brazil, inside or outside government circles. Rose Marie Muraro, one of the first contemporary Brazilians to speak of the liberation of women in her popular books *A mulher na construção do mundo futuro* (Women in the building of a future world) in 1967 and *Libertação sexual da mulher* (Women's sexual liberation) in 1971 advocated the equality of the sexes. But unlike Romy Medeiros da Fonseca, she did not call herself a feminist at this point.[20] However, as director of the publishing house Vozes, Rose Marie Muraro invited Betty Friedan to Rio de Janeiro in 1971 to publicize the publication of the Brazilian edition of *The Feminine Mystique*. (Simone de Beauvoir's *The Second Sex* had appeared in Portuguese in 1949, and later famous feminist works were also published in translation.)

Like Carrie Chapman Catt's trip to Brazil half a century earlier, Betty Friedan's stay was front-page news. But with Brazil under the tight grip of a military dictatorship, Friedan did not find an equivalent women's movement to encourage. Furthermore, even the opposition press often trivialized and ridiculed feminist aspirations. While Betty Friedan's photograph adorned the cover of *O Pasquim*, then the leading member of the small so-called alternative press, which was not controlled or intimidated by the government, that satirical weekly also depicted women as sexual objects. Both Left and Right were upset by Friedan's interviews touching on family planning and abortion. The traditional *Jornal do Brasil*, Rio's leading newspaper, demonstrated its awareness of the differences in perception between male and female reporters covering such a sensitive matter as Friedan's press conference, which was full of hostile questions, by printing two different accounts of this event, one by a male reporter and the other by a female. Both paid as much attention to Betty Friedan's appearance as to what she said, but neither saw or heard quite the same things. The male reporter described Friedan as a vain woman, posturing like a "film star" and always arranging her hair, with "a harsh voice of a markedly masculine timbre; whoever viewed at her at any distance would suppose he were seeing an aging transvestite." In contrast, the female reporter emphasized her energy and contended that "Betty has a husky voice, agreeably nasal, tremendously sexy, sexy principally when she is calm and about to answer questions." While this reporter admitted that Friedan was "ugly," she denied that she was "masculinized."[21]

The next day, the *Jornal do Brasil*'s editorial page displayed a cutting but perhaps accurate comment by Henfil, one of Brazil's best political cartoonists, on many middle- and upper-class women. According to opinion polls conducted by popular magazines like *Manchete*, such women preferred to be the "object" of the men in their lives rather than the "subject of history"; they demonstrated no interest in politics or in attempting to secure the equal salaries theoretically guaranteed them by law, and cared only about motherhood and the family.[22] Henfil's cartoon, entitled "Feminist Leader Visits Brazil," depicts the encounter of this foreign visitor with a Brazilian woman wearing a ball

Henfil

Líder feminista visita o Brasil

"Feminist Leader Visits Brazil"; cartoon by Henfil in the *Jornal do Brasil* during Betty Friedan's 1971 visit to Rio de Janeiro.

Brazilian poster for the 1975 United Nations–proclaimed International Women's Year, when a new women's movement began to emerge. (Centro Informação Mulher, *Agenda, 1986*)

and chain. When the foreign feminist announces that she has "come to bring Brazilian women the good news of women's liberation" and removes the ball and chain from the Brazilian woman, declaring, "You are free! Free from masculine domination!" the Brazilian sniffles and cries, until each woman walks off in a different direction, a perplexed and discouraged foreign feminist and a smiling Brazilian wearing her ball and chain. Not all the repression Brazilian women endured could be directly ascribed to a dictatorial regime.

In the mid 1970s, Brazil began a slow process of transition to civilian rule, which would culminate in the installation of the New Brazilian Republic in 1985. Organized resistance within civil society helped lead to *abertura*, an "opening," a political liberalization permitted by the armed forces themselves. The military regime's policy of gradual decompression and controlled redemocratization fostered the growth of opposition movements, which in turn accelerated the *abertura* process.

Women not only comprised a majority of the participants in most of the new popularly based social movements pressing for change, but many also organized, as women, in defense of their socially ascribed roles as mothers and community caretakers. Their own social identity derived far more from their roles as homemakers and mothers than from any form of paid employment. Since they served as the principal architects of family survival strategies, poor and working-class women were directly affected by the military regime's regressive wage policies and economic development strategies and by rising living costs. All sectors of society could view the women's protests as legitimate efforts to protect family welfare. Like the emerging opposition forces, the Roman Catholic church encouraged women's participation in their programs, helping to provide organizational structures and networks upon which various types of women's movements might later build. However, the mothers' clubs created by local parishes in the 1970s as the church sought to involve women in its pastoral mission served primarily as auxiliary organizations for parish activities, in contrast with the rapidly spreading Christian Base Communities, comprised of both women and men, which built a critical consciousness through religious teachings. While mothers' clubs promoted women's participation in parish and community life, they reinforced women's confinement to traditional roles as wives and mothers. Neighborhood-based feminine associations as well as newly formed feminist groups participated in the challenge to authoritarian rule and the gradual return to political democracy, and in the process began articulating new gender-based political claims.[23]

Amid the opening up of political debate in Brazil in the 1970s and the publicity surrounding the United Nations–proclaimed International Women's Year of 1975, a new women's movement emerged. That year marked the appearance of several small feminist groups in Rio de Janeiro and São Paulo together with the Women's Movement for Amnesty. The Movimento Feminino pela Anistia, founded in São Paulo with links to a similar 1945 movement, was not a feminist or woman-oriented organization, however, but rather an attempt to loosen the grip of the military dictatorship imposed in 1964. United Nations sponsorship of the International Women's Year permitted the creation of women's groups in Brazil when other political activity was discouraged or repressed. As a result, church and leftist political bodies often sought to use these organizations for their own programs.

Led by Terezinha Zerbine, a lawyer married to a general stripped of his political rights, the Women's Movement for Amnesty attempted to mobilize opinion and to stimulate organizations representing broad sectors of civil society to join the fight for a "complete, general, and unrestricted amnesty," for such political amnesty, the women contended, lay at the heart of the struggle for democracy and the rule of law in Brazil. They used the traditional maternal image of women as peacemakers to legitimize their work, which received the public support of a variety of important associations such as the National Conference of Brazilian Bishops, the Order of Brazilian Lawyers, the Brazilian Press Association, student directorates, and the Brazilian Society for the Advancement of Science. And in 1979 the military government approved a limited amnesty project.[24]

The same year which witnessed the formation of the Women's Movement for Amnesty also saw the birth of a new feminist movement in Brazil.[25] A week-long meeting on women held in Rio de Janeiro in June 1975 led to the formation of several feminist groups (although they did not use that term immediately) also involved in the struggle for democracy. Several key groups appeared during the course of that year: first the Centro da Mulher Brasileira (Brazilian Women's Center) in Rio de Janeiro, and then the Centro de Desenvolvimento da Mulher Brasilieira (Center for the Development of Brazilian Women) in São Paulo, and Nós Mulheres (We Women) and Brasil Mulher (Brazil

Women), which published feminist newspapers with those titles. Other groups then arose, not only due to internal divergences within the original associations but also as a result of the activity accompanying Brazil's political "opening." Groups in São Paulo in the late 1970s included the Associação de Mulheres, which had separated from Nós Mulheres in 1978; Pro-Mulher, composed largely of female academics; Grupo Feminista 8 de Março, formed by university students; and Ação Lésbica-Feminista.[26] Most of these associations contained a core of only a few dozen active members. Different groups often dedicated themselves to different tasks, such as health care, women's rights, consciousness raising, publishing feminist newspapers, producing pamphlets on sexuality, conducting research, aiding battered women, and filmmaking or theater. But due to continued disparities and dissimilarities within Brazilian society and the deep cultural differences marking certain regions, especially the Northeast, the feminist movement was still largely limited to certain areas. Feminist groups could be found in south-central cities like Belo Horizonte, Porto Alegre, Curitiba, and Londrina, as well as in Rio de Janeiro and São Paulo; however, those larger metropolises served as the major centers of feminist discourse in Brazil, just as they had earlier in the century.

Amnesty, electricity, water, sewerage, and schools never became the watchwords of contemporary feminism in the developed nations of North America and Western Europe, whose citizens could take for granted minimum levels of comfort and civil liberties. But Brazilian feminists attempted to place so-called specific women's issues within a broader struggle for a democratic, just society and to give priority to the needs and demands of working-class women. Some sought to establish cross-class organizational ties with the far more numerous neighborhood women's associations forming in working-class districts of major manufacturing centers, often under church or banned party sponsorship, and focusing on neighborhood services, especially day care, the high cost of living, and political participation. The demand for day-care facilities, virtually nonexistent in Brazil, led working women and members of church-linked mothers' clubs in São Paulo's lower-class suburbs to petition city hall for the creation of publicly funded and community-based centers in the mid 1970s. With the First Congress of Paulista Women in March 1979, attended mostly by non-feminist groups, an organized day-care movement took shape, at first with middle-class feminist participation, which resulted in government promises to construct far more day care-centers than ever resulted.[27] Despite much greater efforts than those made by their suffragist predecessors (who, however, were also concerned with social issues), feminists found it very difficult to create interclass linkages and to work together for common concrete goals with lower-class women who resisted the feminist label, even to cooperate in such areas as health, work, and education.

Like the women who had once worked for suffrage, most participants in the new feminist groups enjoyed a good education and middle-class status. However, many were also leftist militants with much prior political experience. Unlike the suffragists, who began their campaign under a narrowly based but functioning electoral regime, contemporary feminists first articulated their demands within the framework of opposition to a military dictatorship. The feminist movement developed during a prolonged period of transition to liberal democratic rule, providing them with time to develop their program, for they not only had to challenge state oppression of women, and men, but they also had to assert their claims as women within the opposition movement.

In Brazil, as elsewhere in Latin America, feminism remained open to charges of being a foreign ideology. (Latin America does have a long history of importing ideologies, including Marxism.) For decades, feminism had been viewed as alien to the Latin American character and situation, despised by the Left as a bourgeois capitalist idea, just another imperialist import, and abhorred by the Right as a menace to the Iberian roots of the region. As we have seen, Brazilian feminism did respond to international currents. In the nineteenth century foreign influences on Brazilian feminists had taken the form of useful ideas and examples, and in the early twentieth century the international movement provided Brazil's suffragists with organizational techniques and personal contacts as well. Brazilian feminists in the 1970s, also attuned to developments abroad, could find European attempts to develop a socialist feminism helpful in easing some of the tensions on the Left.

In the late 1970s, amid continued controversy over the legitimacy of feminist claims, Brazil's feminists debated the movement's relationship with the Left.[28] Many women who had gained their first political experiences in leftist groups remained vulnerable to criticism from the Left and to charges that feminism diverted attention from the "real" issue of class conflict. Within the Left, the prevailing assumption was that class exploitation, not gender oppression, explained power imbalances between the sexes. While women tied to certain parties insisted on the primacy of the class struggle, others sought new directions or attempted to conciliate conflicting positions.[29]

In 1979, a split within the Centro da Mulher Brasileira in Rio de Janeiro brought the debate into the open and led to the formation of a new feminist group, the Colectivo de Mulheres. The Collective claimed that the Centro da Mulher Brasileira had been transformed into a "nonfeminist space" which treated as "taboo" issues "concerning women's bodies and sexuality" and neglected the "struggle against discrimination and the oppression of women." "Women's oppression" could "not be reduced to any other form of oppression," and the women's movement had to be "autonomous," not "subordinate," to other groups seeking "the transformation of society."[30] The collective's members, including recently returned political exiles with experience in feminist activities in Europe and the United States, sought to create a less formal hierarchical structure free from the party alliances hindering efforts to deal with issues of personal politics such as sexuality, reproduction, abortion rights, and violence against women.

As the political *abertura* deepened, and more political exiles of both sexes returned after more than a decade abroad, Brazil's small feminist movement displayed increasing vigor.[31] More feminist groups expressed concern with issues relating to reproduction and sexuality as well as with those of education, health, work, child care, living costs, and civil rights. Some still wished to work within the parties to introduce women's issues and elect candidates, but others strove to remain independent. However, most feminist groups in Brazil increasingly couched their political claims in terms of both class exploitation and gender oppression. And for a time the phrase *double activism*, heard in some other Latin American countries, proved popular in Brazil also.

As in many other countries, the new feminist movement did not develop in Brazil without acrimonious debate. But the women's voices were heard, and the questions they raised were discussed in political and intellectual circles. The subject of women emerged as an important scholarly focus. By the early 1980s publishers and educated audiences demonstrated an active interest in studies on women which contrasted sharply with the hostile reception accorded Betty Friedan and the Brazilian translation of her *Feminine Mystique* a decade earlier. What was once a subject for ridicule had become a timely topic.

In the early 1970s the new scholarship on women frequently lacked a feminist perspective. Rather than study gender roles, many scholars then engaged in research on women saw themselves as merely resolving interesting theoretical or methodological questions or exploring social inequalities that could best be explained by the workings of the prevailing sociopolitical system. But by the mid 1980s, thanks in part to the feminist movement, women were accepted as a valid category of analysis rather than simply a focus that could be profitably employed to increase knowledge of Latin American social formations.[32] Nevertheless, the feminist militants and the scholars engaged in research on women in Brazil still generally were not the same individuals, despite some overlap between the two categories.

Even though Brazilian publications on women's history lagged noticeably behind studies by social scientists, as also occurred in other Latin American countries, the younger generation of feminists did rediscover a few pioneers, particularly Bertha Lutz. Her name was given to the Bertha Lutz Tribunal, a mock trial and public forum held in São Paulo in May 1982 that focused on discrimination against working women.[33]

As in the nineteenth century, feminist newspapers played a key role in raising issues, disseminating new ideas, and contributing to the ongoing feminist debate. During the first stage of the new feminist movement, two newspapers made a major impact: *Brasil Mulher* (1975–80), begun in Londrina, Paraná, and subsequently moved to São Paulo, and *Nos Mulheres* (1976–78) in São Paulo. These political papers not only addressed women's issues, but they also formed part of the alternative press resisting military dictatorship. As the feminist movement grew and evolved, with new groups forming and disappearing, these first major feminist newspapers, like lesser ones, ceased publication. But in 1980 *Mulherio*, linked at first to an institution supporting research on women—the Carlos Chagas Foundation—made its appearance in São Paulo. As Brazil's only national feminist newspaper, this professionally produced journal served as a major means of communication for those concerned with women's issues until its demise in 1988.

While the divorce issue did not divide Brazilian feminists in the 1970s as it had a half century earlier, divorce legislation still aroused church hostility. But legalized divorce finally came to Brazil in 1977.

During the previous ten years, according to opinion polls, support for divorce had grown from some 40 percent to over 60 percent of the population. Especially in urban areas and among the young, sentiment favored replacement of the old system of legal separation, or *desquite,* which many felt stimulated concubinage and proved injurious to those caught in a failed marriage. Opposition senator Nelson Carneiro, who spent twenty years fighting for divorce legislation and tried to protect the rights of unmarried women living with men, exploited the political change imposed by President Ernesto Geisel in April 1977 that reduced the requirement for passing a constitutional amendment to a simple majority. Both of the then existing political parties, the MDB (Movimento Democrático Brasileiro, the tolerated opposition party), and the government party, ARENA (Aliança Renovadora Nacional), allowed their members a free vote, and the divorce amendment passed by a majority of fourteen, thereby allowing divorce in Brazil, but only once in any person's lifetime. Although the National Council of Brazilian Bishops issued a protest note, this time bitter campaigning had been avoided. Many bishops realized that any mass mobilization against divorce would strengthen the position of the Right within the church. For the bulk of the MDB, divorce had been their only point of dispute with the church.[34]

As issues of women's reproductive rights and equality within the family emerged more strongly, relationships between the Roman Catholic church and the new feminist movement became more difficult. Fear of offending the "progressive" Roman Catholic church, a major ally of the militant Left and the middle-class opposition in the struggle against authoritarian rule, long kept the parties, just as it had the first new feminist groups, from addressing radical issues like the decriminalization of abortion. Abortion is legal in Brazil under only two conditions: when there is no other way to save the woman's life or if the pregnancy resulted from rape. And the abortion must be performed by a physician. In all other cases the penal code prescribes a series of punishments for those assisting in or undergoing an abortion. Nevertheless, some three million abortions are performed annually, generally under terrible conditions, especially for poor and uneducated women.[35] In the early 1980s the story of a Rio textile worker's unsuccessful efforts to obtain a legal abortion for her young daughter, raped by her stepfather, made Brazil's best-seller list.[36] Although the power of the church remains evident, issues like contraception began to be addressed in political circles by the 1980s, and the distance between the feminist movement and the church widened as the decade progressed.

Family planning also generated controversy and disagreement. In the late 1960s and well into the 1970s, the rightist military regime, committed to an abstract notion of family and dreaming of expanding international influence, contended that Brazil's vast territory and untapped natural resources could support almost unlimited population increase. But by the end of the 1970s key government elements had concluded that a high birthrate impeded progress by giving rise to such social problems as a growing crime rate, an increasing number of abandoned children, and widespread unemployment and underemployment. In its concern for economic development the regime launched a controversial birth control program stressing the use of oral contraceptives, thereby arousing the ire not only of the church but also of segments of the armed forces together with many of their opponents on the Left, who denounced government efforts at family planning as genocidal and imperialist imposed. Feminists voiced fears of coercive government action as well as concern with the side effects of contraceptives on undernourished poor women. Unlike male-led opposition parties, women's groups demanded that the government provide safe, accessible, noncoercive methods of birth control. Health and reproduction, they contended, could not be separated. By the early 1980s, as the debt crisis mounted, family planning issues reverberated within the halls of government and on the floor of Congress, while feminist organizations sought to develop a clear position on reproductive rights with which to meet government proposals.[37]

The ferment of political activity accompanying the redemocratization process in Brazil and the formation of new political parties, which stimulated female participation as well as politicians' awareness of women's importance, increased the need to clarify the relationship of feminist groups with the political parties. The suffragists of the late 1920s had not faced this problem, for their Brazil lacked political parties with clearly defined programs and positions. Unlike the political militants who subsequently became feminists in the late 1970s and early 1980s, the suffragists arrived at their feminism more through personal than through public experiences and activities. They found it easier to remain apart from factional disputes. And, as they lacked the vote, politicians did not actively seek their support. The women's suffrage campaign in Brazil was not tied to any political party or other move-ment. Nor did the suffragists have to deal with questions as contro-versial as those of birth control and abortion, although the FBPF did favor sex education. Sexuality was a major public issue for only a few women in the 1930s.

By the 1980s, many people, particularly middle-class urban intel-lectuals, demonstrated greater willingness to discuss questions of sex-uality publicly. But changes in sexual practices remained more difficult to discern. In 1983 two books on sexuality attained the status of best-sellers in Brazil. One, by feminist author Rose Marie Muraro, *Sexuali-dade da mulher brasileira: Corpo e classe social no Brasil* (Brazilian women's sexuality: Body and class in Brazil), drawn from numerous interviews, focused on the ways in which men and women viewed their bodies, sex lives, and family relations, rather than dealing with their sexual practices. The other book, Marta Suplicy's *Conversando sobre sexo* (Talk-ing about sex), was based on letters received from her television view-ers. For several years this psychoanalyst and sexologist had conducted a five-minute segment on sexual behavior on the popular morning program, "TV Mulher," Brazil's first television program by and for women, which began in 1979. Her willingness to discuss subjects like abortion and masturbation no doubt accounted for the reluctance of some publishers to bring out this book, as well as for her being forced off the air temporarily late in 1982. In the 1970s Brazil's military gov-ernment permitted soft-core pornographic films and encouraged "soc-cer fever" to divert attention from political questions, and in the 1980s television entertainment frequently featured skimpily dressed dancing mulattas, perpetuating pernicious racial as well as sexual stereotypes; but open, serious discussions of sexuality still made many Brazilians uncomfortable. Political debates might seem less daunting.[38]

The return to electoral politics in the early 1980s engendered more debates within feminist circles as to the proper relationship of social movements to party competition. By then, too, many of the earlier feminist entities with their more generalized, consciousness-raising functions had begun to disappear, and a number of small groups arose linked to specific objectives like providing health services, publishing feminist newspapers, producing pamphlets on sexuality, aiding the vic-tims of domestic violence, working for changes in sexist education, and filmmaking and radio programming. As the transition to full civilian rule entered its final stage, more feminists denied any need to organize women separately in the struggle for social justice.[39] And more parties perceived the political dividends they might derive from incorporating women and their least threatening demands into their platforms. Certain issues raised by feminine and feminist groups during the previous decade, including seemingly private issues like day-care centers and violence against women, and apparently public questions like wages and education, received attention. However, as was the case earlier in the century, the politicians and parties endorsing or denying limited feminist demands could not be situated along a strict left-to-right continuum.

With parties seeking to mobilize women as well as men in their search for support, many feminists immersed themselves in the 1982 electoral campaign, the first fairly free national elections since the 1964 military coup d'etat. But it would be far from easy for feminist activists to resist the replication of traditional patterns of feminine subordination within party structures and to assert specific women's demands.

Popular movements in Brazil, as in the rest of Latin America, have long directed themselves toward the state, seeking a better distribution of social services. Many feminists, even those not linked to particular political parties, share a belief in the state as an agency for the promotion of social welfare. With the opposition victories in the 1982 elections, which produced the first popularly elected state governors in Brazil in nearly two decades, some feminist concerns, as well as individual feminists, would be incorporated into government structures. São Paulo, Brazil's richest and most powerful state, with a population of over twenty million, led the way, beginning with the creation of the State Council on the Status of Women (Conselho Estadual da Condição Feminina) in 1983. In the 1930s Bertha Lutz and the FBPF had proposed a women's department to be composed of women dealing with women and their needs, but neither that bureau nor the statute on women became law prior to the establishment of the Estado Novo in 1937. Following his election in 1982, the governor of São Paulo, André Franco Montoro, fulfilled promises to the female participants in his campaign, giving women institutional access to policy-making and implementation. The State Council on the Status of Women addressed a wide range of women's issues, especially education, work, child care, health, and reproductive issues, while also seeking to work with agricultural laborers, black women, and other neglected groups. (In the late 1970s, as labor began to assert itself, women working in such well-organized urban sectors as São Paulo's metallurgical industry held their own assemblies as well as participating in strikes, but in the 1980s, as the economic crisis intensified, some female agricultural laborers in both the Northeast and the south engaged in strikes and violent conflicts over land and wages.) In 1985 the federal government, now in civilian hands, established a similar commission on women (Conselho Nacional dos Direitos da Mulher), which sought to increase women's participation in the Constituent Assembly that drafted a new constitution for Brazil in 1987 and 1988. By 1988 nine of Brazil's twenty-eight states, primarily those in the more populous and prosperous south-central section of the country, had created women's councils.[40] Membership in such bodies gave individual women visibility and provided them with a platform for running for office or assuming high-level government positions.

Ever more women won election to office on both the local and national levels in the 1980s. They profited from the successes of their predecessors' struggle for women's rights, in particular the vote, although they did not all embrace the contemporary women's movement. In 1982 eight women achieved election to the 479-member Chamber of Deputies, twice the number of successful female candidates in 1978, and one woman won a Senate seat.[41] Then, in 1986, twenty-six women were elected to the 559-member Constituent Assembly. Although they occupied less than 5 percent of the congressional seats, these twenty-six women outnumbered all their predecessors combined, for only twenty-one women had served in the national legislature, several for more than one term but others just as substitutes, during the decades from female enfranchisement in 1932 until the 1986 elections. Carlota Pereira de Queiroz was the only woman elected to the Constituent Congress that wrote the 1934 Constitution, although Almerinda Farias Gama also sat in the Constituent Assembly as one of twenty labor union delegates who, together with twenty representatives of employers' associations, comprised the corporate sector of Congress, and both Bertha Lutz and Natércia da Silveira had served on the committee producing a first draft. But no women secured election to the 1946 Constituent Congress.[42]

Although the female politicians who carved out successful careers in the 1980s all benefited from the decades-long struggle for women's rights, they followed different paths to office, besides spanning the political spectrum. For decades, some women have achieved political

Benedita da Silva, the Rio *favela* dweller and Labor party city council member who became the first black woman elected to Congress, in 1986. (Frances O'Gorman et al., *Morro, mulher*)

power through traditional familial means, such as Getúlio Vargas's grandniece, Ivette Vargas, whose long career culminated in her playing a key role in party realignments in the early 1980s as heir to her great-uncle's party, the Partido Trabalhista Brasileira (Brazilian Labor party). Like her spiritual mentor, Carlos Lacerda, a tenacious right-wing opponent of Getúlio Vargas and a supporter of the 1964 military takeover, Sandra Cavalcanti, currently a member of the conservative Partido da Frente Liberal (Party of the Liberal Front), has long been a power in Rio politics, and she played an important role in the last Constituent Assembly.

Although *carioca* voters chose Cavalcanti and rejected the avowed feminist and political neophyte Rose Marie Muraro in 1986, they also selected the distinctive and independent Benedita da Silva in this fragmented election with its exceptionally large field of candidates and political parties. A black slum dweller and women's rights advocate, Benedita da Silva was the only member of her party, the newly formed Partido dos Trabalhadores (Workers' party), elected to the Rio city council in 1982, the only black woman elected in 1986 to the Constituent Congress (or to any other congress), and the only representative whose permanent home is in a *favela*, one of Rio's numerous and enormous shantytowns. Bené, as she is popularly called, carried out her 1986 campaign largely in the *favelas*, working closely with other black candidates in a country where blacks have never been able, or permitted, to organize or demonstrate political strength commensurate with their very large numbers. (The 1980 national census reported that almost 45 percent of Brazil's population declared itself to be black or "brown.")[43] Besides being the only black woman ever elected to Congress, Benedita da Silva is also an evangelical Protestant, a member of one of Brazil's rapidly growing, generally conservative Pentecostal groups known as the Assembly of God.

Under the banner of the Workers' party, a new-style, labor movement–based party with links to the liberationist church and support from many middle-class intellectuals, other women captured major municipalities. First Maria Luiza Fontenelle became mayor of Fortaleza, capital of the northeastern state of Ceará, and then in 1988 Luiza Erundina de Souza won election as mayor of São Paulo, South America's largest city and major industrial center. Born in the poverty-stricken Northeast, like an ever-growing segment of São Paulo's population (among whom she served as a social worker), Erundina won election to the city council in 1982 and to the state assembly in 1986, earning a reputation as a politician who supported popular movements and responded to issues like day care. Unlike Brazil's first female mayor in 1929, Alzira Teixeira Soriano, another *nordestina* but the daughter of a local party chieftain in Rio Grande do Norte, Erundina forged her own political career.

The nineteen-month process of producing Brazil's new 245-article constitution, finally completed late in 1988, demonstrated the divisions existing within the nation on major political issues like land reform— defeated by conservative forces within the Constituent Congress—as well as the difficulties and possibilities of achieving limited feminist demands. Issues such as abortion rights aroused far more opposition than did maternity and even paternity leaves. Due to the influence of the Roman Catholic church together with the unexpected strength of fundamentalist Protestant groups in the Constituent Assembly, the Conselho Nacional dos Direitos da Mulher approached the abortion question very cautiously, advocating that it be treated in ordinary leg- islation rather than in the constitution, as prolife forces desired. Many feminists felt that at best they would be able to maintain the current unsatisfactory situation, blocking a proposed constitutional provision protecting life "since conception," and they succeeded. The extension of maternity leaves to 120 days, the object of numerous public dem- onstrations by women, aroused far less opposition, although the in- stitution of just 5 days of paternity leave had to overcome ridicule and hostility. Women also praised the new definition of the family as a group constituted either by marriage or by stable unions, with equal rights granted to men and women within those families and to all children, whether born in wedlock or not. Family planning is based on a couple's free choice, without coercion, with the state obliged to provide the resources necessary for the exercise of this right, just as day care for children under the age of six also became a duty of the state. But constitutions have long embodied general statements of good intentions and aspirations rather than facts or enforceable provisions.[44]

By the late 1980s gender-conscious political and social movements rather than specifically feminist groupings were increasing. Although feminist organizations remained active in many areas, especially health care, only government bodies received attention from the press and television, which no longer trivialized or ridiculed women's demands. With their command of far greater resources, state agencies sometimes seized the initiative, developing more extensive programs than small feminist groups were able to establish.

Like health and sexuality, violence against women is a cross-class issue which can bring together women of diverse backgrounds and interests in a country marked by the persistence of moral and sexual double standards. A feminist concern in the 1930s, domestic violence served as a major focal point for feminist energies in the 1980s. Once again, violence against women was front-page news throughout Brazil, finally even attracting the attention of U.S. television, which portrayed Brazil as a land of machismo where husbands murdered wives and were exonerated as acting in "legitimate defense of their honor." Brazilian feminists not only organized protest demonstrations over these cases of uxoricide, demanding punishment of those guilty of "crimes of passion," but they also created centers like SOS-Corpo in Recife and SOS-Mulher in São Paulo in 1980 to help battered women. Then, São Paulo's government stepped in. The all-female police precincts that the state established to deal with violence against women met with widespread public approval, and other state governments sought to create similar units.[45]

Although feminists within and outside of government prefer to look forward rather than backward, they could cite a history of accomplishments as well as of frustrations. Despite the problems and obstacles feminists have faced, by the late 1980s the women's movement in Brazil demonstrated more success than elsewhere in South America in organizing, raising a broad range of issues, creating new institutions, and promoting changes in government structures.[46]

In Brazil, as in some other countries, a close connection has existed between the denial of women's demands and the repression of other protest movements, while feminist activities have expanded during periods of political liberalization. The growth of feminist activities in the 1880s and the 1920s reflected the periods' political conjunctures as well as advances in education in an increasingly urbanized and industrialized nation. Under the military dictatorship imposed in 1964, as during the Estado Novo (1937–45), women's organizations, like other popular groups, largely ceased to function, while the return to a system of elective government in the late 1970s and early 1980s facilitated the development of a new feminist movement. But the increasing attention activist women have devoted to party politics in the 1980s, a period of political uncertainty and economic instability, may dissipate some feminist energies. As feminist concerns—and feminists themselves—become incorporated into the governing structure, specific improvements in women's rights and status may result without much growth in feminist consciousness.

Although many feminists praised the programs of government entities they had joined, others saw the women's councils and even the female police precincts as attempts by the power structure to divide and domesticate the women's movement. "Women," in the words of one restless feminist, are "in style. During electoral campaigns everyone talked about his concerns and proposals and made promises to help women. . . . Women are in style . . . but kept under surveillance, limited, and restricted. . . . We, and the blacks, homosexuals, and ecologists, now have our own little space and receive recognition. We are labeled, tagged, and 'accepted,' as long as we behave well."[47] By the late 1980s the feminist movement in Brazil had demonstrated sufficient achievements and women's demands had secured a sufficient degree of public and political recognition to permit such complaints.

Political support is obviously not immutable. Changes in administrations can easily lead to the withdrawal of benefits extended to women. Some of the specific disadvantages of dependence on particular politicians or parties are illustrated by the reductions in funding, activities, and staff suffered by São Paulo's Council on the Status of Women after Orestes Quércia succeeded Franco Montoro as state governor in 1987.

Brazil's pioneer fighters for women's rights and social betterment lacked the heritage of female political activism which their successors possess. Moreover, they could draw on only a tiny pool of professional women to provide leadership for their movement. Even though the percentage of women holding university degrees is still very small, their numbers have grown greatly in recent years. No doubt well-educated professional women will continue to provide the leadership for most groups within and without government seeking specific changes in women's status, although larger numbers of lower-class women gained organizational skills and experience through neighborhood-based associations during the transition to civilian rule. Without middle-class women and the intellectual and financial resources they contribute, the feminist movement would falter. But a movement limited to a relatively small, and largely light-skinned, proportion of the population of this huge country cannot be termed a great success, despite the fact that active feminists remain a minority in all countries. Feminist groups were slow to confront racial issues affecting women, leading some dissatisfied black women in cities like São Paulo to form their own separate feminist organizations.[48] Perhaps the generally Marxist tenor of much political and social debate in Brazil led racial discrimination to be generally subsumed under class considerations. Certainly the race, not just the class, divisions separating Brazilian women will not be easily bridged.

Brazil's feminists are well aware that they face the difficult challenge of confronting the inequalities of class and gender simultaneously, even if they have been less attuned to questions of racial discrimination. They seek to construct a theory and practice of feminism appropriate to Brazilian realities, not simply copied from other countries. However, despite feminists' efforts to build successful interclass coalitions, their construction remains a major problem for women, and for men, struggling for a more equitable society. In the late twentieth century, as in the nineteenth and early twentieth centuries, beneficial change always seems to come more slowly to poor women than to better-off women or to men of any class.

Rather than seeking to integrate women into existing systems without transforming the Brazilian social structure, the new feminism has denied the possibility of liberation without fundamental changes in society. But how this could or should be done is not always clear or easily agreed upon. Radical feminist goals are pursued by few women in Brazil. Far more women would fight for child-care centers or better health-care services than challenge existing power relationships between the sexes. The incorporation of many feminists into government structures in the mid 1980s not only provides them with new resources and support, enabling them to reach more women, but also sets limits to the kind of changes that can be achieved. The boundaries of feminist discourse are blurred as well as expanded. The ever-changing feminist movement has a long history in Brazil, and in its multiple forms the struggle continues.

Appendix A

"To Our Subscribers,"*

by Joana Paula Manso de Noronha

(*O Jornal das Senhoras*, January 1, 1852)

To edit a newspaper is for many men of letters the height of supreme happiness. *I am an editor:* this little phrase said to oneself makes any individual stand two feet taller.

In learned circles the Editor is always treated with the unfailing respect due a man who can say so much in print that is helpful or harmful to anyone. In those other circles of people who consider human progress to be heresy and men of letters to be a breed of idlers (because they know that a hole can be dug with a shovel), intellectual activities are just so much Greek. Therefore the Editor is—just an idler, a useless being.

Well then, a woman editing a newspaper! What kind of Hydra-headed monster will it be? Nevertheless, in France, England, Italy, Spain, the United States, and in Portugal itself, cases abound of women dedicated to literature who contribute to various newspapers.

Perchance shall South America alone stay stationary in its ideas when the entire world marches toward progress and moves toward the moral and material improvement of society?

Well now! That cannot be. Principally society in Rio de Janeiro, the royal court, the capital of empire, the metropolis of South America, will certainly welcome with satisfaction and sympathy *O Jornal das Senhoras* edited by a woman, by a Latin American, who though without talent at least has the will and the desire to spread enlightenment and to strive with all her energy for social betterment and the moral emancipation of women.

*The translation from the Portuguese for this and the following appendixes is by June E. Hahner.

Our campaign has thus begun. The banner of enlightenment waves gracefully in the perfumed breeze of the tropics. Take shelter under it. All you who possess a spark of intelligence, come. We shall be the discreet confidante of your literary works, publishing them anonymously; therefore, do not fear to confide in us, nor fear to give expression to your thoughts. If you possess them it is because they are a gift from God, and that which God gives, men cannot plunder.

By sealed envelope the editor of this newspaper will respond to all ladies desiring to honor our pages. I would be unendingly happy should my dedication obtain your cooperation.

We have the satisfaction to announce that we are already being assisted by a friend of ours, an intelligent and clever young woman, who has done us the favor of taking charge of the section on fashions, in particular, while we preserve her strict anonymity. Let us then read her first article.

Appendix B

"What Do We Want?"

(*O Sexo Feminino*, October 25, 1873)

and "Equality of Rights"

(*O Quinze de Novembro do Sexo Feminino*, April 6, 1890),

by Francisca Senhorinha da Motta Diniz

What Do We Want?

It is quite natural that more than one of those backward souls who form part of our present-day society have asked this question. It is very probable that those who are unconcerned or pessimistic or willfully blind have asked the same question. We will try hard to answer them.

It is definitely a verifiable fact that men have overlooked the need to enlighten women's minds; instead, they remain content to adorn their bodies and flatter their vanity.

It cannot be denied that women (with few exceptions) live in complete ignorance of their rights, unaware even of those due them under our nation's laws—particularly that their public consent is necessary for the conveyance of *real estate*. How many married women are ignorant of the fact that a husband cannot dispose of any piece of the couple's property in any way without the wife's special consent? How many married women are deceived in such matters by husbands who force them to sign those legal documents on which they *automatically scrawl* their names? How many married women write out in their own hand the words dooming all the savings their parents suffered to accumulate but which their wastrel husbands pledged to repay *debts* that were not even contracted for the couple's benefit?

The state of crass and supine ignorance in which women languish, always deceived by their husbands, allows them so often to fool themselves into thinking they are *rich* when some day in fact they will awake to the *sad reality* of not owning anything, of being *poor,* the *poorest possible,* because their husbands have squandered their *inheritance,* wasted it, handed it over to *creditors* who *legally* claim their money. Only then will such women see the abyss in front of their eyes! Is it not very strange in such cases, that after all this has happened, those husbands climax their previous knaveries by abandoning their wives and children?

Many husbands perceive that their wives lack sufficient training to take over their affairs in their absence and carry on as they would do. Other husbands *praise* such ignorance and give thanks for their luck in having wives who understand nothing about those affairs in which men say women *should not meddle!*

How many parents labor unceasingly under the harshest conditions to amass a dowry for their daughter and then deliver her body and soul to a *son-in-law* who will soon squander this dowry? After all, he secured the dowry through a marriage which he viewed not as an *end* in itself but just as a means of obtaining a fortune *without working.* While the true purpose of marriage has always been the legitimization of the *union of man and woman,* so that they will live together as one and love each other as Christ loved his church, in this corrupt, immoral, and irreligious society, *marriage is a means of making one's fortune.* Marriage is the goal of the rascal who does not want to work and who acts like some strange kind of acrobat turning *somersaults* to snare a dowry, no matter if the woman attached to it is pretty or ugly, young or old—all will do. With the social goal of marriage thus perverted, love of family, children, and homeland easily disappears.

Girls must be prepared for *reverses of fortune.* They must receive *education* and *instruction,* so that whether married, single, or widowed, they will know their rights and will be able to judge the *intentions* and *heart* of men requesting their hand in marriage.

To summarize the thesis of this article: We want our emancipation and the regeneration of our customs; we want to regain our lost rights; we want true *education,* which has not been granted us, so that we can educate our children; we want pure *instruction* so we can know our rights and use them appropriately; we want to become familiar with our family affairs so that we can administer them if ever obliged to. In short, we want to *understand* what we do, the *why* and *wherefore* of matters; we want to be our husbands' companions, not their slaves; we want to know how things are done outside the home. What we do not want is to continue to be *deceived*.

Equality of Rights

Like a Columbus at the prow of his ship, like an eagle with his eyes fixed on the sun of the future, the nineteenth century proceeds toward a new world, a new paradise, where women shall have their thrones of honor and receive their radiant queens' crowns not from the sacrilegious hands of an Alcibiades but from the sacred hands of Justice and Right, the true sovereigns, who will depose the false kings seated on their thrones of injustice and iniquity brandishing their scepters of despotism. Yes, we believe that the prophecy of the immortal Victor Hugo will be achieved. We have faith that this century will triumph through the radiant ideal of justice that surrounds it.

We believe, with the strong faith noble causes inspire, that an ideal state will soon be here, when educated women free from traditional prejudices and superstitions will banish from their education the oppression and false beliefs besetting them and will fully develop their physical, moral, and intellectual attributes. Then, linked arm in arm with virtuous, honest, and just men in the garden of spiritual civilization, women will climb the steps of light to have their ephemeral physical beauty crowned with the immortal diadem of true beauty, of science and creativity. In the full light of the new era of redemption we shall battle for the restoration of equal rights and our cause—the Emancipation of Women.

We women do not wish to be the Venus de Milo, but rather the Venus Urania, so that we can brilliantly traverse all the orbits that human endeavor traces at the dawn of humanity and society.

We do not wish to play the role of ornaments in the palaces of the stronger sex. Nor do we wish to continue in the semislavery in which we languish, mutilated in our personalities through laws decreed by men. This is no different from the old days of slave labor when the enslaved could not protest their enslavement.

We are not daunted by such hypocrisy as men's treating us like queens only to give us the scepter of the kitchen, or the procreation machine, etc. We are considered nothing but objects of indispensable necessity! We are cactus flowers and nothing more.

Women's emancipation through education is the bright torch which can dispel the darkness and bring us to the august temple of science and to a proper life in a civilized society.

Moral advancement, which can best lead us to understand our rights and duties, will guide our hearts toward the paradise of goodness and of domestic, social, and human happiness. The union of fine arts with literature, a star in the soul's beautiful sky, will make women men's worthy companions in the struggle for social progress and in the labors of family life.

In short, we want women to be fully aware of their own worth and of what they can achieve with their bodies as well as through their moral beauty and the force of their intellects. We want the lords of the stronger sex to know that although under their laws they can execute us for our political ideas, as they did such ill-fated women as Charlotte Corday and many others, they owe us the justice of equal rights. And that includes the right to vote and to be elected to office.

By right we should not be denied expression in Parliament. We should not continue to be mutilated in our moral and mental personality. The right to vote is an attribute of humanity because it stems from the power of speech. Women are human beings, too.

We Brazilian, Italian, French, and other women of diverse nationalities do not request the vote under the restrictions currently imposed on Englishwomen, but with the full rights of republican citizens. We live in a generous and marvelous country recognized as a world leader in liberal ideas and in the ability to throw off old prejudices.

What we ask is a right never demanded before, and therefore ignored. But it was never deleted from natural law.

Women must publicly plead their cause, which is the cause of right, justice, and humanity. No one should forget that women as mothers represent the sanctity of infinite love. As daughters they represent angelic tenderness. As wives, immortal fidelity. As sisters, the purest dedication and friendship. Moreover, these qualities the Supreme Creator bestowed on them prove their superiority, not their inferiority, and show that equality of action should be put into practice by those men who proclaim the principle of equality.

We Brazilians, Portuguese, French, English, Italian, German, etc., women, like noble Aspasias, side by side with the Hypatiases and Semiramises, etc., are asking for what is due us and what, by natural right, cannot be denied us.

Our ideas are not utopian but instead great and noble, and they will induce humanity to advance toward justice.

This is our political program.

Appendix C

"Our Anniversary,"

by Josefina Alvares de Azevedo

(*A Família*, December 31, 1889)

With this issue *A Família* [The family] begins its second year of publication.

Although it may not have accomplished much for the cause it defends during the period of its publication, nevertheless it has fought for women's rights.

The ancient, stupid prejudices that have long ruled and still rule Brazilian society have always kept us in such an atrophied state that we were not even permitted to have aspirations. Our intellectual activities, carried out under precarious conditions, were bounded by an iron circle.

In more advanced societies, in the principal nations of the Old World, stars of the first magnitude shine. Thus they prove that God did not grant to men alone the dazzling spark of talent, the burning flame of genius. And in undertaking activities in fields reserved for men, they prove they can compete with men without loss of energy, aptitude, and ability. But in Brazil we are not granted any privileges whatsoever, aside from the moral merit of our obscure condition.

The French Revolution, this enormous human epic event that broke forth like a beacon to illuminate the destiny of nations, enshrined in its supremely free laws the cardinal principles of the rights of man. But even so it did not expand the civic capacity of women.

Male egoism, inordinate, fanatical, and intolerant, has not conceded to us anything that we merited based on our abilities.

Thanks to new views which certain eminent individuals later entertained, some things were permitted us, so that we have arrived at the initial period (which is the present time) of our preponderance in society. In Brazil the impenetrable darkness that has enshrouded us up to the present moment is being dispersed, and we are going to conquer a definite place in our society.

With this *desideratum*, that of advocating our emancipation, this newspaper appeared in the generous province of São Paulo, where I then resided, and was later transferred to the nation's capital.

All those who accept the general social principle of the emancipation of women and the new state to which we aspire have maintained a position in the press which I judge correct and competent.

Happily, we see that women are already being granted something more than was the case up to now. Their activities are blazing a necessary trail extending beyond the narrow sphere to which they were confined, through prejudice, so that they can act as complete human beings, intellectually, morally, and materially. This is already a great conquest.

I firmly believe that our complete emancipation will be one of the great events in New World civilization. And the improvements that we are realizing in Brazil give us the right to entertain this hope. With this intention, *A Família* has been fighting for our rights.

We cannot deny how arduous our task has been, but we will not lose heart. When one nurses a hope in one's breast, for hope invigorates and encourages people in precarious positions, then there are no hazards or vicissitudes that can conquer us. Therefore, one year after its appearance *A Família* is stronger than ever and able to continue the struggle.

"To the Young Seamstresses of São Paulo,"

by Tecla Fabbri, Teresa Cari, and Maria Lopes

(*A Terra Livre*, July 29, 1906)

Comrades!

Because of the apathy dominating you which you have not yet shaken off, even in this city where we are so exploited, we resolve to make a new attempt to defend all of us. We hope you will not allow us to remain the only ones demanding our indisputable rights. In all fairness, you should recall that many times some friends have come to our defense in the newspaper columns of *Avanti!*, *La Battaglia*, and *Terra Livre*. But their words were not heard. We hope you will not abandon us also to cry out alone in this wilderness.

We must finally demonstrate that we are capable of demanding our due. If we maintain our solidarity, if you fight with us, if we are heard, we shall begin by exposing the greed of the bloodsucking employers.

The last general strike in this city clearly proved that the seamstresses are the most ignorant and backward group among the working classes. In that movement of worker solidarity all the skilled workers participated, from the mechanics to the cabinetmakers, from the iron workers to the carpenters, plus hat workers, masons, carriage makers, almost all the printers, factory workers in textile, clothing, and match plants, marble cutters, goldsmiths, and many others. In Jundiaí retail commerce made common cause with the strikers by shutting their doors. Here in São Paulo students demonstrated their sympathy and the law school had to be closed. And we, the seamstresses, what did we do?

We remained apathetic and unconcerned while strikers filled the city streets. We still went to our jobs, thereby showing that we had no feelings, that we had no blood in our veins. In the mass of strikers were our fathers, our brothers, our sweethearts, and we walked among them without realizing that they were demanding our rights also. Thus we demonstrated our lack of family affection and love!

Reflect, comrades, that we too must always maintain our solidarity with those struggling for the liberation of labor if we wish any aid from others in achieving our more than just demands.

Comrades! It is essential that we refuse to work night and day, because that is disgraceful and inhuman. Since 1856 men in many places have attained the eight-hour day. But we members of the weaker sex have to work up to sixteen hours a day, double that of the stronger sex! Comrades, think about your futures; if you continue to allow yourselves to be weakened, and the last drop of your blood drained off, then, after you have lost your physical energy, motherhood will be martyrdom and your children will be pale and sickly.

And you, our parents, certainly you will help us, because we do not have the strength to work, so frequently, up to eleven o'clock at night! You should speak about these matters not only with your families but also with our inhuman employers, face to face. After all, their businesses grow and prosper day by day. Go at night to protest and give these thieves a caning if necessary! Come, without delay and energetically pull out the claws of those greedy exploiters! Do you have much to lose? What do they give us—those vultures—in payment for our toil? A ridiculous salary. A miserable pittance!

We too would like to have leisure time to read or study, for we have little education. If the current situation continues, through our lack of consciousness, we shall always be mere human machines manipulated at will by the greediest assassins and thieves.

How can anyone read a book if he or she leaves for work at seven o'clock in the morning and returns home at eleven o'clock at night? We have only eight hours left out of every twenty-four, insufficient time to recuperate our strength and to overcome our exhaustion through sleep! We have no future. Our horizons are bleak. We are born to be exploited and to die in ignorance like animals.

We hope you will not abandon us, comrades, and that you will aid us to lay bare and oppose the employers' infamous outrages, which must be ended. Yes! We count on the support of our sisters and comrades. Then victory will be ours. Let us get to work!

Appendix E

Recollections of a Rio Textile Worker,

by Luiza Ferreira de Medeiros, 1970 (when she was sixty-eight years old; from Edgar Rodrigues, *Alvorado operário. Os congressos operários no Brasil*)

I started working at the Bangú Factory around the time of the First World War when I was seven years old. Work began at 6:00 A.M. and ended around 5:00 P.M., without any set lunch time. It was up to the foremen if we could eat, and our salaries were the same whether or not there was time for lunch. Obviously, all this was after we passed through the first stage of working there for nothing, which was called apprenticeship. In my division you started out earning ten tostões* and you kept going until you became a weaver. We had no place to eat. Meals were taken next to the machines. Since at that time we did not have money to buy clothing, we used the same clothes on the job and on the street. Mill hands wore a kind of clothes called "dried meat" or "drunkard." They were given that name because they were made from cloth with dye stains and broken threads. We had no place to wash ourselves, just one faucet over a slimy tub, which served us as both drinking fountain and wash basin.

I was never paid overtime, even though I worked more hours than the stated workday.

Once Euclides, known as Donga, was caught in a machine and died. The family did not receive a cent, not even anything for the funeral. The funeral expenses were paid with money his fellow workers collected plus something from the Mutual Aid Society the mill hands had organized. Another time Idalina, a pretty girl, lost an arm in a machine. All she got was permission to come back and work with just

*A tostão was a nickle coin worth 100 réis, or a tenth of a milréis.

that one arm once she recuperated. I saw workers get pulled by the ears, as I was, and slapped, and I suffered worse things too. I saw children being beaten!

There was no help or insurance. The factory provided meager medical treatment with old Dr. Paulhaver and nurse Moacyr, who was nicknamed "Dr. Iodine" because all he ever did was daub iodine on injuries.

Mill hands had big families, from five to sixteen children, all working to help out the family. In Bangú we lived this way: most of the workers dwelt in houses with dirt floors, wattle-and-daub walls, and tin or straw roofs. The Martins Júnior school, the only one around, was practically handed over to the girls because the mill hands did not have the means to buy school supplies—books, notebooks, slates, pens, and pencils—and so they could not send the boys to school.

The owners never came near the workers. They gave the impression that we made them nauseous. Threats and brutalism reigned.

Foreman Claúdio Batista shut girls up in his office in order to force them to have sex with him. Many of the mill hands became prostitutes because of that scoundrel! He even suspended women for ten or fifteen days for the slightest shortcomings, or even for no reason, in order to make them submit to his desires. Other times he assigned them to bad machines and gave them defective thread to hamper their work. In his machinations he could count on the aid of Pedro Dias the gatekeeper, who blew the first factory whistle, closing the gate halfway. With the second whistle, he closed the gate a little more. And when the third whistle began, he closed the rest of the gate very fast, locking out workers who arrived at the last minute and who the foreman, therefore, would keep an eye on. He informed on the mill hands, harming many of his coworkers.

The workers who joined the union were always being threatened. Union women were considered prostitutes; or even worse than this, they were seen as repulsive people.

The same foreman who deflowered so many girls prohibited them from wearing low-cut blouses, short or loose sleeves, and skirts which ended more than a couple of inches above the ankle. Their blouses had to be closed at the neck and at the wrists and their skirts had to scrape the floor in order to attest to the "morality" he lacked.

Appendix F

"Women's Letters," by Bertha Lutz

(*Revista da Semana*, December 23, 1918)

For some time I have been following with the greatest interest your columns in the *Revista da Semana*. The last one, that of December 14, pleased me greatly. Ever since I learned of the new electoral status of women in England, I have been very curious as to whether you would have the courage to write what you did. If you had not, I intended to request that you publish a few lines of mine on the matter. Happily, you did it infinitely better than I would have. I am in complete agreement with your ideas and I congratulate and thank you wholeheartedly.

I am a Brazilian, and during the past seven years I have been studying in Europe. It was with great sorrow that I observed upon my return home the situation you described concerning the lack of veneration and respect for women which one sees here in our capital city. The public treatment of women is painful for them and does little to honor our fellow countrymen. More respect, of course, is accorded a woman among the more cultured sectors; but this is superficial and barely conceals the toleration and indulgence with which she is treated, as though she were a spoiled child. In this regard, despite all the national progress achieved in recent years, we find ourselves lagging far behind the peoples who dominate the world today, and behind the new, regenerated France to which this terrible war gave birth.

Surely the greatest portion of the responsibility for this unfortunate state of affairs falls to men, in whose hands rest legislation, politics, and all public institutions. But we also are a bit to blame. You cited the words of one of our greatest contemporaries, President Wilson, concerning American women: "they have shown that they do not differ at all from us in every kind of practical endeavor in which they engage either on their own behalf or on that of the nation." These words should serve to guide us, for they reveal the secret to which emancipated women owe their equal footing with men. I was in Europe during the war, and I spent the tragic days preceding the victory in England and France. The women's war effort was admirable and heroic. Some were brokenhearted by the death of a son, husband, father, or brother, and each one was full of anxiety and horror, but with great simplicity and courage they all took the soldiers' places and carried out the hardest jobs of the absent menfolk. They brought a lively intelligence and an indomitable energy to those tasks, which until now were considered impossible for women. And this heroic example of sacrifice and willpower secured that which all the social and political arguments had failed to accomplish. Today they harvest the fruit of their dedication. Fortunately for our country and for ourselves, we have not been called upon to provide the same proof. But even so we feel that we are worthy of occupying the same position. But how can we obtain it? We should not resign ourselves to being the only subordinates in a world on which liberty smiles. We must become worthy of that position to which we aspire, and we must prove that we merit it. Clearly, at present almost everything depends on men. But one of the greatest forces for emancipation and progress lies within our power: the education of women and men. We must educate women so that they can be intellectually equal and be self-disciplined. We must educate men so that they become aware that women are not toys created for their amusement, and so that, when observing their wives and sisters or remembering their mothers, they understand and are completely convinced of the dignity of women. For us to achieve this result and to demonstrate our equality, both individual and collective efforts are necessary. Practical demonstrations are infinitely more valuable than anything else; only they are truly convincing. You have provided the best example, demonstrating in your columns that the female spirit can rise to the level of large problems, understand new ideas, and express them with elegance and clarity. By achieving first place in a competition, Maria José has also contributed greatly toward the success of our cause. Finally, all the normal school teachers and other women to whom the nation confides the education of its children prove that there are women of great worth in our country also. Such are the excellent examples which moved me to write this letter and to propose that we channel all these isolated efforts so that together they comprise a definitive proof of our equality. For this purpose I am proposing the establishment of a league of Brazilian women. I am not proposing an association of "suffragettes" who would break windows along the street, but rather of Brazilians who understand that a woman ought not to live parasitically based on her sex, taking advantage of man's animal instincts, that she be useful, educate herself and her children, and become capable of performing those political responsibilities which the future cannot fail to allot her. Thus women shall cease to occupy a social position as humiliating for them as it is harmful to men. They shall cease being one of the heavy links that chain our country to the past, and instead become valuable instruments in the progress of Brazil.

Notes

Preface

1. The state of research on the history of Latin American women is discussed by June E. Hahner, "Researching the History of Latin American Women: Past and Future Directions," *Inter-American Review of Bibliography* 23, no. 4 (1983): 545–52; Susan Soeiro, "Recent Work on Latin American Women. A Review Essay," *Journal of Interamerican Studies and World Affairs* 17 (November 1975): 497–516; and Asunción Lavrin, in Lavrin, ed., *Latin American Women: Historical Perspectives* (Westport, Conn.: Greenwood Press, 1978), pp. 302–32, who also suggests thoughtful questions for future investigations.

Bibliographies on women in Latin America published in the United States include the following: Meri Knaster, *Women in Spanish America: An Annotated Bibliography from Pre-Conquest to Contemporary Times* (Boston: G. K. Hall, 1977); K. Lynn Stoner, *Latinas of the Americas. A Source Book* (New York: Garland Publishing, 1989); June E. Hahner, ed., *Women in Latin American History: Their Lives and Views*, rev. ed. (Los Angeles: UCLA Latin American Center, 1980), pp. 177–86; Bertie Cohen Stuart, *Women in the Caribbean: An Annotated Bibliography* (Leiden: Department of Caribbean Studies, Royal Institute of Linguistics and Anthropology, 1979); and Ann Pescatello, "The Female in Ibero-America: An Essay on Research Bibliography and Research Directions," *Latin American Research Review* 7 (Summer 1972): 125–41. Bibliographies also exist for certain individual countries, such as, for Cuba: Nelson Valdés, "A Bibliography on Cuban Women in the Twentieth Century," *Cuban Studies Newsletter* 4 (June 1974): 1–31.

Far fewer bibliographies on women have been published in Latin America. For Brazil, see: Fundação Carlos Chagas, *Mulher brasileira. Bibliografia anotada*, 2 vols. (São Paulo: Editora Brasiliense, 1979–81). The recent surge in Brazilian publications on women and their roles and activities within Brazilian society is analyzed by June E. Hahner, "Recent Research on Women in Brazil," *Latin American Research Review* 20, no. 3 (1985): 163–79.

2. See Hahner, "Recent Research on Women in Brazil."

3. See Anna Macías, *Against All Odds. The Feminist Movement in Mexico to 1940* (Westport, Conn.: Greenwood Press, 1982); Ward M. Morton, *Woman Suffrage in Mexico,* (Gainesville: University of Florida Press, 1962); Elsa M. Chaney, *Supermadre: Women in Politics in Latin America* (Austin: University of Texas Press, 1979); and Marifran Carlson, *Feminismo! The Woman's Movement in Argentina from Its Beginnings to Eva Peron* (Chicago: Academy Chicago Publishers, 1988).

4. Recent research suggests that the terms *feminism* and *feminist* first began to be widely used in France in the early 1890s, principally as a synonym for women's emancipation, then spread to Great Britain and to other European countries by the end of the century. See Karen Offen, "On the French Origin of the Words Feminism and Feminist," *Feminist Issues* 8 (Fall 1988): 45–51.

5. The shift in vocabulary in the United States from the "woman movement" to "feminism" in the early twentieth century is penetratingly analyzed by Nancy F. Cott, *The Grounding of Modern Feminism* (New Haven: Yale University Press, 1987), who gives a

more time-and-place-specific analysis of feminism. But Brazil never experienced a large "woman movement" in the nineteenth century against which twentieth-century feminists could react.

Cott's position may be contrasted with that of a leading feminist scholar and European specialist, Joan Kelly. See *Women, History and Theory. The Essays of Joan Kelly* (Chicago: University of Chicago Press, 1984), which finds feminist theorizing arising in the fifteenth century as well as at other specific points in history when women conscious of their collective oppression engaged in a dialectical opposition to misogyny. In a recent article addressing issues involved in understanding feminism across cultures and centuries, another European specialist, Karen Offen, in "Defining Feminism: A Comparative Historical Approach," *Signs. A Journal of Women in Culture and Society* 14 (Autumn 1988): 119–57, advocates a broad-based definition of feminism, which she views as a developing ideology, diffuse and dynamic.

6. Just as standard histories of Brazil basically ignore women, so do books on the Brazilian press overlook the nineteenth-century women's rights press. Nelson Werneck Sodré, *A história da imprensa no Brasil* (Rio de Janeiro: Civilização Brasileira, 1966), the most complete study of the Brazilian press, mentions more than one thousand journals but ignores the periodicals examined in this book. Information on individual nineteenth-century Brazilian newspapers advocating female emancipation was first published in June E. Hahner, "The Nineteenth-Century Feminist Press and Women's Rights in Brazil," in *Latin American Women: A Historical Perspective*, ed. Asunción Lavrin, pp. 254–85 (Westport, Conn.: Greenwood Press, 1978). A more recent work, Dulcília Helena Schroeder Buitoni, *Mulher de papel. A representação da mulher pela imprensa feminina brasiliera* (São Paulo: Edições Loyola, 1981), focuses on newspapers directed toward women.

While the nineteenth-century Brazilian newspapers advocating the emancipation of women may not be unique in Latin America, the non-Brazilian periodicals tended to be edited by men, not women, and were designed to provide entertainment or moral uplift, not to change women's lives. Although Latin American journals intended for women have received virtually no attention, Jane Herrick has described several in "Periodicals for Women in Mexico during the Nineteenth Century," *The Americas* 14 (October 1957): 135–44. However, with one exception, *El Album de la Mujer* (1883–93), they were edited by men. Herrick does not indicate that this one periodical differed in any major respect from the general run of those concerned with home medicine, cooking, poetry, and pictures. Nor does she consider the fact that a woman owned and edited a journal to be a matter of interest.

7. For a stimulating definition and discussion of gender in historical analysis see Joan W. Scott, "Gender: A Useful Category of Historical Analysis," *American Historical Review* 91 (December 1986): 1053–75.

Introduction

1. John Luccock, *Notes on Rio de Janeiro and the Southern Parts of Brazil Taken during a Residence of Ten Years . . . 1808–1818* (London: S. Leigh, 1820), pp. 112–13.

2. The history of sexuality is a very new field of investigation for Latin America, but a start has been made in Brazil. See Ronaldo Vainfás, ed., *Historia e sexualidade no Brasil* (Rio de Janeiro: Graal, 1986); and Lana Lage da Gama Lima, ed., *Mulheres, adulteros e padres. História e moral na sociedade brasileira* (Rio de Janeiro: Dois Pontos Editôra, 1987). Recent research by U.S.-based historians of Latin America is found in Asunción Lavrin, ed., *Sexuality and Marriage in Colonial Latin America* (Lincoln: University of Nebraska Press, 1989).

3. Maria Odila Leite da Silva Dias, *Quotidiano e poder em São Paulo no século XIX: Ana Gertrudes de Jesús* (São Paulo: Editora Brasiliense, 1984), pp. 11–82.

4. See Sandra Lauderdale Graham's excellent study, *House and Street. The Domestic World of Servants and Masters in Nineteenth-Century Rio de Janeiro* (Cambridge: Cambridge University Press, 1988).

5. Mary Karasch, "Black Worlds in the Tropics. Gilberto Freyre and the Women of Color in Brazil," *Proceedings of the Pacific Coast Council on Latin American Studies* 3 (1974): 25–27; and Graham, *House and Street*, pp. 59–88. For the differences in the lives of free and slave women on nineteenth-century coffee plantations in the Paraíba River valley, see Stanley J. Stein, *Vassouras: A Brazilian Coffee County, 1850–1900* (Cambridge, Mass.: Harvard University Press, 1957), pp. 150–160. In *Mulher e escrava. Uma introdução ao estudo da mulher negra no Brasil* (Petrópolis: Vozes, 1988), Sonia Maria Giacomini, who emphasized the privations suffered by slave women, also analyzes relations between slave and mistress (pp. 73–86). Robert Conrad's documentary collection, *Children of God's Fire. A Documentary History of Black Slavery in Brazil* (Princeton: Princeton University Press, 1983), contains graphic depictions of the exploitation and sufferings of slavery. For slavery in Rio see Mary Karasch's comprehensive study, *Slave Life in Rio de Janeiro, 1808–1850* (Princeton: Princeton University Press, 1987).

6. Robert Walsh, *Notices of Brazil in 1828 and 1829*, 2 vols. (London: Frederick Westley and A. H. Davis, 1830), 2:28.

7. See Tristão de Alencar Araipe, *Código Civil Brazileiro, ou leis civis do Brazil dispostas por ordem de materias em seu estado actual* (Rio de Janeiro: Laemmert, 1885). The Philippine Code, a complex and unwieldy corpus whose structure makes systematic study difficult, rarely mentions women.

8. Maria Dundas Graham [Lady Maria Calcott], *Journal of a Voyage to Brazil and Residence There during Part of the Years 1821, 1822, 1823* (Reprint. New York: Praeger, 1969), p. 305.

9. Walsh, *Notices of Brazil in 1828 and 1829*, 1:153.

10. John Codman, *Ten Months in Brazil, with Incidents of Voyages and Travels, Description of Scenery and Character, Notices of Commerce and Production, Etc.* (Boston: Lee and Shepard, 1867), p. 172.

11. Linda Lewin, *Politics and Parentela in Paraíba. A Case Study of Family-based Oligarchy in Brazil* (Princeton: Princeton University Press, 1987), pp. 184–88.

12. See Araipe, *Código Civil Brazileiro*. Muriel Smith Nazzari's carefully researched doctoral dissertation, "Women, the Family and Property: The Decline of the Dowry in São Paulo, Brazil (1600–1870)" (Ph.D. diss., Yale University, 1986), traces changes in the practice of dowry in São Paulo, where it declined as the region developed a strong market economy and business and the family became separate. In "Dowries and Wills: A View of Women's Socioeconomic Role in Colonial Guadalajara and Puebla, 1640–1790," *Hispanic American Historical Review* 59 (May 1979): 280–304, Asunción Lavrin and Edith Couturier analyze wills and dowries of Hispanic urban women in colonial Mexico, demonstrating how this information can be used to delineate aspects of women's world.

13. Antonio Cândido, "The Brazilian Family," in *Brazil: Portrait of Half a Continent*, ed. T. Lynn Smith and Alexander Marchant, pp. 291–311 (New York: Dryden Press, 1951), provides a concise though not recent survey of the family. Marriage and cohabitation in colonial society, primarily among the upper strata, are analyzed by Maria Beatriz Nizza da Silva, *Sistema de casamento no Brasil colonial* (São Paulo: T. A. Queroz/EDUSP, 1984), while a number of issues concerning the colonial family and white women's roles are raised by A. J. R. Russell-Wood, "Female and Family in the Economy and Society of Colonial Brazil," in *Latin American Women: Historical Perspectives*, ed. Asunción

Lavrin, pp. 60–100 (Westport, Conn.: Greenwood Press, 1978). See also Donald Ramos, "Marriage and the Family in Colonial Vila Rica," *Hispanic American Historical Review* 55 (May 1975): 200–225, and Ramos, "City and Country: The Family in Minas Gerais, 1804–1838," *Journal of Family History* 3 (Winter 1978): 361–75; Maria Luiza Marcílio, *La Ville de São Paulo. Peuplement et Population, 1750–1850* (Rouen: Université de Rouen, 1972); Katia M. de Queiros Mattoso, *Família e sociedade na Bahia do século XIX* (São Paulo: Corrupio, 1988); Angela Mendes de Almeida, ed., *Pensando a família no Brasil. Da colonia a modernidade* (Rio de Janeiro: Espação e Tempo, 1987); Eni de Mesquita Samara, *A família brasileira* (São Paulo: Editora Brasiliense, 1983); and Elizabeth Ann Kuznesof, "The Role of the Female-Headed Household in Brazilian Modernization: São Paulo, 1765–1836," *Journal of Social History* 13 (Summer 1980): 589–613. The history of an elite family in the modernizing south-central section of Brazil is given by Darrell E. Levi, *The Prados of São Paulo, Brazil: An Elite Family and Social Change, 1840–1930* (Athens: University of Georgia Press, 1987); while Linda Lewin's study of the extended family and its public role in Brazil, *Politics and Parentela in Paraíba*, focuses on the Northeast, analyzing the rise and fall of an oligarchy dominating political life in Paraíba in the late nineteenth and early twentieth centuries. Maria Suely Kofes de Almeida, Antonio Augusto Arantes, Carlos Rodrigues Brandão, Mariza Corrêa, Bela Feldman-Bianco, Verena Stolche, and Alba Zalvar, *Colcha de retalhos. Estudos sobre a família no Brasil* (São Paulo: Editôra Brasiliense, 1982), a collection of anthropological essays on the contemporary family, demonstrates the diversity of families still found in Brazil; this volume also contains a perceptive, historically oriented essay by Mariza Corrêa on the patriarchal family, "Repensando a família patriarcal brasileira," pp. 13–38.

14. For general studies of the empire see Sérgio Buarque de Hollanda, ed., *História geral da civilização brasileira*, vols. 2–7: *O Brasil monárquico* (São Paulo: Difusão Européia do Livro, 1962–72); Manoel de Oliveira Lima, *O Império Brasileiro (1821–1889)*, 4th ed. (São Paulo: Edições Melhoramentos, 1962); João Camillo de Oliveira Torres, *A democracia coroada. Teoria política do Império do Brasil*, 2d ed. (Petrópolis: Vozes, 1964).

15. Johann B. von Spix and Karl F. P. von Martius, *Travels in Brazil in the Years 1817–1820*, 2 vols., trans. H. E. Lloyd (London: Longman, Hurst, Rees, Orme, Brown and Green, 1824), 1:159.

16. James C. Fletcher and Daniel Parish Kidder, *Brazil and the Brazilians Portrayed in Historical and Descriptive Sketches*, 7th ed. (Boston: Little, Brown, 1867), pp. 163–70. Seeking to improve sanitation and health, medical reformers in nineteenth-century Brazil advocated changes in home construction and in women's activities, stressing the need to admit air and light to closed colonial homes built to protect inhabitants from "dangerous airs." Upper-class women should leave their small, dark, damp bedrooms and alcoves and get some air and exercise; thus illness might be prevented and their children's health improved. Marriages between women aged eighteen or twenty to men in their mid-twenties, rather than between young girls and old men, would also produce better babies. The nineteenth-century hygienists defended physical education designed to promote sound bodies, replacing flaccid, sickly colonials. But age and sex determined the proper exercises. While some doctors advised boys to jump, race, swim, or ride horses, they considered singing, recitation, and playing the piano sufficient to develop female respiratory organs. However, both sexes might dance. See Jurandir Freire Costa, *Ordem médica e norma familiar*, 2d ed. (Rio de Janeiro: Graal, 1983), pp. 110–23, 184–87, 219–26.

17. Louis Agassiz and Elizabeth C. Agassiz, *A Journey in Brazil* (Boston: Ticknor and Fields, 1868), pp. 270, 479, 481.

18. Herbert H. Smith, *Brazil. The Amazons and the Coast* (New York: Charles Scribner's Sons, 1879), pp. 50, 122–123.

19. Ibid., pp. 467, 501.

20. William Scully, *Brazil. Its Provinces and Chief Cities* (London: Murray, 1866), p. 11.

21. Luccock, *Notes on Rio de Janeiro*, p. 111; Richard F. Burton, *The Highlands of Brazil, with a Full Account of the Gold and Diamond Mines*, 2 vols. (London: Tinsley Brothers, 1869), 1:398–99; Graham, *Journal of a Voyage to Brazil*, pp. 135–36, 244; Scully, *Brazil*, pp. 56, 155; John Mawe, *Travels in the Interior of Brazil, Particularly in the Gold and Diamond Districts of that Country* (Philadelphia: M. Carey, 1816), pp. 88–89.

22. Christopher Columbus Andrews, *Brazil. Its Condition and Prospects* (New York: D. Appleton, 1887), pp. 32–33; Gilberto Amado, *História da minha infancia* (Rio de Janeiro: José Olympio, 1954), p. 40; João Chagas, *De bond. Alguns aspectos da civilisação brazileira* (Lisbon: Livraria Moderna, 1897), pp. 89–90; Smith, *Brazil. The Amazons and the Coast*, p. 50.

23. Andrews, *Brazil. Conditions and Prospects*, pp. 39–40; Amado, *História da minha infancia*, p. 40; Antonio Corrêa de Sousa Costa, *Qual a alimentação de que usa a classe pobre do Rio de Janeiro e sua influencia sobre a mesma classe* (Rio de Janeiro: Perseverança, 1865), p. 32; *Revista Typographica* (Rio de Janeiro), May 26, 1888, p. 5; Chagas, *De bond*, p. 156.

24. The definition and historical treatment of the middle class is a problem that extends well beyond the boundaries of Brazilian studies, but it is particularly marked for Brazil, since the urban middle classes have been far less studied than the elite or even urban labor. Actual historical studies, like those by Decio Saes, *Classe média e política na Primeira República Brasileira (1889–1930)* (Petrópolis: Vozes, 1975); or Nícia Villela Luz, "O papel das classes médias no movimento republicano," *Revista de História* 57 (January–March 1964): 13–27, who concludes that the middle class lacked decisive political strength as well as social and ideological cohesion at the time of the fall of the empire in 1889, are rare. Such works as Nelson Werneck Sodré, *Formação histórica do Brasil* (São Paulo: Editôra Brasiliense, 1964); Virginio Santa Rosa, *Que foi o tenentismo* (Rio de Janeiro: Civilização Brasileira, 1964); and Hélio Jaguaribe, *Desenvolvimento econômico e político* (Rio de Janeiro: Paz e Terra, 1969), view the urban middle classes as major historical opponents of regional oligarchies and elite policies.

In *Estratificação social no Brasil. Suas origens históricas e suas relações com a organização política do país* (São Paulo: Difusão Européia do Livro, 1965), João Camillo de Oliveira Torres attempts a historical survey of social classes in Brazil, emphasizing political organization. A brief description of social structure during the monarchy is found in Leoncio Basbaum, *História sincera da República*, vol. 1: *Das origens ate 1889*, 2d ed. (São Paulo: Edições LB, 1962), pp. 200–227. In *A República Velha (Instituições e classes sociais)* (São Paulo: Difusão Européia do Livro, 1970), pp. 145–245, Edgard Carone discusses social classes and class actions at the end of the empire and through the Old Republic. The accounts of perceptive foreigners like Smith, *Brazil. The Amazons and the Coast*, are most useful in understanding occupational and social distinctions. The variety of such marginals as beggars, thieves, and swindlers is described in Alexandre José de Mello Filho, *Factos e memórias* (Rio de Janeiro: Garnier, 1903), pp. 1–93; and Paulo Barreto [João do Rio, pseud.], *A alma encantadora das ruas* (Rio de Janeiro: Garnier, 1908), pp. 35–44; 193–210. For an investigation into perceived relative status and prestige of occupations in Brazil in the mid-twentieth century see Bertram Hutchins, "The Social Grading of Occupations in Brazil," *British Journal of Sociology* 8 (June 1957): 176–189.

25. Brazil, Directoria Geral de Estatística, *Recenseamento da população do Império do Brazil a que se procedeu no dia 1 de agosto de 1872*, 21 vols. in 22 (Rio de Janeiro: Leuzinger, 1873–1876), Quadros gerais, 21:1; Município Neutro, 21:61; São Paulo, 19:427–29; Bahia, 3:508–10; Pernambuco, 13:214–15; Pará, 10:211–12; São Pedro do Rio Grande do Sul, 17:205–6.

26. Thomas Ewbank, *Life in Brazil; or, a Journal of a Visit to the Land of the Cocoa and the Palm* (New York: Harper and Brothers, 1856), pp. 74–75, 92–94, 113–15; Walsh, *Notices of Brazil in 1828 and 1829*, 1:137–138, 391–92, 501–2; 2:18–19; Daniel P. Kidder, *Sketches of Residence and Travel in Brazil*, 2 vols. (Philadelphia: Sorin and Ball, 1848), 1:125–26; Graham, *Journal of a Voyage to Brazil*, pp. 161–167; Luccock, *Notes on Rio de Janeiro*, p. 15; Mary C. Karasch, *Slave Life in Rio de Janeiro, 1808–1850* (Princeton: Princeton University Press, 1987), pp. 206–7; Carl N. Degler, *Neither Black nor White. Slavery and Race Relations in Brazil and the United States* (New York: Macmillan, 1971), p. 70.

27. Brazil, *Recenseamento da população . . . 1872*, Quadros gerais, 19:5.

28. Brazil, *Recenseamento da população . . . 1872*, Município Neutro, 21:61; Brazil, Directoria Geral de Estatística, *Recenseamento do Brazil realizado em 1 de setembro de 1920*, 5 vols. in 18 (Rio de Janeiro: Typ. da Estatística, 1922–1930), 2:514.

29. Brazil, *Recenseamento da população . . . 1872*, Quadros gerais, 19:1–2, 61.

30. Luccock, *Notes on Rio de Janeiro*, p. 111.

31. Antonio Muniz de Souza, *Viagens e observações de hum brasileiro, que, desejando ser util á sua patria, se dedicou a estudar os usos e costumes de seos patricios, e os tres reinos de natureza, em varios lugares e sertões do Brasil, offerecidas á nação brasileira* (Rio de Janeiro: Typ. Americana de I. P. da Costa, 1834), p. 64. Professor Mary Karasch of Oakland University kindly called my attention to this account.

32. Luis Edmundo da Costa, *O Rio de Janeiro no tempo dos Vice-Reis*, 3d ed., 2 vols. (Rio de Janeiro: Editôra Aurora, 1951), 1:261.

> Menina que sabe muito
> É menina atrapalhada,
> Para ser mãe de família
> Saiba pouco ou saiba nada.

33. Charles Expilly, *Mulheres e costumes do Brasil*, trans. Gastão Penalva (São Paulo: Companhia Nacional do Livro, 1935), p. 401.

34. Hermann Burmeister, *Viagem ão Brasil através das provincias do Rio de Janeiro e Minas Gerais visando especialmente a historia natural dos distritos auri-diamantíferros*, trans. Manoel Salvaterra and Hubert Schoenfeld (São Paulo: Livraria Martins, 1952), p. 64.

35. Fletcher and Kidder, *Brazil and the Brazilians*, p. 164.

36. Agassiz and Agassiz, *A Journey in Brazil*, pp. 478–79.

37. Joaquim Manuel de Macedo, *A moreninha*, 13th ed. (São Paulo: Edições Melhoramentos, 1967), p. 100. Professor Muriel Nazzari of Indiana University kindly called my attention to this aspect of the novel.

38. Lígia Lemos, "Pioneiras do intelectualismo feminino no Brasil," *Formação* (November 1947): 51–52; Ivan Lins, *História do positivismo no Brasil* (São Paulo: Companhia Editôra Nacional, 1967), pp. 19–26; Heleith Iara Bongiovani Saffioti, *A mulher na sociedade de classes. Mito e realidade* (São Paulo: Quatro Artes, 1969), p. 270; Tancredo Moraes, *Pela emancipação integral da mulher* (Rio de Janeiro: Editôra Pongetti, 1971), pp. 88–90; Ignez Sabino, *Mulheres illustres do Brazil* (Rio de Janeiro: Garnier, [1889]), pp. 171–77.

Chapter 1. Pioneers for Women's Rights

1. For discussions of social and economic changes during the last decades of the empire see Richard Graham, *Britain and the Onset of Modernization in Brazil, 1850–1914* (Cambridge: Cambridge University Press, 1968), pp. 23–50; Octavio Ianni, *Industrialização e desenvolvimento social no Brasil* (Rio de Janeiro: Civilização Brasileira, 1963), pp. 75–114; Emília Viotti da Costa, *Da senzala à colônia* (São Paulo: Difusão Européia do Livro, 1966), pp. 428–41.

2. See such general works on Brazilian urban history as Richard M. Morse, *From Community to Metropolis. A Biography of São Paulo* (Gainesville: University of Florida Press, 1958); and Morse, "Brazil's Urban Development: Colony and Empire," in *From Colony to Nation: Essays on the Independence of Brazil*, ed. A. J. R. Russell-Wood, pp. 155–81 (Baltimore: Johns Hopkins University Press, 1975); Pedro Pinchas Geiger, *Evolução da rêde urbana brasileira* (Rio de Janeiro: Instituto Nacional de Estudos Pedagógicos, Ministério da Educação e Cultura, 1963); Paul Singer, *Desenvolvimento económico e evolução urbana (Analise da evolução económica de São Paulo, Blumenau, Pôrto Alegre, Belo Horizonte e Recife* (São Paulo: Companhia Editôra Nacional, 1968); Michael L. Conniff, Melvin K. Hendrix, and Stephen Nohlgren, "Brazil," in *The Urban Development of Latin America, 1750–1920*, ed. Richard M. Morse, pp. 36–52 (Stanford: Stanford University Press, 1971).

3. Christopher Columbus Andrews, *Brazil. Its Condition and Prospects* (New York: D. Appleton, 1887), p. 22; Herbert H. Smith, *Brazil. The Amazons and the Coast* (New York: Charles Scribner's Sons, 1879), pp. 453, 457.

4. James C. Fletcher and Daniel Parish Kidder, *Brazil and the Brazilians Portrayed in Historical and Descriptive Sketches*, 7th ed. (Boston: Little, Brown, 1867), pp. 30–31.

5. Andrews, *Brazil. Conditions and Prospects*, pp. 28–29.

6. Fletcher and Kidder, *Brazil and the Brazilians*, pp. 22–36; Andrews, *Brazil. Conditions and Prospects*, pp. 22–23; Smith, *Brazil. The Amazons and the Coast*, pp. 450–60; William Scully, *Brazil. Its Provinces and Chief Cities* (London: Murray, 1866), pp. 151–57; William Hadfield, *Brazil and the River Plate in 1868. Showing the Progress of Those Countries since His Former Visit in 1853* (London: Bates, Hendy, 1869), pp. 31–37; Frank Vincent, *Around and about South America. Twenty Months of Quest and Query*, 5th ed. (New York: D. Appleton, 1895), pp. 215, 225.

7. Alberto Ribeiro Lamengo, *O homem e a Guanabara* (Rio de Janeiro: Conselho Nacional de Geografia, 1948), pp. 322–23; Adolfo Morales de los Rios Filho, *O Rio de Janeiro Imperial* (Rio de Janeiro: A Noite, 1946), pp. 83–95; Hadfield, *Brazil and the River Plate in 1868*, pp. 34–37; Geiger, *Evolução da rede urbana brasileira*, p. 151; Antonio Martins de Azevedo Pimentel, *Subsídios para o estudo de hygiene do Rio de Janeiro* (Rio de Janeiro: Carlos Gaspar da Silva, 1890), pp. 76–77, 226–36; Ferreira da Rosa, *Rio de Janeiro. Notícia histórica e descritiva da Capital do Brasil* (Rio de Janeiro: Typ. do Annuario do Brasil, 1924), p. 7; Alfred Agache, *Cidade do Rio de Janeiro. Extensão, remodelação, embellezamento* (Paris: Foyer Brésilien, 1930), pp. 64–65. See also Charles J. Dunlop, *Subsídios para a história do Rio de Janeiro* (Rio de Janeiro: Rio Antigo, 1957).

8. Fletcher and Kidder, *Brazil and the Brazilians*, p. 23.

9. Andrews, *Brazil. Conditions and Prospects*, p. 20; Smith, *Brazil. The Amazons and the Coast*, pp. 459–60.

10. *Gazeta dos Operarios* (Rio de Janeiro), Dec. 20, 1875, p. 1; Dec. 21, 1875, p. 1; *Revista Typographica* (Rio de Janeiro), March 31, 1882, p. 2; Azevedo Pimental, *Subsídios para o estudo de hygiene*, p. 189; Antonio Corrêa de Sousa Costa, *Qual a alimentação de que usa a classe pobre do Rio de Janeiro e sua influencia sobre a mesma classe* (Rio de Janeiro: Perseverança, 1865), p. 31; Américo de Castro to D. Pedro II, Rio de Janeiro, Dec. 18, 1884, Arquivo Geral da Cidade do Rio de Janeiro, 40-4-45; *Gazeta da Tarde* (Rio de Janeiro), Feb. 21, 1884, p. 21.

11. For education under the empire see the multivolumed studies by Primitivo Moacyr, *A instrução e as provincias*, 3 vols. (São Paulo: Companhia Editôra Nacional, 1939–40), and *A instrução e o império*, 3 vols. (São Paulo: Companhia Editôra Nacional, 1938). An extensive study of women's education, but just for São Paulo, is Leda Maria Pereira Rodrigues, *A instrução feminina em São Paulo. Subsídios para sua história até a proclamação da República* (São Paulo: Faculdade de Filosofia "Sedes Sapientine," 1962).

12. Rui Barbosa, *Reforma do ensino primario e varias instituições complimentares da instru-ção pública.* Vol. 10, tomo 1 of *Obras completas de Rui Barbosa* (Rio de Janeiro: Ministério da Educação e Saude, 1947), pp. 9–11.

13. Brazil, Ministério do Império, *Relatório da Inspectoria Geral da instrucção primaria e secundaria do Municipio da Corte apresentado em 18 de abril de 1874 ao illm. e exm. sr. conselheiro João Alfredo Corrêa de Oliveira ministro e secretario d'estado dos negocios do império pelo consel-heiro dr. Antonio Felix Martins* (Rio de Janeiro: Cinco de Março, 1874), tables 33, 36, and 37.

14. Heleith Iara Bongiovani Saffioti, *A mulher na sociedade de classes, Mito e realidade* (São Paulo: Quarto Artes, 1969), pp. 202–12; Reynaldo Kuntz Bush, *O ensino normal em São Paulo* (São Paulo: Livraria Record, 1935), pp. 41–43; Rodrigues, *A instrução feminina em São Paulo,* pp. 151–62.

15. Antonio da Silva Jardim, Secretary of the Normal School, to the President of the Province of São Paulo, São Paulo, April 25, 1881, Arquivo do Estado de São Paulo, Escola Normal de São Paulo, Ordem 5130, Lata 2; São Paulo, *Relatorio com que o exm. sr. dr. João Baptista Pereira presidente da provincia de S. Paulo passou a administração ao 2° vice presidente exm. sr. Barão de Tres Rios* (Santos: "Diario de Santos," 1879), pp. 25–27; São Paulo, *Relatorio apresentado à assembléa legislativa provincial de S. Paulo pelo presidente da provincia Laurindo Abelardo de Brito no dia 13 de janeiro de 1881* (Santos: "Diario de Santos," 1881), pp. 21–23; Relatorio de José E. C. de Sá e Benevides, Interim Director of the Escola Normal, to Barão de Parnaíba, President of the Province of São Paulo, São Paulo, Oct. 26, 1886; and Sá e Benevides to Barão de Parnaíba, São Paulo, March 6, 1887, Arquivo do Estado de São Paulo, Escola Normal de São Paulo, Ordem 5131, Lata 3; São Paulo, *Relatorio apresentado ao sr. dr. presidente do estado de São Paulo pelo dr. Cesario Motta Junior secretario d'estado dos negocios do interior em 28 de marco de 1894* (São Paulo: Vanordem, 1894), Relatório of Director of the Escola Normal, Dec. 30, 1893, pp. 24–25; Leonor Maria Tanuri, *O ensimo normal no estado de São Paulo, 1890–1930* (São Paulo: Universidade de São Paulo, 1979), pp. 13–43.

16. Brazil, Ministério do Império, *Relatorio da Inspectoria Geral da instrucção primaria e secundaria, 1874,* p. 39. See also Mauricio Lamberg, *O Brazil,* trans. Luiz de Castro (Rio de Janeiro: Nunes, 1896), pp. 59–61; and Ernest Michel, *A travers l'hemisphere sud on mon second voyage autour du monde. Portugal, Sénégal, Brésil, Uruguay, République Argentine, Chile, Pérou* (Paris: Libraire Victor Palmé, 1887), pp. 44–45.

17. Affonso A. de Freitas, *A imprensa périodica de São Paulo desde seus primoridos em 1823 até 1914* (São Paulo: "Diario Official," 1915), p. 95; Memorial of D. Anna Joaquina da Silva Cajueiro to Marquês de Olinda, Rio de Janeiro, Nov. 26, 1861, Instituto Histórico e Geográfico Brasileiro, Marquês de Olinda Collection, L. 26, D. 53.

18. *O Domingo* (Rio de Janeiro), June 14, 1874, p. 6.

19. Felix Ferreira, *A educação da mulher. Notas collegidas de varios autores* (Rio de Janeiro: Hildebrandt, 1881), p. x.

20. *O Sexo Feminino* (Campanha, M.G., until September 1874; thereafter Rio de Janeiro), Sept. 7, 1873, p. 3; Sept. 27, 1873, p. 4; Nov. 8, 1873, p. 4; March 12, 1874, p. 4; April 11, 1874, p. 3; Aug. 18, 1874, p. 4; July 29, 1875, p. 2.

21. For an interesting and insightful account of Brazil's patriarchal families and the difficulties of teaching their children, see the letters of Ina von Binzer, *Os meus romanos. Alegrias e tristezas de uma educadora alemã no Brasil,* trans. Alice Rossi and Luisita da Gama Cerqueira (Rio de Janeiro: Paz e Terra, 1980), a German schoolteacher who came to Brazil in 1881 under contract to a *fazendeiro* in the province of Rio de Janeiro to instruct his seven children; she later worked in a private secondary school in Rio de Janeiro and then taught in homes once more.

22. Alice Brandt, *The Diary of "Helena Morley,"* trans. Elizabeth Bishop (New York: Ecco Press, 1957), pp. 13–14, 55–56, 93–94.

23. In *A história da imprensa no Brasil* (Rio de Janeiro: Civilização Brasileira, 1966), Nelson Werneck Sodré presents a wealth of detail on the role of the press in Brazil.

24. *O Sexo Feminino,* Sept. 27, 1873, p. 1; Nov. 8, 1873, p. 2.

25. *O Jornal das Senhoras* (Rio de Janeiro), Jan. 1, 1852, p. 1; Jan. 11, 1852, pp. 12, 14; Feb. 8, 1852, p. 42; César H. Guerrero, *Mujeres de Sarmiento* (Buenos Aires: Artes Gráficas Bartolomé U. Chiesivo, 1960), p. 79; Innocêncio Francisco da Silva, *Diccionario bibliographico portuguez,* 22 vols. (Lisbon: Imprensa Nacional, 1858–1923), 10:144; 11:275. See also Jim Levy, *Juana Manso: Argentine Feminist.* Occasional Paper no. 1 (Bundoora: La Trobe University, Institute of Latin American Studies, 1977).

26. Luccock, *Notes on Rio de Janeiro,* p. 114.

27. *O Jornal das Senhoras,* Jan. 1, 1852, p. 5; Jan. 11, 1852, p. 12.

28. Ibid., Jan. 11, 1852, pp. 12–13.

29. Ibid., Jan. 11, 1852, pp. 12, 14.

30. Ibid., Jan. 1, 1852, p. 6; Jan. 11, 1852, pp. 13–14.

31. Ibid., Jan. 1, 1852, pp. 1, 2; Jan. 11, 1852, p. 14; Feb. 8, 1852, p. 44.

32. Ibid., July 4, 1852, p. 1; Innocêncio Francisco da Silva, *Diccionario bibliographico portuguez,* 7:450; Augusto Victorino Alves Sacramento Blake, *Diccionario bibliographico brazileiro,* 7 vols. (Rio de Janeiro: Imprensa Nacional, 1883–1902), 2:182–86; 7:386–87; First Secretary of Conservatório Dramático Brasileiro to Violante Atabalipa de Bivar e Vellasco, Rio de Janeiro, July 3, 1850, Biblioteca Nacional, Secção de Manuscritos, I. 1, 725; Olímio Barros Vidal, *Precursoras brasileiras* (Rio de Janeiro: A Noite, 1955), pp. 121–31.

Following a family crisis and the fall of the Argentine dictator Juan Manuel de Rosas in 1852, Joana Manso and her two daughters returned to Argentina, where she achieved a distinguished but difficult career as an educator and follower of the educational principles of Domingo Faustino Sarmiento until her death in 1875. In 1854 she had edited a short-lived periodical for women, *Album de Senoritas.* See Guerrero, *Mujeres de Sarmiento,* pp. 81–101; Levy, *Juana Manso: Argentine Feminist.*

33. *O Jornal das Senhoras,* Sept. 19, 1852, pp. 89–90; Oct. 3, 1852, pp. 106–7; June 5, 1853, p. 177; Barros Vidal, *Precursoras brasileiras,* p. 131.

34. *O Bello Sexo* (Rio de Janeiro), Aug. 21, 1862, pp. 1–2; Sept. 12, 1862, p. 1.

35. Brazil, Directoria Geral de Estatística, *Recenseamento do Brazil realizado em 1 de setembro de 1920,* 5 vols. in 18 (Rio de Janeiro: Typ. da Estatística, 1922–30), vol. 4, pt. 4, pp. xii, xvi.

36. *O Sexo Feminino,* Dec. 27, 1873, p. 4; Jan. 28, 1874, p. 4; April 25, 1874, p. 2; *O Domingo,* Jan. 18, 1874, p. 2; April 19, 1874, p. 2.

37. *Leque* (São Paulo), Jan. 16, 1887, p. 1; *A Violeta* (São Paulo), June 17, 1887, p. 1.

38. *O Sexo Feminino,* Sept. 7, 1873, p. 1; Sept. 14, 1873, p. 2; Sept. 20, 1873, p. 1; Oct. 25, 1873, pp. 1–2.

39. Ibid., Sept. 14, 1873, p. 2.

40. Ibid., Nov. 8, 1873, p. 2; Nov. 29, 1873, p. 2; Jan. 14, 1874, p. 2; July 22, 1875, p. 2; July 29, 1875, p. 2; Sept. 5, 1875, pp. 1–2; Oct. 10, 1875, p. 3; Oct. 31, 1875, pp. 1–2; Dec. 12, 1875, p. 1.

41. Ibid., Sept. 7, 1873, p. 1; Sept. 20, 1873, p. 1; Oct. 18, 1873, p. 2; Nov. 8, 1873, p. 4; April 7, 1874, p. 1; May 2, 1874, p. 2; July 18, 1874, p. 4; July 22, 1875, p. 2; Aug. 29, 1875, p. 3.

42. *O Domingo,* Dec. 14, 1873, p. 3; Dec. 21, 1873, p. 3; Dec. 28, 1873, p. 3; Jan. 18, 1874, p. 3; *Echo das Damas* (Rio de Janeiro), April 18, 1879, p. 1.

43. *O Sexo Feminino*, Nov. 15, 1873, pp. 2–3; July 29, 1875, p. 3; Aug. 14, 1875, p. 2; Aug. 29, 1875, p. 3.

44. Ibid., Sept. 7, 1874, p. 1; July 22, 1875, p. 1.

45. Brazil, Directoria Geral de Estatística, *Recenseamento da população do Império do Brazil a que se procedeu no dia 1 de agosto de 1872*, 22 vols. (Rio de Janeiro: Leuzinger, 1873–76), Minas Gerais, 9:1070.

46. *O Sexo Feminino*, Nov. 15, 1873, p. 4; Aug. 8, 1875, p. 1; Nov. 21, 1875, p. 2.

47. *O Sexo Feminino*, April 2, 1876, p. 1; *Primaveira* (Rio de Janeiro), Aug. 29, 1880, p. 1; *O Quinze de Novembro do Sexo Feminino* (Rio de Janeiro), Dec. 15, 1889, pp. 3–4.

48. Brazil, *Recenseamento do Brazil . . . 1920*, vol. 4, pt. 1, p. x; pt. 4, p. xiii.

49. *O Domingo*, March 22, 1874, p. 1; Barros Vidal, *Precursoras brasileiras*, p. 138.

50. Barbara J. Berg argues this position, perhaps to excess, in *The Remembered Gate: Origins of American Feminism. The Woman and the City, 1800–1860* (New York: Oxford University Press, 1978).

51. *O Bello Sexo*, Sept. 7, 1862, pp. 2–4.

52. Ibid., Aug. 21, 1862, p. 2; Sept. 7, 1862, p. 2.

53. A pioneering study of voluntary associations in Brazil is provided by Michael L. Conniff, "Voluntary Associations in Rio, 1870–1945. A New Approach to Urban Social Dynamics," *Journal of Interamerican Studies and World Affairs* 17 (February 1975): 64–81.

54. The two major studies of the abolition of slavery in Brazil are Robert Conrad, *The Destruction of Brazilian Slavery, 1850–1888* (Berkeley: University of California Press, 1972); and Robert Brent Toplin, *The Abolition of Slavery in Brazil* (New York: Atheneum, 1971). Unlike Richard Graham, in his earlier perceptive essay, "Causes for the Abolition of Negro Slavery in Brazil: An Interpretive Essay," *Hispanic American Historical Review* 46 (May 1966): 123–37, Conrad argues that until 1886 *paulista* coffee planters were strong defenders, not opponents, of slavery. Emília Viotti da Costa's thorough and suggestive *Da senzala à colônia* (São Paulo: Difusão Européia do Livro, 1966), which studies slavery, the coffee economy, and abolition, deals extensively with São Paulo. The final years of slavery and abolition in the Northeast are analyzed by Peter L. Eisenberg, "Abolishing Slavery: The Process on Pernambuco's Sugar Plantations," *Hispanic American Historical Review* 52 (November 1972): 580–97; and J. H. Galloway, "The Last Years of Slavery on the Sugar Plantations of Northeastern Brazil," *Hispanic American Historical Review* 51 (November 1971): 586–605. For the abolition movement in the city of Rio de Janeiro, see Rebecca Baird Bergstresser, "The Movement for the Abolition of Slavery in Rio de Janeiro, Brazil, 1880–1889" (Ph.D. diss., Stanford University, 1973); for the Campos region of the province of Rio de Janeiro see Cleveland Donald, Jr., "Slave Resistance and Abolitionism in Brazil: The Campista Case, 1879–1888," *Luso-Brazilian Review* 13 (Winter 1976): 182–93. Also of value is the older account by Evaristo de Moraes, *A campanha abolicionista (1879–1888)* (Rio de Janeiro: Freitas Bastos, 1924). Carolina Nabuco has written a biography of her father, the celebrated abolitionist and patrician planter from Pernambuco, *The Life of Joaquim Nabuco*, trans. Ronald Hilton (Stanford: Stanford University Press, 1950). Recent articles on the aftermath of abolition are found in *The Abolition of Slavery and the Aftermath of Emancipation in Brazil* (Durham, N.C.: Duke University Press, 1988).

55. Brazil, *Recenseamento da população do Império do Brazil . . . 1872*, Quadros gerais, 19:1; Perdigão Malheiro, *A escravidão no Brasil*, 3d ed. (Petrópolis: Vozes, 1976), 2:150–51. While the 1819 estimate is based on fairly reliable church data, the 1864 figures are only rough estimates. Even the later government figures present problems, for numbers of slaves could be exaggerated or undercounted depending on particular political and economic circumstances.

The relative importance of the interregional slave trade in supplying the labor needs of the expanding coffee economy is open to debate. Herbert S. Klein questions the degree to which this traffic ever reached high levels, especially after 1870, and suggests that needed fieldhands were supplied by declining areas within the south-central provinces. See his "The Internal Slave Trade in Nineteenth-Century Brazil: A Study of Slave Importations into Rio de Janeiro in 1852," *Hispanic American Historical Review* 51 (November 1971): 580–83.

56. Brazil, Ministério da Agricultura, *Relatório*, May 14, 1888, p. 24; Brazil, *Recenseamento do Brazil . . . 1920*, 4:ix.

57. Ignez Sabino, *Mulheres illustres do Brazil* (Rio de Janeiro: Garnier, [1899]), pp. 251–57; *Jornal do Comércio* (Rio de Janeiro), Oct. 5, 1880, p. 2; *Gazeta da Tarde* (Rio de Janeiro), Nov. 3, 1880, p. 2; Moraes, *A campanha abolicionista*, p. 24; *A Mãi de Família* (Rio de Janeiro), March 15, 1884, p. 38.

58. Statutes of the Associação Protetora dos Escravos, *Arquivo: Boletim Histórico e Informativo* 1 (September–December 1980): 41–48; Charles Pradez, *Nouvelles études sur le Brésil* (Paris: Ernest Thorin, 1872), pp. 194–95, 203; Moraes, *A campanha abolicionista*, pp. 24, 37, 41; José Jacintho Ribeiro, *Chronologia paulista; ou Relação histórica dos factos mais importantes ocorridos em S. Paulo desde a chegada de Martim Affonso de Souza em S. Vicente até 1898*, 3 vols. (São Paulo: N.p. 1899–1901), vol. 2, pt. 1, p. 59; *Galeria nacional. Vultos proeminentes da história brasileira. 6 Fascículo* (Rio de Janeiro: Jornal do Brasil, 1933), pp. 562–63; Mello Barreto Filho and Hermeto Lima, *História da polícia do Rio de Janeiro. Aspectos da cidade e da vida carioca*, 3 vols. (Rio de Janeiro: A Noite, 1944), 2:148; Morse, *From Community to Metropolis*, p. 147; *Gazeta da Tarde*, Oct. 5, 1885, p. 1. See also Thereza Caiuby Crescenti, "Mulher e libertação dos escravos" (mimeo; paper presented to Segundo Simposio de História do Vale do Paraíba, Pindamonhangabe, July 19–24, 1976), which contains information on what different writers and sources have noted concerning women and abolition.

59. *Echo das Damas*, Feb. 6, 1886, p. 3; *O Sexo Feminino* (Rio de Janeiro), Nov. 7, 1875, pp. 2–3; *Voz da Verdade* (Rio de Janeiro), May 12, May 28, and June 25, 1885; Moraes, *A campanha abolicionista*, pp. 37, 230; Sacramento Blake, *Diccionario bibliographico brazileiro*, 6:225; *A Família* (Rio de Janeiro), special number 1889, p. 3; Dec. 31, 1889, p. 7.

60. Otelia Cromwell, *Lucretia Mott* (Cambridge, Mass.: Harvard University Press, 1958), pp. 47–49, 67–72; Alma Lutz, *Crusade For Freedom. Women of the Anti-Slavery Movement* (Boston: Beacon Press, 1968), pp. 21–22; Blanche Glassman Hersh, *The Slavery of Sex. Feminist-Abolitionists in America* (Urbana: University of Illinois Press, 1978), pp. 6–38. An 1851 photograph of the Executive Committee of the Philadelphia Anti-Slavery Society depicts five women and seven men (reproduced in Judith Papachristou, ed., *Women Together. A History in Documents of the Women's Movement in the United States*. A Ms. Book [New York: Alfred A. Knopf, 1976], p. 19).

Chapter 2. The Quest for Education, Employment, and Suffrage

1. Numerous works have described the political system of the Brazilian empire, ranging from the Marxist, such as Leoncio Basbaum, *História sincera da República*, vol. 2: *Das origens até 1889*, 2d ed. (São Paulo: Edições LB, 1962), to the monarchist, such as João Camillo de Oliveira Torres, *A democracia coroada. Teoria política do Império do Brasil*, 2d ed. (Petrópolis: Vozes, 1964). Like the older work, José Maria dos Santos, *A política geral do Brasil* (São Paulo: J. Magalhães, 1930), Oliveira Torres pictures the monarchy as a democracy preferable to its republican successor. Newer studies concentrating on particular aspects of imperial politics, particularly the elite, include Thomas Flory, "Judicial Politics in Nineteenth-Century Brazil," *Hispanic American Historical Review* 55 (November

1975): 664–92; Eul Soo Pang and Ron L. Seckinger, "The Mandarins of Imperial Brazil," *Comparative Studies in Society and History* 14 (March 1972): 215–44; and Roderick Barman and Jean Barman, "The Role of the Law Graduate in the Political Elite of Imperial Brazil," *Journal of Interamerican Studies and World Affairs* 18 (November 1976): 423–50. On the early decades of the empire see Roderick J. Barman, *Brazil: The Forging of a Nation* (Stanford: Stanford University Press, 1988). Among the most important treatments of local politics are Victor Nunes Leal, *Coronelismo, ensada e voto. O município e o regime representativo no Brasil (Da colônia à Primeira República)* (Rio de Janeiro: Forense, 1948); and Maria Isaura Pereira de Queiroz, *O mandonismo local na vida política brasileira* (São Paulo: Instituto de Estudos Brasileiros, 1969). Also of interest are Joseph L. Love, "Political Participation in Brazil, 1881–1969," *Luso-Brazilian Review* 7 (December 1970): 3–24, an analytical overview of political participation in Brazil; and Raymundo Faoro, *Os donos do poder. Formação do patronato político brasileiro* (Pôrto Alegre: Editôra Globo, 1958).

2. Works on Pedro II range from the antagonistic to the eulogistic, with the latter surpassing critical accounts of him, both as man and as emperor. Among the laudatory biographies are Mary Wilhelmine Williams, *Dom Pedro the Magnanimous. Second Emperor of Brazil* (Chapel Hill: University of North Carolina Press, 1937), a synthesis of imperial panegyrics; and the extensive study by Pedro Calmon, *História de D. Pedro II*, 4 vols. (Rio de Janeiro: José Olympio, 1975). In sharp contrast stand the writings of some of Pedro II's republican antagonists, such as Anfriso Fialho, *História da fundação da República* (Rio de Janeiro: Laemmert, 1891), pp. 17–22, 33–35. Few take the more balanced approach of republican Cristiano Benedito Ottoni in his *D. Pedro de Alcântara* (Rio de Janeiro: Typ. Jornal do Commercio, 1893), written shortly after the emperor's death; or Heitor Lyra, in his multivolume, highly favorable biography, *História de Dom Pedro II*, 3 vols. (São Paulo: Companhia Editôra Nacional, 1940).

3. The major statement on the abolition of slavery by Joaquim Nabuco is available in English: *Abolitionism. The Brazilian Antislavery Struggle*, trans. Robert Conrad (Urbana: University of Illinois Press, 1977).

4. Antonio de Almeida Oliveira, *Obra destinada a mostrar o estado em que se acha, e as reformas, que exige a instrucção publica no Brazil* (Maranhão: Typ. do Paiz, 1874), pp. 8–24, 466.

5. José Liberto Barroso, *A instrução publica no Brazil* (Rio de Janeiro: Garnier, 1867), pp. xvi–xvii.

6. Christopher Columbus Andrews, *Brazil. Its Condition and Prospects* (New York: D. Appleton, 1887), pp. 172–75.

7. Félix Ferreira, *A educação da mulher. Notas colligidas de varios autores* (Rio de Janeiro: Hildebrandt, 1881), pp. vii–xi.

8. Maria Beatriz Nizza da Silva, *Cultura no Brasil Colônia* (Petrópolis: Vozes, 1981), pp. 68–81.

9. Oliveira, *Obra destinada*, pp. 137–38, 443–66.

10. Barroso, *A instrução publica no Brazil*, p. xxix.

11. José Liberto Barroso, *Conferencias populares* (Rio de Janeiro: J. Villeneuve, 1876), 5:100–118.

12. Louis Agassiz and Elizabeth C. Agassiz, *A Journey in Brazil* (Boston: Ticknor and Fields, 1868), p. 480.

13. Félix Ferreira, *Noções da vida domestica, adaptadas, com accrescimos do original frances á instrucção do sexo feminino nas Escolas Brazileiras* (Rio de Janeiro: Dias da Silva Junior, 1879), p. vi.

14. Joaquim Manoel de Macedo, *Mulheres celebres* (Rio de Janeiro: Garnier, 1878), pp. 18–19, 83–86, 93.

15. Josephina Alvares de Azevedo, *Galeria illustre (Mulheres celebres)* (Rio de Janeiro: A Vapor, 1897).

16. Brazil, Ministério do Império, *Relatorio apresentado a Assembléa Geral Legislativa na quarta sessão da decima quinta legislatura pelo ministro e secretario d'estado dos negocios do imperio Dr. João Alfredo Corrêa de Oliveira* (Rio de Janeiro: Typ. Nacional, 1875), report of Dr. Joaquim Monteiro Caminhoá, "Faculdade de Medicina do Rio de Janeiro. Memoria historica dos acontecimentos notaveis do anno lectivo de 1874," pp. 23–24.

17. Guilherme Bellegarde, Félix Ferreira, and José Maria da Silva Júnior, eds., *Commemorativa da inauguração das aulas para o sexo feminino do Imperial Lyceo de Artes e Officios* (Rio de Janeiro: Lombaerts, 1881). I am indebted to Maria Thereza Caiuby Criscente Bernardes for calling this book to my attention.

18. Ibid., pp. 1, 4–9, 21, 26, 44, 86, 92, 102, 106.

19. Ibid., pp. 14, 20–25, 27, 34, 47, 48, 61, 69, 76, 81–85, 86, 92, 96.

20. Ibid., pp. 61, 76, 86.

21. Ibid., pp. 17–22, 26, 38–40, 44, 53, 56, 57, 59, 60, 63, 73, 75, 76, 83, 95, 96, 98, 103, 105.

22. Ibid., pp. 14, 22, 23, 28–29, 44, 67–68, 73, 81, 97, 100.

23. Ferreira, *A educação da mulher,* pp. 43–44; Ferreira, *Noções da vida domestica,* pp. 104–5, 116; Félix Ferreira, *O Lyceo de Artes e Officios e as aulas de dezenho para o sexo feminino* (Rio de Janeiro: Typ. Nacional, 1881), p. 25.

24. Ferreira, *A educação da mulher,* p. 51.

25. See Susan Groag Bell, "Christine de Pizan (1364–1430): Humanism and the Problem of a Studious Woman," *Feminist Studies* (Spring–Summer 1976): 173–84. An excellent selection of documents presenting the debate in Europe and the United States over women and their claims to freedom, focusing on the controversies over women's legal status, education, employment, and participation in political life from the Enlightenment to the mid-twentieth century, is given in Susan Groag Bell and Karen M. Offen, eds., *Women, the Family, and Freedom. The Debate in Documents,* 2 vols. (Stanford: Stanford University Press, 1983).

26. *Escrínio* (Porto Alegre), June 12, 1901, p. 3; Pedro Maia Soares, "Feminism no Rio Grande do Sul: Primeiros apontamentos (1835–1945)," in *Vivência. História, sexualidade e imagens femininas,* ed. Maria Cristina A. Bruschini and Fúlvia Rosemberg, pp. 136–38 (São Paulo: Editora Brasiliense, 1980), pp. 136–138; *Mulheres brasileiras. Galeria da Fundação Osório* (Rio de Janeiro: N.p., 1950), p. 91.

27. *O Domingo* (Rio de Janeiro), Nov. 30, 1873, p. 1.

28. *Echo das Damas* (Rio de Janeiro), April 18, 1879, p. 1.

29. *O Sexo Feminino* (Campanha, M.G.), May 2, 1874, p. 2.

30. *O Domingo,* March 1, 1874, pp. 1–2.

31. *Aurora Brasileira* (Ithaca, N.Y.), Oct. 22, 1873, p. 1; Jan. 20, 1874, p. 1. For a description of the actual discriminatory treatment accorded women at Cornell University, see Charlotte Williams Conable, *Women at Cornell: The Myth of Equal Education* (Ithaca, N.Y.: Cornell University Press, 1977). Barbara Miller Solomon, *In the Company of Women. A History of Women and Higher Education in America* (New Haven: Yale University Press, 1985), provides a historical overview of women's higher education in the United States.

32. *O Sexo Feminino,* Jan. 28, 1874, pp. 3–4.

33. Interview with Ivonne Moraes de Pinho, granddaughter of Maria Estrela, Rio de Janeiro, June 18, 1983; Belarmino Barreto, *Biographia da exm. sra. D. Maria Augusta Generosa Estrella natural do Rio de Janeiro filha do illm. sr. Albino Augusto Generoso Estrella e futura doutora em medicina pela Academia de Nova York* (Bahia: Typ. do "Correio da Bahia," 1878), pp. 19–76; *A Mulher* (New York), April 1881, pp. 26, 30; Guilherme Auler, *Os*

bolsistas do Imperador (Petrópolis: Tribuna de Petrópolis, 1956), pp. 1, 19, 51; Alberto Silva, *A primeira médica do Brasil* (Rio de Janeiro: Irmões Pongetti, 1954), pp. 33–37.

34. Barreto, *Biographia,* p. 109.

35. Interview with Ivonne Moraes de Pinho, June 18, 1983; "Eighteenth Annual Commencement of the New York Medical College and Hospital for Women," March 29, 1881, in possession of Ivonne Moraes de Pinho; *Echo das Damas,* May 2, May 20, July 20, 1879; *Jornal do Comércio* (Rio de Janeiro), Nov. 1, Nov. 11, 1882; *Gazeta de Notícias* (Rio de Janeiro), Jan. 3, 1878, Nov. 1, 1882; *O Globo* (Rio de Janeiro), Nov. 12, 1882.

36. Roberto Bego, "O 'Diccionario Bibliografico Brasileiro de Sacramento Blake' revisto, anotado e corrigido na parte referente a medicina e aos medicos" (typescript), Instituto Histórico e Geográfico Brasiliero, 1971 (Professor Roderick Barman of the University of British Columbia kindly called my attention to the existence of this uncatalogued typescript); *Revista Americana* (Rio de Janeiro) 3 (April 1910): 143–55; Tobias Barreto, *Estudos de sociologia* (Rio de Janeiro: Instituto Nacional do Livro, 1962), pp. 59–87; *A Mulher,* April 4, 1881, p. 26; Brasil, Ministério do Império, *Relatorio apresentado a assembléa geral legislativa na segunda sessão da décima setima legislatura pelo ministro e secretario de estado dos negócios do império conselheiro Leoncio de Carvalho* (Rio de Janeiro: Typ. Nacional, 1879), Anexo A, "Decreto n. 7247 de 19 de abril de 1879," pp. 1–15.

37. *A Mulher,* April 1881, p. 26.

38. Ibid., Jan. 1881, pp. 2, 6; Feb. 1881, p. 16; March 1881, pp. 18, 22; April 1881, pp. 26–30; *A Mulher* (Recife), Feb. 15, 1883.

39. *America Illustrada* (Recife), Feb. 13, 1881, pp. 2–7.

40. *A Mulher,* April 1881, p. 27; June 6, 1881, pp. 43, 47.

41. *Echo das Damas,* April 18, 1879, p. 1.

42. Brazil, Ministério do Império, *Relatório,* 1875, report of Dr. Joaquim Monteiro Caminhoá, "Faculdade de Medicina do Rio de Janeiro," 1874, p. 25.

43. *A Mulher,* June 6, 1881, pp. 43, 46.

44. Oliveira, *Obra destinada,* pp. 133–39; *Aurora Brasileira,* May 20, 1874, p. 57; June 20, 1874, pp. 66–67; Macedo, *Mulheres celebres,* p. 161.

45. Andrews, *Brazil. Conditions and Prospects,* p. 180.

46. Luiz Gastão de Escragnolle Doria, *Memória histórica do Collegio de Pedro Segundo, 1837–1937* (Rio de Janeiro: Ministério da Educação, 1937), pp. 170–73; Sylvia Tigre Maia, "A evolução intelectual da mulher no Brasil. Subsídio para a história da educação. 1 parte: No Império," *Formação* 5 (September 1943): 49–50.

47. *Gazeta da Tarde* (Rio de Janeiro), Oct. 1, 1885, p. 1; Oct. 3, 1885, p. 2.

48. *Inauguração das aulas para o sexo feminino no Imperial Lyceo de Artes e Officios em 11 de outubro de 1881* (Rio de Janeiro: Hildebrandt, 1881), pp. iv–v; *A imprensa e o Lyceu de Artes e Officios. Aulas para o sexo feminino* (Rio de Janeiro: Hildebrandt, 1881), pp. iii, 5, 12, 25; Bellegarde, *O Lyceu de Artes e Officios e as aulas para o sexo feminino,* p. 27; Brazil, Ministério do Império, *Relatorio apresentado á assembléa geral legislativa na primeira sessão da decima sexta legislatura pelo ministro e secretario de estado dos negocios do império conselheiro dr. José Bento da Cunha e Figueiredo* (Rio de Janeiro: Typ. Nacional, 1877), Anexo C, "Instrucção publica primeira e secundaria," pp. 1–6; Brazil, Ministério do Império, *Relatorio apresentado á assembléa geral legislativa na primeira sessão da decima setima legislatura pelo ministro e secretario de estado dos negocios do imperio conselheiro Carlos Leoncio de Carvalho* (Rio de Janeiro: Typ. Nacional, 1878), Anexo C, "Decreto N. 6884 de 20 de abril de 1878," pp. 1–5; Brazil, Ministério do Império, *Relatorio apresentado á assembléa geral legislativa na terceira sessão da decima setimo legislatura pelo ministro e secretario de estado dos negocios do imperio Barão Homem de Mello* (Rio de Janeiro: Typ. Nacional, 1880), pp. 25–28; Anexo C, "Decreto N. 7684 de 6 de marco de 1880," pp. 1–12; *Programma do ensino na escola normal da corte* (Rio de Janeiro: Lyra de Apollo, 1874), pp. 3–18.

49. Mauricio Lamberg, *O Brazil*, trans. Luiz de Castro (Rio de Janeiro: Nunes, 1896), p. 59.

50. Amélia Diniz and Elysa Diniz to Princess Imperial Isabel, Rio de Janeiro, Nov. 11, 1882, and "Programma de Estudos do Lyceo Santa Izabel," Arquivo Nacional, Seção de Arquivos Particulares, no. 17, Item. Doc. Cx. 15; *Voz da Verdade* (Rio de Janeiro), May 12, 1885, p. 4; May 28, 1885, p. 4; *O Quinze de Novembro do Sexo Feminino* (Rio de Janeiro), Feb. 1889, p. 4; Alfredo Valladão, *Campanha da Princeza*, 3 vols. (São Paulo: Empreza Graphica da "Revista dos Tribunaes," 1942), 3:252.

51. Brazil, Ministério do Império, *Relatorio apresentado á assembléa geral legislativa na terceira sessão da decima setimo legislatura pelo ministro e secretario de estado dos negocios do imperio Barão Homem de Mello* (Rio de Janeiro: Typ. Nacional, 1880), Visconde de Santa Izabel, "Relatorio do Director da Faculdade de Medicina do Rio de Janeiro," Jan. 21, 1880, p. 13; and José Alves de Mello, "Memoria historica da Faculdade de Medicina da Bahia relativa ao anno de 1879," March 1, 1880, p. 18; Brazil, Ministério do Império, *Relatorio apresentado á assembléa geral legislativa na segunda sessão da decima oitava legislatura pelo ministro e secretario de estado dos negocios do Império Rodolpho Epiphanio de Souza Dantas* (Rio de Janeiro: Typ. Nacional, 1882), p. 26; Brazil, Ministério do Império, *Relatorio apresentado á assembléa geral legislativa na quarta sessão da decima oitava legislatura pelo ministro e secretario de estado dos negocios do império Francisco Antunes Maciel* (Rio de Janeiro: Typ. Nacional, 1884), p. 24; Brazil, Ministério do Império, *Relatorio apresentado á assembléa geral legislativa na primeira sessão da decima nona legislatura pelo ministro e secretario dos negocios do imperio João Florentino Meira de Vasconcellos* (Rio de Janeiro: Imprensa Nacional, 1885), Carlos Ferreira de Souza Fernandes, "Relatorio do Director da Faculdade de Medicina do Rio de Janeiro," Jan. 21, 1885, p. 53; Brazil, Ministério do Império, *Relatorio apresentado á assembléa geral legislativa na primeira sessão da vigesima legislatura pelo ministro e secretario de estado dos negocios do império Barão de Mamoré* (Rio de Janeiro: Imprensa Nacional, 1886), p. 35; Brazil, Ministério do Império, *Relatorio apresentado á assembléa geral legislativa na segunda sessão da vigesima legislatura pelo ministro e secretario de estado dos negocios do império Barão de Mamoré* (Rio de Janeiro: Imprensa Nacional, 1887), p. 47; Brazil, Ministério do Império, *Relatorio apresentado á assembléa geral legislativa na terceira sessão da vigesima legislatura pelo ministro e secretario de estado dos negocios do imperio José Fernandes da Costa Pereira Junior* (Rio de Janeiro: Imprensa Nacional, 1888), p. 53; Francisco Bruno Lobo, "A primeira médica formada no Brasil," *Revista de História* 42 (April–June 1971): 484.

52. *Gazeta Academica* (Bahia) 2 (August 1886): 146–52, 166–77. Professor Donald Cooper of Ohio State University kindly provided me with a copy of sections of this journal.

53. *Echo das Damas*, Jan. 4, 1888, p. 1.

54. Amanda Labarca Hubertson, *Feminismo contemporaneo* (Santiago: Zig Zag, 1947), pp. 125, 133; Laureana Wright de Kleinhans, *Mujeres notables mexicanas* (Mexico: Económica, 1910), p. 539; Elsa M. Chaney, *Supermadre. Women in Politics in Latin America* (Austin: University of Texas Press, 1979), p. 56.

55. Alberto Silva, *A primeira médica do Brasil* (Rio de Janeiro: Irmões Pongetti, 1954), pp. 52, 94, 122, 196–98; Lobo, "A primeira médica formada no Brasil," p. 483; *A Mensageira* (São Paulo), Jan. 15, 1898, p. 106; Olímio Barros Vidal, *Precursoras brasileiras* (Rio de Janeiro: A Noite, 1955), pp. 207–29.

56. *A Família* (São Paulo), Nov. 30, 1889, p. 6.

57. Brazil, *Informações apresentado pela Commissão Parlamentar de Inquerito ao corpo legislativo na terceira sessão da decima oitava legislatura* (Rio de Janeiro: Typ. Nacional, 1883), p. 138.

58. *O Domingo*, Nov. 30, 1873, p. 11; Barros Vidal, *Precursoras brasileiras*, pp. 69–74, 167–80.

59. Maria Josephina Matilde Durocher, *Ideas por coordenar á respeito da emancipção* (Rio de Janeiro: Typ. do Diario do Rio de Janeiro, 1871), p. 18.

60. Joaquim José da França Junior, *As doutoras. Comedia em 4 actos* (Rio de Janeiro: Sociedade Brasileira de Autores Theatraes, 1932). Information on the play, its performance, and its author is given by Luiz Gastão de Escragnolle Doria, "Cousas do passado," *Revista do Instituto Histórico e Geográfico Brasileiro* 71, pt. 2 (1908): 295–97. Additional biographical information can be found in Sacramento Blake, *Diccionario bibliográphico brazileiro*, 4:163–65. The dramatic work of França Junior is ably and engagingly analyzed by Roderick J. Barman, "Politics on the Stage: The Late Brazilian Empire as Dramatized by França Junior," *Luso-Brazilian Review* 13 (Winter 1976): 244–60.
Some of the strongest opposition in the United States to women entering the professions also centered on medicine; see, e.g., Eleanor Flexner, *Century of Struggle: The Woman's Rights Movement in the United States* (Cambridge, Mass.: Harvard University Press, 1959), p. 119. The problems of women in medicine in the United States and the opposition to them are treated in Mary Roth Walsh, *"Doctors Wanted: No Women Need Apply." Sexual Barriers in the Medical Profession, 1835–1975* (New Haven: Yale University Press, 1977). See also Judy Barrett Litoff, *American Midwives, 1860 to the Present* (Westport, Conn.: Greenwood Press, 1978).

61. Azevedo, *A mulher moderna*, pp. 145–47.

62. *A Família*, Nov. 14, 1889, pp. 2–3.

63. *Revista Illustrada* (Rio de Janeiro), March 9, 1889, p. 7.

64. *A Mensageira* (São Paulo), Oct. 15, 1899, pp. 169, 174; Dec. 15, 1899, pp. 201–4; Jan. 15, 1900, pp. 217–21; *A Família*, June 16, 1889, p. 2; Nov. 30, 1889, p. 6; Barros Vidal, *Precursoras brasileiras*, pp. 231–49; Evaristo de Moraes, *Reminiscencias de um rabula criminalista* (Rio de Janeiro: Leite Ribeiro, 1922), pp. 121–28; *Report of the Royal Commission on the Status of Women in Canada* (Ottawa: Information Canada, 1970), p. 165.

65. Bellegarde, Ferreira, and Silva Júnior, *Commemorativa da inauguração das aulas para o sexo feminino*, pp. 109–13.

66. *Revista Illustrada*, no. 425 (1886), reproduced in Dulcília Helena Schroeder Buitoni, *Mulher de papel. A representação da mulher na imprensa feminina brasileira* (São Paulo: Edições Loyola, 1981), pp. 16–17.

67. See, for example, the writings of virulent republican Afriso Fialho, *História da fundação da republica*, pp. 33–36.

68. Anna Eurydice Eufrozina de Barandas, *O ramalhete ou flores escolhidas no jardim da imaginação* (Pôrto Alegre: I. J. Lopes, 1845), pp. 51–64.

69. *O Domingo*, Dec. 14, 1873, p. 1.

70. *Echo das Damas*, April 18, 1879, p. 1; Aug. 7, 1886, p. 2.

71. *O Sexo Feminino*, Dec. 20, 1873, p. 3; Jan. 14, 1874, p. 2; March 7, 1874, p. 4; April 11, 1874, pp. 3–4.

72. *O Quinze de Novembro do Sexo Feminino*, April 6, 1890, p. 2.

73. Azevedo, *A mulher moderna*, pp. 28, 78.

74. *O Quinze de Novembro do Sexo Feminino*, April 6, 1890, p. 1.

75. *A Família*, July 6, 1889, pp. 1–2, 8; Oct. 3, 1889, pp. 1, 3–4; Nov. 30, 1889, p. 1; Dec. 31, 1889, p. 1; Azevedo, *A mulher moderna*, p. 124.

76. Barros Vidal, *Precursoras brasileiras*, p. 165; *A Família*, July 6, 1889, p. 8; Nov. 23, 1889, p. 3; Dec. 31, 1889, p. 2; Azevedo, *A mulher moderna*, p. 14.

77. *A Família*, Nov. 23, 1889, p. 3.

78. *O Quinze de Novembro do Sexo Feminino*, April 6, 1890, p. 2.

79. Azevedo, *A mulher moderna*, pp. 23, 25, 30–73.

80. *A Família*, Oct. 19, 1889, p. 1.

81. Azevedo, *A mulher moderna*, p. 20.

82. *O Quinze de Novembro do Sexo Feminino*, June 16, 1890, p. 1.

83. Azevedo, *A mulher moderna*, pp. 31–73.

84. Tito Livio de Castro, *A mulher e a sociogenia. Obra posthuma* (Rio de Janeiro: Francisco Alves [1894]). He believed that female mental development through education was essential for the evolution of the species.

85. Brazil, Câmara dos Deputados, *Annaes do Congresso Constituinte da República*, 2d ed., 3 vols. (Rio de Janeiro: Imprensa Nacional 1924–26), 2:544, session of Jan. 14, 1891.

86. *Annaes do Congresso Constituinte*, 2:456, session of Jan. 12, 1891.

87. Similar antisuffrage arguments were employed in the United States. See Kraditor, *The Ideas of the Woman Suffrage Movement*; and Mara Mayor, "Fears and Fantasy of the Anti-Suffragists," *Connecticut Review* 7 (April 1973): 64–74.

88. See Raimundo Teixeira Mendes, *A mulher. Sua preeminência social e moral, segundo os ensinos da verdadeira siencia pozitiva*, 4th ed. (Rio de Janeiro: Igreja Pozitivista do Brazil, 1958). For studies of positivism in Brazil see Ivan Lins, *História do positivismo no Brasil* (São Paulo: Companhia Editôra Nacional, 1964); João Cruz Costa, *O positivismo na república. Notas sobre a história do positivismo no Brasil* (São Paulo: Companhia Editôra Nacional, 1956); João Camillo de Oliveira Torres, *O positivismo no Brasil* (Petrópolis: Vozes, 1943). Also useful is João Cruz Costa, *A History of Ideas in Brazil. The Development of Philosophy in Brazil and the Evolution of Natural History*, trans. Suzette Macedo (Berkeley: University of California Press, 1964).

89. *Annaes do Congresso Constituinte*, 2:478, session of Jan. 13, 1891.

90. Azevedo, *A mulher moderna*, p. 109.

91. *Annaes do Congresso Constituinte*, 2:543, session of Jan. 14, 1891; vol. 3, session of Jan. 29, 1891.

92. Ibid., 1:276, 438–39.

93. Eneida de Morais, *História do carnaval carioca* (Rio de Janeiro: Editôra Civilização Brasileira, 1956), p. 79.

Chapter 3. Contrasting Women's Worlds in the Early Twentieth Century

1. *Renascença* (Rio de Janeiro), July 1904, p. 181.

2. Luiz Edmundo da Costa, *O Rio de Janeiro do meu tempo*, 3 vols. (Rio de Janeiro: Imprensa Nacional, 1938), 1:26.

3. Alured Gray Bell, *The Beautiful Rio de Janeiro* (London: William Heinenmann, 1914), p. 49.

4. *Progresso Suburbano* (Piedade, Rio de Janeiro), Aug. 6, 1902, p. 1; Aug. 23, 1902, p. 1; *O Suburbio* (Meier, Rio de Janeiro), July 2, 1904, p. 1; July 16, 1904, p. 1; *A Noite* (Rio de Janeiro), March 22, 1919, p. 1; Donat Alfred Agache, *Cidade do Rio de Janeiro. Extensão, remodelação, embellezamento* (Paris: Foyer Brésilien, 1930), p. 188; João Chagas, *De bond. Alguns aspectos da civilisação brasileira* (Lisbon: Livraria Moderna, 1897), pp. 86, 112–13.

5. *Renascença*, March 1905, p. 92.

6. Ibid.

7. Alice R. Humphrey, *A Summer Journey to Brazil* (New York: Boswell, Silver, 1900), pp. 46–47.

8. Nevin Otto Winter, *Brazil and Her People of To-Day; An Account of the Customs, Characteristics, Amusements, History and Advancement of the Brazilians, and the Development and*

Resources of Their Country (Boston: L. C. Page, 1910), p. 51; Clayton Sedgwick Cooper, *The Brazilians and Their Country* (New York: Frederick A. Stokes, 1917), p. 272.

9. Bell, *Beautiful Rio de Janeiro*, p. 22.

10. Ibid., p. 192.

11. Cooper, *The Brazilians and Their Country*, p. 126.

12. Marie Robinson Wright, *The New Brazil: Its Resources and Attractions, Historical, Descriptive and Industrial* (Philadelphia: George Barrie and Son, 1901), p. 444.

13. Ibid., p. 442.

14. Cooper, *The Brazilians and Their Country*, pp. 125, 127, 129.

15. On women and the Civil Code of 1916 see Clovis Bevilacqua, *Código Civil dos Estados Unidos do Brasil: Comentários* (Rio de Janeiro: Editôra Rio, 1965), pp. 601–29.

16. Afonso Henriques de Lima Barreto, *Clara dos Anjos*, 2d ed. (São Paulo: Editôra Brasiliense, 1962).

17. See, for example, Donald Pierson's study of life in a small town in São Paulo in the 1940s, *Cruz das Almas* (Washington, D.C.: U.S. Government Printing Office, 1948). In *A Grain of Mustard Seed. The Awakening of the Brazilian Revolution* (Garden City, N.Y.: Doubleday Anchor Press, 1973), Marcio Moreira Alves comments on the virtual segregation of women from male visitors that he encountered in his cousin's home in the interior of Minas Gerais in the 1960s when he was fleeing the wrath of Brazil's military dictatorship.

18. José Pacheco, *A mulher no lugar do homem* (N.p., n.d.), pp. 3–4.

> O trabalho da mulher
> para que não fale o povo,
> é amarrar uma cabra,
> dar leite a um gato novo,
> tratar duma bacorinha
> botar milho p'ra galinha
> e reparar se tem ovo.
>
> São os trabalhos caseiros
> cada qual mais conhecido,
> é varrar casa e fiar
> catar pulga no vestido,
> e trator dos seus filhinhos
> e também catar bichinhos
> nas barbas de seu marido.

19. Maria Lacerda de Moura, *"A mulher é uma degenerada,"* 3d ed. (Rio de Janeiro: Civilização Brasileira, 1932), p. 25.

20. *A Barricada* (Rio de Janeiro), July 1, 1915, reprinted in Edgar Rodrigues, *Nacionalismo e cultura social, 1913–1922* (Rio de Janeiro: Laemmert, 1972), p. 94.

21. Wright, *The New Brazil*, p. 446.

22. *A Mensageira* (São Paulo), Oct. 15, 1897, p. 4; Dec. 30, 1897, p. 92.

23. *Escrínio* (Pôrto Alegre), Aug. 26, 1901, p. 2.

24. Andradina América Andrada de Oliveira, *Divórcio?* (Pôrto Alegre: Livraria Universal, 1912), p. 224.

25. Moura, *"A mulher é uma degenerada,"* p. 90.

26. Manoel Francisco Pinto Pereira, *A mulher no Brazil* (São Paulo: C. Teixeira, 1916), pp. 88–91.

27. Olímio Barros Vidal, *Precursoras brasileiras* (Rio de Janeiro: A Noite, 1955), p. 235.

28. Brazil, Directoria Geral de Estatística, *Estatística da instrucção. Estatística escolar* (Rio de Janeiro: Typ. da Estatística, 1916), pp. clxi–clxiii; *A Mensageira*, Jan. 15, 1898, p. 106; July 15, 1898, p. 303; Heleieth I. B. Saffioti, *Women in Class Society,* trans. Michael Vale (New York: Monthly Review Press, 1978), pp. 165–69; Sylvia Tigre Maia, "A evolução intelectual feminina no Brasil. II parte. Na República," *Formação* 6 (December 1943): 33–39.

29. Brazil, Directoria Geral de Estatística, *Estatística da instrucção,* pp. vii, clxxx, cxcii, 302, 304, 307.

30. Brazil, Directoria Geral de Estatística, *Recenseamento da população do Império do Brazil a que se procedeu no dia 1 de agosto de 1872,* 22 vols. (Rio de Janeiro: Leuzinger, 1873–76), Município Neutro, 21:61; *Recenseamento do Rio de Janeiro (Districto Federal) realizado em 20 de setembro de 1906,* 2 vols. (Rio de Janeiro: Leuzinger, 1907), 1:104; *Recenseamento do Brazil realizado em 1 de setembro de 1920,* 5 vols. in 18 (Rio de Janeiro: Typ. da Estatística, 1922–30), vol. 4, pt. 5, tomo 1, pp. 24–27.

31. *O Funccionário* (São Paulo), Sept. 7, 1888, p. 1; *A Mensageira,* Oct. 15, 1897, p. 4; Dec. 30, 1897, p. 92; Richard M. Morse, *From Community to Metropolis. A Biography of São Paulo, Brazil* (Gainesville: University of Florida Press, 1958), p. 215; *A Noite* (Rio de Janeiro), Oct. 16, 1930; *Echo Lusitano* (Belém), Feb. 27, 1909, p. 4.

32. Jorge Amado, *Gabriela, Clove and Cinnamon* (New York: Avon Books, 1974), pp. 252–53.

33. *Revista Feminina* (São Paulo), Dec. 1920 (unpaginated); *O Imparcial* (Rio de Janeiro), Jan. 18, 1923, p. 1; *A Rolha* (São Paulo), May 14, 1918, p. 11; *A Defesa* (Rio de Janeiro), Aug. 7, 1925; *O Jornal* (Rio de Janeiro), June 17, 1930.

34. *O Domingo* (Rio de Janeiro), June 21, 1874, p. 11; *Correio da Manhã* (Rio de Janeiro), Jan. 5, 1923; *Nosso Jornal* (Rio de Janeiro), Aug. 1920; Ferreira da Rosa, *Associação dos Empregados no Comércio do Rio de Janeiro. Meio Século. Narrativa histórica* (Rio de Janeiro: Paulo, Pongetti, 1930), pp. 189, 290, 307, 334–36; Mariana Coelho, *Evolução do feminismo. Subsídios para a sua história* (Rio de Janeiro: Imprensa Moderna, 1933), p. 218.

35. J. C. Oakenfull, *Brazil: Past, Present, and Future* (London: John Bale, Sons and Danielson, 1919), pp. 761–62.

The milreis, the standard currency in Brazil until 1942, was divided into a thousand reis. The dollar sign separated the milreis and the reis, so that, for example, 2 milreis and 500 reis would be written 2$500.

36. Clodoveu Doliveira, *O trabalhador brasileiro* (Rio de Janeiro: A Balança, 1933), pp. 115–16.

37. Ibid., p. 118.

38. Lola de Oliveira, *Hontem e hoje* (São Paulo: Paulista, 1928), p. 138.

39. Mary C. Karasch, *Slave Life in Rio de Janeiro, 1808–1850* (Princeton: Princeton University Press, 1987), p. 362. Other studies of Brazilian slavery include Robert Edgar Conrad, ed., *Children of God's Fire. A Documentary History of Black Slavery in Brazil* (Princeton: Princeton University Press, 1983); Kátia de Queirós Mattoso, *To Be a Slave in Brazil,* trans. Arthur Goldhammer (New Brunswick, N.J.: Rutgers University Press, 1986); and Suely Robles Reis de Queiroz, *Escravidão negra em São Paulo* (Rio de Janeiro: Livraria José Olympio, 1977).

40. Florestan Fernandes, *The Negro in Brazilian Society,* trans. Jacqueline D. Skiles, A. Brunel, and Arthur Rothwell (New York: Columbia University Press, 1969), pp. 96–117.

41. *O Imperial* (Rio de Janeiro), Jan. 18, 1923, p. 1.

42. "These apresentada pela União dos Empregados no Commercio do Rio de Janeiro á 1ª Conferencia pelo Progresso Feminino, realisada no Rio de Janeiro sob auspices da Federação Brasileira das Ligas pelo Progresso Feminino," Dec. 21, 1922, Arquivo

Nacional, Arquivo Particular no. 46, Arquivo da Federação Brasileira pelo Progresso Feminino (uncatalogued).

43. *A Terra Livre* (São Paulo), July 29, 1906, p. 2.

44. Ibid., Feb. 17, 1906, p. 4; J. C. Oakenfull, *Brazil in 1911* (London: Butler and Tanner, 1912), p. 355.

45. *Renascença*, March 1905, pp. 89–90; *O Imperial*, Jan. 18, 1923, p. 1; "Condições do trabalho na industria de chapeus," São Paulo (state), *Boletim do Departamento Estadual do Trabalho* 1, no. 3 (2d trimester 1912): 226–27; "O trabalho domiciliar," São Paulo, *Boletim* 4, no. 17 (4th trimester 1915): 613–20; "O trabalho domiciliar," São Paulo, *Boletim* 6, no. 25 (4th trimester 1917): 617–20; "Hygiene e segurança do trabalho e a industria em domicilio," Brazil, Congress, Câmara dos Deputados, *Documentos Parlamentares. Legislação social*, 3 vols. (Rio de Janeiro: Typ. do Jornal do Commercio, 1919–22), 3:7–125.

46. Historical studies of aspects of prostitution in Brazil are just now beginning to appear. See Luiz Carlos Soares, "Da necessidade do bordel higienizado. Tentativas de controle da prostituição carioca no século XIX," and Magali G. Engel, "O médico, a prostituta e os significados do corpo," in *História e sexualidade no Brasil*, ed. Ronaldo Vainfás (Rio de Janeiro: Graal, 1986). Even scholarly work by social scientists on contemporary prostitution are not very common. Sociologist Renan Springer de Freitas, *Bordel, bordéis: Negociando identidades* (Petrópolis: Vozes, 1985); and social anthropologist Maria Dulce Gaspar, *Garotas de programa. Prostituição em Copacabana e identidade social* (Rio de Janeiro: Jorge Zahar Editora, 1985), focus on prostitution and social identity in Belo Horizonte and in Rio de Janeiro, respectively, in studies which began as Masters' theses. In *Divergência e prostituição. Uma analise sociologica da comunidade prostituicional do Maciel* (Rio de Janeiro and Salvador: Tempo Brasileiro/Fundação Cultural do Estado da Bahia, 1984), Grey Espinheira describes the organization of prostitution and the prostitutes living in the old colonial center of the city of Salvador; while Jefferson Alfonso Bacelar, *A família da prostituta* (São Paulo: Editôra Ática, 1982), examines the family structure of prostitutes in the same city. Often considered just a matter of morality, prostitution continues to receive attention from those publishing journalistic accounts about it or from those attempting to combat it, including the Roman Catholic church, whose concern with prostitutes and prostitution has resulted in such printed works as: Antonio Batista Fragoso et al., *O grito de milhões de escravas. A cumplicadade do siléncio*, 2d ed. (Petrópolis: Vozes, 1986); Conselho Nacional dos Bispos Brasileiros, Comissão Episcopal de Pastoral, *Prostituição. Desafio à sociedade e à igreja* (São Paulo: Edições Paulinas, 1976); Angelo Assis et al., *A prostituição em debate* (São Paulo: Faculdade de Teologia N. Sra. da Assunção/ Edições Paulinas, 1982).

47. Donna J. Guy, "White Slavery, Public Health, and the Socialist Position on Legalized Prostitution in Argentina, 1913–1936," *Latin American Research Review* 23 (November 3, 1988): 60–80.

48. Ludgero Gonçalves da Silva, "Relatorio do Chefe de Policia da Corte," in *Relatorio apresentado à assembléa geral legislativa na quarta sessão da decima quinta legislatura pelo ministro e secretario de Estado dos Negocios da Justiça Dr. Manoel Antonio Duarte de Azevedo* (Rio de Janeiro: Americana, 1875), p. 183.

49. Herculano Augusto Lassance Cunha, *Dissertação sobre a prostituição em particular na cidade do Rio de Janeiro. These apresentada à faculdade de medicina do Rio de Janeiro, em 17 de dezembro de 1845* (Rio de Janeiro: Typ. Imparcial de Francisco de Paula Brito, 1845), pp. 18–24.

50. *A Voz do Povo* (Rio), 1920, in Edgar Rodrigues, *Alvorádo operário. Os congressos operarios no Brasil* (Rio de Janeiro: Mundo Livre, 1979), pp. 207–8.

51. Rodrigues, *Alvorado operário*, p. 214.

52. União Geral dos Pintores, "Relatorio Histórico do Movimento Sociologico desta Associação," 1913, Arquivo Geral da Cidade do Rio de Janeiro (hereinafter AGCRJ), Cx. 5, Doc. 155.

53. J. C. Oakenfull, *Brazil: Past, Present, and Future*, p. 671.

54. Ferreira da Rosa, *O lupanar* (Rio de Janeiro: N.p., 1896), pp. 11–21, 194–96, 253–55; *O Cruzeiro* (Rio de Janeiro), Sept. 3, 1879, p. 2; Carl von Koseritz, *Imagens do Brasil* (São Paulo: Livraria Martins, 1943), p. 224.

55. Von Koseritz, *Imagens do Brasil*, pp. 224–25; Ferreira da Rosa, *O lupanar*, p. 13.

56. Cynthia Jeffress Little, "Moral Reform and Feminism. A Case Study," *Journal of Interamerican Studies and World Affairs* 17 (November 1975): 386–97.

57. Brazil, Directoria Geral de Estatística, *Recenseamento do Brazil . . . 1920*, vol. 5, pt. 5, tomo 1, pp. xii–xiii, xv, xxii.

58. Brazil, Ministério da Justiça, *Relatorios*, 1867, p. 69; 1870, p. 29; 1875, p. 214; 1877, p. 258; 1878, pp. 59–60.

59. Christopher Columbus Andrews, *Brazil: Its Condition and Prospects* (New York: D. Appleton, 1887), p. 39. For a literary portrayal of the ethnic and national mix of Rio's working classes and the occupations of both men and women, including laundresses and prostitutes, and their characteristic form of housing, the *cortiço*, see Aluízio Azevedo, *O cortiço* (São Paulo: Livraria Martins, 1965). This novel, first published in 1890, was very popular at the time.

60. Some of the most valuable historical studies concerning industrialization in Brazil are Warren Dean, *The Industrialization of São Paulo, 1880–1945* (Austin: University of Texas Press, 1969); Stanley J. Stein, *The Brazilian Cotton Manufacture: Textile Enterprise in an Underdeveloped Area, 1850–1950* (Cambridge, Mass.: Harvard University Press, 1957); Nícia Villela Luz, *A luta pela industrialização do Brazil 1808 á 1930)* (São Paulo: Difusão Européia do Livro, 1961); Annibal Villanova Villela and Wilson Suzigan, *Política do governo e crescimento da economia brasileira, 1889–1945* (Rio de Janeiro: IPEA/INPES, 1973).

61. "Relatorio do Sindicato dos Trabalhadores em Fabricas de Tecidos Para o 2° Congresso operario Brazilerio," 1913, AGCRJ, Cx. 5, Doc. 154; "Federação Operária do Rio de Janeiro," *A Voz do Trabalhador*, Oct. 15, 1913, reprinted in *A classe operária no Brasil. Documentos (1889 á 1930)*, 2 vols., ed. Paulo Sérgio Pinheiro and Michael M. Hall, 1:164 (São Paulo: Editôra Alfa Omega, 1979–81); *A Terra Livre*, March 24, 1906, p. 2; *O Operário* (Sorocaba), Jan. 2, 1910, p. 1; Jan. 9, 1910, p. 2; April 3, 1910, p. 2; *A Noite*, June 22, 1917, p. 4; "Condições do trabalho na industria textil no Estado de S. Paulo," São Paulo (state), *Boletim do Departamento Estadual do Trabalho* 1, nos. 1 and 4 (4th trimester 1911 and 1st trimester 1912): 36; *Gazeta Operária*, Nov. 28, 1902, p. 3; *A Tribuna do Povo* (Rio de Janeiro), March 18, 1909, pp. 1–2; April 18, 1909, p. 3; *A Voz do Trabalhador*, Nov. 22, 1908, p. 1; June 1, 1909, p. 2.

62. On the textile industry see Stein, *The Brazilian Cotton Manufacture*.

63. *Gazeta Operária*, Nov. 2, 1902, p. 1; Nov. 9, 1902, p. 2; *A Terra Livre*, Dec. 30, 1905, p. 3; March 24, 1906, p. 2; *A Tribuna do Povo*, March 18, 1909, p. 2; April 18, 1909, p. 3.

64. *União Operária* (Recife), June 4, 1905, p. 4; Nov. 5, 1905, p. 3; *O Imparcial*, Jan. 18, 1923, p. 1; *Diário da Bahia* (Salvador), Nov. 11, 1931; Ferreira da Rosa, *O Rio de Janeiro em 1900. Visitas e excursões*, 2d ed. (N.p., n.d.), p. 73; "Condições do trabalho na industria textil no Estado de S. Paulo, São Paulo (state), *Boletim do Departamento Estadual do Trabalho* 1, nos. 1 and 4 (4th trimester 1911 and 1 trimester 1912): 46, 57, 60.

65. Brazil, *Recenseamento do Brazil . . . 1920*, vol. 5, pt. 2, pp. vi–vii, ix, xiv.

66. "Relatorio do Sindicato dos Trabalhadores em Fabricas de Tecidos para o 2° Congresso operario Brazileiro," 1913, AGCRJ, Cx. 5, Doc. 154.

67. Brazil, *Recenseamento do Brazil* . . . *1920*, vol. 2, pt. 2 p. lxiv; vol. 4, pt. 5, tomo 1, pp. 24–27. Although census data provide the most comprehensive source on the number of working women and their occupations in Brazil for the period under consideration, they present numerous problems. Only in 1872 did Brazil conduct its first national census, preceded by an 1870 census of the capital. The 1872 census remains one of the most accurate ever carried out in Brazil. The problems with the 1890 census are especially great regarding occupations. The 1900 census was very poorly conducted; its results for Rio de Janeiro were set aside, and another census was conducted there in 1906. The census of 1910 was not completed. While that of 1920 investigated some areas, such as industry, in more detail than did previous censuses, it also contained errors. Brazilian censuses were neither standardized nor precise. This obviously hinders linkage of data. Part-time or irregular women's employment tends to be excluded from the census of the active population in Brazil as in other countries. A comparison of the national census of 1970 with the PNAD (Pesquisa Nacional por Amostra de Domicílios) for the same year has demonstrated that the number of women in the labor force in nonagricultural activities was undercounted by about 30 percent. At least half the women self-employed or in commercial and related fields and two-thirds of those working without pay in family enterprises were omitted. See Felicia R. Madeira and Paulo I. Singer, *Estrutura do emprego e trabalho feminino no Brasil, 1920–1970*, Cadernos CEBRAP 13 (São Paulo: CEBRAP, 1973), p. 25.

68. Brazil, *Recenseamento do Brazil* . . . *1920*, vol. 4, pt. 5, tomo 1, pp. xii–xiii.

69. *O Sexo Feminino* (Rio de Janeiro), July 29, 1875, p. 2.

70. See Esther Bosserup, *Women's Role in Economic Development* (New York: St. Martin's Press, 1970); and Nadia Haggag Youssef, *Women and Work in Developing Societies* (Berkeley: Institute of International Studies, University of California, 1974).

71. See Madeira and Singer, *Estrutura do emprego e trabalho feminino no Brasil*, p. 25.

72. Brazil, Directoria Geral de Estatística, *Recenseamento da população do Império do . . . 1872*, Município Neutro, 21:xxi, 61; Brazil, Directoria Geral de Estatística, *Recenseamento do Rio de Janeiro . . . 1906*, 1:100, 104; Brazil, *Recenseamento do Brazil . . . 1920*, vol. 5, pt. 5, tomo 1, pp. 24–27.

73. Evelyne Sullerot, *Women, Society, and Change*, trans. Margaret Scotford Archer (New York: McGraw-Hill, 1971), p. 111.

74. "Relatorio do Sindicato dos Trabalhadores em Fabricas de Tecidos para o 2° Congresso operario Brazileiro," 1913, AGCRJ, Cx. 5, Doc. 154; Leo de Affonseca Junior, *O custo da vida na cidade do Rio de Janeiro* (Rio de Janeiro: Imprensa Nacional, 1920), p. 13; J. C. Oakenfull, *Brazil (1913)* (London: Butler and Tanner 1914), pp. 571–74.

75. *O País*, Feb. 19, 1893, p. 3; Feb. 20, 1893, p. 3; Feb. 21, 1893, p. 3; *Renascença*, May 1905, pp. 185–89.

76. "Relatorio do Sindicato dos Trabalhadores em Fabricas de Tecidos para o 2° Congresso operario Brazileiro," 1913, AGCRJ, Cx. 5, Doc. 154. See also *O Imparcial*, Jan. 18, 1923, p. 1.

77. "These apresentada pela União dos Empregados no Commercio do Rio de Janeiro a 1ª Conferencia pelo Progresso Feminino, realisada no Rio de Janeiro sob auspices da Federação Brasileira das Ligas pelo Progresso Feminino," Dec. 21, 1922, Arquivo Nacional, Arquivo Particular no. 46, Arquivo da FBPF (uncatalogued).

78. Studies of the Brazilian labor movement include Boris Fausto, *Trabalho urbano e conflito social (1890–1920)* (São Paulo: Difel/Difusão Editorial, 1976); José Albertino Rodrigues, *Sindicato e desenvolvimento no Brasil* (São Paulo: Difusão Européia do Livro, 1968); Leoncio Rodrigues, *Conflito industrial e sindicalismo no Brasil* (São Paulo: Difusão Européia do Livro, 1966); Edgar Rodrigues, *Socialismo e sindicalismo no Brasil, 1675–1913* (Rio de

Janeiro: Laemmert, 1969); and Rodrigues, *Nacionalismo e cultura social, 1913–1922* (Rio de Janeiro: Laemmert, 1972); Azis Simão, *Sindicato e estado. Suas relações na formação do proletariado de São Paulo* (São Paulo: Dominus Editôra, 1966); John W. F. Dulles, *Anarchists and Communists in Brazil, 1900–1935* (Austin: University of Texas Press, 1973); and Sheldon L. Maram, *Anarquistas, imigrantes e o movimento operário brasileiro, 1890 á 1920* (Rio de Janeiro: Paz e Terra, 1979). On the struggle to create effective forms of worker resistance during the first two decades of the twentieth century, see also June E. Hahner, *Poverty and Politics. The Urban Poor in Brazil, 1870–1920* (Albuquerque: University of New Mexico Press, 1986), pp. 221–60.

79. Eulália Maria Lahmeyer Lobo, *História do Rio de Janeiro (Do capital comercial ao capital industrial e financeiro)*, 2 vols. (Rio de Janeiro: Instituto Brasileiro de Mercado de Capitais, 1978), 2:523.

80. See manuscript list of delegates to the 1913 Second Brazilian Labor Congress, AGCRJ, Cx. 5, Doc. 178. Delegates to the 1906 First Labor Congress as well as to the 1913 congress are found in Pinheiro and Hall, *A classe operária no Brasil*, 1:44–45, 182–85. Edgar Rodrigues, *Socialismo e sindicalismo no Brasil*, pp. 180, 239–40, gives delegates to the First São Paulo State Labor Congress in 1906 and the Second São Paulo Labor Congress in 1908. See also photograph of delegates to the 1906 First Labor Congress in Rodrigues, *Socialismo e sindicalismo no Brasil*, as well as photographs in Pinheiro and Hall, *A classe operária no Brasil*, vol. 1. However, Francisco Correia, "Mulheres libertárias: Um roteiro," in *Libertários no Brasil. Memoria, lutas, cultura*, ed. Antonio Arnoni Prado, pp. 38–63 (São Paulo: Editôra Brasiliense, 1986), gives the names of several women attending anarchist congresses around 1920. While Correia attempts to demonstrate the importance of female contributions to anarchism in Brazil, most of the women he cites apparently confined their public political activities to participation in anarchist plays, which he considers to have been a major means of spreading anarchistic views.

81. Maxime Molyneux, "No God, No Boss, No Husband. Anarchist Feminism in Nineteenth-Century Argentina," *Latin American Perspectives* 13 (Winter 1986): 119–45.

82. *A Tribuna do Povo*, March 18, 1904, p. 4.

83. *Brazil Operário* (Rio de Janeiro), August (first fortnight), 1903, p. 4.

84. "Documentos do movimento operário. Congresso Operário de 1912," *Estudos Sociais* 5 (June 1963): 77.

85. *O Estado de São Paulo*, Aug. 28, 1902, p. 3.

86. *O Amigo do Povo*, May 28, 1904, p. 3.

87. Giovanni Rossi to Alfred G. Sanftleben, Taquary, November 29, 1896, cited in Eric Gordon, Michael M. Hall, and Hobart A. Spalding, Jr., "A Survey of Brazilian and Argentine Materials at the International Instituut voor Sociale Geschiedenis in Amsterdam," *Latin American Research Review* 8 (Fall 1973): 39.

88. *Brazil Operário* (Rio de Janeiro), August (first fortnight), 1903, p. 4; *A Terra Livre*, Feb. 17, 1906, p. 4; July 29, 1906, p. 2; August 15, 1906, p. 4.

89. *A Terra Livre*, July 29, 1906, p. 2.

90. Ibid.; Michael M. Hall, "Immigration and the Early São Paulo Working Class," *Jahrbuch für Geschichte von Staat, Wirtschaft und Gesellschaft Lateinamerikas* 12 (1975): 402.

91. "Relatorio tranzitorio que a União dos Alfaiates apresenta ao Segundo Congresso Operario reunido nesta capital nos dias 8, 9, 10, 11, 12, 13, 14 de setembro de 1913 na séde do Centro Cosmopolita a Rua do Senado 273," AGCRJ, Cx. 5, Doc. 153.

92. "Documentos do movimento operário. Resoluções do Primeiro Congresso Operário Brasileiro," *Estudos Sociais* 4, no. 16 (March 1963): 396.

93. *O Componeador* (Rio de Janeiro), May 1, 1909, p. 3.

94. Augusto Olympio Viveiros de Castro, *A questão social* (Rio de Janeiro: Livraria Editôra Conselheiro Candido de Oliveira, 1920), pp. 193–201.

95. See, for example, Viveiros de Castro, *A questão social;* A. de Sampaio Doria, *A questão social. Quaes os principios scientificios a adoptar na formação da legislação social do Brasil?* (São Paulo: Monteiro Lobato, 1922); and Celso Vieira, *Defesa social. Estudos jurídicos* (Rio de Janeiro: Imprensa Nacional, 1920).

96. Viveiros de Castro, *A questão social,* pp. 202–6.

97. *O Sexo Feminino,* Oct. 11, 1873, p. 2. Some of the poetry and prose of Narcisa Amália de Campos are found in Antônio Simões dos Reis, ed., *Bibliografia Brasileira. Narcisa Amália* (Rio de Janeiro: Organizações Simões, 1949).

98. *A Família,* Feb. 2, 1889, p. 4; May 25, 1889, p. 5; July 6, 1889, p. 4; Nov. 14, 1889, pp. 4, 6; *Echo das Damas,* Jan. 31, 1888, pp. 1–2; Aug. 26, 1888, p. 2; *O Quinze de Novembro do Sexo Feminino,* Dec. 6, 1890, p. 2; *A Mensageira,* Oct. 15, 1897, p. 3; Nov. 30, 1897, p. 58; Sacramento Blake, *Diccionario bibliographico brazileiro,* 3:279–80, 5:241–42, 6:231; José Brito Broca, *A vida literária no Brasil: 1900,* 2d ed. (Rio de Janeiro: José Olympio, 1960), p. 252.

99. *A Mensageira,* Oct. 15, 1897, pp. 3–5; Júlia Lopes de Almeida, *Livro das noivas,* 3d ed. (Rio de Janeiro: Companhia Nacional Editôra, 1896), pp. 13, 38, 205. Addressed to prospective wives, this book combined the sentimental and the practical, with both household hints and moral exhortations. On Júlia Lopes de Almeida see Jeffrey D. Needell, *A Tropical Belle Epoque. Elite Culture and Society in Turn-of-the-Century Rio de Janeiro* (New York: Cambridge University Press, 1988), pp. 135–36, 212–15; and José Brito Broca, *A vida literária no Brasil,* p. 124.

100. Cooper, *The Brazilians and Their Country,* p. 125.

101. J. C. Oakenfull, *Brazil: Past, Present, and Future,* pp. 662–63; Jacob Penteado, *Belènzinho, 1910 (Retrato de uma época)* (São Paulo: Livraria Martins, 1962), pp. 52, 59–60; José Joaquim de Campos da Costa Medeiros e Albuquerque, *O perigo americano* (Rio de Janeiro: Leite Ribeiro and Maurillo, 1919), p. 9.

102. *O Escrínio* (Terezinha), Feb. 21, 1909, p. 3.

103. Pinto Perreira, *A mulher no Brasil,* pp. 5, 86–88.

104. Reis Carvalho [Oscar d'Alva], "A questão feminino," *Kosmos* (Rio de Janeiro), Jan., Feb., March, and April 1904 (unpaginated).

105. Eunapio Deiró, "A mulher perante as religiões antigas e o christianismo," *Kosmos,* Dec. 1904.

106. Article from *O Jornal do Comercio* reprinted in *A Mensageira,* Aug. 31, 1899, pp. 113, 137.

107. Josephina Alvares de Azevedo, *A mulher moderna. Trabalhos de propaganda* (Rio de Janeiro: Montenegro, 1891), pp. 116–17.

108. *Escrínio,* Aug. 26, 1901, p. 2.

109. Quoted in Andradina América Andrada de Oliveira, *Divórcio?* (Pôrto Alegre: Livraria Universal, 1912), p. 21.

110. Quoted in Oliveira, *Divórcio?,* p. 208.

111. Ibid., pp. 8–18.

112. *Escrínio,* June 12, 1901, p. 2; Oliveira, *Divórcio?,* pp. 8–18, 75–90; Lola de Oliveira, *Minha mãe* (Rio de Janeiro: [Livraria Laemmert], 1958), pp. 97–100; Pedro Maia Soares, "Feminismo no Rio Grande do Sul: Primeiros apontamentos (1835–1945)," in *Vivência. História, sexualidade e imagens femininas,* ed. Maria Cristina A. Bruschini and Fúlvia Rosemberg, pp. 142–45 (São Paulo: Editôra Brasiliense, 1980).

Chapter 4. The Women's Suffrage Movement

1. John Nist, *The Modernist Movement in Brazil* (Austin: University of Texas Press, 1967), discusses the Modern Art Week and the modernist movement. See also Mário da

Silva Brito, *História do modernismo brasileiro*, 2d rev. ed. (Rio de Janeiro: Civilização Brasileira, 1964).

2. See, for example, Francisco Figueira de Mello e Vasconcellos, *Educação sexual da mulher (These inaugural apresentada á Faculdade de Medicina do Rio de Janeiro em 5 de novembro de 1915)* (Rio de Janeiro, 1915).

3. Susan Kent Besse, "Freedom and Bondage: The Impact of Capitalism on Women in São Paulo, Brazil, 1917–1937" (Ph.D. diss., Yale University, 1983), pp. 183–88. This excellent study deals with both public and private aspects of the lives of middle- and upper-class *paulista* women, including education, work, and marriage, and their integration into a consumer society.

4. Besse, "Freedom and Bondage," pp. 277–83. On the life of Tarsila do Amaral, see Aracy A. Amaral, *Tarsila. Sua obra e seu tempo*, 2 vols. (São Paulo: Editora Perspectiva, 1975). The activities of women in the modernist movement are analyzed by Mary Lombardi, "Women in the Modern Art Movement in Brazil: Salon Leaders, Artists, and Musicians, 1917–1930" (Ph.D. diss., University of California, Los Angeles, 1973).

5. See, for example, Mariana Coelho, *Evolução do feminismo. Subsídios para a sua história* (Rio de Janeiro: Imprensa Moderna, 1933), p. 509.

6. Theodoro de Moraes, "Escolas Normaes Livres," *Educação* (São Paulo) 4 (July–September 1928): 151.

7. Olímio Barros Vidal, *Precursoras brasileiras* (Rio de Janeiro: A Noite, 1955), pp. 272–73; Antonio Austregesilo Lima, *Perfil da mulher brasileira (Esbôço acêrca do feminismo no Brasil)* (Paris: Livrarias Aillaud e Bertrand, 1923), p. 146; Adalzira Bittencourt, *A mulher paulista na historia* (Rio de Janeiro: Livros de Portugal, 1954), pp. 203–6.

8. For the election figures and an incisive study of political participation in Brazil see Joseph L. Love, "Political Participation in Brazil, 1881–1969," *Luso-Brazilian Review* 7 (December 1970): 3–24. An excellent set of coordinated regional political studies is provided by Love, *São Paulo in the Brazilian Federation* (Stanford: Stanford University Press, 1980); together with John D. Wirth, *Minas Gerais in the Brazilian Federation, 1889–1937* (Stanford: Stanford University Press, 1977); and Robert M. Levine, *Pernambuco in the Brazilian Federation, 1889–1937* (Stanford: Stanford University Press, 1978). See also Joseph L. Love, *Rio Grande do Sul and Brazilian Regionalism, 1882–1930* (Stanford: Stanford University Press, 1971); and Eul-Soo Pang, *Bahia in the First Republic. Coronelismo and Oligarchies, 1889–1934* (Gainesville: University of Florida Press, 1979). Michael L. Conniff ably analyzes politics in Rio de Janeiro in *Urban Politics in Brazil. The Rise of Popularism, 1925–1945* (Pittsburgh: University of Pittsburgh Press, 1981).

9. Salvador de Moya, *Culto a mulher (Tem a mulher, naturalmente, perante a sociedade, os mesmos direitos do homem?)* (São Paulo: Imprensa Methodista, 1912).

10. Manoel Francisco Pinto Pereira, *A mulher no Brasil* (São Paulo: C. Teixeira, 1916), p. 145.

11. Article from *Gazeta de Petrópolis*, cited in *A Mensageira*, Dec. 15, 1897, pp. 70–71.

12. Austregesilo Lima, *Perfil da mulher brasileira*, p. 149.

13. *Tribuna Feminina* (Rio de Janeiro), Nov. 25, 1916, pp. 1–2.

14. Coelho, *Evolução do feminismo*, pp. 218–221; Fanny Tabak, "O status da mulher no Brasil—Victórias e preconceitos," *Cadernos da PUC* 7 (August 1971): 180. The most important statement of this nationalism is Olavo Bilac, *A defesa nacional (Discursos)* (Rio de Janeiro: Liga da Defesa Nacional, 1917).

15. "A mulher na bureaucracia e no magistério," *Nosso Jornal* (Rio de Janeiro), April 30, 1920, (unpaginated); Coelho, *Evolução do feminismo*, pp. 254–60, 499–502; Diva Nolf Nazario, *Voto feminino e feminism. Um anno de feminismo entre nós* (São Paulo: N.p., 1923), pp. 13–15; "O feminismo no Brasil," *Revista Feminina* (São Paulo), Oct. 1918 (unpagin-

ated); "O feminismo em marcha," *Revista Feminina*, July 1919; "Vida feminina," *Revista Feminina*, July 1919; "O feminismo no Brasil," *Revista Feminina*, Aug. 1919; "O feminismo no Brasil," *Revista Feminina*, Sept. 1919; "A mulher e o magistério superior. Mais uma victoria da mulher brasileira," *Revista Feminina*, July and Aug. 1924; Lina Hirsh, "These New 'Amazons,'" *Independent Woman*, Feb. 1935, p. 72; *Revista da Semana* (Rio de Janeiro), July 2, 1932.

16. Schoolteachers and educators figured prominently in different women's rights movements throughout the Western Hemisphere, from Susan B. Anthony, perhaps the most famous suffragist in the United States, to Maria Jesus Alvarado Rivera of Peru, to Amanda Labarca Hubertson, who pioneered the suffrage movement in Chile. On the latter two women see Elsa M. Chaney, *Supermadre. Women in Politics in Latin America* (Austin: University of Texas Press, 1979), chap. 3, pp. 58–86.

17. *O Sexo Feminino* (Rio de Janeiro), Oct. 4, 1873, p. 3; July 22, 1875, p. 4; Nov. 7, 1875, p. 1; *Voz da Verdade* (Rio de Janeiro), May 28, 1885, p. 4; *O Quinze de Novembro do Sexo Feminino* (Rio de Janeiro), Dec. 15, 1889, p. 4; Augusto Victorino Alves Sacramento Blake, *Diccionario bibliographico brazileiro*, 7 vols. (Rio de Janeiro: Imprensa Nacional 1883–1902), 2:371; Ignez Sabino [Pinho Maia], *Mulheres illustres do Brazil* (Rio de Janeiro: Garnier, [1889]), pp. 247–50; Adalzira Bittencourt, *Dicionário bio-biográfico de mulheres ilustres, notaveis e intelectuais*, 2 vols. (Rio de Janeiro: Editôra Pongetti, 1969), 1:116–17.

18. *Nosso Jornal*, Oct. 15, 1919.

19. Ibid., April 30, 1920.

20. "Para uma senhora ganhar dinheiro em casa. Prendas domésticas," *Revista Feminina*, Dec. 1916; "Nossa exposição de trabalhos," *Revista Feminina*, May 1917; "A nossa Revista," *Revista Feminina*, Dec. 1917; "A Revista Feminina no I Congresso Brasileiro de Jornalistas," *Revista Feminina*, Oct. 1918; "O nosso triumpho," *Revista Feminina*, Nov. 1920; São Paulo (state), "Custo de vida. Alimentação. Custo provável da alimentação na cidade de São Paulo," *Boletim do Departamento Estadual do Trabalho* 9, nos. 34 and 35 (1st and 2d trimesters, 1920): 15; Léo de Affonseca Júnior, *O custo da vida no cidade do Rio de Janeiro* (Rio de Janeiro: Imprensa Nacional, 1920), p. 13; Brazil, Directoria Geral de Estatística, *Recenseamento do Brasil realizado em 1 de setembro de 1920*, 5 vols. in 18 (Rio de Janeiro: Typ. da Estatística, 1922–1930), vol. 5, pt. 2, p. xi.

21. "As senhoras brasileiras," *Revista Feminina*, July 1918.

22. "Curriculum vitae" of Bertha Lutz, Arquivo da Federação Brasileira pelo Progresso Feminino, Arquivo Nacional, Arquivo Particular 46 (hereinafter cited as Arquivo da FBPF), Cx. 68. (The Arquivo Nacional is in the process of cataloguing and reclassifying the archive of the federation, and this and following citations of particular box numbers may well no longer be accurate. But since no other classifications yet exist, these may still be of use to other researchers and so are cited herein.) Austregesilo Lima, *Perfil da mulher brasileira*, pp. 42–44; Nazario, *Voto feminino e feminismo*, p. 3.

23. *Revista da Semana*, Dec. 28, 1918.

24. *Nosso Jornal*, Nov. 15, 1919; Roy F. Nash, "The Brains of Brazil's Woman Movement," *The Woman Citizen*, March 25, 1922, pp. 9, 16–17; Mary Gray Peck, *Carrie Chapman Catt. A Biography* (New York: R. W. Wilson, 1944); Edgar Rodrigues, *Novos rumos (História do movimento operário e das lutas sociais no Brasil) (1922–1946)* (Rio de Janeiro: Mundo Livre, n.d.), pp. 49–52.

25. Maria Lacerda de Moura to Bertha Lutz, Oct. 21, 1920, Arquivo da FBPF, Cx. 69.

26. On the life and thought of Maria Lacerda de Moura, see Miriam Lifchitz Moreira, *Outra face do feminismo: Maria Lacerda de Moura* (São Paulo: Editora Ática, 1984).

27. Bertha Lutz to Mrs. Adams, Dec. 18, 1920 (copy), Arquivo da FBPF, Cx. 69.

28. See Bertha Lutz's interviews in *Boa Noite* (Rio de Janeiro), June 4, 1921; *A Noite* (Rio de Janeiro), Oct. 11, 1921; and *O Imperial* (Rio de Janeiro), Nov. 2, 1921.

29. Bertha Lutz to Deputy Maurício de Lacerda, Rio, Nov. 9, 1920 (copy); Lutz to Senator Lopes Gonçalves, Rio, May 13, 1921 (copy); Lutz to Senator Raul Soares, Rio, May 13, 1921 (copy); Lutz to Deputy Nogueira Penido, Rio; Lutz to Caetano Lopes Junior, Director of Estrada de Ferro Central do Brasil, Rio, Nov. 28, 1922 (copy); Lutz to Baron Ramiz Galvão, President of Conselho Superior do Ensino, Rio, May 28, 1921 (copy); Paulina Luisi to Bertha Lutz, Montevideo, July 14, Sept. 12, Oct. 20, and Nov. 28, 1921, Arquivo da FBPF, Cx. 46.

30. Draft of speech by Bertha Lutz to FBPF, Aug. 9, 1930, Arquivo da FBPF, Cx. 68.

31. *Nosso Jornal,* Aug. 1920; *Feminismo Internacional* (New York), Oct. 1923, p. 10.

32. Carrie Chapman Catt, "The History of the Origin of the International Alliance of Women" (unpublished typescript), New York Public Library, Carrie Chapman Catt Collection, Box 5; Peck, *Carrie Chapman Catt,* pp. 121–23, 137–67; Ida Husted Harper, *The Life and Work of Susan B. Anthony,* 3 vols. (Indianapolis: Hollenbeck Press, 1908), 3:1244–47, 1315–28. Regine Deutsch provides a short history of the alliance in *The International Woman Suffrage Alliance. Its History from 1904 to 1929* (London: The International Woman Suffrage Alliance, 1929). A brief discussion of the international movement is given by Edith F. Hurwitz, "The International Sisterhood," in *Becoming Visible. Women in European History,* ed. Renate Bridenthal and Claudia Koonz, pp. 327–45 (Boston: Houghton Mifflin, 1977).

33. Catt, "The History of the Origin of the International Alliance of Women"; Peck, *Carrie Chapman Catt,* pp. 347–51.

34. Francesca Miller, "The International Relations of Women of the Americas, 1890–1930," *The Americas* 43 (October 1986): 171–82.

35. Dorothy N. Hubert, League of Women Voters, to Bertha Lutz, Washington, D.C., Dec. 17, 1921; and Bertha Lutz to Edwin Morgan, U.S. Ambassador to Brazil, Rio, Nov. 24, 1921, Arquivo da FBPF, Cx. 25; "A Significant Pan American Conference," *Bulletin of the Pan American Union* 55 (July 1922): 10–35; Peck, *Carrie Chapman Catt,* pp. 356–61.

36. Heleieth I. B. Saffioti, *A mulher na sociedade de classes. Mito e realidade* (São Paulo: Quatro Artes, 1969), p. 27.

37. The interview is reprinted in Austregesilo Lima, *Perfil da mulher brasileira,* pp. 132–42. See also the statements made by Lutz in the United States, reported in "The Latin Point of View," *Independent Woman,* Oct. 1922, p. 21.

38. Carrie Chapman Catt to Bertha Lutz, London, Sept. 8, 1922, Arquivo da FBPF, Cx. 14; "A Significant Pan American Conference," pp. 28–29; Carrie Chapman Catt, "Summing up South America," *The Woman Citizen,* June 2, 1923, pp. 7–8, 26; Austregesilo Lima, *Perfil da mulher brasileira,* p. 136; Peck, *Carrie Chapman Catt,* pp. 373–74; Coelho, *Evolução do feminismo,* pp. 401–17.

39. "Relatório da Federação Brasileira pelo Progresso Feminino, 1922–1924," Arquivo da FBPF, Cx. 7; Bernice Martins Prates to Valentina Biosca, Belo Horizonte, Oct. 17, Nov. 15, and Nov. 26, 1922; Evelina de Arruda Pereira to Bertha Lutz, São Paulo, Nov. 24, 1922; Hayda Arruda to Bertha Lutz, São Paulo, Dec. 27, 1923; Bertha Lutz to Katherine Bompas, Rio, Feb. 26, 1923 (copy), Arquivo da FBPF, Cx. 69.

40. *Estatutos da Federação Brasileira pelo Progresso Feminino* (Rio de Janeiro: Olympica, 1936), pp. 3–4.

41. "Conferencia pelo Progresso Feminino"; "O Trabalho feminino nas fabricas. These apresentada á Primeira Conferencia pelo Progresso Feminino em dezembro de 1922"; "These apresentada pelo União dos Empregados do Commercio de Rio de Janeiro

a la Conferencia pelo Progresso feminino, realisada no Rio de Janeiro sob os auspícios da Federação Brasileira das Ligas pelo Progresso Feminino," Arquivo da FBPF, Cx. 14; *O Brasil* (Rio de Janeiro), Dec. 9 and Dec. 23, 1922; *Jornal do Brasil* (Rio de Janeiro), Dec. 23, 1922; Austregesilo Lima, *Perfil da mulher brasileira*, pp. 145–46; Coelho, *Evolução do feminismo*, pp. 248–51; Carrie Chapman Catt, "Busy Women in Brazil," *The Woman Citizen*, March 24, 1923, pp. 9–10; "Conferencia Brasileira pelo progresso feminino. Alliança Brasileira pelo Suffrágio Feminino," *Revista Feminina*, Jan. 1923.

42. "Relatório da Federação Brasileira pelo Progresso Feminino, 1922–1924," Arquivo da FBPF, Cx. 7; "Estatutos da Alliança pelo Suffrágio Feminino," Arquivo da FBPF, Cx. 42; Carrie Chapman Catt, "Busy Women in Brazil," pp. 9–10; Nazario, *Voto feminino e feminismo*, pp. 60–68.

43. Carrie Chapman Catt, "Summing up South America," p. 26.

44. Carrie Chapman Catt, Typescript copy of speech given in New York City, 1924, New York Public Library, Carrie Chapman Catt Collection, Box 3.

45. Carrie Chapman Catt, "Busy Women in Brazil," p. 9.

46. Bertha Lutz to Carrie Chapman Catt, July 24, 1940 (copy), New York Public Library, Carrie Chapman Catt Collection, Box 5; Lutz to Catt, Sept. 20, 1939 (copy), Arquivo da FBPF.

47. Catt, "Summing up South America," p. 7; Catt, "Anti-Feminism in South America," *Current History Magazine*, April–Sept. 1923, p. 1033.

48. Interview with Carmen Velasco Portinho, Rio de Janeiro, June 11, 1984.

49. Ibid.

50. Hirsh, "These New Amazons," *Independent Woman*, Feb. 1935, pp. 46, 72; Austregesilo Lima, *Perfil da mulher brasileira*, p. 146; *Boletim da Federação Brasileira pelo Progresso Feminino* 1 (February 1935): 2, 4; Nash, "The Brains of Brazil's Woman Movement," pp. 9, 16.

51. Interview with Carmen Portinho, Rio de Janeiro, June 20, 1983.

52. Interviews with Carmen Portinho, Rio de Janeiro, June 20, 1983, and June 11, 1984; Nazario, *Voto feminino e feminismo*, pp. 2–30; Coelho, *Evolução do feminismo*, pp. 213–14, 218–19, 253, 266–68.

53. Interview with Carmen Portinho, Rio de Janeiro, June 11, 1984.

54. Austregesilo Lima, *Perfil da mulher brasileira*, pp. 121–23.

55. João Batista Cascudo Rodrigues, *A mulher brasileira. Direitos políticos e civís* (Fortaleza: Imprensa Universitária do Ceará, 1962), pp. 46–52; Nazario, *Voto feminino e feminismo*, p. 59; Coelho, *Evolução do feminismo*, pp. 227–32; Morris Blachman, "Eve in an Adamocracy: The Politics of Women in Brazil" (Ph.D. diss., New York University, 1976), pp. 140–43.

56. See, for example, articles by and about her in *The Woman Citizen*, March 25, 1922; *Equal Rights*, Aug. 22, 1931; *Independent Woman*, Feb. 1935.

57. Peck, *Carrie Chapman Catt*, p. 360.

58. Interview with Carmen Portinho, Rio de Janeiro, June 11, 1984.

59. Interview with Maria Rita Soares de Andrade, Rio de Janeiro, June 21, 1983.

60. Telephone interview with Elisa Pinho Osborne, Rio de Janeiro, June 11, 1984.

61. Response of Lylia Guedes to questionnaire of Departmento de Propaganda da Federação Brasileira pelo Progresso Feminino, September 1936, Arquivo da FBPF.

62. *Rio Jornal* (Rio de Janeiro), Dec. 13, 1921.

63. Memorandum from Executive Committee of Federação Brasileira pelo Progresso Feminino to Deputy Basílio Magalhães, 1924, reprinted in Coelho, *Evolução do feminismo*, p. 245.

64. Elisabeth Bastos, *Justiça, alegria, felicidade (Os novos rumos do feminismo brasileiro)* (Rio de Janeiro: Livraria Jacintho [1935]), pp. 45, 74, 78, 83.

65. Lola de Oliveira, *Hontem e hoje* (São Paulo: Paulista, 1928), p. 61.

66. Else Nascimento Machado, *O progresso feminino e sua base* (São Paulo: Imprensa Methodista, 1922), 72.

67. "Agosto," *Revista Feminina*, Aug. 1919; "Janeiro," *Revista Feminina*, Jan. 1920; "Mulheres assassinadas," *Revista Feminina*, March 20, 1920; "Vida Feminina," *Revista Feminina*, March 1920; "O assassinos de mulheres," *Revista Feminina*, April 1920; "O jury esperança dos assassinos," *Revista Feminina*, Aug. 1920; "Os assassinos de mulheres," *Revista Feminina*, Feb. 1921; "Os direitos da mulher," *Revista Feminina*, Sept. 1921; "Abril," *Revista Feminina*, April 1922; "Junho," *Revista Feminina*, June 1922; "Liquidações femininas," *Revista Feminina*, June 1922; "O julgamento de uma mulher," *Revista Feminina*, June 1922.

68. Maria Eugenia Afonso Celso, *De relance . . . Chronicas de B.F.* (São Paulo: Monteiro Lobato, 1923), pp. 31–35.

69. Coelho, *Evolução do feminismo*, p. 12.

70. Ibid., pp. 22, 566–68; Bastos, *Justiça, alegria, felicidade*, pp. 85–88; Bertha Lutz, *13 princípios básicos. Suggestões ao Ante-projecto da Constituição* (Rio de Janeiro: Federação Brasileira pelo Progresso Feminino, 1933), pp. 54, 57. On the moral reform campaigns in Uruguay and Argentina, including attempts to abolish regulated prostitution, see Cynthia Little, "Moral Reform and Feminism. A Case Study," *Journal of Interamerican Studies and World Affairs* 17 (November 1975): 386–97. The little-known life of Ercília Cobra has been researched by Maria Lucia de Barros Mott, "Biografia de uma revoltada: Ercília Nogueira Cobra," *Cadernos de Pesquisa* 58 (August 1986): 89–102. Writings by and about Patrícia Galvão are collected in Augusto de Campos, ed., *Pagú. Patrícia Galvão: Vida-obra* (São Paulo: Editora Brasiliense, 1982); while Susan K. Besse provides a brief biography, "Pagú: Patrícia Galvão—Rebel," in *The Human Tradition in Latin America. The Twentieth Century*, ed. William H. Beezley and Judith Ewell, pp. 103–17 (Wilmington, Del.: Scholar-Resources, 1987).

71. Coelho, *Evolução do feminismo*, pp. 221–26; Tabak, "O status da mulher no Brasil," p. 181; Blachman, "Eve in an Adamocracy, " p. 142.

72. Interview with Carmen Portinho, Rio de Janeiro, June 11, 1984.

73. *Boletim da Federação Brasileira pelo Progresso Feminino* 1 (February 1935): 2; Coelho, *Evolução do feminismo*, pp. 237–38.

74. Nazario, *Voto feminino e feminismo*, p. 30.

75. Ibid., p. 87.

76. Austregesilo Lima, *Perfil da mulher brasileira*, pp. 125–26.

77. *O Jornal*, Jan. 1, 1928; Coelho, *Evolução do feminismo*, p. 265.

78. Jorge Americano, *São Paulo naquelle tempo (1895-1915)* (São Paulo: Edição Saraiva, 1957), pp. 418–19.

79. Maria Lacerda de Moura. *"A mulher é uma degenerada,"* 3d ed. (Rio de Janeiro: Civilização Brasileira, 1932), pp. 80, 85.

80. *A Cigarra* (São Paulo), Jan. 1, 1922.

81. Moura, *"A mulher é uma degenerada,"* pp. 63–64.

82. Afonso Henriques de Lima Barreto, *Coisas do reino do jambón*, 2d ed. (São Paulo: Editôra Brasileira, 1961), pp. 54, 65.

83. Lima Barreto, *Coisas do reino do jambón*, pp. 55–62, 70–74; Lima Barreto, *Marginália*, 2d ed. (São Paulo: Editôra Brasileira, 1961), p. 147; *Vida urbana*, 2d ed. (São Paulo: Editôra Brasileira, 1961), p. 279.

84. Machado, *O progresso feminino e sua base*, pp. 55–59.

85. Interview with Carmen Portinho, Rio de Janeiro, June 11, 1984.

86. Interview with Maria Rita Soares de Andrade, Rio de Janeiro, June 21, 1984.

87. *A Reacção* (São Paulo), Aug. 22, 1931, p. 4.

88. See, for example: Celso, *De relance*, pp. 25–30; "A Revista Feminina no I Congresso Brasileiro de Jornalistas," *Revista Feminina*, Oct. 1918; Marieta Lopes de Souza, "O feminismo que eu amo," *Brasil Feminino* (Rio de Janeiro), Feb. 1932, p. 2.

89. Maria Lacerda de Moura, *Religião do amor e da belleza*, 2d ed. (São Paulo: Empreza Typographica Editôra "O Pensamento," 1929), pp. 44–49, 104–7; Moura, *Amai e . . . não vos multipliqueis* (Rio de Janeiro: Civilização Brasileira, 1932), p. 187.

90. Austregesilo Lima, *Perfil da mulher brasileira*.

91. Moura, *Amai e . . . não vos multipliqueis*, pp. 37–38.

92. Historical studies of the Roman Catholic church and politics in Brazil include José Oscar Beozzo, "A Igreja entre a Revolução de 1930, O Estado Novo e a redemo-cratização," in *História geral da civilização brasileira III. O Brasil republicano 4. Economia e cultura (1930–1964)*, 2d ed., ed. Boris Fausto, pp. 271–341 (São Paulo: Difel, 1986); Margaret Todaro Williams, "Integralism and the Brazilian Catholic Church," *Hispanic American Historical Review* 54 (August 1974): 431–52; Williams, "The Politicization of the Brazilian Catholic Church. The Catholic Electoral League," *Journal of Interamerican Studies and World Affairs* 16 (Aug. 1974): 301–25, on the 1930s; and, concentrating on the post-1930 period, Thomas C. Bruneau, *The Church in Brazil. The Politics of Religion* (Austin: University of Texas Press, 1982); and Scott Mainwaring, *The Catholic Church and Politics in Brazil, 1916–1985* (Stanford: Stanford University Press, 1986). For a detailed biography of Cardinal Leme, see Sister Maria Regina do Santo Rosario [Laurita Pessoa Gabaglia], *O cardeal Leme (1882–1942)* (Rio de Janeiro: José Olympio, 1962).

93. Interviews with Zéia Pinho Rezende, Rio de Janeiro, June 14,1984; and Carmen Portinho, Rio de Janeiro, June 20, 1983.

94. Interviews with Maria Luiza Bittencourt, Rio de Janeiro, June 13, 1984; Maria Sabina de Albuquerque, Rio de Janeiro, June 21, 1983; Maria Rita Soares de Andrade, Rio de Janeiro, June 8, 1984; Carmen Portinho, Rio de Janeiro, June 20, 1983, and June 14, 1984.

95. Anna Macías, *Against All Odds. The Feminist Movement in Mexico to 1940* (Westport, Conn.: Greenwood Press, 1982).

96. Chaney, *Supermadre*, pp. 69–73; Carrie Chapman Catt, "Picturesque Peru," *The Woman Citizen*, May 19, 1923, pp. 9–10, 24–25.

97. Rodrigues, *A mulher brasileira*, pp. 55–72; Blachman, "Eve in an Adamocracy," pp. 139–41. In Mexico, too, action by one state governor could provide a striking contrast with events elsewhere. Salvador Alvarado, appointed governor of Yucatán in 1915, introduced women's rights legislation during his three years in office; see Anna Macías, *Against All Odds*, pp. 67–81.

98. "Desde que uma só exista não ha motivo para que não sejam eleitoras todas as mulheres habilitadas no Brasil," Arquivo do Instituto Histórico e Geográfico Brasileiro, Misc. 206, 9, 4, no. 13. The actual list of signatures, headed by Bertha Lutz's, is found in the Arquivo da FBPF, Cx. 42.

99. *A Vanguarda* (Rio de Janeiro), May 11, 1928.

100. Coelho, *Evolução do feminismo*, pp. 266–68; *Boletim da Federação Brasileira pelo Progresso Feminino* 1 (February 1935): 2.

101. *Educação* 3 (April–June 1928): 212.

102. On the demise of the Old Republic and the beginnings of the Vargas period see Jordan M. Young, *The Brazilian Revolution of 1930 and the Aftermath* (New Brunswick, N.J.: Rutgers University Press, 1967); and Boris Fausto, *A revolução de 1930. Historiografia e história* (São Paulo: Editôra Brasiliense, 1972).

103. Coelho, *Evolução do feminismo,* p. 268.

104. José Francisco Assis Brazil, *Democracia representativa. Do voto e do modo de votar,* 4th ed. (Rio de Janeiro: Imprensa Nacional, 1931), pp. 51–57.

105. See Andrew Rosen, *Rise Up, Women! The Militant Campaign of the Women's Social and Political Union, 1903–1914* (London: Routledge and Kegan Paul, 1974).

106. Coelho, *Evolução do feminismo,* p. 269; interview with Maria Luiza Bittencourt, Rio de Janeiro, June 13, 1984.

107. Alzira Vargas do Amaral Peixoto, *Getúlio Vargas, meu pai* (Rio de Janeiro: Editôra Globo, 1960), p. 98.

108. *Diário de Notícias* (Rio de Janeiro), Oct. 31, 1931; *O Globo* (Rio de Janeiro), Nov. 4, 1930, and Jan. 13, 1931; transcription of speech by Bertha Lutz, c. 1973, "A Federação Brasileira pelo Progresso Feminino. Movimento Feminista de 1931–1937. Extrato de uma gravação em Uher," Arquivo da FBPF, Cx. 68; Coelho, *Evolução do feminismo,* pp. 269–70; Blachman, "Eve in an Adamocracy," pp. 151–58; Rodrigues, *A mulher brasileira,* pp. 75–79.

109. Adalzira Bittencourt, *Dicionário bio-bibliográphico de mulheres,* 2:329–32; *Aurora Social* (Recife), June 26, 1906, p. 3; *Echo das Damas* (Rio de Janeiro), Jan. 14, 1888, p. 1; *A Família* (São Paulo), Feb. 2, 1889, p. 3; July 6, 1889, p. 4; *A Mensageira* (São Paulo), March 31, 1898, pp. 177–79; May 15, 1898, pp. 239–40; Feb. 15, 1899, pp. 6–9.

110. *Renascença* (São Paulo), Feb. 1923.

111. Zélia Gattai, *Anarquistas, graças a Deus* (Rio de Janeiro: Editôra Record, 1979), p. 210.

112. See the documentary study edited by Susan Groag Bell and Karen M. Offen, *Women, the Family, and Freedom,* 2 vols. (Stanford: Stanford University Press, 1983).

113. Studies of the tensions between organized socialism and the European women who espoused socialist-feminist theories include Marilyn Jacoby Boxer and Jean H. Quataert, eds., *Socialist Women: European Socialist Feminism in the Nineteenth and Twentieth Centuries* (New York: Elsevier Press, 1978); Jane Slaughter and Robert Kern, eds., *European Women on the Left: Socialism, Feminism, and the Problems Faced by Political Women, 1880 to the Present* (Westport, Conn.: Greenwood Press, 1981); Charles Sowerwine, *Sisters or Citizens? Women and Socialism in France Since 1876* (Cambridge: Cambridge University Press, 1982); and Jean H. Quataert, *Reluctant Feminists in German Social Democracy, 1885–1917* (Princeton: Princeton University Press, 1979).

114. *O Estado de São Paulo* (São Paulo), Aug. 28, 1902, p. 3; *Gazeta Operaria* (Rio de Janeiro), Sept. 28, 1902, pp. 1–3.

115. On Argentine feminism see Asunción Lavrin, *The Ideology of Feminism in the Southern Cone, 1900–1914,* Working Paper no. 169, Latin American Program (Washington, D.C.: The Wilson Center, 1986); and Marifran Carlson, *Feminismo! The Woman's Movement in Argentina from Its Beginnings to Eva Peron* (Chicago: Academy Chicago Publishers, 1988). For a review of the literature of feminism in Latin America see Sandra McGee Deutsch, "Feminist Studies," in *Latinas of the Americas: A Source Book,* ed. K. Lynn Stoner, pp. 129–74 (New York: Garland, 1989).

116. "Livro de Matrícula"; "Atas. Anos: 1922–1931 Vol. 1," Arquivo da FBPF, Cx. 68.

117. Membership list of the Federação Mattogrossense pelo Progresso Feminino, August 1934, Arquivo da FBPF, Cx. 36.

118. Interview with Carmen Portinho, Rio de Janeiro, June 20, 1983.

119. Minutes of the meetings of the Directorate of the Federação Brasileira pelo Progresso Feminino, June 19, Aug. 10, Sept. 16, and Nov. 17, 1924, "Atas. Anos: 1922–1931, Vol. 1," Arquivo da FBPF, Cx. 68.

120. *A Noite,* Nov. 20, 1924, p. 7.

121. *A Reacção* (São Paulo), Aug. 15, 1931, p. 1.

122. *Diário de Notícias* (Rio de Janeiro), June 26, 1931; *A Noite,* June 26, 1931.

123. *Boletim da Federação Brasileira pelo Progresso Feminino* 2 (March 1936): 9.

124. Lutz, *13 princípios básicos,* p. 119.

125. Bertha Lutz to President of the Republic, Rio de Janeiro, Dec. 29, 1921 (draft), Arquivo da FBPF, Cx. 42; Alice Pinheiro Coimbra, "Histórico do feminismo no Brasil" (typescript), Arquivo da FBPF, Cx. 68; FBPF to Geraldo de Paula e Souza, Head of the Sanitation Service of São Paulo, Rio de Janeiro, March 20, 1924 (draft), Arquivo da FBPF, Cx. 42; Judge José Candido de Albuquerque Mello Mattos to Bertha Lutz, Rio de Janeiro, Feb. 23, 1924, Arquivo da FBPF, Cx. 42; João Luiz Alves to Bertha Lutz, Rio de Janeiro, Feb. 26, 1924, Cx. 42; *A Noite,* Nov. 20, 1924, p. 7; Adalzira Bittencourt, *A mulher paulista na história* (Rio de Janeiro: Livros de Portugal, 1954), p. 300.

126. Petition to Minister of Agriculture, Industry, and Commerce, Rio de Janeiro, June 19, 1924 (copy), Arquivo da FBPF, Cx. 53.

127. *Boletim da Federação Brasileira pelo Progresso Feminino* 2 (December 1934): 2–3.

128. Brazil, Câmara dos Deputados, Commissão de Estatuto da Mulher, *O trabalho feminino. A mulher na ordem economica e social. Documentação organizada por Bertha Lutz Presidente da Commissão* (Rio de Janeiro: Imprensa Nacional, 1937), pp. 70–72.

129. Brazil, *O trabalho feminino,* pp. 65–68.

130. *O Globo,* Jan. 13, 1931; *A Batalha* (Rio de Janeiro), June 5, 1931; *Brasil Feminino* (Rio de Janeiro), May, 1932, p. 26; Blachman, "Eve in an Adamocracy," pp. 158–60.

131. Brazil, *O trabalho feminino,* pp. 11–19; Lutz, *13 princípios básicos; Boletim da Federação Brasileira pelo Progresso Feminino* 1 (February 1935): 3; Bertha Lutz, *A nacionalidade da mulher casada* (Rio de Janeiro: Irmões Pongetti, 1933).

132. Interviews with Carmen Portinho, Rio de Janeiro, June 20, 1983, and June 11, 1984.

133. Interview with Maria Rita Soares de Andrade, Rio de Janeiro, June 21, 1983.

134. *A Noite,* Jan. 25, 1933; *Boletim da Federação Brasileira pelo Progresso Feminino* 2 (January 1936): 2.

135. "Vida Feminina," *Revista Feminina,* Jan. 1917; "As reivindicações da mulher," *Revista Feminina,* July 1919; "O feminismo no Brasil. Uma candidata a intendente municipal," *Revista Feminina,* Oct. 1919; "O Feminismo no Brasil. Por que e para que foi creado o 'Partido Liberal Feminista,'" *Revista Feminina,* April 1925; Coelho, *Evolução do feminismo,* pp. 104; 218–21; Lima Barreto, *Coisas do reino do jambón,* p. 60; Lima Barreto, *Marginália,* p. 279.

136. *Nosso século. 1930–1945. A era de Vargas* (São Paulo: Abril Cultura, 1980), p. 105.

137. "Conferencia pelo Progresso Feminino," 1922, Arquivo da FBPF, Cx. 14; Bittencourt, *A mulher paulista na história,* p. 296; Carolina Ribeiro, "A mulher paulista em 32," *Revista do Instituto Histórico e Geográfico de São Paulo* 59 (1961): 247–62; Moema Toscano, "Mulher, trabalho e política. Caminhos cruzados do feminismo" (Thesis of livredocência, Pontificada Universidade Católica do Rio de Janeiro, 1975), pp. 52–53; Carlota Pereira de Queiroz, "Discurso pronunciado na Câmara dos Deputados pela Dra. Carlota Pereira de Queiroz (da Bancada Paulista) em 8 de agosto de 1935" (Rio de Janeiro: Oficinas Gráficas do "Jornal do Brasil," 1936); Ilan Rachum, "Feminism, Woman Suffrage, and National Politics in Brazil: 1922–1937," *Luso Brazilian Review* 14 (Summer 1977): 126–27; Rodrigues, *A mulher brasileira,* p. 80; Blachman, "Eve in an Adamocracy," p. 161.

138. *Boletin da Federação Brasileira pelo Progresso Feminino* 1 (December 1934): 3; and 2 (September 1936): 6; Bittencourt, *A mulher paulista na história*, p. 296.

139. Saffioti, *A mulher na sociedade de classes*, pp. 282–89; Rachel Soihet, "Bertha Lutz e a ascensão social da mulher, 1919–1937," (Master's thesis, Universidade Federal Fluminense, 1974), pp. 38–45. The text of the ante-projecto do Departamento Nacional da Mulher presented by Bertha Lutz is found in Brazil, *Trabalho feminino*, pp. 151–54.

140. On the Aliança Nacional Libertadora see Robert W. Levine, *The Vargas Regime. The Critical Years, 1934–1938* (New York: Columbia University Press, 1970), pp. 58–80.

141. *O Imparcial* (Santo André), June 13, 1935, p. 1; July 11, 1935, p. 1. Professor John French of Florida International University kindly supplied me with copies of these newspaper articles.

142. Plínio Salgado, *A mulher no século XX*, in *Obras completas de Plínio Salgado*, 20 vols. (São Paulo: Editôra das Américas, 1955), 8:259–301.

143. See Hélgio Trinidade, *Integralismo (O fascismo brasileiro na década de 30)* (São Paulo: Difusão Européia do Livro, 1974); and Levine, *The Vargas Years*, pp. 81–99.

144. Richard Bourne, *Getúlio Vargas of Brazil, 1883–1954. Sphinx of the Pampas* (London: Charles Knight, 1974); pp. 97–98; Mary M. Cannon, *Women in Brazil Today* (Washington, D.C.: U.S. Department of Labor, 1943), p. 8; "Feminism in Brazil," *Bulletin of the Pan American Union* 70 (December 1936): 981–82; interviews with Maria Rita Soares de Andrade, Rio de Janeiro, June 21, 1983, and Maria Sabina de Albuquerque, Rio de Janeiro, June 21, 1983; transcription of speech by Bertha Lutz, c. 1973, "A Federação Brasileira pelo Progresso Feminino. Movimento Feminista de 1931–1937. Extrato de uma gravação em Uher," Arquivo da FBPF, Cx. 68; "Carmen Portinho Lutz (Notas biográphicas)," Arquivo da FBPF, Cx. 36; Maria Rita Soares de Andrade to Raimundo Magalhães, Rio de Janeiro [1950], Arquivo da FBPF, Cx. 53.

145. Bertha Lutz to President Getúlio Vargas, Rio de Janeiro, July 7, 1932 (copy), Arquivo da FBPF, Cx. 53.

146. "Relatório sobre as inscrições ao concurso para provimento de cargos de consul de 3ª classe, do quadro único do Ministério das Relações Exteriores," Rio de Janeiro, June 28, 1937, and Processo no. 2158, Arquivo Nacional, Documentação da Presidência, DASP, Série: Pessoal, Subsérie: Seleção, Concursos Diplomata, (unclassified); information supplied by D. Nadir Duarte Ferreira, head of the Arquivo Histórico do Ministério das Relações Exteriores, Dec. 1986; Brazil, *Coleção das leis da República dos Estados Unidos do Brasil de 1938*, vol. 4: *Decretos-leis* (Rio de Janeiro: Imprensa Nacional, 1939), p. 30; Flávio Mendes de Oliveira Castro, *História da organização do Ministério das Relações Exteriores* (Brasília: Editôra Universidade de Brasília, 1983), p. 335; Sérgio Bath, *História da legislação do Instituto Rio Branco* (Brasília: Instituto Rio Branco, 1975), p. 9.

147. Artur de Souza Costa, Ministro do Estado da Fazenda, to Presidente do Departamento Administrativo do Serviço Público, Rio de Janeiro, July 15, 1942; Presidente do Departamento Administrativo do Serviço Público to Ministro do Estado da Fazenda, Rio de Janeiro, Sept. 28, 1942; Ovídio Paulo de Menezes Gil, Chefe do Gabinete, to Presidente do Departamento Administrativo do Serviço Público, Rio de Janeiro, Oct. 19, 1942, Arquivo Nacional, Documentação da Presidência, DASP, Série: Pessoal, Subsérie: Seleção, Concursos Contador (unclassified).

148. Relatório of Edmundo Perry, Departamento Nacional de Seguros Privados e Capitalização, Sept. 9, 1944, Arquivo Nacional, Documentação da Presidência, DASP, Série: Pessoal, Subsérie: Seleção, Concursos (unclassified).

149. Process no. 3, 747/47, Arquivo Nacional, Documentação Presidência, DASP, Série: Pessoal, Subsérie: Seleção, Concursos Escrivão de Polícia, 1941–43, 1945–49.

150. Bertha Lutz to Carrie Chapman Catt, July 24, 1940 (copy), New York Public Library, Carrie Chapman Catt Collection, Box 5.

Epilogue: Fifty Years Later

1. John D. French with Mary Lynn Pederson, "Women and Working Class Mobilization in Postwar São Paulo, 1945–1948," *Latin American Research Review* 24, no. 3 (1989): 108–10. Some activities of the Brazilian Federation of Women and other women's organizations are recalled by one of the federation's founders, Ana Montenegro, in *Ser ou não ser feminista* (Recife: Guarapes, 1981), pp. 63–77. Maria Augusta Tibiriçá Miranda provides a biography of her mother in *Alice Tibiriçá. Lutas e ideais* (Rio de Janeiro: PLG Comunicação, 1980). Alice Tibiriçá was born into a traditional *mineiro* family and married into a leading *paulista* family; she participated actively in the women's suffrage movement and fought in various public health campaigns, particularly that against leprosy in the 1920s, and then became the first president of the Brazilian Federation of Women and a leading figure in the campaign for a state monopoly on petroleum in the 1940s.

2. Few attempts have been made at comparative studies of women and politics in Latin America, such as the discussions by Jane Jacquette, "Female Political Participation in Latin America," in *Sex and Class in Latin America,* ed. June Nash and Helen Icken Safa, pp. 221–44 (New York: Praeger, 1976); and "Female Political Participation in Latin America: Raising Feminist Issues," in *Women in the World, 1975–1985. The Women's Decade,* ed. Lynne B. Iglitzin and Ruth Ross, pp. 243–69 (Santa Barbara, Calif.: ABC Clio Information Services, 1986); Elsa M. Chaney's book, dealing largely with Peru and Chile, *Supermadre. Women in Politics in Latin America* (Austin: University of Texas Press, 1980); and Sonia E. Alvarez's fine detailed dissertation focusing on Brazil, "The Politics of Gender in Latin America: Comparative Perspectives on Women in the Brazilian Transition to Democracy" (Ph.D. diss., Yale University, 1986).

3. A striking portrait in novel form of the role and the problems faced by the leading women in a reform party in Peru, Víctor Raul Haya de la Torre's Alianza Popular Revolucionária Americana (APRA), is drawn by Madga Portal in *La trampa* (Lima: Ediciones Raiz, 1956).

4. See Eva Alterman Blay, *As prefeitas. A participação da mulher no Brasil* (Rio de Janeiro: Avenir Editora, 1981); Fanny Tabak and Moema Toscano, *Mulher e politica* (Rio de Janeiro: Paz e Terra, 1982); and Fanny Tabak, *Autoritarismo e participação da mulher* (Rio de Janeiro: Graal, 1983).

5. Maria Rita Soares de Andrade to Raimundo Magalhães [1950], (copy), Arquivo da Federação Brasileira pelo Progresso Feminino, Arquivo Nacional, Arquivo Particular 46, Cx. 53.

6. Ruth Marie Barbosa Goulart [Ruth Bueno, pseud.], *Regime jurídica da mulher casada,* 2d ed. (Rio de Janeiro: Forense, 1970), pp. 9–70; Ruth Bueno, "A estrutura dos direitos e deveres da mulher no anteprojeto de Código Civil," *Jurídica* (1972): 3–16.

7. Studies which discuss women and politics during the Allende years include Michele Mattelart, "The Feminine Version of the Coup d'Etat," in *Sex and Class in Latin America,* ed. June Nash and Helen Icken Safa, pp. 279–301 (New York: Praeger, 1974); Elsa Chaney, "The Mobilization of Women in Allende's Chile," in *Women in Politics,* ed. Jane Jacquette, pp. 267–80 (New York: John Wiley, 1974); Maria de los Angeles Crummet, "El Poder Feminino: The Mobilization of Women against Socialism in Chile," *Latin American Perspectives* 4 (Fall 1977): 103–13; Carol Andreas, "The Chilean Woman: Reform, Reaction and Resistance," *Latin American Perspectives* 4 (Fall 1977): 121–25.
Other cases in which women played important roles in reactionary or right-wing

movements in twentieth-century Latin America include Mexico's Cristero Rebellion and Argentina's Liga Patriótica in the 1920s; see Barbara Ann Miller, "The Roles of Women in the Mexican Cristero Rebellion: *Las señoras y las religiosas*," *The Americas* 40 (January 1984): 303–24; Sandra F. McGee, "The Visible and Invisible Liga Patriótica Argentina, 1919–28: Gender Roles and the Right Wing," *Hispanic American Historical Review* 64 (May 1984): 233–58; and McGee, "Right-Wing Female Activists in Buenos Aires, 1900–1932," in *Women and the Structures of Society: Selected Research from the Fifth Berkshire Conference on the History of Women*, ed. Barbara J. Harris and Joann McNamara, pp. 85–97 (Durham, N.C.: Duke University Press, 1984).

8. Thomas E. Skidmore provides an able political history of the period from Getúlio Vargas's ascension to power in 1930 until João Goulart's overthrow in 1964 in *Politics in Brazil, 1930–1964* (New York: Oxford University Press, 1967), and of the period after Goulart's overthrow in *The Politics of Military Rule in Brazil, 1964–85* (New York: Oxford University Press, 1988). John W. F. Dulles gives a detailed chronology of a decade of events in *Unrest in Brazil: Political-Military Crises, 1955–1964* (Austin: University of Texas Press, 1970). One of the most searching attempts to explain the economic and political causes of the 1964 coup d'etat is that by a leading Brazilian social scientist, Otávio Ianni, *O colapso do populismo no Brasil* (Rio de Janeiro: Civilização Brasileira, 1968).

9. "Dona Amélia Molina Bastos: Ou como e onde marcha a CAMDE," interview given to Stella M. Senra Pollanah, *Livro de Cabeceira da Mulher* I (Rio de Janeiro: Editôra Civilização Brasileira, 1967), 5:159–174.

10. See Solange de Deus Simões, *Deus, pátria e família. As mulheres no golpe de 1964* (Petrópolis: Vozes, 1984).

11. For a general discussion of this phenomenon in an international context see Esther Boserup, *Women's Role in Economic Development* (New York: St. Martin's Press, 1970).

12. On the structure of female employment in the twentieth century see Felicia R. Madeira and Paul I. Singer, *Estrutura do emprego e trabalho feminino no Brasil: 1920–1970*, Cadernos CEBRAP 13 (São Paulo: CEBRAP, 1973). Although a number of studies dealing with questions relating to women and work have appeared in Brazil in recent years, most are case studies of women in particular industries or areas. Among the few broader treatments of women in the work force are Cristina Bruschini, *Mulher e trabalho* (São Paulo: Nobel and Conselho Estadual da Condição Feminina, 1985); and Carmen Barroso, *Mulher, sociedade e estado no Brasil* (São Paulo: Editora Brasiliense, 1982).

13. Madeira and Singer, *Estrutura do emprego e trabalho feminino no Brasil*, p. 17.

14. *Cadernos de Debate*, 2: *Mulher. Depoimentos sobre um trabalho* (São Paulo: Editôra Brasiliense, 1976), p. 46.

15. The position of black women in the work force and the double discrimination they endure is described by Leila González, *Mulher negra*, *Mulherio* 1 (September–October 1981): 8–9; and Sueli Carneiro and Thereza Santos, *Mulher negra*, in *Mulher negra. Política governamental e a mulher*, ed. Sueli Carneiro, Thereza Santos, and Albertina Gordo de Oliveira Costa, pp. 1–54 (São Paulo: Nobel and Conselho Estadual da Condição Feminina, 1985). *Mulher negra: Dossiê sobre a discriminação racial* (São Paulo: Conselho Estadual da Condição Feminina, 1986) provides examples of racial discrimination in other areas as well.

16. *Cadernos de Debate*, 2: *Mulher. Depoimentos sobre um trabalho*, p. 45.

17. Rose Marie Muraro, "Libertação feminina? Existe sim!" *Nova* 7 (April 1974): 96.

18. Among the few studies carried out in Brazil on domestic servants are Heliethe I. B. Saffioti, *Emprego doméstico e capitalismo* (Petrópolis: Vozes, 1978); Zaira Ary Farias, *Domesticidade. "Cativeiro" feminino?* (Rio de Janeiro: Achiamé and Centro da Mulher Brasileira, 1983); and Ely Souto dos Santos, *As domésticas. Um estudo interdisciplinar da realidade social, politica, econômica e jurídica* (Porto Alegre: Editora da Universidade, 1983).

19. Articles on aspects of this congress appeared in *Jornal do Brasil* (Rio de Janeiro), Oct. 25, Oct. 27, and Oct. 28, 1972; and *O Globo* (Rio de Janeiro), Oct. 26, 1972.

20. Interviews with Rose Marie Muraro, Rio de Janeiro, July 6, 1974; Romy Medeiros da Fonseca, Rio de Janeiro, July 11, 1974; "Feminista, sim senhor," interview with Romy Medeiros da Fonseca by Raul Giudicelli, *Ultima Hora* (Rio de Janeiro), Aug. 18, 1972; "Mulher à brasileira," *Jornal do Brasil*, Jan. 11, 1972, sec. B, p. 5.

21. *Jornal do Brasil*, April 14, 1971, p. 14.

22. *Manchete* (Rio de Janeiro), Dec. 1, 1974, pp. 29–34.

23. Jany Chiriac and Solange Padilha, "Características e limites das organizações de base femininas," in *Trabalhadoras do Brasil*, ed. Maria Cristina A. Bruschini and Fúlvia Rosemberg, pp. 191–203 (São Paulo: Editôra Brasiliense, 1982); *Que história é essa? Clube de mães e grupos de mulheres de São Paulo* (São Paulo: Grupo de Educação Popular, 1985); Alvarez, "The Politics of Gender in Latin America," pp. 223–327. For a succinct description of the Christian Base Communities see Afonso Borges Filho [Frei Betto], *O que é comunidade eclesial de base* (São Paulo: Editora Brasiliense, 1981).

24. *Nos Mulheres* (São Paulo) 1 (November–December 1976): 10; "Movimento feminino pela anistia. O papel da mulher na conjuntura brasileira," Congresso Nacional de Anistia, São Paulo, Nov. 1978 (mimeo). Four years of her interviews, talks, and statements, beginning with a key March 1975 interview in *O Pasquim* are collected in Therezinha Godoy Zerbine, *Anistia. Semente da liberdade* (São Paulo: Escolas Profissionais Salesianas, 1979). *Maria Quitéria* (São Paulo, 1977), the bulletin published by the Movimento Feminino pela Anistia, was symbolically named after the "heroine" of the early nineteenth-century independence movement who had participated in the fighting in Bahia disguised as a man.

25. Aspects of the new feminist movement in Brazil have received attention from some social scientists and from some participants in feminist debates, including Eva Alterman Blay, "Women, Redemocratization, and Political Alternatives," in *Brazil's Economic and Political Future*, ed. Julian M. Chacel, Pamela S. Falk, and David V. Fleischer, pp. 199–213 (Boulder, Colo.: Westview Press, 1988); Sonia E. Alvarez, "Politicizing Gender and Engendering Democracy," in *Democratizing Brazil. Problems of Transition and Consolidation*, ed. Alfred Stepan, pp. 205–51 (New York: Oxford University Press, 1988); Alvarez, "The Politics of Gender in Brazil"; Cornelia Butler Flora, "Socialist Feminism in Latin America," in *The United Nations Decade for Women World Conference*, ed. Nyomi Lynn, pp. 69–93 (New York: Hayworth Press, 1984); Marianne Schmink, "Women in Brazilian *Abertura* Politics," *Signs: Journal of Women in Culture and Society* 7 (Autumn 1981): 115–34; Joan Myers Weimer, "The Mother, the Macho, and the State," *International Journal of Women's Studies* 1 (January–February 1978): 73–82; Jane S. Jacquette, "Women, Feminism, and the Transition to Democracy in Latin America," in *Latin America and Caribbean Contemporary Record*, vol. 5, ed. Abraham F. Lowenthal (New York: Holmes and Meier, 1987); Cynthia Sarti, "Feminismo no Brasil: Uma trajétoria particular," *Cadernos de Pesquisa* 64 (February 1988): 38–47; Maria Lygia Quartim de Moraes, *Mulheres em movimento* (São Paulo: Nobel and Conselho Estadual da Condição Feminina, 1985); Anette Goldberg, "Feminismo em regime autoritário: A experiencia do movimento de mulheres no Rio de Janeiro" (Paper presented at the Twelfth Congress of the International Political Science Association, August 1982); Madel T. Luz, ed., *O lugar da mulher (Estudos sobre a condição feminina na sociedade atual)* (Rio de Janeiro: Graal, 1982); *Encontros com a Civilização Brasileira*, no. 26: *Mulher hoje* (Rio de Janeiro: Civilização Brasileira, 1980); Elizabeth Souza Lobo and Maria Celia Paoli, "Notas sobre o movimento no feminino," *Desvios* 1 (November 1982): 46–57.

26. Statements summarizing the positions of some of these groups are found in *O*

movimento de mulheres no Brasil. Cadernos da Associação das Mulheres 3 (São Paulo: Associação das Mulheres, 1979).

27. See Maria da Gloria Marcondes Gohn, *A forca da periféria. A luta das mulheres por creches em São Paulo* (Petrópolis: Vozes, 1985); and Fúlvia Rosemberg, "O movimento de mulheres e a abertura politica no Brasil. O caso da creche," *Cadernos de Pesquisa* 51 (November 1984): 73–79.

28. Aspects of the debate appeared in *Nós Mulheres, Brasil Mulher,* and *Mulherio,* all published in São Paulo.

29. For a statement on women and revolutionary politics as practiced by a shadowy Maoist organization called MR-8, which once advocated armed struggle and then sought to disrupt or take over various feminist meetings and activities, see *A mulhere a revolução brasileira. MR 8: Resoluções sobre o trabalho entre as mulheres* (São Paulo: Editora Quilombo, 1980).

30. *O movimento de mulheres no Brasil,* pp. 43–55.

31. *Memórias do exílio,* vol. 2: *Memórias das mulheres no exílio,* ed. Albertina de Oliveira Costa, Maria Teresa Porciuncula Moraes, Norma Marzola, and Valentina da Rocha Lima, (Rio de Janeiro: Graal, 1980), contains the personal testimonies of some three dozen Brazilian women who endured political exile in the years following the 1964 military coup d'etat. This second volume of *Memórias do exílio* contrasts strongly with the first volume, published in Portugal in 1976 and in Brazil two years later, which focused on male political activities and reactions to exile and contained few accounts by women.

32. See June E. Hahner, "Recent Research on Women in Brazil," *Latin American Research Review* 20, no. 3 (1985): 163–79.

33. *Mulherio* (São Paulo), July–Aug. 1982, pp. 4–5. Less than two years earlier, two books had been published in Brazil which dealt in large part with Bertha Lutz and the suffrage movement: Branca Moreira Alves, *Ideologia e feminismo. A luta da mulher pelo voto no Brasil* (Petrópolis: Vozes, 1980); and June E. Hahner, *A mulher brasileira e suas lutas sociais e políticas, 1850–1937* (São Paulo: Editora Brasiliense, 1981).

34. Heloneida Studart, "Os brasileiros querem o divórcio," *Manchete,* June 1, 1974, pp. 12–13; Nelson Carneiro, *A luta pelo divórcio* (Rio de Janeiro: Livraria São José, 1973); *Latin America* 9 (May 16, 1975): 151; *Latin American Political Report* 11 (July 1, 1977): 198.

35. Romy Medeiros da Fonseca, "A questão ideologica," in *A condição feminina,* ed. Nanci Valadares de Carvalho, pp. 32–38 (São Paulo: Vértice, 1988); *Veja,* June 17, 1987, p. 146.

36. Cícera Fernandes de Oliveira and Danda Prado, *Cícera. Um destino de mulher. Autobiografia duma emigrante nordestina, operária têxtil* (São Paulo: Editora Brasiliense, 1981).

37. *Latin American Economic Report* 7 (June 1, 1979): 163; *Latin American Regional Reports. Brazil,* Nov. 9, 1979, pp. 3–4, and Sept. 12, 1980, pp. 3–4; Alvarez, "Politicizing Gender and Engendering Democracy," pp. 214–25. See also the debates in *Brasil Mulher* (1975–80) and *Nós Mulheres* (1976–78).

38. Rose Marie Muraro, *Sexualidade da mulher brasileira: Corpo e classe social no Brasil* (Petrópolis: Vozes, 1983); Marta Suplicy, *Conversando sobre sexo* (São Paulo: Published by the author, 1983).

39. See, for example, Maria Malta Campos, "Feminismo e separatismo," *Mulherio* 2 (September–October 1982): 3.

40. Blay, "Women, Redemocratization, and Political Alternatives," p. 207.

41. *Informe Mulher* (Brasília) 5 (April 1988): 3.

42. *Mulherio* (December–February 1987): 11–17.

43. Brazil, Secretaria de Planejamento da Presidência da República, Fundação Instituto Brasileiro de Geográfia e Estatística, *IX Recenseamento geral do Brasil. 1980,* vol. 1, tomo 4, no. 1 (Rio de Janeiro: IBGE 1983), p. 10.

44. Brazil, *Constituição. República Federativa do Brasil. 1988.* (Brasília: Centro Gráfica do Senado Federal, 1988); *Nexo* (São Paulo) 1 (June 1988): 26; *New York Times*, Sept. 3, 1988.

45. In *Mulheres espancadas. A violência denunciada* (São Paulo: Cortez Editora, 1985), Maria Amélia Azevedo, following a general discussion of the question, details domestic violence reported to the police in São Paulo in the early 1980s. Bila Sorj and Paula Montero describe feminist efforts to combat domestic violence and aid battered women in Recife in "SOS-Mulher e a luta contra a violência," in *Perspectivas antropológicas da mulher* (Rio de Janeiro: Zahar, 1985), 4:101–7. Mariza Corrêa, *As crimes da paixão* (São Paulo: Editora Brasiliense, 1981), discusses "crimes of passion," the "rules of the game" and the way they apply for men and for women, the history of the concepts of "passion" and "honor" in Brazilian law, the role of the jury, and defense strategies employed by lawyers; her more detailed study, *Morte em família. Representações jurídicas de papeis sexuais* (Rio de Janeiro: Graal, 1983), focuses on the crimes committed in Campinas, São Paulo, between 1952 and 1972 and clearly demonstrates the effects of unequal gender roles in the judicial process and the asymmetrical nature of relations between the sexes.

46. Jacquette, "Women, Feminism, and the Transition to Democracy in Latin America," in *Latin American and Caribbean Contemporary Record*, vol. 5, ed. Abraham Lowenthal.

47. Rachel Moreno, "De feminismos, de feministas, de mulheres," p. 50.

48. See the critical view of many urban intellectuals and members of the middle class, including feminists reluctant to engage in day-to-day struggles or do concrete work to help particular women like prostitutes, expressed by a black activist telling her life history in Daphne Patai, *Brazilian Women Speak. Contemporary Life Stories* (New Brunswick, N.J.: Rutgers University Press, 1988), pp. 79–108.

Bibliography

Archives

Arquivo do Estado de São Paulo. São Paulo.
Arquivo do Instituto Histórico e Geográfico Brasileiro. Rio de Janeiro.
Arquivo do Instituto Histórico e Geográfico de São Paulo. São Paulo.
Arquivo do Museu Imperial. Petrópolis.
Arquivo Geral da Cidade do Rio de Janeiro. Rio de Janeiro.
Arquivo Histórico do Ministério das Relações Exteriores (Itamarati). Rio de Janeiro.
Arquivo Nacional. Rio de Janeiro.
Arquivo Público do Estado de Pernambuco. Recife.
Biblioteca Nacional do Rio de Janeiro. Secão de Manuscritos. Rio de Janeiro.
Centro Informação Mulher. São Paulo.
National Archives. Washington, D.C.
New York Public Library. New York.
Sophia Smith Collection, Smith College. Northampton, Mass.

Interviews

Albuquerque, Maria Sabina de. Rio de Janeiro, June 21, 1983.
Andrade, Maria Rita Soares de. Rio de Janeiro, June 21, 1983, and June 8, 1984.
Bittencourt, Maria Luiza. Rio de Janeiro, June 13, 1984.
Fonseca, Romy Medeiros de. Rio de Janeiro, July 11, 1974.
Lutz, Bertha. (Telephone interview.) Rio de Janeiro, June 28, 1974.
Muraro, Rose Marie. Rio de Janeiro, July 5, 1974.
Osborne, Elisa Pinho. (Telephone interview.) Rio de Janeiro, June 11, 1984.
Pinho, Ivonne Moraes de. Rio de Janeiro, June 18, 1983.
Portinho, Carmen Velasco. Rio de Janeiro, June 20, 1983, and June 11, 1984.
Rezende, Zéia Pinho de. Rio de Janeiro, June 14, 1984.

Printed Materials

Periodicals

Dates of periodicals are given for periodicals of limited duration and for the period in which they were consulted in their entirety.

America Illustrada, Recife (1881).
O Amigo do Povo, São Paulo (1903–4).
Aurora Brasiliense, Ithaca, N.Y. (1873–75).
Aurora Social, Recife (1902, 1906–7).
Avanti!, São Paulo.

A Batalha, Rio de Janeiro (1931).

O Bello Sexo, Rio de Janeiro (1862).

Boletim da Federação Brasileira pelo Progresso Feminino, Rio de Janeiro (1935).

Brasil Feminino, Rio de Janeiro (1932, 1935).

Brasil Mulher, São Paulo (1975–80).

Brasil Operario, Rio de Janeiro (1903–4).

A Cigarra, São Paulo (1922).

O Combate, Fortaleza (1891, 1896).

O Componeador, Rio de Janeiro (1909).

Correio das Modas, Rio de Janeiro (1839–40).

A Defesa, Rio de Janeiro (1925).

Diário da Bahia, Salvador (1931).

Diário de Noticias, Rio de Janeiro (1931).

O Domingo, Rio de Janeiro (1873–75).

Echo das Damas, Rio de Janeiro (1879–80, 1885–88).

Educação, São Paulo (1928).

Escrínio, Porto Alegre (1901).

O Escrínio, Terezinha (1909).

O Estado de São Paulo, São Paulo.

A Família, São Paulo (1888–89); Rio de Janeiro (1889).

Feminismo Internacional, New York (1922–23).

A Folha, São Paulo (1918).

O Funccionário, São Paulo (1888).

Gazeta Academica, Salvador (1886).

Gazeta da Tarde, Rio de Janeiro.

Gazeta de Notícias, Rio de Janeiro.

Gazeta dos Operarios, Rio de Janeiro (1875–76).

Gazeta Operaria, Rio de Janeiro (1902–3).

O Globo, Rio de Janeiro (1882).

A Hora Social, Recife (1919).

O Imperial, Rio de Janeiro (1923).

Informe Mulher, Brasília (1988).

O Jornal, Rio de Janeiro (1930).

Jornal das Famílias, Rio de Janeiro and Paris (1863–78).

O Jornal das Senhoras, Rio de Janeiro (1852–55).

Jornal do Brasil, Rio de Janeiro.

Jornal do Comércio, Rio de Janeiro.

Kosmos, Rio de Janeiro (1904–8).

Kultur, Rio de Janeiro (1904).

Leque, São Paulo (1886–87).

A Mãi de Família, Rio de Janeiro (1884).

Manchete, Rio de Janeiro.

A Mensageira, São Paulo (1898–1900).

A Mulher, New York (1881); Recife (1883).

Mulherio, São Paulo (1981–88).

Nexo, São Paulo (1988).

A Noite, Rio de Janeiro.

Nós Mulheres, São Paulo (1976–78).

Nosso Jornal, Rio de Janeiro (1919–20).

Novo Correio das Modas, Rio de Janeiro (1852–54).

O Operário, Sorocaba, S.P. (1910).
O País, Rio de Janeiro.
Primaveira, Rio de Janeiro (1880).
Progresso Suburbano, Piedade [Rio de Janeiro] (1902).
O Quinze de Novembro do Sexo Feminino, Rio de Janeiro (1889–94).
A Razão, Rio de Janeiro (1919–20).
A Reacção, São Paulo (1931).
Recreio do Bello Sexo, Rio de Janeiro (1852–56).
Renascença, Rio de Janeiro (1904–5).
Renascença, São Paulo (1923).
Revista Americana, Rio de Janeiro (1910).
Revista Feminina, São Paulo (1916–25).
Revista Illustrada, Rio de Janeiro.
Revista Typographica, Rio de Janeiro (1882).
Semana Operaria, Rio de Janeiro (1908).
O Sexo Feminino, Campanha, M.G. (1873–74); Rio de Janeiro (1875–76, 1889).
O Socialista, Rio de Janeiro (1893).
O Socialista, São Paulo (1896).
O Suburbio, Rio de Janeiro (1904).
A Terra Livre, São Paulo (1905–7, 1910); Rio de Janeiro (1907–8).
O Trabalhador Graphico, São Paulo (1904–6).
A Tribuna do Povo, Rio de Janeiro (1909).
Tribuna Feminina, Rio de Janeiro (1916).
Tribuna Operaria, Belém (1892–93).
Ultima Hora (Rio de Janeiro).
União Operaria, Engenho de Dentro, [Rio de Janeiro] (1904).
A Vanguarda, Rio de Janeiro (1928).
A Violeta, São Paulo (1887).
Voz da Verdade, Rio de Janeiro (1885).
A Voz do Operario, Salvador (1891, 1894).
A Voz do Povo, Bangú [Rio de Janeiro] (1911).
A Voz do Trabalhador, Rio de Janeiro (1908–9).

Public Documents

Actas e pareceres do congresso de instrucção do Rio de Janeiro. Rio de Janeiro, Typ. Nacional, 1884.
Album cartográfico do Rio de Janeiro (séculos XVIII e XIX). Organized with text by Lygia da Fonseca Fernandes da Cunha. Rio de Janeiro: Biblioteca Nacional, 1971.
Arquivo do Distrito Federal. *Revista de documentos para a história da cidade do Rio de Janeiro, 1500–1900.* Rio de Janeiro: Prefeitura do Distrito Federal, 1952.
Associação dos Empregados no Comercio do Rio de Janeiro. *Relatório.* 1880–1915.
Brazil. *Annuário Estatística do Brasil.* 1939–40.
———. *Coleção das leis da República dos Estados Unidos do Brasil do 1938.* Vol. 4, *Decretos-leis.* Rio de Janeiro: Imprensa Nacional, 1939.
———. Comissão Parlamentar Mista de Inquerito para Examinar a Situação da Mulher em Todos os Setores de Atividades. *Relatório, conclusões e recomendações.* Brasília: Senado Federal 1978.
———. Congress. Câmara dos Deputados. *Annaes do Congresso Constituinte da República.* 2d ed. 3 vols. Rio de Janeiro: Imprensa Nacional, 1924–25.

———. Congress. Câmara dos Deputados. Commissão de Estatuto da Mulher. *O trabalho feminino. A mulher na ordem econômica e social. Documentação organisada por Bertha Lutz, presidente da commissão.* Rio De Janeiro: Imprensa Nacional, 1937.

———. Congress. Câmara dos Deputados. *Documentos parlamentares. Legislação social.* 3 vols. Rio de Janeiro: Typ. do Jornal do Commercio, 1919–22.

———. Conselho Nacional dos Direitos da Mulher. *Mulher, cidadã brasileira.* Brasília: Conselho Nacional dos Direitos da Mulher [1985].

———. Conselho Nacional dos Direitos de Mulher. *Mulher e constituinte.* Brasília: Conselho Nacional dos Direitos da Mulher, 1985.

———. Conselho Nacional dos Direitos da Mulher. *Mulher trabalhadora.* Brasília. Conselho Nacional dos Direitos da Mulher, 1986.

———. Conselho Nacional dos Direitos da Mulher. *Violência contra a mulher. Relatório I. Encontro Nacional de Delegadas Lotadas em Delegacias de Defesa da Mulher.* Brasília: Conselho Nacional dos Direitos da Mulher, 1986.

———. *Constituição. República Federativa do Brasil. 1988.* Brasília: Centro do Senado Federal, 1988.

———. Diretoria Geral de Estatística. *Estatística de instrucção. Estatística escolar.* Rio de Janeiro: Typ. da Estatística, 1916.

———. Diretoria Geral de Estatística. *Recenseamento do Brazil realizado em 1 de setembro de 1920.* 5 vols. in 18. Rio de Janeiro: Typ. da Estatística, 1922–30.

———. Diretoria Geral de Estatística. *Recenseamento geral da República dos Estados Unidos do Brazil em 31 de dezembro de 1890. Districto Federal (Cidade do Rio de Janeiro), Capital da República dos Estados Unidos do Brazil.* Rio de Janeiro: Leuzinger, 1895.

———. Diretoria Geral de Estatística. *Recenseamento da população do Império do Brazil a que se procedeu no dia 1 de agosto de 1872.* 22 vols. Rio de Janeiro: Leuzinger, 1873–76.

———. Diretoria Geral de Estatística. *Recenseamento do Rio de Janeiro (Districto Federal) realizado em 20 de setembro de 1906.* 2 vols. Rio de Janeiro: Officina da Estatística, 1907.

———. *Informações apresentades pela Commissão Parlamentar de Inquerito ao Corpo Legislativo na terceira sessão da decima oitava legislatura.* Rio de Janeiro: Typ. Nacional, 1883.

———. Ministério do Império. *Relatório.* 1875–88.

———. Ministério de Justiça. *Relatório.* 1866–1924.

———. *Relatorio apresentado so sr. ex. o Ministro da Fazenda pela Commissão de Inquerito Industrial.* Rio de Janeiro: Typ. Nacional, 1882.

———. Secretaria de Planejamento da Presidencia da República. Fundação Instituto Brasileiro de Geografia e Estatística. *IX Recenseamento geral do Brasil. 1980.* 26 vols. Rio de Janeiro: IBGE, 1983.

———. Senado Federal. Comissão Parlamentar Mista de Inquerito. *CPI da Mulher.* 2 vols. Brasília: Senado Federal, 1978.

Centro Industrial do Brasil. *O Brasil. Suas riquezas naturaes. Suas industrias.* Vol. 3. Rio de Janeiro: M. Orosco, 1909.

Comissão de Mulheres do MUB e Centro Comunitária de Duque de Caxias. *Dossiê Caxias: Maternidades maltratando mulheres e bebês causam até mortes! Dossiê apresentado a Comissão Especial dos Direitos da Reprodução da Asembleia Legislativa do Rio de Janeiro.* Rio de Janeiro: Reproarte, 1986.

"Documentos do movimento operário. Congresso operário de 1912." *Estudos Sociais* 5 (June 1963): 69–87.

"Documentos do movimento operário. Pela Paz!" *Estudos Sociais* 4 (December 1962): 285–93.

"Documentos do movimento operário. Um relatório datado de 1913." *Estudos Sociais* 5 (November 1963): 195–206.

"Documentos do movimento operário. Resoluções do primeiro congresso operário brasileiro." *Estudo Sociais* 4 (March 1963): 387–98.

Instituto de Ação Cultural. *As mulheres em movimento.* Rio de Janeiro: Editora Marco Zero, n.d.

Liga da Defesa Nacional. *Estatutos da Liga da Defesa Nacional.* Rio de Janeiro: Typ. do Jornal do Commercio, 1916.

Movimento de mulheres no Brasil. Cadernos da Associação das Mulheres 3. São Paulo: Associação das Mulheres, 1979.

Mulher negra: Dossiê sobre a discriminção racial. São Paulo: Conselho Estadual da Condição Feminina, 1986.

As mulheres e o trabalho. Em Tempo. São Paulo: A Editora Aparte, 1983.

Paraná. Conselho Estadual da Condição Feminina. *O que é a Constituinte.* Curitiba: Conselho Estadual da Condição Feminina, 1986.

Pernambuco. *Falla que o presidente da provincia . . . dirigio à assemblêa legislativa no dia de sua instalação . . .* 1886–88.

Revista do Instituto Histórico e Geográfico Brasileiro.

Rio de Janeiro [city]. *Assistencia pública e privada no Rio de Janeiro (Brasil). História e estatística.* Rio de Janeiro: Typ. do "Annuario do Brasil," 1922.

São Paulo [state]. *Boletim do Departamento Estadual do Trabalho.* 1911–20.

————. Conselho Estadual da Condição Feminina. *O direito de ter ou não ter filhos no Brasil.* São Paulo: Conselho Estadual da Condição Feminina, 1986.

———— [province and state]. *Relatorio apresentado à assemblêa legislativa provincial de São Paulo pelo presidente da provincia . . .* 1876–94.

———— [state]. Repartição de Estatística e Arquivo. *Relatório.* 1894–95.

Books, Articles, and Unpublished Dissertations

Affonseca Júnior, Léo de. *O custo da vida na cidade do Rio de Janeiro.* Rio de Janeiro: Imprensa Nacional, 1920.

Agache, Donat Alfred. *Cidade do Rio de Janeiro. Extensão, remodelação, embellezemento.* Paris: Foyer Brésilien, 1930.

Agassiz, Louis, and Elizabeth C. Agassiz. *A Journey in Brazil.* Boston: Ticknor and Fields, 1868.

Alambert, Zuleika. *Feminismo. O ponte de vista marxista.* São Paulo: Nobel, 1986.

————. *A situação e organização da mulher.* Cadernos do Centro da Mulher Brasiliera, no. 1. São Paulo: Global Editora, 1980.

Albuquerque, J. A. Guilhon, ed. *Classes médias e política no Brasil.* Rio de Janeiro: Paz e Terra, 1977.

Albuquerque, José Joaquim de Campos da Costa Madeiros e. *O perigo americano.* Rio de Janeiro: Leite Ribeiro and Maurillo, 1919.

Almeida, Angela Mendes de, ed. *Pensando a família no Brasil. Da côlonia à modernidade.* Rio de Janeiro: Espaço e Tempo/Editôra da UFRRJ, 1987.

Almeida, Júlia Lopes de. *Livro das noivas.* Rio de Janeiro: Companhia Nacional Editôra, 1890.

Almeida, Maria Suely Kofes de, Antonio Augusto Arantes, Carlos Rodrigues Brandão, Mariza Corrêa, Bela Feldman-Bianco, Verena Stolche, and Alba Zalvar. *Colcha de retalhos. Estudos sobre a família no Brasil.* São Paulo: Editora Brasiliense, 1982.

Alvarez, Sonia E. "Politicizing Gender and Engendering Democracy." In *Democratizing Brazil. Problems of Transition and Consolidation.* Ed. Alfred Stepan. New York: Oxford University Press, 1989.

———. "The Politics of Gender in Latin America: Comparative Perspectives on Women in the Brazilian Transition to Democracy." Ph.D. diss., Yale University, 1986.

Alves, Branca Moreira. *Ideologia e feminismo. A luta pelo voto no Brasil.* Petropólis: Vozes, 1980.

Alves, Branca Moreira, and Jacquelline Pitanguy. *O que é feminismo.* Coleção Primeiros Passos 44. São Paulo: Editora Brasiliense, 1981.

Alves, Branca Moreira, Jacqueline Pitanguy, Leila Linhares Barsted, Mariska Ribeiro, and Sandra Boschi (Grupo Ceres). *Espelho de Vênes. Identidade social da mulher.* São Paulo: Editora Brasiliense, 1981.

Alves, Márcio Moreira. *A Grain of Mustard Seed. The Awakening of the Brazilian Revolution.* Garden City, N.Y.: Doubleday Anchor Press, 1973.

Amado, Gilberto. *História da minha infancia.* Rio de Janeiro: José Olympio, 1954.

Amado, Jorge. *Gabriela, Clove and Cinnamon.* New York: Avon Books, 1974.

Amaral, Aracy A. *Tarsila. Sua obra e seu tempo.* 2 vols. São Paulo: Editora Perspectiva, 1975.

Americano, Jorge. *São Paulo naquelle tempo (1895–1915).* São Paulo: Edição Saraiva, 1957.

Andreas, Carol. "The Chilean Woman: Reform, Reaction, and Resistance." *Latin American Perspectives* 10 (Fall 1977): 121–25.

Andrews, Christopher Colombus. *Brazil: Its Condition and Prospects.* New York: D. Appleton, 1887.

Araipe, Tristão de Alencer. *Código Civil Brazileiro, ou leis civis do Brazil dispostas por ordem de matérias em seu estado actual.* Rio de Janeiro: Laemmert, 1885.

Araujo, Antonio Amaury Correa de. *Lampião: As mulheres e o congaço.* São Paulo: Traco Editora, 1985.

Araujo, Elysio de. *As linhas de tiro.* Rio de Janeiro: Almanak Laemmert, 1940.

———. *Atravez do meu século. Notas históricas.* São Paulo: São Paulo Editôra, 1932.

Arestizábel, Irma. *J. Carlos. 100 anos.* Rio de Janeiro: FUNARTE and PUC/RJ, 1984.

Arrom, Silvia Marina. *The Women of Mexico City, 1790–1857.* Stanford: Stanford University Press, 1985.

As mulheres. Um protesto por uma mãe. Bahia: Typ. do Bazar 65, 1887.

Associação das Mulheres. *Mulher profissão secretária.* São Paulo: Associação das Mulheres, n.d.

Associação das Mulheres and Associação das Donas de Casa. *A nossa história 1. O trabalho da dona de casa.* São Paulo: Associação das Mulheres and Associação das Donas de Casa, 1979.

Associação das Mulheres and Grupo Feminista "8 de Março." *A contracepção e o aborto.* São Paulo: N.p., n.d.

Associação dos Geógrafos Brasileiros (Secção do Rio de Janeiro). *Aspectos da geografia carioca.* Rio de Janeiro: Conselho Nacional de Geografia, 1962.

Auler, Guilherme. *Os bolsistas do Imperador.* Petrópolis: Tribuna de Petrópolis, 1956.

Azevedo, Aluízio. *O cortiço.* São Paulo: Livraria Martins, 1965.

Azevedo, Arnoldo, ed. *A cidade de São Paulo. Estudos de geografia urbana.* Vol. 2: *A evolução urbana.* São Paulo: Companhia Editôra Nacional, 1958.

Azevedo, Fernando. *Brazilian Culture. An Introduction to the Study of Culture in Brazil.* Trans. William Rex Crawford. New York: Macmillan, 1950.

Azevedo, Josephina Alvares de. *A mulher moderna. Trabalhos de propaganda.* Rio de Janeiro: Montenegro, 1891.

Azevedo, Maria Amélia. *Mulheres espancadas. A violência denunciada.* São Paulo: Cortez Editora, 1985.

Backheuser, Everardo. *Habitações populares. Relatório apresentado ao exm. sr. dr. J. J. Seabra, Ministro da Justiça e Negocios Interiores.* Rio de Janeiro: Imprensa Nacional, 1906.

Bakota, Carlos Steven. "Crisis and the Middle Classes. The Ascendancy of Brazilian Nationalism: 1914–1922." Ph.D. diss., University of California, Los Angeles, 1973.

Barandas, Anna Eurydice Eufrozina de. *O ramalhete ou flores escolhidas no jardim da imaginação.* Porto Alegre: I. J. Lopes, 1845.

Barbosa, Luiz. *Serviços de assistencia no Rio de Janeiro.* Rio de Janeiro: Ao Luzeiro, 1908.

Barbosa, Maria Benedita de Oliveira [Zaira Americana, pseud.]. *Zaira Americana mostra as immensas vantagens que a sociedade inteira obtem da mulher, como mãi e esposa do homem.* Rio de Janeiro: Empreza Typ. Dous de Dezembro de Paula Brito, 1853.

Barbosa, Rui. *Reforma do ensino primário e varias instituições complimentares da instrução pública.* Vol. 10, tomo 1, of *Obras completas de Rui Barbosa.* Rio de Janeiro: Ministério da Educação e Saude, 1947.

Barcelar, Jefferson Afonso. *A família da prostituta.* São Paulo: Editora Ática, 1982.

Barman, Roderick J. *Brazil. The Forging of a Nation, 1798–1852.* Stanford: Stanford University Press, 1988.

———. "Politicians on the Stage: The Late Brazilian Empire as Dramatized by França Junior." *Luso-Brazilian Review* 3 (Winter 1976): 244–60.

Barman, Roderick J., and Jean Barman. "The Role of the Law Graduate in the Political Elite of Imperial Brazil." *Journal of Interamerican Studies and World Affairs* 18 (November 1976): 423–50.

Barreto, Belarmino. *Biographia da exm. sra. D. Maria Augusta Generosa Estrella natural do Rio de Janeiro filha do illm. sr. Albino Augusto Generosa Estrella a futura doutora em medicina pela Academia de Nova York.* Bahia: Typ. do "Correio da Bahia," 1878.

Barreto, Filho, João Paulo de Melo, and Hermeto Lima. *História da polícia do Rio de Janeiro. (Aspectos da cidade e da vida carioca).* 3 vols. Rio de Janeiro: A Noite, 1939–44.

Barreto, Paulo [João do Rio, pseud.]. *A alma encantadora das ruas.* Paris: Garnier, 1908.

Barreto, Tobias. *Estudos de sociologia.* Rio de Janeiro: Instituto Nacional do Livro, 1962.

Barroso, Carmen. *Mulher, sociedade e estado no Brasil.* São Paulo: Editora Brasiliense, 1982.

———. *A saude da mulher.* São Paulo: Nobel and Conselho Estadual da Condição Feminina, 1985.

Barroso, Carmen, and Cristina Bruschini. *Educação sexual. Debate aberto.* Petrópolis: Vozes, 1982.

Barroso, Carmen, and Albertina Oliveira Costa, eds. *Mulher, mulheres.* São Paulo: Cortez Editora and Fundação Carlos Chagas, 1983.

Barroso, José Liberto. *Conferencias populares.* Rio de Janeiro: J. Villeneuve, 1876.

———. *A instrução pública no Brasil.* Rio de Janeiro: Garnier, 1867.

Basbaum, Leôncio. *História sincera da República.* 4 vols. Vols. 1–3, São Paulo: Edições LB, 1962; Vol. 4, São Paulo: Editôra Fulgor, 1968.

Bastos, Elizabeth. *Justiça, alegria, felicidade (Os novos rumos do feminismo brasileiro).* Rio de Janeiro: Livraria Jacintho, 1935.

Bath, Sérgio. *História da legislação do Instituto Rio Branco.* Brasília: Instituto Rio Branco, 1975.

Bell, Alured Grey. *The Beautiful Rio de Janeiro.* London: William Heinenmann, 1914.

Bell, Susan Groag. "Christine de Pizan (1364–1430): Humanism and the Problem of a Studious Woman." *Feminist Studies* (Spring–Summer 1976): 173–84.

Bell, Susan Groag, and Karen N. Offen, eds. *Women, the Family, and Freedom. The Debate in Documents.* 2 vols. Stanford: Stanford University Press, 1983.

Bellegarde, Guilherme. *O Lyceu de Artes e Officios e as aulas para o sexo feminino.* Rio de Janeiro: Typ. Nacional, 1881.

Bellegarde, Guilherme, Felix Ferreira, and José Maria da Silva Junior. *Commemorativa da inauguração das aulas para o sexo feminino do Imperial Lyceo de Artes e Officios.* Rio de Janeiro: Lombaerts, 1881.

Beozzo, José Oscar. "A Igreja entre a Revolução de 1930, O Estado Novo e a redemocratização." In *História geral da civilização.* III. *O Brasil republicano.* 4. *Economia e cultura (1930–1964).* 2d ed. Ed. Boris Fausto. São Paulo: Difel, 1986.

Berg, Barbara J. *The Remembered Gate: Origins of American Feminism. The Woman and the City, 1800–1860.* New York: Oxford University Press, 1978.

Bergstresser, Rebecca Baird. "The Movement for the Abolition of Slavery in Rio de Janeiro, Brazil, 1880–1889." Ph.D. diss., Stanford University, 1973.

Bernardes, Maria Thereza Caiuby Crescenti. "Mulheres educadas. Rio de Janeiro do século XIX (1840–1890)." Ph.D. diss., Universidade de São Paulo, 1983.

Besse, Susan Kent. "Freedom and Bondage: The Impact of Capitalism on Women in São Paulo, Brazil, 1917–1937." Ph.D. diss., Yale University, 1983.

————. "Pagú: Patrícia Galvão—Rebel." In *The Human Tradition in Latin America. The Twentieth Century.* Ed. William H. Beezley and Judith Ewell. Wilmington, Del.: Scholarly Resources, 1987.

Bevilacqua, Clovis. *Código Civil dos Estados Unidos do Brasil: Comentários.* Rio de Janeiro: Editôra Rio, 1965.

Bilac, Elizabeth Doria. *Família de trabalhadores: Estratégia de sobrevivência.* São Paulo: Edições Símbolo, 1978.

Bilac, Olavo. *A defesa nacional (Discursos).* Rio de Janeiro: Liga da Defesa Nacional, 1917.

Binzer, Ina von. *Os meus romanos. Alegrias e tristezas de uma educadora alemã no Brasil.* Trans. Alice Rossi and Luisita da Gama Cerqueira. Rio de Janeiro: Paz e Terra, 1980.

Bittencourt, Adalzira. *Dicionario bio-bibliográphico de mulheres ilustres, notáveis e intelectuais do Brasil.* 2 vols. Rio de Janeiro: Editora Pongetti, 1970, vol. 1.

————. *A mulher paulista na história.* Rio de Janeiro: Livros de Portugal, 1954.

Blachman, Morris. "Eve in an Adamocracy: The Politics of Women in Brazil." Ph.D. diss., New York University, 1976.

Blake, Augusto Victorino Alves Sacramento. *Diccionario bibliographico brazileiro.* 7 vols. Rio de Janeiro: Imprensa Nacional, 1883–1902.

Blay, Eva Alterman. *As prefeitas: A participação política da mulher no Brasil.* Rio de Janeiro: Avenir Editora, 1981.

————. *Trabalho domesticado: A mulher na indústria paulista.* São Paulo: Editôra Ática, 1978.

————. "Women, Redemocratization, and Political Alternatives." In *Brazil's Economic and Political Future.* Ed. Julian M. Chacel, Pamela S. Falk, and David V. Fleischer. Boulder: Westview Press, 1988.

Boehrer, George C. A. *Da monarquia à república. História do Partido Republicano do Brasil (1870–1889).* Trans. Berenice Xavier. Rio de Janeiro: Ministério da Educação e Cultura, 1954.

Borges Filho, Afonso [Frei Betto]. *O que é comunidade eclesial de base.* Coleção Primeiros Passos 19. São Paulo: Editora Brasiliense, 1981.

Borges, Wanda Rose. *A profissionalização feminina. Uma experiência no ensino pública.* São Paulo: Edições Loyola, 1980.

Boserup, Esther. *Women's Role in Economic Development.* New York: St. Martin's Press, 1970.

Bourne, Richard. *Getúlio Vargas of Brazil, 1883–1954. Sphinx of the Pampas.* London: Charles Knight, 1974.

Boxer, Marilyn Jacoby, and Jean J. Quataert, eds. *Socialist Women: European Socialist Feminism in the Nineteenth and Twentieth Centuries.* New York: Elsevier Press, 1978.

Boyer, Richard E., and Keith A. Davies. *Urbanization in 19th Century Latin America: Statistics and Sources.* Supplement to the *Statistical Abstract of Latin America.* Los Angeles: UCLA Latin American Center, 1973.

Brant, Alice. *The Diary of "Helena Morley."* Trans. Elizabeth Bishop. New York: Ecco Press, 1957.

Brazil, José Francisco Assis. *Democracia representativa. Do voto e do modo de votar.* 4th ed. Rio de Janeiro: Imprensa Nacional, 1931.

Brito, Mário da Silva. *História do modernismo brasileiro.* 2d rev. ed. Rio de Janeiro: Civilização Brasileira, 1964.

Broca, José Brito. *A vida literária no Brasil, 1900.* Rio de Janeiro: José Olympio, 1960.

Bruneau, Thomas C. *The Church in Brazil. The Politics of Religion.* Austin: University of Texas Press, 1982.

Bruno, Ernani Silva. *História e tradições da cidade de São Paulo.* 2d ed. 3 vols. Rio de Janeiro: José Olympio, 1954.

Bruschini, Cristina. *Mulher e trabalho.* São Paulo: Nobel and Conselho Estadual da Condição Feminina, 1985.

Bruschini, Maria Cristina A., and Fúlvia Rosemberg, eds. *Trabalhadoras do Brasil.* São Paulo: Editora Brasiliense, 1982.

———. *Vivência: História, sexualidade e imagens femininas.* São Paulo: Editora Brasiliense, 1980.

Bryce, James. *South America. Observations and Impressions.* New York: Macmillan, 1912.

Buitoni, Dulcília Helena Schroeder. *Mulher de papel. A representação da mulher pela imprensa feminina brasileira.* São Paulo: Edições Loyola, 1981.

Burmeister, Herman. *Viagem ao Brasil através das provincias do Rio de Janeiro e Minas Gerais visando especialmente a história natural dos distritos auri-diamantíferros.* Trans. Manoel Salvaterra and Hubert Schoenfeld. São Paulo: Livraria Martins, 1952.

Burns, E. Bradford. *A History of Brazil.* New York: Columbia University Press, 1970.

———. *The Poverty of Progress. Latin America in the Nineteenth Century.* Berkeley: University of California Press, 1980.

Burton, Richard F. *The Highlands of Brazil, with a Full Account of the Gold and Diamond Mines.* 2 vols. London: Tinsley Brothers, 1869.

Bush, Reyaldo Kuntz. *O ensino normal em São Paulo.* São Paulo: Livraria Record, 1935.

Cadernos de Debate. Vol. 2, *Mulher. Depoimentos sobre um trabalho.* São Paulo: Editora Brasiliense, 1982.

Cadernos de Debate. Vol. 6, *A estructura familiar na opressão feminina.* São Paulo: Editora Brasiliense, 1980.

Cadernos de Pesquisa. Revista de Estudos e Pesquisas em Educação. Vol. 37. São Paulo: Fundação Carlos Chagas, 1981.

Calmon, Pedro. *História de D. Pedro II.* 4 vols. Rio de Janeiro: José Olympio, 1975.

———. *História do Brasil na poesia do povo.* Rio de Janeiro: A Noite, 1949.

Campos, Augusto de, ed. *Pagú. Patrícia Galvão: Vida-obra.* São Paulo: Editora Brasiliense, 1982.

Campos, Maria Malta. "Feminismo e separatismo." *Mulherio* 2 (September–October 1982): 3.

Candido, Antonio. "The Brazilian Family." In *Brazil: Portrait of Half a Continent.* Ed. T. Lynn Smith and Alexander Marchant. New York: Dryden Press, 1951.

———. *Teresina etc.* Rio de Janeiro: Paz e Terra, 1980.

Cannon, Mary M. *Women in Brazil Today.* Washington, D.C.: U.S. Department of Labor, 1934.

Cardoso, Irede. *O direito da mulher na constituição nova.* São Paulo: Global Editora, 1986.

————. *Mulher e trabalho: Discriminações e barreiras no mercado de trabalho.* São Paulo: Cortez Editora, 1980.

————. *Os tempos dramáticos da mulher brasileira.* Coleção História Popular, no. 2. São Paulo: Centro Editorial Latino-Americano, 1981.

Carlson, Marifran. *Feminismo! The Woman's Movement in Argentina from Its Beginnings to Eva Perón.* Chicago: Academy Chicago Publishers, 1988.

Carneiro, José Fernando. *Imigração e colonização no Brasil.* Rio de Janeiro: Universidade do Brasil, 1950.

Carneiro, Nelson. *A luta pelo divórcio.* Rio de Janeiro: Livraria São José, 1973.

Carneiro, Sueli Tereza Santos, and Albertina Gordo de Oliveira Costa. *Mulher negra. Política governamental e a mulher.* São Paulo: Nobel and Conselho Estadual da Condição Feminina, 1985.

Carone, Edgard. *A Primeira República (1889–1930). Texto e contexto.* São Paulo: Difusão Européia do Livro, 1969.

————. *A República Velha (Instituições e classes sociais).* São Paulo: Difusão Européia do Livro, 1970.

————. *A República Velha II (Evolução política).* São Paulo: Difusão Européia do Livro, 1971.

Carvalho, Nanci Valadares de, ed. *A condição feminina.* São Paulo: Vértice, 1988.

Carvalho, Reis [Oscar d'Alva]. "A questão feminina." *Kosmos* (Rio de Janeiro) January, February, March, and April 1904.

Castro, Augusto Olympio Viveiros de. *A questão social.* Rio de Janeiro: Livraria Editôra Conselheiro Candido de Oliveira, 1920.

Castro, Oliveira. *História da organização do Ministério das Relações Exteriores.* Brasília: Editôra Universidade de Brasília, 1983.

Castro, Tito Livio de. *A mulher e a sociogenia. Obra postuma.* Rio de Janeiro: Francisco Alves, 1984.

Catt, Carrie Chapman. "Anti-Feminism in South America." *Current History Magazine* (April–September 1923): 1028–36.

————. "Busy Women in Brazil." *The Woman Citizen,* March 24, 1923, pp. 9–10.

————. "Picturesque Peru." *The Woman Citizen,* May 19, 1923, pp. 9–10, 24–25.

————. "Summing up South America." *The Woman Citizen,* June 2, 1923, pp. 7–8, 26.

Celso, Maria Eugenia Afonso. *De relance . . . Chronicas de B. F.* São Paulo: Monteiro Lobato, 1923.

Chacon, Vamireh. *História das idéias socialistas no Brasil.* Rio de Janeiro: Civilização Brasileira, 1965.

Chagas, João. *De bond. Alguns aspectos da civilisação brasileira.* Lisbon: Livraria Moderna, 1897.

Chalhoub, Sidney. *Trabalho, lar e botequim. O cotidiano dos trabalhadores no Rio de Janeiro da Belle Epoque.* São Paulo: Editora Brasiliense, 1986.

Chaney, Elsa. "The Mobilization of Women in Allende's Chile." In *Women in Politics.* Ed. Jane Jacquette. New York: John Wiley, 1974.

————. *Supermadre. Women in Politics in Latin America.* Austin: University of Texas Press, 1979.

Chiriac, Jany, and Solange Padilha. "Características e limites das organizações de base femininas." In *Trabalhadoras do Brasil.* Ed. Maria Cristina A. Bruschini and Fúlvia Rosemberg. São Paulo: Editora Brasiliense, 1982.

Coaracy, Vivaldo. *Todos contam sua vida.* Rio de Janeiro: José Olympio, 1959.

Codman, John. *Ten Months in Brazil, with Incidents of Voyages and Travels, Description of Scenery and Character, Notices of Commerce and Production, Etc.* Boston: Lee and Shepard, 1867.

Coelho, Mariana. *Evolução do feminismo. Subsídios para a sua história.* Rio de Janeiro: Imprensa Moderna, 1933.

Conable, Charlotte Williams. *Women at Cornell. The Myth of Equal Education.* Ithaca, N.Y.: Cornell University Press, 1977.

Conniff, Michael L. *Urban Politics in Brazil: The Rise of Populism, 1925–1945.* Pittsburgh: University of Pittsburgh Press, 1981.

———. "Voluntary Associations in Rio, 1870–1945. A New Approach to Urban Social Dynamics." *Journal of Interamerican Studies and World Affairs* 17 (February 1975): 64–81.

Conniff, Michael L., Melvin K. Hendrix, and Stephen Nohlgren. "Brazil." In *The Urban Development of Latin America, 1750–1920.* Ed. Richard M. Morse. Stanford: Stanford University Press, 1971.

Conrad, Robert Edgar. *Children of God's Fire. A Documentary History of Black Slavery in Brazil.* Princeton: Princeton University Press, 1983.

———. *The Destruction of Brazilian Slavery, 1850–1888.* Berkeley: University of California Press, 1972.

Constatt, Oscar. *Brasil. Terra e gente.* Trans. Eduardo de Lima Castro. Rio de Janeiro: Conquista, 1975.

Cooper, Clayton Sedgwick. *The Brazilians and Their Country.* New York: Frederick A. Stokes, 1917.

Corrêa, Mariza. *Os crimes da paixão.* Tudo é História, no. 33. São Paulo: Editora Brasiliense, 1981.

———. *Morte em família: Representações jurídicas de papeis sexuais.* Rio de Janeiro: Graal, 1983.

Costa, Albertina de Oliveira, Maria Teresa Porciuncula Moraes, Norma Marzola, and Valentina da Rocha Lima. *Memórias do exílio.* Vol. 2: *Memórias das mulheres no exílio.* Rio de Janeiro: Graal, 1980.

Costa, Antonio Corrêa de Sousa. *Qual a alimentação de que usa a classe pobre do Rio de Janeiro e sua influencia sobre a mesma classe.* Rio de Janeiro: Perseverança, 1865.

Costa, Emília Viotti da. *Da senzala à colônia.* São Paulo: Difusão Européia do Livro, 1966.

Costa, João Cruz. *A History of Ideas in Brazil. The Development of Philosophy in Brazil and the Evolution of Natural History.* Trans. Suzette Macedo. Berkeley: University of California Press, 1964.

———. *O positivismo na República. Notas sobre a história do positivismo no Brasil.* São Paulo: Companhia Editôra Nacional, 1956.

Costa, Luiz Edmundo da. *De um livro de memórias.* 5 vols. Rio de Janeiro: Imprensa Nacional, 1958.

———. *Recordações do Rio antigo.* Rio de Janeiro: A Noite, 1950.

———. *O Rio de Janeiro do meu tempo.* 3 vols. Rio de Janeiro: Imprensa Nacional, 1938.

Cott, Nancy F. *The Grounding of Modern Feminism.* New Haven: Yale University Press, 1987.

Covarrubias, Paz, and Rolando Franco, eds. *Chile: Mujer y Sociedad.* Santiago: UNICEF, 1978.

Crescenti, Thereza Caiuby. "Mulher e libertação dos escravos." Mimeo. Paper presented to Segundo Simposio de História do Vale do Paraíba, Pindamonhangaba, July 19–24, 1976.

Cromwell, Otelia. *Lucretia Mott.* Cambridge, Mass.: Harvard University Press, 1958.

Cruls, Gastão. *Aparencia do Rio de Janeiro.* 2 vols. Rio de Janeiro: José Olympio, 1965.

Crummet, Maria de los Angeles. "El Poder Feminino: The Mobilization of Women against Socialism in Chile." *Latin American Perspectives* 4 (Fall 1977): 103–13.

Cunha, Delfina Benigna da. *Colleção de várias poesias dedicadas á Imperatriz-Viuva como tributo de gratidão*. Rio de Janeiro: Laemmert, 1846.

———. *Poesias offercidas ás senhoras rio-grandenses*. Rio de Janeiro: Austral, 1838.

Cunha, Herculano Augusto Lassance. *Dissertação sobre a prostituição em particular na cidade do Rio de Janeiro. These apresentada a faculdade de medicina do Rio de Janeiro, em 17 de dezembro de 1845*. Rio de Janeiro: Typ. Imparcial de Francisco de Paula Brito, 1845.

Cunha, Maria Clementina Pereira. *O espelho do mundo. Juquery. A história de um asilo*. Rio de Janeiro: Paz e Terra, 1986.

Dean, Warren. *The Industrialization of São Paulo, 1880–1945*. Austin: University of Texas Press, 1969.

———. *Rio Claro. A Brazilian Plantation System, 1820–1920*. Stanford: Stanford University Press, 1976.

Degler, Carl N. *Neither Black nor White. Slavery and Race Relations in Brazil and the United States*. New York: Macmillan, 1974.

Deiró, Eunapio. "A mulher perante as religiões antigas e o christianismo." *Kosmos*, December 1904.

Denis, Pierre. *Brazil*. Trans. Bernard Miall. London: T. Fisher Unwin, 1911.

Dent, Charles Hastings. *A Year in Brazil*. London: Kegan, Paul, Trench, 1886.

Deutsch, Regine. *The International Woman Suffrage Alliance. Its History from 1904 to 1929*. London: The International Woman Suffrage Alliance, 1929.

Deutsch, Sandra McGee. "Feminist Studies." In *Latinas of the Americas: A Source Book*. Ed. K. Lynn Stoner. New York: Garland, 1989.

Dias, Everardo. *História das lutas sociais no Brasil*. São Paulo: Editôra Edaglit, 1962.

Dias, Maria Odila Leite da Silva. *Quotidiano e poder em São Paulo no século XIX: Ana Gertrudes de Jesus*. São Paulo: Editora Brasiliense, 1984.

Diégues Júnior, Manuel. *Imigração, urbanização e industrialização (Estudo sobre alguns aspectos da contribuição cultural do imigrante no Brasil)*. Rio de Janeiro: Centro Brasileiro de Pesquisas Educacionaes, Instituto Nacional de Estudos Pedagógicos, Ministério da Educação e Cultura, 1964.

Diniz, Edinha. *Chiquinha Gonzaga. Uma história de vida*. Rio de Janeiro: Editora Codecri, 1984.

Doliveira, Clodoveu. *O trabalhador brasileiro*. Rio de Janeiro: A Balança, 1933.

"Dona Amélia Molina Bastos; ou como e onde marcha a CAMDE." Interview given to Stella M. Senra Pollanah. In *Livro de Cabeceira da Mulher* I. Vol. 5. Rio de Janeiro: Civilização Brasileira, 1967.

Donald, Cleveland, Jr. "Slave Resistance and Abolitionism in Brazil: The Campista Case, 1879–1888." *Luso-Brazilian Review* 13 (Winter 1976): 182–93.

Doria, A. de Sampaio. *A questão social. Quaes os princípios scientíficos a adoptar na formação da legislação social do Brasil?* São Paulo: Monteiro Lobato, 1922.

Doria, Luiz Gastão de Escragnolle. "Cousas do passado." *Revista do Instituto Histórico e Geográfico Brasileiro* 71, pt. 2 (1908): 295–97.

———. *Memória histórica do Collejio de Pedro Segundo. 1837–1937*. Rio de Janeiro: Ministério da Educação, 1937.

Doxiadis Associates. *Guanabara: A Plan for Urban Development*. Athens: K. Papadimitropoulos, 1966.

DuBois, Ellen Carol. *Feminism and Suffrage. The Emergence of an Independent Women's Movement in America, 1848–1869*. Ithaca, N.Y.: Cornell University Press, 1978.

Dulles, John W. F. *Anarchists and Communists in Brazil, 1900–1935*. Austin: University of Texas Press, 1973.

————. *Unrest in Brazil: Political-Military Crises, 1955–1964*. Austin: University of Texas Press, 1970.

————. *Vargas of Brazil: A Political Biography.* Austin: University of Texas Press, 1967.

Dunlop, Charles J. *Subsídios para a história do Rio de Janeiro.* Rio de Janeiro: Editôra Rio Antigo, 1957.

Durocher, Maria Josephina Matilde. *Ideas por coordenar á respeito da emancipação.* Rio de Janeiro: Typ. do Diario de Rio de Janeiro, 1871.

Eisenberg, Peter L. "Abolishing Slavery: The Process on Pernambuco's Sugar Plantations." *Hispanic American Historical Review* 52 (November 1972): 586–605.

Encontros com a Civilização Brasileira. No. 26, *Mulher hoje.* Rio de Janeiro: Civilização Brasileira, 1980.

Ewbank, Thomas. *Life in Brazil; or a Journal of a Visit to the Land of the Cocoa and the Palm.* New York: Harper and Brothers, 1856.

Expilly, Charles. *Mulheres e costumes do Brasil.* Trans. Gastão Penalva. São Paulo: Companhia Nacional do Livro, 1935.

Faoro, Raymundo. *Os donos do poder. Formação do patronato político brasileiro.* Pôrto Alegre: Editôra Globo, 1958.

Farias, Zaira Ary. *Domesticidade. "Cativeiro" feminino?* Rio de Janeiro: Achiamé and Centro da Mulher Brasileira, 1983.

Fausto, Boris. *Crime e cotidiano. A criminalidade em São Paulo (1890–1920).* São Paulo: Editora Brasiliense, 1984.

————. *A revolução de 1930. Historiografia e história.* São Paulo: Editora Brasiliense, 1972.

————. *Trabalho urbano e conflito social (1890–1920).* São Paulo: Difel/Difusão Editorial, 1976.

————, ed. *História geral da civilização brasileira.* Vols. 8–11, *O Brasil republicano.* São Paulo: Difel/Difusão Editorial, 1975–86.

Federação Brasileira pelo Progresso Feminino. *Estatutos da Federação Brasileira pelo Progresso Feminino.* Rio de Janeiro: Olympica, 1936.

"Feminism in Brazil." *Bulletin of the Pan American Union* (December 1936): 981–82.

Fernandes, Floristan. *The Negro in Brazilian Society.* Trans. Jacqueline D. Skiles, A. Brunel, and Arthur Rothwell. New York: Columbia University Press, 1969.

Ferreira, Félix. *A educação da mulher. Notas colligidas de varios autores.* Rio de Janeiro: Hildebrandt, 1881.

————. *O Lyceo de Artes e Officios e as aulas de dezenho para o sexo feminino.* Rio de Janeiro: Hildebrandt, 1881.

————. *Noções da vida domestica, adaptadas, com accrescimos do original francez á instrucção do sexo feminino nas escolas brasileiras.* Rio de Janeiro: Dias da Silva Junior, [1879].

Ferrez, Gilberto. *O Rio antigo do fotógrafo Marc Ferrez. Paisagens e tipos humanos do Rio de Janeiro.* São Paulo: Editôra Ex Libris, 1984.

Ferrez, Gilberto, and Weston J. Naef. *Pioneer Photographers of Brazil, 1840–1920.* New York: Center for Inter-American Relations, 1976.

Fialho, Anfriso. *História da fundação da republica.* Rio de Janeiro: Laemmert, 1891.

Fletcher, James C., and Daniel Parish Kidder. *Brazil and the Brazilians Portrayed in Historical and Descriptive Sketches.* 7th ed. Boston: Little, Brown, 1867.

Flexner, Eleanor. *Century of Struggle. The Woman's Rights Movement in the United States.* Cambridge, Mass.: Harvard University Press, 1959.

Flora, Cornelia Butler. "Socialist Feminism in Latin America." In *The United Nations Decade for Women World Conference.* Ed. Nyomi Lynn. New York: Hayworth Press, 1984.

Flory, Thomas. "Judicial Politics in Nineteenth-Century Brazil." *Hispanic American Historical Review* 55 (November 1975): 664–92.

Forester, Robert F. *The Italian Emigration of Our Times.* Cambridge, Mass.: Harvard University Press, 1924.

Foot, Francisco. *Nem pátria nem patrão. Vida operária e cultura anarquista no Brasil.* São Paulo: Editora Brasiliense, 1983.

Foot, Francisco, and Victor Leonardi. *História da indústria e do trabalho no Brasil. Das origens aos anos vinte.* São Paulo: Global Editora, 1982.

Fowler, Robert Booth. *Carrie Catt. Feminist Politician.* Boston: Northeastern University Press, 1986.

França Júnior, Joaquim José de. *As doutoras. Comedia em 4 actos.* Rio de Janeiro: Sociedade Brasiliera de Autores Theatraes, 1932.

Franchetto, Bruna, Maria Laura V. C. Cavalcanti, Maria Luiza Heilborn, and Tânia Salem. *Perspectivas Antropológicas da Mulher.* Vol. 1. Rio de Janeiro: Zahar Editora, 1981.

Franco, Alipio. *Escola Normal da Bahia. Memória histórica. 1836 a 1936.* Bahia: Imprensa Official do Estado, 1936.

Freitas, Affonso A. de. *A imprensa periodica de São Paulo desde seus primoridos em 1823 até 1914.* São Paulo: Typ. do "Diario Official," 1915.

French, John D., with Mary Lynn Pedersen. "Women and Working Class Mobilization in Postwar São Paulo, 1945–1948." *Latin American Research Review* 24, no. 3 (1989): 101–23.

Freyre, Gilberto. *The Masters and the Slaves.* Trans. Samuel Putnam. New York: Alfred A. Knopf, 1946.

Fulford, Roger. *Votes for Women. The Story of a Struggle.* London: Faber and Faber, 1957.

Fundação Carlos Chagas. *Mulher brasileira. Bibliografia anotada.* 2 vols. São Paulo: Editora Brasiliense, 1979–81.

Furtado, Celso. *The Economic Growth of Brazil. A Survey from Colonial to Modern Times.* Trans. Ricardo W. de Aguiar and Eric Charles Drysdale. Berkeley: University of California Press, 1965.

Galeria Nacional. *Vultos prominentes da história brasileira.* Rio de Janeiro: Officinas Graphicas do Jornal do Brasil, 1931.

Garrido, C. de Sampayo. *Emigração portuguesa. Relatório consular.* São Paulo: Julio Costa, 1920.

Gattai, Zélia. *Anarquistas, graças a Deus.* Rio de Janeiro: Editora Record, 1979.

Geiger, Pedro Pinchas. *Evolução da rêde urbana brasileira.* Rio de Janeiro: Instituto Nacional de Estudos Pedagógicos, Ministério de Educação e Cultura, 1963.

Giacomini, Sonia Maria. *Mulher e escrava. Uma introdução ao estudo da mulher negra no Brasil.* Petrópolis: Vozes, 1988.

Gohn, Maria da Glória Marcondes. *A força da periferia. A luta das mulheres por creches em São Paulo.* Petrópolis: Vozes, 1985.

Goldberg, Anette. "Feminismo em regime autoritário: A experiencia do movimento de mulheres no Rio de Janeiro." Paper presented at the Twelfth Congress of the International Political Science Association, August 1982.

Goldberg, Maria Amélia Azevedo. *Violência contra a mulher.* São Paulo: Conselho Estadual da Condição Feminina, n.d.

González, Leila. "Mulher negra." *Mulherio* 1 (September–October 1981): 8–9.

Gordon, Eric, Michael Hall, and Hobart A. Spalding, Jr. "A Survey of Brazilian and Argentine Materials at the International Instituut Voor Sociale Geschiedenis in Amsterdam." *Latin American Research Review* 8 (Fall 1973): 27–77.

Goulart, Ruth Maria Barbosa [Ruth Bueno, pseud.]. "A estrutura dos direitos e deveres da mulher no anteprojeto de Código Civil." *Jurídica* (1972): 3–16.

——. *Regime jurídica da mulher casada.* 2d ed. Rio de Janeiro: Forense, 1970.

Graham, Maria Dundas [Lady Maria Calcott]. *Journal of a Voyage to Brazil and Residence There during Part of the Years 1821, 1822, 1823.* Reprint. New York: Praeger, 1969.

Graham, Richard. *Britain and the Onset of Modernization in Brazil, 1850-1914.* Cambridge: Cambridge University Press, 1968.

————. "Causes for the Abolition of Negro Slavery in Brazil: An Interpretive Essay." *Hispanic American Historical Review* 46 (May 1966): 123-37.

Graham, Sandra Lauderdale. *House and Street. The Domestic World of Servants and Masters in Nineteenth-Century Rio de Janeiro.* Cambridge: Cambridge University Press, 1988.

Grupo Feminista "8 de Março." *A mulher no mercado de trabalho.* São Paulo: Grupo Feminista "8 de Março," 1979.

Guerrero, César E. *Mujeres de Sarmiento.* Buenos Aires: Artes Gráficas Bartolomé U. Chiesivo, 1960.

Guimarães, Joaquim da Silva Mello. *Instituições de previdencia fundadas no Rio de Janeiro.* Rio de Janeiro: Typ. Nacional, 1883.

Guy, Donna J. "White Slavery, Public Health, and the Socialist Position on Legalized Prostitution in Argentina, 1913-1936." *Latin American Research Review* 23, no. 3 (1988): 60-80.

Hadfield, William. *Brazil and the River Plate in 1868. Showing the Progress of Those Countries since His Former Visit in 1853.* London: Bates, Hendy, 1869.

Hahner, June E. "Feminism, Women's Rights, and the Suffrage Movement in Brazil, 1850-1932." *Latin American Research Review* 15, no. 1 (1980): 65-111.

————. "The Nineteenth-Century Feminist Press and Women's Rights in Brazil." In *Latin American Women: Historical Perspectives.* Ed. Asunción Lavrin. Westport, Conn.: Greenwood Press, 1978.

————. *Poverty and Politics: The Urban Poor in Brazil, 1870-1920.* Albuquerque: University of New Mexico Press, 1986.

————. "Recent Research on Women in Brazil." *Latin American Research Review* 20, no. 3 (1985): 163-79.

————. "Women and Work in Brazil, 1850-1920: A Preliminary Investigation." In *Essays concerning the Socioeconomic History of Brazil and Portuguese India.* Ed. Dauril Alden and Warren Dean. Gainesville: University Presses of Florida, 1977.

————. "'Women's Place' in Politics and Economics in Brazil since 1964." *Luso-Brazilian Review* 19 (Summer 1982): 83-91.

————, ed. *A mulher no Brasil.* Rio de Janeiro: Civilização Brasileira, 1978.

————, ed. *Women in Latin American History. Their Lives and Views.* Rev. ed. Los Angeles: UCLA Latin American Center, 1981.

Hall, Michael M. "Immigration and the Early São Paulo Working Class." *Jahrbuch für Geschichte von Staat, Wirtschaft und Gesellschaft Lateinamerikas* 12 (1975): 393-407.

————. "Reformadores de classe média no Império Brasileiro: A Sociedade Central de Imigração." *Revista de História* 53, no. 105 (1976): 141-71.

Harper, Ida Husted. *The Life and Work of Susan B. Anthony.* 3 vols. Indianapolis: Hollenbeck Press, 1908.

Hasenbalg, Carlos. *Discriminação e desigualdades raciais no Brasil.* Trans. Patrick Burgin. Rio de Janeiro: Graal, 1979.

Hauser, Philip M., ed. *Urbanization in Latin America.* New York: International Documents Service, 1961.

Herrick, Jane. "Periodicals for Women in Mexico during the Nineteenth Century." *The Americas* 14 (October 1957): 135-44.

Hersh, Blanche Glassman. *The Slavery of Sex. Feminist Abolitionists in America.* Urbana: University of Illinois Press, 1978.

Hirsh, Lina. "These New Amazons." *Independent Woman* 14 (February 1935): 46–47, 72.

Hoffnagel, Marc Jay. "O movimento republicano em Pernambuco, 1870–1889." *Revista do Instituto Arqueológico, Histórico, e Geográfico Pernambucano* 49 (January 1977): 31–59.

Hollanda, Sérgio Buarque de, ed. *História geral da civilização brasileira*. Vols. 3–7, *O Brasil monárquico*. São Paulo: Difusão Européia do Livro, 1962–72.

Huggins, Martha Knisely. *From Slavery to Vagrancy in Brazil: Crime and Social Control in the Third World*. New Brunswick, N.J.: Rutgers University Press, 1984.

Hume, Leslie Parker. *The National Union of Women's Suffrage Societies, 1897–1914*. New York: Garland, 1982.

Humphrey, Alice R. *A Summer Journey to Brazil*. New York: Boswell, Silver, 1900.

Hurwitz, Edith F. "The International Sisterhood." In *Becoming Visible. Women in European History.* Ed. Renate Bridenthal and Claudia Koonz. Boston: Houghton Mifflin, 1972.

Ianni, Otávio. *O colapso do populismo no Brasil*. Rio de Janeiro: Civilização Brasileira, 1968.

———. *Industrialização e desenvolvimento social no Brasil*. Rio de Janeiro: Civilização Brasileira, 1963.

A imprensa e o Lyceo de Artes e Officios. Aulas para o sexo feminino. Rio de Janeiro: Hildebrandt, 1881.

Inauguração das aulas para o sexo feminino no Imperial Lyceo de Artes e Officios em 11 de outubro de 1881. Rio de Janeiro: Hildebrandt, 1881.

Jacquette, Jane S. "Female Political Participation in Latin America." In *Sex and Class in Latin America*. Ed. June Nash and Helen Icken Safa. New York: Praeger, 1976.

———. "Female Political Participation in Latin America: Raising Feminist Issues." In *Women in the World. 1975–1985. The Women's Decade*. Ed. Lynne B. Iglitzin and Ruth Ross. Santa Barbara, Calif.: ABC Clio Information Services, 1986.

———. "Women, Feminism, and the Transition to Democracy in Latin America." In *Latin American and Caribbean Contemporary Record*. Vol. 5. Ed. Abraham F. Lowenthal. New York: Holmes and Meier, 1987.

Jaguaribe, Hélio. *Desenvolvimento econômico e político*. Rio de Janeiro: Paz e Terra, 1969.

Jesús, Carolina Maria de. *Child of the Dark: The Diary of Carolina Maria de Jesús*. Trans. David St. Clair. New York: E. P. Dutton, 1962.

———. *Diario de Bitita*. Rio de Janeiro: Editora Nova Fronteira, 1986.

Karasch, Mary. "Black Worlds in the Tropics. Gilberto Freyre and the Women of Color in Brazil." *Proceedings of the Pacific Coast Council on Latin American Studies* 3 (1974): 19–29.

———. "From Porterage to Proprietorship: African Occupations in Rio de Janeiro, 1808–1850." In *Race and Slavery in the Western Hemisphere: Quantitative Studies*. Ed. Stanley L. Engerman and Eugene D. Genovese. Princeton: Princeton University Press, 1975.

———. *Slave Life in Rio de Janeiro, 1808–1850*. Princeton: Princeton University Press, 1987.

Kelly, Joan. *Women, History, and Theory. The Essays of Joan Kelly*. Chicago: University of Chicago Press, 1984.

Kent, Susan Kingsley. *Sex and Suffrage in Britain, 1860–1914*. Princeton: Princeton University Press, 1987.

Kerber, Linda K. *Women of the Republic. Intellect and Ideology in Revolutionary America*. Chapel Hill: University of North Carolina Press, 1980.

Kleinhaus, Laureana Wright de. *Mujeres notables mexicanas*. México, D.F.: Económica, 1910.

Knaster, Meri. *Women in Spanish America: An Annotated Bibliography from Pre-Conquest to Contemporary Times*. Boston: G. K. Hall, 1977.

Kohn Loncarica, Alfredo G. *Cecilia Grierson. Vida y obra de la primeira médica argentina.* Buenos Aires: Stilcograf, 1976.

Korth, Eugene H., and Della M. Flysche. "Dowry and Inheritance in Colonial Spanish America: Peninsular Law and Chilean Practice." *The Americas* 43 (April 1987): 395–410.

Kraditor, Aileen S. *The Ideas of the Woman Suffrage Movement, 1890–1920.* New York: Columbia University Press, 1965.

Kuznesof, Elizabeth Ann. "The Role of the Female-Headed Household in Brazilian Modernization: São Paulo 1765–1836." *Journal of Social History* 13 (Summer 1980): 589–613.

Labarca Hubertson, Amanda. *¿A donde va la mujer?* Santiago: Ediciones Extra, 1934.

———. *Feminismo contemporaneo.* Santiago: Zig Zag, 1947.

Lacerda, Maurício de. *Entre duas revoluções.* Rio de Janeiro: Editôra Leite Ribeiro, 1927.

———. *Evolução legislativa do direito social brasileiro.* Rio de Janeiro: Ministério do Trabalho, Indústria e Comércio, 1960.

———. *História de um covardia.* Rio de Janeiro: Livraria Editôra Freitas Bastos, 1931.

Lacerda, Maurício Caminha de. "Maurício de Lacerda, meu pai." *Revista Brasileira* 6 (September–October 1960): 195–217.

Lamberg, Maurício. *O Brasil.* Trans. Luiz de Castro. Rio de Janeiro: Nunes, 1896.

Lamengo, Alberto Ribeiro. *O homem e a Guanabara.* Rio de Janeiro: Conselho Nacional de Geografia, 1948.

Lapouge, Maryvonne, and Clelia Pisa. *As brasileiras. Voix, crits du Brésil.* Paris: Des femmes, 1977.

Lavrin, Asunción. *The Ideology of Feminism in Southern Cone, 1900–1914.* Working Paper no. 169, Latin American Program. Washington, D.C.: The Wilson Center, 1986.

———, ed. *Latin American Women: Historical Perspectives.* Westport, Conn.: Greenwood Press, 1978.

———, ed. *Sexuality and Marriage in Colonial Latin America.* Lincoln: University of Nebraska Press, 1989.

Lavrin, Asunción, and Edith Couturier. "Doweries and Wills: A View of Women's Socioeconomic Role in Colonial Guadalajara and Puebla, 1640–1790." *Hispanic American Historical Review* 59 (May 1979): 280–304.

Leacock, Seth, and Ruth Leacock. *Spirits of the Deep: A Study of an Afro-Brazilian Cult.* New York: Natural History Press, 1972.

Leal, Victor Nunes. *Coronelismo, enxada e voto. O município e o regime representativo no Brasil. (Da colônia a Primeira República).* Rio de Janeiro: Forense, 1948.

Leite, Miriam Lifchitz Moreira. *Outra face do feminismo: Maria Lacerda de Moura.* São Paulo: Editora Ática, 1984.

———, ed. *A condição feminina no Rio de Janeiro. Século XIX.* São Paulo: Editôra Hucitec, and Brasília: Instituto Nacional do Livro, 1984.

Leite, Rosalina de Santa Cruz. *A operária metalúrgica: Estudo sobre as condições de vida e trabalho de operárias metalúrgicas na cidade de São Paulo.* São Paulo: Editora Semente, 1982.

Lemos, Carlos A. C. *Cozinhas, etc.* São Paulo: Editora Perspectiva, 1976.

Lemos, Lígia. "Pioneiras do intelectualismo feminino no Brasil." *Formação* (November 1947): 51–52.

Levi, Darrell E. *The Prados of São Paulo, Brazil. An Elite Brazilian Family and Social Change, 1840–1930.* Athens: University of Georgia Press, 1987.

Levine, Robert M. *Pernambuco in the Brazilian Federation, 1889–1937.* Stanford: Stanford University Press, 1978.

———. *The Vargas Regime. The Critical Years, 1934–1938.* New York: Columbia University Press, 1970.

Levy, Jim. *Juana Manso: Argentine Feminist.* Occasional Paper no. 1. Institute of Latin American Studies. Bundoora: La Trobe University, 1977.

Lewin, Linda. *Politics and Parentela in Paraíba. A Case Study of Family-Based Oligarchy in Brazil.* Princeton: Princeton University Press, 1987.

Lima, Antonio Austregesilo. *Perfil da mulher brasileira (Esboco acerca do feminismo no Brasil).* Paris: Livrarias Aillaud e Bertrand, 1923.

Lima, Lana Lage da Gama, ed. *Mulheres, adúlteros e padres. História e moral na sociedade brasileira.* Rio de Janeiro: Dois Pontos Editora, 1987.

Lima Barreto, Afonso Henriques de. *Clara dos Anjos.* 2d ed. São Paulo: Editôra Brasiliense, 1962.

———. *Coisas do reino do jambón.* 2d ed. São Paulo: Editôra Brasiliense, 1961.

———. *Marginália.* 2d ed. São Paulo: Editôra Brasiliense, 1961.

———. *Vida urbana.* 2d ed. São Paulo: Editôra Brasiliense, 1961.

Lins, Ivan. *História do positivismo no Brasil.* São Paulo: Companhia Editôra Nacional, 1964.

Litoff, Judy Barrett. *American Midwives, 1860 to the Present.* Westport, Conn.: Greenwood Press, 1978.

Little, Cynthia. "Moral Reform and Feminism. A Case Study." *Journal of Interamerican Studies and World Affairs* 17 (November 1975): 386–97.

Lobo, Elizabeth Souza, and Maria Celia Paoli. "Notas sobre o movimento no feminino." *Desvios* 1 (November 1982): 45–57.

Lobo, Eulália Maria Lahmeyer. *História do Rio de Janeiro (Do capital comercial ao capital industrial e financeiro).* 2 vols. Rio de Janeiro: Instituto Brasileiro de Mercado de Capitais, 1978.

Lobo, Francisco Bruno. "A primeira médica formada no Brasil." *Revista de História* 42 (April–June 1971): 483–86.

Lombardi, Mary. "Women in the Modern Art Movement in Brazil: Salon Leaders, Artists, and Musicians, 1917–1930." Ph.D. diss., University of California, Los Angeles, 1973.

Love, Joseph L. "Political Participation in Brazil, 1881–1969." *Luso-Brazilian Review* 7 (December 1970): 3–24.

———. *Rio Grando do Sul and Brazilian Regionalism, 1882–1930.* Stanford: Stanford University Press, 1971.

———. *São Paulo in the Brazilian Federation, 1889–1937.* Stanford: Stanford University Press, 1980.

Luccock, John. *Notes on Rio de Janeiro and the Southern Parts of Brazil Taken during a Residence of Ten Years . . . 1808–1818.* London: S. Leigh, 1820.

Lutz, Alma. *Crusade for Freedom. Women of the Anti-Slavery Movement.* Boston: Beacon Press, 1968.

Lutz, Bertha. *A nacionalidade da mulher casada.* Rio de Janeiro: Irmões Pongetti, 1933.

———. *13 princípios básicos. Sugestões ao Ante-projeto da Constituição.* Rio de Janeiro: Federação Brasileira pelo Progresso Feminino, 1933.

Luz, Madel T., ed. *O lugar da mulher (Estudos sobre a condição feminina na sociedade atual).* Rio de Janeiro: Graal, 1982.

Luz, Nícia Vilela. *A luta pela industrialização do Brasil (1808 à 1930).* São Paulo: Difusão Européia do Livro, 1961.

———. "O papel das classes médias no movimento republicano." *Revista de História* 57 (January–March 1964): 13–27.

Macedo, Joaquim Manoel de. *A moreninha.* 13th ed. São Paulo: Edições Melhoramentos, [1967].

———. *Mulheres celebres*. Rio de Janeiro: Garnier, 1878.

McGee, Sandra F. "Right-Wing Female Activists in Buenos Aires, 1900–1932." In *Women and the Structure of Society: Selected Research from the Fifth Berkshire Conference on the History of Women*. Ed. Barbara J. Harris and Joann McNamara. Durham, N.C.: Duke University Press, 1984.

———. "The Visible and Invisible Liga Patriotica Argentina, 1919–28: Gender Roles and the Right Wing." *Hispanic American Historical Review* 64 (May 1984): 233–58.

Machado, Else Nascimento. *O progresso feminino e sua base*. São Paulo: Imprensa Methodista, 1922.

Macías, Anna. *Against All Odds. The Feminist Movement in Mexico to 1940*. Westport, Conn.: Greenwood Press, 1982.

Mackenzie, Midge, ed. *Shoulder to Shoulder. A Documentary by Midge Mackenzie*. New York: Alfred A. Knopf, 1975.

Madeira, Felicia R., and Paulo I. Singer. *Estrutura do emprego e trabalho feminino no Brasil, 1920–1970*. Cadernos CEBRAP 13. São Paulo: CEBRAP, 1973.

Maia, Ignez Sabino Pinho. *Mulheres illustres do Brazil*. Rio de Janeiro: Garnier [1899].

Maia, Sylvia Tigre. "A evolução intelectual feminina no Brasil. Subsídios para a história da educação. I Parte. No Império." *Formação* 5 (September 1943): 45–51.

———. "A evolução intelectual feminina no Brasil. II Parte. Na República." *Formação* 6 (December 1943): 33–39.

Mainwaring, Scott. *The Catholic Church and Politics in Brazil, 1916–1985*. Stanford: Stanford University Press, 1986.

Maram, Sheldon L. "Anarcho-Syndicalism in Brazil." In *Latin America: Power and Poverty. Proceedings of the Fourth Pacific Coast Council on Latin American Studies*, 1975.

———. *Anarquistas, imigrantes e o movimento operário brasileiro, 1890 a 1920*. Rio de Janeiro: Paz e Terra, 1979.

———. "The Immigrant and the Brazilian Labor Movement, 1890–1920." In *Essays concerning the Socioeconomic History of Brazil and Portuguese India*. Ed. Dauril Alden and Warren Dean. Gainesville: University Presses of Florida, 1977.

———. "Labor and the Left in Brazil, 1890–1921: A Movement Aborted." *Hispanic American Historical Review* 57 (May 1977): 254–72.

Marcílio, Maria Luiza. *La Ville de São Paulo. Peuplement e Population, 1750–1850*. Rouen: Université de Rouen, 1972.

Mariz, Zélia Maria Bezerra. *Nísia Floresta Brasileira Augusta*. Natal: Editora Universitária, 1982.

Mattelart, Michele. "The Feminine Version of the Coup d'Etat." In *Sex and Class in Latin America*. Ed. June Nash and Helen Icken Safa. New York: Praeger, 1974.

Mattoso, Kátia M. de Queirós. *Bahia: A cidade do Salvador e seu mercado no século XIX*. São Paulo: Editora Hucitec, 1978.

———. *Família e sociedade na Bahia do século XIX*. Trans. James Amado. São Paulo: Corrupio, 1988.

———. *To Be a Slave in Brazil, 1550–1888*. Trans. Arthur Goldhammer. New Brunswick, N.J.: Rutgers University Press, 1986.

Mawe, John. *Travels in the Interior of Brazil, Particularly in the Gold and Diamond Districts of that Country*. Philadelphia: M. Carey, 1816.

Mayer, Arno J. "The Lower Middle Class as Historical Problem." *Journal of Modern History* 47 (September 1975): 409–36.

Mayor, Mara. "Fears and Fantasy of the Anti-Suffragists." *Connecticut Review* 7 (April 1974): 64–74.

Melder, Keith E. *Beginnings of Sisterhood. The American Woman's Rights Movement, 1800–1850.* New York: Schocken Books, 1977.

Mello, Morais Filho, Alexandre José de. *Factos e memórias.* Rio de Janeiro: Garnier, 1903.

———. *Festas e tradições populares do Brasil.* 3d ed. Rio de Janeiro: F. Briguiet, 1946.

———. *Mythos e poemas. Nacionalismo.* Rio de Janeiro: G. Leuzinger e Filhos, 1884.

———. *Serenatas e saráos.* 3 vols. Rio de Janeiro: Garnier, 1901–2.

Melo, Henrique Capitolino Pereira de. *Pernambucanas illustres.* Pernambuco: Mercantil, 1879.

Melo Franco, Afonso Arinos de. *Rodrigues Alves. Apogeu e declínio do presidencialismo.* 2 vols. Rio de Janeiro: José Olympio, and São Paulo: Editora da Universidade de São Paulo, 1973.

Mendes, Raimundo Teixeira. *A mulher. Sua preeminência social e moral, segundo os ensinos da verdadeira scencia pozitiva.* 4th ed. Rio de Janeiro: Igreja Pozitivista do Brazil, 1958.

Michel, Ernest. *A travers l'hemisphere sud on mon second voyage autour du monde. Portugal, Sénégal, Brésil, Uruguay, République Argentine, Chile, Pérou.* Paris: Libraire Victor Palmé, 1887.

Miller, Barbara Ann. "The Roles of Women in the Mexican Cristero Rebellion: Las señoras y las religiosas." *The Americas* 40 (January 1984): 303–24.

Miller, Francesca. "The International Relations of Women in the Americas, 1890–1928." *The Americas* 43 (October 1986): 171–82.

Miranda, Maria Augusta Tibiriçá. *Alice Tibiriçá. Lutas e ideais.* Rio de Janeiro: PLG Comunicação, 1980.

Mitchell, David J. *The Fighting Pankhursts.* New York: Macmillan, 1967.

Moacyr, Primitivo. *A instrução e as provincias.* 3 vols. São Paulo: Companhia Editôra Nacional, 1939–40.

Moisés, José Alvaro, et al. *Cidade, povo e poder.* Rio de Janeiro: Centro de Estudos de Cultural Contemporânea and Paz e Terra, 1982.

———. *Contradições urbanas e movimentos sociais.* 2d ed. Rio de Janeiro: Centro de Estudos de Cultura Contemporânea and Paz e Terra, 1978.

Molyneux, Maxime. "No God, No Boss, No Husband. Anarchist Feminism in Nineteenth-Century Argentina." *Latin American Perspectives* 13 (Winter 1986): 119–45.

Montenegro, Ana. *Mulheres. Participação nas lutas populares.* Salvador: M&S Gráfica e Editora, 1985.

———. *Ser ou nao ser feminista.* Recife: Guararapes, 1981.

Moraes, Evaristo de. *Apontamentos de direito operario.* Rio de Janeiro: Imprensa Nacional, 1905.

———. *A campanha abolicionista (1879–1888).* Rio de Janeiro: Freitas Bastos, 1924.

———. *Reminiscencias de um rabula criminalista.* Rio de Janeiro: Leite Ribeiro, 1922.

Moraes, Maria Lygia Quartim de. *Mulheres em movimento.* São Paulo: Nobel and Conselho Estadual da Condição Feminina, 1985.

———. "Struggling for Democracy and Equality in Brazil." *AfriAsia* 30 (June 1986): 40–42.

———. *Vida de mulher.* Rio de Janeiro: Editôra Marco Zero, 1981.

Moraes, Tancredo. *Pela emancipação integral da mulher.* Rio de Janeiro: Editora Pongetti, 1971.

Moraes, Theodoro de. "Escolas Normaes Livres." *Educação* 4 (July–September 1928).

Morais, Eneida de. *História do carnaval carioca.* Rio de Janeiro: Civilização Brasileira, 1955.

Morse, Richard M. *From Community to Metropolis. A Biography of São Paulo, Brazil.* Gainesville: University of Florida Press, 1958.

————, ed. *The Urban Development of Latin America, 1750–1920.* Stanford: Center for Latin American Studies, Stanford University, 1971.

Morton, Ward. *Woman Suffrage in Mexico.* Gainesville: University of Florida Press, 1962.

Moses, Claire Goldberg. *French Feminism in the Nineteenth Century.* Albany: State University of New York Press, 1984.

Mott, Maria Lucia de Barros. "Biografia de uma revoltada: Ercília Nogueira Cobra." *Cadernos de Pesquisa* 58 (August 1986): 89–102.

Moura, Esmeralda Blanco B. de. *Mulheres e menores no trabalho industrial: Os fatores sexo e edade no dinámica do capital.* Petrópolis: Vozes, 1982.

Moura, Maria Lacerda de. *Amai e . . . não vos multipliqueis.* Rio de Janeiro: Civilização Brasileira, 1932.

————. *"A mulher é uma degenerada."* 3d ed. Rio de Janeiro: Civilização Brasileira, 1932.

————. *Religião do amor e da belleza.* 2d ed. São Paulo: Typ. Editôra "O Pensamento," 1929.

Moura, Roberto. *Tia Ciata e a pequena África no Rio de Janeiro.* Rio de Janeiro: FUNARTE, 1983.

"Movimento feminino pela anistia. O papel da mulher na conjuntura brasileira." Mimeo. Congresso Nacional de Anistia, São Paulo, November 1978.

Moya, Salvador de. *Culto á mulher (Tem a mulher, naturalmente, perante a sociedade, os mesmos direitos do homen?* São Paulo: Imprensa Methodista, 1912.

A mulher e a revolução brasileira. MR 8: Resoluções sobre o trabalho entre as mulheres. São Paulo: Editora Quilombo, 1980.

Muraro, Rose Marie. "Libertação feminina? Existe sim!" *Nova* 7 (April 1974): 95–97.

————. *Libertação sexual da mulher.* 2d ed. Petrópolis: Vozes, 1971.

————. *A mulher na construção do mundo futuro.* Petrópolis: Vozes, 1967.

————. *Sexualidade da mulher brasileira: Corpo e classe social no Brasil.* Petrópolis: Vozes, 1983.

Nabuco, Joaquim. *Abolitionism. The Brazilian Antislavery Struggle.* Trans. Robert Conrad. Urbana: University of Illinois Press, 1977.

Nash, Roy F. "The Brains of Brazil's Woman Movement." *The Woman Citizen,* March 25, 1922, pp. 9, 16–17.

Nazario, Diva Wolf. *Voto feminino e feminismo. Um anno de feminismo entre nós.* São Paulo: N.p., 1923.

Nazzari, Muriel Smith. "Women, the Family and Property: The Decline of the Dowry in São Paulo, Brazil (1600–1870)." Ph.D. diss., Yale University, 1986.

Needell, Jeffrey D. *A Tropical Belle Epoque. Elite Culture and Society in Turn-of-the-Century Rio de Janeiro.* New York: Cambridge University Press, 1988.

Newhall, Beatrice. "Woman Suffrage in the Americas." *Bulletin of the Pan American Union* 70 (May 1936): 424–28.

Nist, John. *The Modernist Movement in Brazil.* Austin: University of Texas Press, 1967.

Nosso século. 1930–1945. A era de Vargas. São Paulo: Abril Cultura, 1980.

Oakenfull, J. C. *Brazil: A Century of Independence, 1822–1922.* Freiburg, Germany: C. A. Wagner, 1922.

————. *Brazil in 1911.* London: Butler and Tanner, 1912.

————. *Brazil (1913).* London: Butler and Tanner, 1914.

————. *Brazil: Past, Present, and Future.* London: John Bale, Sons, and Danielsson, 1919.

Offen, Karen. "Defining Feminism: A Comparative Historical Approach." *Signs. Journal of Women in Culture and Society* 14 (Autumn 1988): 119–57.

O'Gorman, Frances, et al. *Morro, mulher.* São Paulo: Edições Paulinas, 1984.

Oliveira, Andradina América de. *Divorcio?* Pôrto Alegre: Livraria Universal, 1912.

Oliveira, Antonio de Almeida. *Obra destinada a mostrar o estado em que se acha, e as reformas, que exige a instrução publica no Brazil.* Rio de Janeiro: Garnier, 1867.

Oliveira, Cícera Fernandes de, and Danda Prado. *Cícera. Um destino de mulher. Autobiografia duma emigrante nordestina, operária têxtil.* São Paulo: Editôra Brasiliense, 1981.

Oliveira, João Gualberto de. "A primeira mulher diplomada pela Faculdade de Direito de São Paulo." *Revista Bancaria Brasileira* 31 (November 30, 1962): 28, 31.

Oliveira, Lola de. *Hontem e hoje.* São Paulo: Paulista, 1928.

————. *Minha mãe.* Rio de Janeiro: [Livraria Laemmert], 1958.

O'Neill, William L. *Everyone Was Brave. A History of Feminism in America.* Chicago: Quadrangle Books, 1969.

Ottoni, Cristiano Benedito. *D. Pedro de Alcantara.* Rio de Janeiro: Typ. Jornal do Commercio, 1893.

Pacheco, José. *A mulher no lugar do homem.* N.p, n.d.

Pang, Eul Soo, and Ron L. Seckinger. "The Mandarins of Imperial Brazil." *Comparative Studies in Society and History* 14 (March 1972): 215–44.

Papachristou, Judith, ed. *Women Together: A History in Documents of the Women's Movement in the United States.* A Ms. Book. New York: Alfred A. Knopf, 1976.

Patai, Daphne. *Brazilian Women Speak. Contemporary Life Stories.* New Brunswick, N.J.: Rutgers University Press, 1988.

Peck, Mary Gray. *Carrie Chapman Catt. A Biography.* New York: R. W. Wilson, 1944.

Peixoto, Alzira Vargas do Amaral. *Getúlio Vargas, meu pai.* Rio de Janeiro: Editôra Globo, 1960.

Pena, Maria Valéria Junior. *Mulheres e trabalhadoras. Presença feminina na constitutição do sistema fabril.* Rio de Janeiro: Paz e Terra, 1981.

Penteado, Jacob. *Belènzinho, 1910 (Retrato de uma época).* Rio de Janeiro: Livraria Martins, 1962.

Pereira, Manoel Francisco Pinto. *A mulher no Brasil.* São Paulo: C. Teixeira, 1916.

Peres, Tirsa Regazzini. "A instrução secundária feminina no Brasil: 1889–1930." *Didática* 15 (1979): 35–43.

Pescatello, Ann. "The Female in Ibero-America: An Essay on Research Bibliography and Research Directions." *Latin American Research Review* 7 (Summer 1972): 125–41.

————. *Power and Pawn: The Female in Iberian Families, Societies, and Cultures.* Westport, Conn.: Greenwood Press, 1976.

————, ed. *Female and Male in Latin America: Essays.* Pittsburgh: University of Pittsburgh Press, 1973.

Pierson, Donald. *Cruz das Almas.* Washington, D.C.: U.S. Government Printing Office, 1948.

Pimentel, Antonio Martins de Azevedo. *Quaes os melhoramentos hygienicos que devem ser introduzidos no Rio de Janeiro para tornar esta cidade mais saudavel.* Rio de Janeiro: Moreira Maximino, 1884.

————. *Subsidios para o estudo de hygiene do Rio de Janeiro.* Rio de Janeiro: Carlos Gaspar da Silva, 1890.

Pimentel, Silvia. *A mulher e a constituinte. Uma contribuição ao debate.* São Paulo: Cortez Editora and EDUC, 1985.

Pinheiro, Paulo Sérgio, and Michael M. Hall, eds. *A classe operária no Brasil. Documentos (1889–1930).* 2 vols. São Paulo: Editora Alfa Omega, 1979, and Editora Brasiliense, 1982.

Portal, Magda. *La trampa.* Lima: Ediciones Raiz, 1956.

Pradez, Charles. *Nouvelles études sur le Brésil.* Paris: Ernest Thorin Editeur, 1872.

Prado, Antonio Arnoni, ed. *Libertários no Brasil. Memória, lutas, cultura.* São Paulo: Editora Brasiliense, 1986.

Prado, Danda. *O que é família. Coleção Primeiros Passos 50.* São Paulo: Editora Brasiliense, 1981.

Programma do ensino na escola normal da corte. Rio de Janeiro: Lyra de Apollo, 1874.

Quataert, Jean H. *Reluctant Feminists in German Social Democracy, 1885–1917.* Princeton: Princeton University Press, 1979.

Que história é essa? Clube de mães e grupos de mulheres de São Paulo. São Paulo: Grupo de Educação Popular, 1985.

Queiroz, Carlota Pereira de. "Discurso pronunciada na Camara de Deputados pela Dra. Carlota Pereira de Queiroz (da Bancada Paulista) em 8 de agosto de 1935." Rio de Janeiro: Oficinas Gráficas do "Jornal do Brasil," 1936.

Queiroz, Isaura Pereira de. *O mandonismo local na vida política brasileira.* São Paulo: Instituto de Estudos Brasileiros, 1969.

Queroz, Suely Robles Reis de. *Escravidão negra em São Paulo.* Rio de Janeiro: José Olympio, 1977.

Rachum, Ilan. "Feminism, Woman Suffrage, and National Politics in Brazil: 1922–1937." *Luso-Brazilian Review* 14 (Summer 1977): 118–33.

Rago, Margareth. *Do cabare ao lar. A utopia da cidade disciplinar. Brasil: 1890–1930.* Rio de Janeiro: Paz e Terra, 1985.

Ramos, Donald. "City and Country: The Family in Minas Gerais, 1804–1838." *Journal of Family History* 3 (Winter 1978): 361–75.

————. "Marriage and the Family in Colonial Vila Rica." *Hispanic American Historical Review* 55 (May 1975): 200–225.

Reis, Antônio Simões dos, ed. *Bibliografia brasileira. Narcisa Amália.* Rio de Janeiro: Organizações Simões, 1949.

Report of the Royal Commission on the Status of Women in Canada. Ottawa: Information Canada, 1970.

Ribeiro, Carolina. "A mulher paulista em 32." *Revista do Instituto Histórico e Geográfico de São Paulo* 59 (1961): 247–62.

Ribeiro, José Jacintho. *Chronologia paulista; ou relação histórica dos factos mais importantes ocorridos em S. Paulo desde a chegada de Martim Affonso de Souza em S. Vicente até 1898.* 3 vols. São Paulo: N.p., 1899–1901.

Ribeyrolles, Charles. *O Brasil pittoresco.* 2 vols. Rio de Janeiro: Typ. Nacional, 1859–61.

Rios Filho, Adolfo de los. *O Rio de Janeiro imperial.* Rio de Janeiro: A Noite, 1946.

Rodrigues, Aracky Martins. *Operário, operária: Estudo exploratório sobre o operariado industrial da Grande São Paulo.* São Paulo: Edições Símbolo, 1978.

Rodrigues, Edgar. *Alvorado operário. Os congressos operários no Brasil.* Rio de Janeiro: Mundo Livre, 1979.

————. *Nacionalismo e cultura social, 1913–1922.* Rio de Janeiro: Laemmert, 1972.

————. *Novos rumos (história do movimento operário e das lutas sociais no Brasil) (1922–1946).* Rio de Janeiro: Mundo Livre, n.d.

————. *Socialismo e sindicalismo no Brasil, 1675–1913.* Rio de Janeiro: Laemmert, 1969.

Rodrigues, Jessita Martins. *A mulher operária. Um estudo sobre tecelãs.* São Paulo: Editora Hucitec, 1979.

Rodrigues, João Batista Cascudo. *A mulher brasileira. Direitos políticos e civís.* Fortaleza: Imprensa Universitária do Ceará, 1962.

Rodrigues, José Albertino. *Sindicato e desenvolvimento no Brasil.* São Paulo: Difusão Européia do Livro, 1968.

Rodrigues, Leda Maria Pereira [Madre Maria Angela]. *A instrução feminina em São Paulo:*

Subsídios para sua história até a proclamação da República. São Paulo: Faculdade de Filosofia "Sedes Sapientiae," 1962.

Rodrigues, Leôncio. *Conflito industrial e sindicalismo no Brasil.* São Paulo: Difusão Européia do Livro, 1966.

Rosa, Ferreira da. *Associação dos Empregados no Comércio do Rio de Janeiro. Méio seculo. Narrativa histórica.* Rio de Janeiro: Paulo, Pongetti, 1930.

―――. *O lupanar.* Rio de Janeiro: N.p., 1896.

―――. *O Rio de Janeiro em 1900. Visitas e excursões.* 2d ed. N.p., n.d.

―――. *Rio de Janeiro. Notícia histórica e descritiva da Capital do Brasil.* Rio de Janeiro: Typ. do Annuario do Brasil, 1924.

Rosário, Sister Maria Regina do Santo [Laurita Pessoa Gabaglia]. *O cardeal Leme (1882–1942).* Rio de Janeiro: José Olympio, 1962.

Rosemberg, Fúlvia. "O movimento de mulheres e a abertura política no Brasil. O caso da creche." *Cadernos de Pesquisa* 5 (November 1984): 73–79.

Rosemberg, Fúlvia, Regina P. Pinto, and Esmeralda V. Negrao. *A educação da mulher no Brasil.* São Paulo: Global Editora, 1982.

Rosen, Andrew. *Rise Up, Women! The Militant Campaign of the Women's Social and Political Union, 1903–1914.* London: Routledge and Kegan Paul, 1974.

Rover, Constance. *Women's Suffrage and Party Politics in Britain, 1886–1914.* London: Routledge and Kegan Paul, 1967.

Russell-Wood, A. J. R. "Female and Family in the Economy and Society of Colonial Brazil." In *Latin American Women: Historical Perspectives.* Ed. Asunción Lavrin. Westport, Conn.: Greenwood Press, 1978.

―――, ed. *From Colony to Nation: Essays on the Independence of Brazil.* Baltimore: Johns Hopkins University Press, 1975.

Saes, Décio. *Classe média e política na Primeira República Brasileira (1889–1930).* Petrópolis: Vozes, 1975.

Saffioti, Heleith Iara Bongiovani. *Do artesanal ao industrial. A exploração da mulher: Um estudo de operárias têxtis e de confecções no Brasil e nos Estados Unidos.* São Paulo: Editora Hucitec, 1981.

―――. *Emprego doméstico e capitalismo.* Petrópolis: Vozes, 1978.

―――. *Mulher brasileira: Opressão e exploração.* Rio de Janeiro: Achiamé, 1984.

―――. *A mulher na sociedade de classes. Mito e realidade.* São Paulo: Quatro Artes, 1969.

Salgado, Plínio. *A mulher no século XX.* In *Obras completas de Plínio Salgado.* São Paulo: Editôra das Américas, 1955.

Samara, Eni de Mesquita. *A família brasileira. Tudo é história 71.* São Paulo: Editora Brasiliense, 1983.

Santa Rosa, Virgínio. *Que foi o tenentismo.* Rio de Janeiro: Civilização Brasileira, 1964.

Santos, Ely Souto dos. *As domésticas. Um estudo interdisciplinar da realidade social, política, econômica e jurídica.* Porto Alegre: Editora da Universidade, 1983.

Santos, José Maria. *Bernardino de Campos e o Partido Republicano Paulista. Subsídios para a história da República.* Rio de Janeiro: José Olympio, 1960.

―――. *A política geral do Brazil.* São Paulo: J. Magalhães, 1930.

―――. *Os republicanos paulistas e a abolição.* São Paulo: Livraria Martins, 1965.

Sarti, Cynthia. "Feminismo no Brasil: Uma trajetoria particular." *Cadernos de Pesquisa* 64 (February 1988): 38–47.

Schmink, Marianne. "Women in Brazilian *Abertura* Politics." *Signs: Journal of Women in Culture and Society* 7 (Autumn 1981): 115–34.

Scott, Rebecca J., et al. *The Abolition of Slavery and the Aftermath in Brazil.* Durham, N.C.: Duke University Press, 1988.

Scully, William. *Brazil. Its Provinces and Chief Cities.* London: Murry, 1866.

Silva, Alberto. *A primeira médica do Brasil.* Rio de Janeiro: Irmões Pongetti, 1954.

Silva, Innocêncio Francisco da. *Diccionario bibliographico portuguez.* 22 vols. Lisbon: Imprensa Nacional, 1858–1923.

Silva, Joaquim Norberto Souza. *Brasileiras celebres.* Rio de Janeiro: Garnier, 1862.

Silva, Maria Beatriz Nizza da. *Cultura no Brasil Colônia.* Petrópolis: Vozes, 1981.

———. *Sistema do casamento no Brasil colonial.* São Paulo: T. A. Queiroz/EDUSP, 1984.

Simão, Azis. *Sindicato e estado. Suas relações na formacão do proletariado de São Paulo.* São Paulo: Dominus Editôra, 1966.

Simões, Solange de Deus. *Deus, patria e família. As mulheres no golpe de 1964.* Petrópolis: Vozes, 1984.

Singer, Paulo. *Desenvolvimento econômico e evolução urbana (Ánalise da evolução econômica de São Paulo, Blumenau, Pôrto Alegre, Belo Horizonte e Recife).* 2d ed. São Paulo: Companhia Editôra Nacional, 1977.

Skidmore, Thomas E. *Politics in Brazil, 1930–1964.* New York: Oxford University Press, 1967.

———. *The Politics of Military Rule in Brazil, 1964–85.* New York: Oxford University Press, 1988.

Slaughter, Jane, and Robert Kern, eds. *European Women on the Left. Socialism, Feminism, and the Problems Faced by Political Women, 1880 to the Present.* Westport, Conn.: Greenwood Press, 1981.

Smith, Herbert E. *Brazil. The Amazons and the Coast.* New York: Charles Scribner's Sons, 1879.

Soares, Pedro Maia. "Feminismo no Rio Grande do Sul: Primeiros apontamentos (1835–1945)." In *Vivência. História, sexualidade, e imagens femininas.* Ed. Maria Cristina A. Bruschini and Fúlvia Rosemberg. São Paulo: Editora Brasiliense, 1980.

Sodré, Nelson Werneck. *Formação histórica do Brasil.* São Paulo: Editôra Brasiliense, 1964.

———. *A história da imprensa no Brasil.* Rio de Janeiro: Civilização Brasileira, 1966.

Soeiro, Susan. "Recent Work on Latin American Women. A Review Essay." *Journal of Interamerican Studies and World Affairs* 17 (November 1975): 497–516.

Soihet, Rachel. "Bertha Lutz e a ascensão social da mulher, 1919–1937." Master's thesis, Universidade Federal Fluminense, 1974.

Solomon, Barbara Miller. *In the Company of Women. A History of Women and Higher Education in America.* New Haven: Yale University Press, 1985.

Sorj, Bila, and Paula Montero. "SOS-Mulher e a luta contra a violência." In *Perspectivas antropológicas da mulher.* Vol. 4. Rio de Janeiro: Zahar, 1985, 4:103–7.

Souza, Antonio Muniz de. *Viagens e observações de hum brasileiro, que, desejando ser util á sua patria, se dedicou a estudar os usos e costumes de seos patricios, e os tres reinos de natureza, em varios lugares e sertões do Brasil, offerecidas á nação brasileira.* Rio de Janeiro: Typ. Americana de I. P. da Costa, 1834.

Sowerwine, Charles. *Sisters or Citizens? Women and Socialism in France since 1876.* Cambridge: Cambridge University Press, 1982.

Spalding, Hobart A., Jr. *Organized Labor in Latin America. Historical Case Studies of Urban Workers in Dependent Societies.* New York: Harper and Row, 1977.

Spix, Johann B. von, and Karl F. F. von Martius. *Travels in Brazil in the Years 1817–1820.* 2 vols. Trans. H. E. Lloyd. London: Longman, Hurst, Rees, Orme, Brown, and Green, 1824.

Stein, Ingrid. "As figuras femininas nos romances de Machado de Assis." Ph.D. diss., Rheinischen Friedrich-Wilhelms-Universität, 1983.

Stein, Stanley J. *The Brazilian Cotton Manufacture. Textile Enterprise in an Underdeveloped Area, 1850–1950.* Cambridge, Mass.: Harvard University Press, 1957.

————. *Vassouras: A Brazilian Coffee County, 1850–1900.* Cambridge, Mass.: Harvard University Press, 1957.

Stolcke, Verena. *Cafeicultura. Homens, mulheres e capital (1850–1980).* São Paulo: Editora Brasiliense, 1986.

Stoner, K. Lynn. *Latinas of the Americas. A Source Book.* New York: Garland, 1989.

Stuart, Bertie Cohn. *Women in the Caribbean: An Annotated Bibliography.* Leiden: Department of Caribbean Studies, Royal Institute of Linguistics and Anthropology, 1979.

Studart, Heloneida. "Os brasileiros querem o divórcio." *Manchete,* June 1, 1974, pp. 12–13.

————. *A mulher brinquedo do homem?* Petrópolis: Vozes, 1969.

————. *Mulher objeto de cama e mesa.* Petrópolis: Vozes, 1974.

Sullerot, Evelyne. *Women, Society, and Change.* Trans. Margaret Scotford Archer. New York: McGraw-Hill, 1971.

Suplicy, Marta. *Conversando sobre sexo.* São Paulo: Published by the author, 1983.

Tabak, Fanny. *Autoritarismo e participação política da mulher.* Rio de Janeiro: Graal, 1983.

————. "O status da mulher no Brasil. Vitórias e preconceitos." *Cadernos da PUC* 7 (August 1971): 165–201.

Tabak, Fanny, and Moema Toscano. *Mulher e política.* Rio de Janeiro: Paz e Terra, 1982.

Tanuri, Leonor Maria. *O ensino normal no estado de São Paulo.* São Paulo: Universidade de São Paulo, 1979.

Tappen, Kathleen B. *The Status of Women in Brazil.* Washington, D.C.: Office of the Coordinator on Inter-American Affairs, 1944.

Toplin, Robert Brent. *The Abolition of Slavery in Brazil.* New York: Atheneum, 1971.

Torres, João Camillo de Oliveira. *A democracia coronada. Teoria política do Império do Brasil.* 2d ed. Petrópolis: Vozes, 1964.

————. *Estratificação social no Brasil. Suas origens históricas e suas relações com a organização política do país.* São Paulo: Difusão Européia do Livro, 1965.

————. *O positivismo no Brasil.* 2d ed. Petrópolis: Vozes, 1957.

Toscano, Moema. "Mulher, trabalho, e política. Caminhos cruzados do feminismo." Thesis of livre-docência. Pontificada Universidade Católica do Rio de Janeiro, 1975.

Trinidade, Hélgio. *Integralismo (O fascismo brasileiro na década de 30).* São Paulo: Difusão Européia do Livro, 1974.

Vainfás, Ronaldo, ed. *História e sexualidade no Brasil.* Rio de Janeiro: Graal, 1986.

Valdés, Nelson. "A Bibliography on Cuban Women in the Twentieth Century." *Cuban Studies Newsletter* 4 (June 1974).

Valladão, Alfredo. *Campanha da Princeza.* 3 vols. São Paulo: Empreza Graphica da "Revista dos Tribunaes," 1942.

Vasconcellos, Francisco Figueira de Mello e. *Educação sexual da mulher (These inaugural apresentada á faculdade de Medicina do Rio de Janeiro).* Rio de Janeiro, 1915.

Velasco y Arias, María. *Juana Paula Manso. Vida y acción.* Buenos Aires: N.p., 1937.

Verucci, Florisa, and Ediva Marino. *Os direitos da mulher.* São Paulo: Nobel and Conselho Estadual da Condição Feminina, 1985.

Vidal, Olímio Barros. *Precursoras brasileiras.* Rio de Janeiro: A Noite, 1955.

Vieira, Celso. *Defesa social. Estudos jurídicos.* Rio de Janeiro: Imprensa Nacional, 1920.

Villela, Annibal Villanova, and Wilson Suzigan. *Política do governo e crescimento da economia brasileira, 1889–1945.* Rio de Janeiro: Instituto de Planejamento Economico e Social/Instituto de Pesquisas, 1973.

Vincent, Frank. *Around and about South America. Twenty Months of Quest and Query.* New York: D. Appleton, 1890.

Von Koseritz, Carl. *Imagens do Brasil.* São Paulo: Livraria Martins, 1943.

Walsh, Mary Roth. *"Doctors Wanted: No Women Need Apply." Sexual Barriers in the Medical Profession, 1835–1975.* New Haven: Yale University Press, 1977.

Walsh, Robert. *Notices of Brazil in 1828 and 1829.* 2 vols. London: Frederick Westley and A. H. Davis, 1830.

Weimer, Joan Myers. "The Mother, the Macho, and the State." *International Journal of Women's Studies* 1 (January–February, 1978): 73–82.

Williams, Margaret Todaro. "Integralism and the Brazilian Catholic Church." *Hispanic American Historical Review* 54 (August 1974): 301–25.

————. "The Politization of the Brazilian Catholic Church. The Catholic Electoral League." *Journal of Interamerican Studies and World Affairs* 16 (August 1974): 301–25.

Williams, Mary Wilhelmine. *Dom Pedro the Magnanimous. Second Emperor of Brazil.* Chapel Hill: University of North Carolina Press, 1937.

Winter, Nevin Otto. *Brazil and Her People of To-day: An Account of the Customs, Characteristics, Amusements, History, and Advancement of the Brazilians, and the Development of Their Country.* New York: Frederick A. Stokes, 1927.

Wirth, John D. *Minas Gerais in the Brazilian Federation, 1889–1937.* Stanford: Stanford University Press, 1977.

Wirth, John D., and Robert L. Jones, eds. *Manchester and São Paulo. Problems of Rapid Urban Growth.* Stanford: Stanford University Press, 1978.

Women Workers in Brazil. Women's Bureau Bulletin 206. Washington, D.C.: U.S. Department of Labor, 1946.

Wright, Marie Robinson. *The New Brazil: Its Resources and Attractions, Historical, Descriptive, Industrial.* Philadelphia: George Barrie and Son, 1901.

Young, Jordan M. *The Brazilian Revolution of 1930 and the Aftermath.* New Brunswick, N.J.: Rutgers University Press, 1967.

Youssef, Nadia Haggag. *Women and Work in Developing Societies.* Berkeley: Institute of International Studies, University of California, 1974.

Zerbine, Therezinha Godoy. *Anistia. Semente da liberdade.* São Paulo: Escolas Profissionais Salesianas, 1979.

Index

Abolition, xvi, 14, 15, 38–40, 42, 43, 49, 234 n.54, 236 n.53; comparison of Brazilian and U.S. women's role in, 39–40; and employment of black women, 91; position of women in abolitionist organizations, 39–40; and women's organizations, 37, 39–40; and women's publications, 15, 36, 39, 40

Aliança Nacional de Mulheres, 160–61, 169–70

Almeida, Júlia Lopes de, 114–15, 118, 131–33, 136, 137, 142 (picture), 144

Almeida, Presciliana Duarte de, 36, 66

Amado, Jorge, 88

Amaral, Tarsila do, 123

Andrade, Maria Rita Soares de Andrade, 148, 153, 171, 183

Andrade, Oswaldo de, 123, 124

Arts, women in the, 39, 51, 54, 57, 122, 123, 131, 137, 143, 193; foreign influence on, 57, 123; training of, 51, 57, 123; as women's activity, 39, 51, 54, 160; and the women's movement, 166

Augusta, Nísia Floresta Brasileira, 14–15, 114

Azevedo, Josefina Alvares de, 36, 37 (picture), 50–51, 70–73, 74, 118

Barandas, Ana Euridice Eufrosina de, 68

Barreto, Afonso Henriques de Lima, 82, 152–53, 171

O Bello Sexo, 30, 34–35, 36, 37

Campos, Mirtes de, 66, 86, 118, 131, 151, 164

Campos, Narcisa Amália de Campos, 114

Castro, Augusto Olympio Viveiros de, 111–13

Catholic church and Brazilian women, 5, 49, 67, 117–18, 134, 136, 176; compared to other countries, 155; and divorce, 118, 119, 155, 196–97; and domestic roles, 191; and education, 23, 48, 60, 61, 88, 155, 176; and employment, 111, 112–13; and liberationists, 191, 203; and lower classes, 112; and marriage, 6, 8; in politics, 154–55, 176; and prostitution, 96, 244 n.4; and reproduction, 198; and suffrage, 155; and women's movements, 137, 154, 155, 185, 191–93, 197; and women's publications, 134, 136. See also Religion

Catt, Carrie Chapman, 139, 141, 142–43, 146, 156, 179, 189

Celso, Maria Eugenia Alfonso, 144, 150, 158

Civil Code of Brazil (1916), 6, 81–82; revision, 184

Coeducation, 23, 24, 60–62, 179; foreign influence on, 60; resistance to, 23, 60, 179

Conselho Nacional dos Direitos da Mulher (National Council of Women's Rights), 201, 204

Constituent Assembly of 1987–88: and women's issues, 201, 204; women's participation in, 201. See also specific constitutions

Constitution of 1891: and women's issues, xvii, 73, 75, 159

Constitution of 1934, xvii, 170, 179; women's participation in, 169–70, 172–73, 177, 201

Constitution of 1937, 179

Constitution of 1946, 201

Council on the Status of Women, São Paulo State (Conselho Estadual da Condição Feminina), 200, 205

Couto, Amélia Carolina da Silva, 31, 34, 36, 39, 55, 59

Daltro, Leolinda de Figuereido, 129–30, 145, 153, 171

About the Author

June E. Hahner is Professor of History at the State University of New York at Albany, where she served as the first director of the Women's Studies program. Her books include *Poverty and Politics: The Urban Poor in Brazil, 1870–1920,* winner of the 1987 NECLAS book prize, *Civilian-Military Relations in Brazil, 1889–1898,* and the documentary studies *Women in Latin American History: Their Lives and Views* and *A Mulher no Brasil.* She has also contributed numerous articles to scholarly journals in the United States and Latin America. She is a member of the board of editors of *The Americas* and a past chair of the Brazilian Studies Committee of the Conference on Latin American History.

Library of Congress Cataloging-in-Publication Data

Hahner, June Edith, 1940–
   Emancipating the female sex : the struggle for women's rights in Brazil, 1850–1940
/ June E. Hahner.
    p. cm.
   Includes bibliographical references.
   ISBN 0-8223-1051-1. — ISBN 0-8223-1069-4 (pbk.)
   1. Women's rights—Brazil—History—19th century. 2. Women's rights—Brazil—
History—20th century. 3. Feminism—Brazil—History—19th century.
4. Feminism—Brazil—History—20th century. 5. Women—Brazil—Social
conditions. I. Title.
HQ1236.5.B6H34 1990
305.42'0981—dc20   90-31833
                                      CIP